# Portraits of FAITHFUL Saints

## *by* Herman Hanko

Reformed Free Publishing Association
Grandville, Michigan

*Book design by Jeff Steenholdt*

Individual essays originally copyrighted by Reformed Free Publishing Association in series entitled "Cloud of Witnesses" in the *Standard Bearer* magazine from October 15, 1989, to July 1, 1997

Illustrations from public domain courtesy of the Hekman Library of Calvin College and Seminary, Grand Rapids, Mich., and of the library at the Protestant Reformed Seminary, Grandville, Mich.

Address all inquiries to:
*Reformed Free Publishing Association*
*4949 Ivanrest Ave.*
*Grandville, MI 49418-9709 USA*
*(616-224-1518)*

ISBN 0-916206-60-2
LC 98-066842

*Dedicated to my children and grandchildren, concerning whom it is my earnest prayer that they may hold fast to the faith of their fathers*

# Contents

# *Foreword*

"We believe that the same God, after he had created all things, did not forsake them, or give them up to fortune or chance, but that he rules and governs according to his holy will, so that nothing happens in this world without his appointment . . ."

So run the wise affirmations of Article 13 ("Of Divine Providence") in the Belgic Confession. Founded firmly on Holy Scripture, the Confession gives no room for any notion that the events of human history take place by chance. It affirms that God is totally in control, not only of human history in general, but especially of the history of the Christian church. Church history is the most important part of any historical study because it describes God's activities, both supernatural and ordinary, among His redeemed people.

By contrast, the wicked, who "receiveth not the things of the Spirit of God: for they are foolishness unto him" (I Cor. 2:14), are predisposed to interpret all the phenomena of life—past, present, and future—as being under the direction of some grand cosmic lottery of Fortune and Chance. They describe these vain notions in their philosophy, evolutionary science, relativistic ethics, and in their very religion. Fortune, Chance, and Free Will figure prominently in the Pantheon of their gods. So pervasive is this attitude toward history in the modern mind that even those scholars who specialize in historical research express skepticism as to whether final and complete understanding of the past can ever be achieved. The idea that history has a meaning, a purpose, and a goal is a truth foreign to the halls of modern academia.

Sad to say, this same attitude has permeated many of today's churches. Worship has become, in a thousand sanctuaries, an orgy of self-enjoyment; doctrinal teaching has been forsaken; and the history of Christianity is largely forgotten or misinterpreted. Modern evangelicals consider the Reformation at best a shadowy thing of the past and, at worst, an outright mistake. Nominal Christians give the distinct impression that since the death of the apostle John, nothing of worth has happened. Ask them "Who was Augustine?" or "Who was John Calvin?" or "What happened at the Reformation?" or "What are the Canons of Dordt?" and one finds they do not know and really care less.

John Calvin was right: "We must look . . . at God's more especial care of the human race, which is such that the life and death of men, the public destinies of kingdoms and of nations, and the private cases of individuals, and whatsoever men usually ascribe to fortune, are under His heavenly rule and disposal. And . . . we must contemplate that peculiar protection by which God defends His Church, in which protection He more expressly manifests His presence and His power" ("The Secret Providence of God" in *Calvin's Calvinism*, p. 227 of Henry Cole translation, Grand Rapids, Michigan, Reformed Free Publishing Association, 1987).

To study history is not to do research in a thicket of meaningless chance; it is to study the works of God in His providential government of the world. More particularly, to study the history of the church of God is to behold that realm where, as Calvin says, God "manifests His presence by clearer and brighter proofs; He there shows Himself as the Father of His family, and condescends to grant a nearer view of Himself" ("The Secret Providence of God," p. 226).

To study church history is to come to know the work of God in Christ among His people. It is a work covering the centuries; it is a work continuing to the present. To slight church history is to slight God and to treat His most wonderful works of redemption through the ages as not worthy of serious contemplation.

Strife and heresy have lunged with vicious blades at the heart of the church, all under the inscrutable hand of God's providence. The godliest of men stumbled and fell. It is part of the necessary education of Christians in all ages that they learn the past. "Whatsoever things were written aforetime," said Paul, "were written for our learning, that we through patience and comfort of the Scriptures might have hope" (Rom. 15:4). What Paul wrote is applicable as well to our study of the works of God in subsequent church history.

One cannot understand an oak tree without understanding how such a living thing has developed from a little acorn. The whole tree is a testimony of growth. The giant trunk and the sturdy limbs tell of the tree's health and history. Without all that, it could not bear leaves in the present. Every "present" has a past. So it is with the church.

The disparities between denominations, between creeds, between individuals, all have a start in human history. There we find the records of how the majestic truths of the Scriptures were drawn forth in crises and controversies. We see how the faithful suffered for their adherence to truth, yet we also see how those truths triumphed.

When the present leaves of the great oak are detached from their age-old parent, then they are adrift on the wind. Modern churches are blown about by the icy winds of today's spiritual winter. They are "tossed to and fro, and carried about with every wind of doctrine, by the sleight of men, and cunning craftiness, whereby they lie in wait to deceive" (Eph. 4:14). They are easy prey to the charismatic phenomenon, dispensationalism, ritualism, new ageism, feminism, ecumenism: one fad after another, and often all together.

Even in the Reformed and Presbyterian churches—long bastions of biblical orthodoxy—multitudes have forsaken the heritage of their Christian forebears. The creeds and confessions of their churches are held lightly by hosts of their officebearers, whose backs are turned on the past. The uncertain light of a new age illuminates the shrine where they worship. "Strange fire" punctuates their liturgy. They have turned away from the Reformation, and justification by faith has been perverted by some of their learned theologians into what seems better termed as "justification by doubt."

To keep before Christians their precious heritage, Professor Herman Hanko has collected the history of the struggles and ultimate triumphs of those who lived out their faith from the time of early church history onward. The author has drawn for us "portraits" whereby we can gain close-up views of God's works in the lives and times of the faithful who lived before us. Facts about their lives are the fruit of the author's years of research and teaching church history at the Protestant Reformed Seminary.

This series of short biographies, first published in the *Standard Bearer*, is now brought together in one volume. Between its covers, history comes alive. The reader's imagination is captured, his spirit engaged, his mind and heart enlightened, and his spirit edified in a simple yet meaningful way. The relatively short chapters are what is needed by those pressed for time by the frantic pace of modern life. *Portraits of Faithful Saints* is a book to read to the youth of the church and is not too difficult for them to read for themselves. In a family library, this book should become a standard reference, one worth rereading through the years and passing down through the generations.

For a believer to read of these saints, of his dear brothers and sisters in Christ, is to read of the one family of the elect of God, of which he is, by grace, a member. Above all, *Portraits of Faithful Saints* is a book that should lead one to worship the Most High, by whose power, by whose sovereign purpose, the saints were born again and upheld in the course of their lives as an on-going testimony to the truth of the work of Christ in redemption.

HUGH L. WILLIAMS, Editor
*British Reformed Journal*

# Preface

In writing the biographies of saints from bygone years and centuries, two dangers must be avoided.

It is possible, and in fact increasingly common in our day, to write about saints of the past in such a way that while the story of their lives is interesting and entertaining, there is no significance in what they did and said for us who face the complexities of our modern twentieth-century life. Entertainment? Yes. Instruction and edification? No. The times in which these people lived were different; the faith they held is different; the calling they attempted to fulfill is totally irrelevant to our day.

Such an attitude is born out of a serious error. It fails to recognize that God so works in history in the gathering of His church that the church of all ages is one, united by the one great truth of God, revealed in Christ, and made known to the church by the Spirit of Christ. Such an attitude finds the truth confessed in past centuries a mere opinion of the church which, while perhaps useful at the time, is of no value today to a church facing the towering problems of our modern technological age. And in turning its back on that truth, it turns its back on those who fought for it and sometimes died for it.

The opposite danger is to consider those whom God has used in the past in the defense of the faith to be such noble men that we are not only to worship them, but also to worship the ground on which they walked, the stakes at which they were burned, the prisons in which they suffered the cruel tortures of their oppressors. The danger of a kind of hero-worship that rises in the church is that our present-day religion consists of very little more than a veneration of saints from the past—as if we fulfill our calling in the world as God's church by paying homage to faithful people of God in long ago centuries.

The danger is real. Some seem to do little else than "garnish the graves of the prophets." But if one were to look for the truth for which these saints fought and died, one would need a lantern to find it.

Does this mean that a book dedicated to past saints can be of no value for the church today? No, that cannot be. Scripture itself points us in a different direction. As an introduction to the sad book of Judges, Scripture informs us that upon the death of Joshua and the elders that outlived Joshua, "there arose another generation after them, which knew not the Lord, nor yet the works which he had done for Israel" (Judg. 2:10). Israel's subsequent apostasy and oppression at the hand of heathen nations was the result.

Two things are brought to our attention. One is that it is what the Lord does for Israel that is important. That is, not what man does counts, but a memory of what the Lord does is what saves the church from apostasy. The second is (and one need only read what the Lord did for Israel) that the Lord does His mighty deeds through men whom He raises up: an Abraham, a Joseph, a Moses, a Joshua. We cannot know the Lord's mighty deeds without knowing about these men.

The important thing, then, is the Lord's mighty deeds. They have continued in the church until the present. We wish to know them. To know those mighty deeds we must know the men through whom the Lord worked them. That will keep us from apostasy.

Hebrews 11 reminds us of the heroes of faith and recounts their stirring deeds of faith. The purpose is not that we may be reminded of some significant biographical detail, but "Wherefore seeing we also are compassed about with so great a cloud of witnesses, let us lay aside every weight, and the sin which doth so easily beset us, and let us run with patience the race that is set before us, looking unto Jesus the author and finisher of our faith; who for the joy that was set before him endured the cross, despising the shame, and is set down at the right hand of the throne of God" (Heb. 12:1, 2).

We run a race in this life. It is a marathon that requires endurance; but it is the race of faith. The saints of bygone years, heroes of faith, are, so to speak, standing alongside the race course which has been laid out, cheering us on. They have run the race before us and are now entered into their reward. Their lives of faith encourage us and spur us on in our own difficult and exhausting race when the course seems all but impossible.

If the faith God gave them enabled them to perform such mighty exploits, their voices echoing from the past down the corridors of time will give us courage—us whose course in the race is usually not as difficult as was theirs.

But it is the faith that counts. And Jesus is the Author and Finisher of our faith—as He was the Author and Finisher of the faith of those who have run the course before us. We hear their encouraging shouts that faith will overcome, and so are strengthened; but we look to Jesus for that faith which we need to run without dropping of exhaustion in our own race from here to glory.

We speak of the saints who have been before us, therefore, only that we may learn of their faith and its power in their lives. Because Christ is the Author and Finisher of that faith (the term "Finisher" is also extremely important), that faith which enabled them to do what they did can only enable us to do what we are called to do.

Jaroslav Pelikan put it well in his book, *The Christian Tradition*: "Tradition is the living faith of the dead; traditionalism is the dead faith of the living."

These chapters first appeared in a series of articles written for the *Standard Bearer*. The choice of what saints to include in that series and subsequently in this book has been, necessarily, somewhat arbitrary. Undoubtedly our readers will wonder why some whom they expected to find between these covers were omitted, while others will wonder why the ones included were deemed worthy of this special attention.

While I indeed confess to a certain arbitrariness in the choices made, nevertheless, certain criteria did dictate the choices. It might be well to mention these criteria briefly.

Without exception, people were included who were truly saints (insofar as we are able to judge them by their lives) and who have now gone to join the company of just men made perfect. They rightly belong to that cloud of witnesses of which the author of the epistle to the Hebrews spoke.

Each one had something unique to contribute to an understanding of God's work in the salvation of the church of His Son. Other saints may have done equally great deeds and made equally important contributions, but to include them would have been to some extent repetitious. I picked saints whose role in the wonderful works of God in the church can be clearly seen and defined; and the description of each one's life is to demonstrate the place God gave to him or her in the broader scope of God's eternal purpose.

If these saints are to speak to us today, they quite obviously had to have something to say. And so, another criterion was the inspiration which we could derive in our own calling and life from the work they did and the courage of faith they manifested. Each must, in his own way, be a witness to us in our life and calling.

In some instances I have included a sketch of someone with whom I have strong disagreements. These disagreements are spelled out. But this did not dim the strength and power of their witness and testimony, nor did their errors obscure the important role they played in the work of the church and the defense of the faith once for all delivered to the saints.

While others may disagree with my assessments, no book can be permitted to become so unwieldy as to include all those who rightfully have a place in the roll call of the heroes of faith. Surely, we freely admit that God's judgments are different from ours and that only heaven will reveal how God used each saint in the work of the church for the good of His cause and kingdom. But we are not yet in heaven, and earth's perspectives and judgments shall have to be sufficient for the time being.

Many of the readers of the *Standard Bearer* were kind enough to express appreciation for the articles and to suggest that they be reprinted in book form. The Reformed Free Publishing Association has graciously consented to do this. The necessary editing has now been completed, and this material is presented to the public with the prayer that God will use it to enable the saints today who are called to live in such perilous times to run the race set before them, inspired by the cloud of witnesses who shout their encouragement from the glories of heaven, where they have attained the victory which shall presently be ours.

HERMAN HANKO

# Part One

## Ancient Period
### 100-750

# Part One:

## Ancient Period *(100-750)*

| | | |
|---|---|---|
| | **50** | |
| | | **Polycarp** c.69-c.154 |
| Death of Apostle John c.100 | **100** | **Justin Martyr** c.100-c.165 |
| | | **Tertullian** b: c.145-160 |
| | **150** | d: c.220-240 |
| | **200** | |
| | **250** | **Anthony** 251-356 |
| | | **Athanasius** 296-373 |
| Reign of Constantine over | **300** | |
| Roman Empire 324-337.... | | |
| Council of Nicea 325 .......... | | **John Chrysostom** 347-407 |
| | **350** | **Augustine** 354-430 |
| Council of Constantinople | | |
| 381.............................. | | **Patrick** b: c.389; d: c.461-493 |
| | **400** | |
| Council of Chalcedon 451.... | | |
| Fall of Rome 476............... | | |
| | **500** | |
| | | **Columba** c.521-597 |
| | **550** | |
| | **600** | |
| | **650** | |
| | | **Boniface** c.675-754 |
| | **700** | |
| | **750** | |

## Chapter 1

# *Polycarp*
### *Martyr of*
### *Christ*

### *Introduction*

*The church of Jesus Christ, while in the world, is always in persecution. It is its lot in this life to suffer for righteousness' sake. We ought not be surprised by this, for the Scriptures speak of it in countless places. What Paul told the churches which he organized on his first missionary journey is true for all time: "We must through much*

tribulation enter into the kingdom of God" (Acts 14:22).

This incessant persecution has produced a list of heroes of faith—saints, men, women, and sometimes children—who loved not their lives unto death and who sealed their faith with their blood.

Among all these is the ancient Polycarp, elder and minister in the church of Smyrna. He is not the first of the martyrs. He did not suffer more than many others. His death was not necessarily more illustrious than the death of other saints. But he provides for us an example of faithfulness in martyrdom, a testimony to the power of the grace of Christ in great suffering, and an enduring encouragement for God's saints today who suffer for the sake of the gospel of Jesus Christ.

### *His Early Life*

The date of Polycarp's birth is about A.D. 69, near the date of Paul's martyrdom in Rome. Polycarp was not born in a Christian home. In fact, his birthplace is unknown, for he appeared on the scene of the history of the church in a strange and perplexing way, a way that is an evidence of the mysterious ways of God's providence.

It all started in Smyrna. If you will look at a map, you will find Smyrna less than fifty miles north by northwest of Ephesus on the western coast of the province of Asia in Asia Minor. Smyrna was a city in which a church had been established early, perhaps by the apostle Paul during those years of labor in Ephesus when "all they which dwelt in Asia heard the word of the Lord Jesus" (Acts 19:10). The Lord Himself wrote a letter from heaven to the church of Smyrna. He had nothing about which to reprimand the church; He had only words of encouragement and comfort in its sufferings at the hands of its persecutors (Rev. 2:8–11). It is possible that Polycarp was minister in the church at the time this letter arrived in Smyrna and that he read it to his congregation, little knowing that it spoke of his own martyrdom at the hands of the wicked.

At any rate, some years earlier a man named Strataeas, a brother of Timothy, was either elder or minister in the church at Smyrna. A wealthy woman named Callisto, a member of the church and one noted for her works of charity, dreamed that she was to go to the gate of the city called the Ephesian Gate and redeem there a young boy who was a slave of two men. This she did and brought Polycarp to her own house where she gave him a Christian home, taught him the ways of the Lord, provided for his education, and adopted him as her son.

Soon after the boy came into Callisto's home, he gave evidence of the work of the Spirit of Christ in his heart. He was grave and reserved, kind towards those with whom he associated, much given to the study of Scripture, and diligent in witnessing to others of his faith. An outstanding feature of his conduct was his self-denial, something which undoubtedly was used by the Lord to prepare him for future martyrdom. It is difficult to see how self-indulgent, excessively pampered people, who have much too much of this world's goods and who always crave more, can face martyrdom if it should be required of them.

Perhaps one of the most intriguing aspects of Polycarp's early manhood was his acquaintance with the apostle John. Twenty years they knew each other, and Polycarp had the privilege of studying at John's feet. It is easy to envy Polycarp. One can imagine listening to Jesus' beloved disciple speak of his years with the Lord and teach what Christ had taught him. All this careful training prepared him for work in the church.

### His Work in Smyrna

The work which the Lord called Polycarp to perform in Smyrna was extensive and important. He was, first of all, a deacon in the church laboring for the care of the poor. This was an especially important work in the early church, for persecution was the lot of the saints, and persecution brought much work to deacons. They had to care for women and children whose husbands and fathers were in prison or had been killed. They had to visit the saints in prison to comfort them and encourage them in faithfulness, while at the same time trying as best they could to ease their sufferings by bringing them food and clothing and salves for their lacerated backs. And they had to gather money from a congregation of people who themselves had very little of this earth's goods.

Because of his learning, however, Polycarp was soon called to be an elder in the church—a presbyter, as Scripture calls those who held this office. Upon the death of the minister (then already called the bishop), Polycarp became pastor and minister in the congregation. An old tradition has it that the apostle John ordained him to the ministry. This tradition, if not true, could at least mean that John was present to witness the event. Polycarp's fame and influence extended throughout Asia Minor. Not only was he respected because of his close association with the apostle John, but for his own piety he gained a name among the saints in that part of the world.

There were several interesting events in these years of labor in the church. Ignatius, bishop of Antioch, the city where Paul had begun his labors in Asia Minor on his first missionary journey, came through Smyrna on his way to Rome and martyrdom there. Ignatius and Polycarp spent a few pleasant days together in Smyrna, recalling their past friendship when Ignatius lived in Smyrna and the times they had both studied under the apostle John.

Somewhat later, Polycarp traveled to Rome. A dispute over the date of the commemoration of our Lord's death and resurrection had threatened to tear the church apart. The churches in Asia Minor commemorated these events at the same time of the year as they had taken place; in other words, the commemoration began on the 14th of Nisan, the day of the Passover when the Lord ate the last supper with His disciples. This meant, of course, that these events in the Lord's life were observed each year on a different day of the week, and the resurrection was not celebrated on the first day of the week every year. This tradition, according to Polycarp, was apostolic, for

both Paul and John had taught these churches this practice. But the other churches, led by Rome, wanted the resurrection of the Lord celebrated on the first day of the week. They had instituted the practice of celebrating it on the first Lord's day after the first day of spring. The question was a minor one, of course, but it threatened to split the early church into two factions.

In the interests of settling the matter, Polycarp traveled to Rome to talk with Anicetus, the minister in the congregation there. They discussed the matter at length, but neither could persuade the other. The result was that they decided to allow the churches the liberty of celebrating these events of the Lord's life on the date they chose, without rancor, bitterness, or strife. As a gesture of their friendly parting, Anicetus asked Polycarp to preside at the administration of the Lord's Supper in the church of Rome, which Polycarp did.

## Polycarp's Martyrdom

The threat of persecution always hung over the head of the church in those days. There were times of relative peace and surcease from persecution in its most brutal forms, but there were also times when persecution broke out in fury. The church was hated in the Roman Empire, especially by the Jews and pagan Romans. Every natural calamity, whether flood or earthquake or drought, was blamed on the Christians and on their refusal to worship Caesar as God.

When Polycarp was an old man, at least eighty-five years old, a flurry of persecution broke out in Smyrna, brought on by the mobs who were thirsting for the blood of the Christians. Fourteen Christians were seized and dragged to the public arena where they were fed to wild beasts. All but one died gloriously, one even slapping a wild animal that seemed to be too lazy to attack the Christian who was intended to be its dinner.

The crowd was not placated and began to shout for more. Particularly, they began to shout for Polycarp, whom they knew to be minister in the church and who was, at the urging of his flock, in hiding. The police were sent to find him. They finally did find him, after exacting information of his hiding place from a servant, who was subjected to hideous torture.

The crowd and the local magistrate were present in the arena when Polycarp was apprehended. He was brought before the magistrate in the stands of the arena and immediately tried and convicted while the frenzied crowd shouted for his blood. It was a

most unusual and illegal trial that went something like this, the magistrate speaking first:

"Swear by the fortune of Caesar!  Repent!  Declare: Death to the atheists!"

Turning to the mob, with a lift of his head and a wave of his hand, Polycarp shouted, "Death to the atheists!"

But the magistrate knew what Polycarp meant. "Apostatize! Swear, and I will set you free at once!  You have but to insult Christ."

"I have served Him for eighty-six years and He has never done me any wrong. Why then should I blaspheme against my King and my Savior?"

"Swear by Caesar's fortune!"

"You flatter yourself if you hope to persuade me. In all truth I solemnly declare to you: I am a Christian."

"I have the lions here, to use as I think fit."

"Give your orders. As for us Christians, when we change it is not from good to bad: it is splendid to pass through evil into God's justice."

"If you do not repent, I shall have you burned at the stake since you are so contemptuous of the lions."

"You threaten me with a fire that burns for an hour and then dies down. But do you know the eternal fire of the justice that is to come? Do you know the punishment that is to devour the ungodly? Come, don't delay!  Do what you want with me."

The condemnation was proclaimed; the mob rushed from the seats to gather sticks and faggots, with the Jews gleefully helping along. Polycarp told the soldiers in charge of the execution that they need not fasten him to the stake, for he had no intention of fleeing. The flames leaped high, while from the flames could be heard this prayer from the lips of Christ's faithful servant:

> Lord God Almighty, Father of Thy beloved and blessed Son, Jesus Christ, through whom we have received the grace of knowing Thee, God of angels and powers, and the whole creation, and of the whole race of the righteous who live in Thy presence; I bless Thee for deigning me worthy of this day and this hour that I may be among Thy martyrs and drink of the cup of my Lord Jesus Christ...I praise Thee for all Thy mercies; I bless Thee, I glorify Thee, through the eternal High Priest, Jesus Christ, Thy beloved Son, with whom to Thyself and the Holy Spirit, be glory both now and forever. Amen.

It is an abiding lesson to us that those who died for their faith with prayers and songs of praise on their lips were those who knew what they believed, loved that truth, and were prepared to die for it. Polycarp had made his love for the truth clear in a letter he wrote to the church at Philippi, in which he warned them against heresies already appearing in the church. He said,

> Whoever doth not confess that Jesus Christ is come in the flesh, is antichrist, and whoever doth not confess the mystery of the cross, is of the devil; and he, who wrests the words of the Lord according to his own pleasure, and saith, there is no resurrection and judgment, is the first-born of Satan. Therefore would we forsake the empty babbling of this crowd and their false teachings, and turn to the word which hath been given us from the beginning...

Knowing that persecution soon will be upon the church also today, ought not we take heed to these things?

## Chapter 2

# Justin Martyr
### Convert from Heathendom

*Introduction*
*When the Son of*
*God gathers His*
*church by His Word*
*and Spirit, He*
*brings individual*
*elect saints to the*
*fellowship of the*
*church in different*
*ways. Some are*
*born and raised*
*within the covenant*
*and drink the truths*
*of the Scriptures*
*with their mother's*
*milk. Some are*
*brought into the*
*fellowship of the*
*church from darkest*
*heathendom through*
*a sudden turning*
*from the darkness of*

idolatry to the light of the gospel. Some live for years on the periphery of the church, attending only infrequently a church where only the faintest glimmerings of the gospel are heard, but who come to conversion and faith gradually, through a long period of time, even though they had some acquaintance with the gospel from childhood. Some walk a long and difficult spiritual pilgrimage as they travel through the strange teachings of some sect; then through rampant Arminianism; only finally to emerge into the light of the truth of sovereign grace. God leads His own to the fellowship of the church in sometimes strange and wonderful ways.

In the early history of the church of Jesus Christ, even during the apostolic period, the same principle was true. The church of that ancient day was composed of Jews who had been brought up in the Old Testament Scriptures but who were brought to faith in Christ by the same wonder of salvation which saved the Gentiles. Some were proselytes, Gentile converts to the Jewish religion, also finally brought into the fellowship of the church through the sovereign work of the Spirit of Christ. Especially in the day when first the gospel was preached throughout the Mediterranean world, the majority in the church were converts from paganism and heathendom. But even then, the conversion wrought by God was not always the sudden bursting of the light of salvation into the darkness of unbelief; it was sometimes, even in heathendom, a sojourn, a journey long and arduous, that finally brought peace and salvation.

This is the story of one such convert from paganism: the church father Justin Martyr.

### *His Conversion*

Justin's surname was not really "Martyr." He received that name because he died a martyr's death. But this is not quite the point of this story, as important as it is that he sealed his confession with his blood.

Justin was actually born in Samaria, although for many years he had almost no acquaintance with the Jewish religion or with the Christian faith. He was born of a Greek father by the name of Priscus. Priscus and his wife were sent by the Roman emperor Vespasian, along with a rather large number of Roman citizens, to settle in Flavia Neopolis, a town known in Bible times as Shechem. His birth date is somewhere around the turn of the century—A.D. 100. It seems as if this colony of Roman citizens was a rather close-knit community, and contact with the surrounding people was unusual. A.D. 100 is, however, about thirty years after the destruction of Jerusalem by the armies of Titus, and very few Jews were left in the area.

Justin was an unusually brilliant student. At a fairly young age he traveled throughout the empire in search of teachings which would satisfy him. He himself tells us of these years.

Already as a teenager Justin experienced deep longings in his soul which were impossible to satisfy, but which centered in the question of man's relation to God. What is man's relation to God? How is it established? What must one expect from it? The questions would not stay down. They troubled him deeply, and the answers seemed to him more important than anything else. He would spend his life, if necessary, searching for the answers to these questions.

After his conversion, Justin understood that these questions and this deep unsatisfied longing for something he knew not what, were the work of Christ in his soul. It is doubtful that God ever brings anyone to salvation and the knowledge of Christ without creating in

him a deep longing, an unsatisfied thirst, a hunger for something which he does not have. Augustine, three centuries later, put it this way in his *Confessions:* "My soul can find no rest until it rests in Thee." This longing, finally, is born out of the knowledge of sin and the hopelessness and emptiness of one's life brought about by the hopelessness of sin. Salvation is by faith in Christ; but only the empty sinner needs Christ; only the thirsty sinner drinks at the Fountain of Living Waters; only the hungry sinner eats the Bread of Life; only the laboring and heavy-laden come to Christ to find rest for their souls. It is the general rule of the Holy Spirit to bring to faith in Christ by sovereignly showing the sinner the need for Christ. That Justin had this deep longing is not strange. That it was a part of his life for ever so many years before peace came is a remarkable providence of God.

Justin traveled widely throughout the empire in order to find those teachings which would satisfy his soul. The polytheism (worship of many gods) of paganism seemed to him foolish and absurd in the extreme and not something to satisfy the soul. He tells us of these years of wandering—wandering from land to land, but wandering spiritually as well.

Justin went to the Stoics—a school of philosophy concerned mainly with ethics. They told him that questions about a man's relation to God were relatively unimportant and he ought not to be bothered by them, at least not at first. But for Justin they were the only important thing.

He went to the Peripatetics—a school of teachers who traveled about to spread their teachings. After about three days with Justin, one such teacher would not continue his teaching until he had assurance from Justin that he would pay his tuition. It was Justin's position that if the teacher were more interested in money than in teaching, he could have nothing to say which would ease the ache in his soul.

He went to the Pythagoreans—philosophers of an ancient school who told him that they could not help him until he mastered music, astronomy, and geometry, for the truth could be learned only through a mastery of these subjects.

Then he discovered that ancient school of Greek philosophy called Platonism. He tells us about it:

> [Here I shall] soon have the intuition of God, for is not this the aim of Platonic philosophy?

> Under the influence of this notion it occurred to me that I would
> withdraw to some solitary place, far from the turmoil of the world,
> and there, in perfect self-collection, give myself to my own
> contemplations. I chose a spot by the seaside.

Justin was probably at Ephesus at this time, a city of Asia Minor near the sea, but also near a church of Christ established by Paul. While Justin was giving himself over to his meditations by the seaside, an old man met him and began a conversation with him. The old man was a Christian. Justin argued vehemently with the old man in the defense of his pet philosophy and received very little argument in return. But finally the old man curtly cut him off: "You are a mere dealer in words, but no lover of action and truth; your aim is not to be a practicer of good, but a clever disputant, a cunning sophist." Finally, Justin put the question to the old man, "Where then is truth?" The old man replied, "Search the Scriptures, and pray that the gates of light may be opened to thee, for none can perceive and comprehend these things except God and His Christ grant them understanding."

We are sometimes not only ashamed to witness of the truth to others, but we readily excuse our failure to witness by an appeal to the superior knowledge of those with whom we dispute. It remains, however, a striking fact of the church in the immediate post-apostolic years that the rapid spread of the gospel throughout the whole Mediterranean world was through the faithful witness of the people of God. There were few if any missionaries in these days after the great missionary labors of Paul. Only faithful and often uneducated people of God, testifying of the truth and manifesting in their lives the joy of salvation, were the means God used to spread the gospel throughout the known world. Here we have an instance of that: the learned Justin, brought to his knees in sorrow for sin by a humble and childlike old man on the seaside near Ephesus.

The importance of the influence of Christian witnessing is evident in another aspect of Justin's conversion. He tells in one of his later writings that some of the unrest that stirred in his soul before his conversion was the unflinching faith of Christians who were tortured for their faith and put to death because they confessed Christ. He had witnessed such public spectacles from time to time and had been deeply impressed by the stalwart courage of young girls and old men. He secretly wondered what kind of strength was theirs to be faithful under such circumstances. This witness too was important.

The power of salvation is not the power of an eloquent defense of the faith; it is the power of God—even when He is pleased to use human means. Justin became a faithful servant of Christ and valiant defender of the faith.

## His Life As a Christian

After Justin became a Christian and was joined to the church of Christ, he spent his time traveling around the empire writing and teaching.

Schools in those days were not like schools today. A gifted and learned man (and sometimes an ungifted and stupid man) would stop in a certain town or city and begin teaching. If his instruction was considered worthwhile enough, he would soon gather some students around him who would then study under him. If he was an exceptionally able man, he might even establish a fairly permanent school that would be continued by his pupils beyond his own life.

It was something like this that Justin made his life's work. He would not, however, attempt to establish any kind of a permanent school. Rather, he was interested in using his knowledge and ability to instruct others in the Christian faith and teach others the truths of God's Word. Many times, when the opportunity presented itself, he would engage in public debates with defenders of pagan religions and philosophies. It was this practice that finally led to his martyrdom.

In the meantime, he also did a great deal of writing. Some of his writings have survived the ravages of time and are available today. He was one of the very first of the defenders of Christianity who used his writing ability to answer the critics. In fact, so effective were his writings that he became known in later times as an apologist (in other words, one who defended the faith).

A brief survey of Justin's writings will give you a bit of an idea of what he did. He attacked paganism head-on by showing the utter absurdity and stupidity of worshiping twelve or fifteen gods. He made an emphatic point of it that paganism could not possibly be a religion that was true when it brought forth horrible immoralities: the Roman Empire in those days was dying from a moral rot that was eating at its vitals and that condoned every horrible sin under heaven.

Pagans, growing ever more wary and fearful of Christianity as it spread through the world and gained converts in every walk of life, began to attack it viciously. Christians were accused of atheism for refusing to worship Caesar. They were accused of treason because they spoke of a King greater than Caesar. Strangely enough, they were accused of cannibalism because they claimed, in their celebration of the Lord's Supper, to be eating the body of the Lord and drinking His blood. They were accused of immorality because they held "love feasts," which were intended to express the communion of the saints and give material help to the poor, but which were interpreted as immoral orgies. All these foolish and wild charges Justin took the time to answer carefully and patiently.

But he also set about proving the truth of the Christian religion. He did this in especially two ways: 1) He pointed to the Old Testament prophets and showed how their prophecies were exactly fulfilled in the work and death of Christ. This was a striking argument and one which our own Belgic Confession uses in Article 5 in defense of the authority of Scripture. 2) Probably chiefly because the New Testament Scriptures, so recently written, were not widely known, he appealed to miracles as being proofs of the authentic character of the Christian faith, a purpose for which the Lord gave the power of miracles to the early church.

I suppose, however, that in one respect Justin would be considered a heretic by today's standards. It is not, I think, right to call him a heretic, for the church knew very little of the truth in the infancy of its New Testament existence. Sometimes mistakes were made through ignorance, which the church in later years would never make—at least one would think so. Justin believed, having come out of paganism himself, that the pagan philosophers possessed the germ of the truth in their hearts, which germ of the truth was Christ Himself, the Logos of John 1. Since these men possessed this germ of the truth, it was possible, Justin believed, that the best of them were saved without faith in Christ. This germ of truth came to expression in their philosophies.

This was wrong, yet there are those in our day who call themselves Reformed who teach the same thing.

### *His Martyrdom*

The time had come for Justin to earn the surname Martyr. This name would be given him by a church who held the memory of his martyrdom in reverence.

In the course of his travels Justin came twice to Rome. The second time he enraged a pagan philosopher, who, since he could not get the best of Justin in debate, determined to have him killed. So he reported to the authorities that Justin was a Christian guilty of all sorts of awful crimes. Justin was summoned before the magistrates and tried. The record of his trial stirs the blood of the child of God. The faithfulness and courage which Justin showed is sometimes overwhelming to us who know not what suffering for Christ's sake is.

But the story, written so long ago, ends like this: "Rusticus the prefect [magistrate] pronounced sentence, saying, 'Let those who have refused to sacrifice to the gods and to yield to the command of the emperor be scourged, and led away to suffer the punishment of decapitation, according to the laws.' The holy martyrs having glorified God, and having gone forth to the accustomed place, were beheaded, and perfected their testimony in the confession of the Saviour. And some of the faithful having secretly removed their bodies, laid them in a suitable place, the grace of our Lord Jesus Christ having wrought along with them, to whom be glory for ever and ever. Amen."

Chapter 3

# Tertullian
## Theologian of the Trinity

*Introduction*
*Although Paul writes to the Corinthians that the general rule of God in the church of Christ is that "not many wise men after the flesh, not many mighty, not many noble, are called" (I Cor. 1:26); nevertheless, God is sometimes pleased to give to the church of Christ men of outstanding ability and great intellectual, moral, and spiritual strength, who stand as giants in the annals of the* church's history.

Such a man was Tertullian. Though he is little known, and though the Roman Catholic Church, with some reason, considers him a heretic and apostate, he remains a towering figure whose importance in the church stands on a par with such men as Augustine, Luther, and Calvin.

Much of Tertullian's life has been lost in the dusty past. Only the sketchiest of details have come down to us. He was from Carthage, a city in North Africa of some importance in the history of the Roman Empire, and a city known to the youngest of school boys who have learned a bit of ancient history.

The church of the third century had spread throughout the Roman Empire. It was divided geographically and nationally into two parts. The Eastern church, including Palestine, Syria, Asia Minor, Greece, and Egypt, was basically Greek. It spoke the Greek language and possessed the speculative Greek mind. The Western church, including Italy, Spain, Gaul, and North Africa, was Latin. It spoke the Latin language and was under the influence of the

practical Roman mind with its emphasis on law. Tertullian belonged
to the Western church.

Christianity had come to North Africa early, probably from Italy.
But the Lord's work there brought much fruit, and by the middle of
the third century ninety ministers were laboring in the area of the
province in which Carthage was found. Tertullian had reminded the
pagans of God's work in their land.

> If we wanted to act not simply as secret avengers but as open enemies, what
> effective opposition could be offered us? We are but of yesterday, and yet we
> have filled all the places that belong to you—cities, islands, forts, towns,
> exchanges; the military camps themselves, tribes, town councils, the palace,
> the senate, the market-place; we have left you nothing but your temples.

The church in North Africa had come to know what persecution
was, for the sands of this part of Africa had been soaked with the
blood of countless martyrs. Tertullian spoke out of personal
experience when he wrote that "the blood of the martyrs is the seed
of the church." In an angry defense of the Christians, Tertullian had
charged the empire with unjust hatred against Christianity.

> The term "conspiracy" should not be applied to us but rather to those who
> plot to foment hatred against decent and worthy people, those who shout for
> the blood of the innocent and plead forsooth in justification of their hatred
> the foolish excuse that the Christians are to blame for every public disaster and
> every misfortune that befalls the people. If the Tiber rises to the walls, if the
> Nile fails to rise and flood the fields, if the sky withholds its rain, if there is
> earthquake or famine or plague, straightway the cry arises: "The Christians to
> the lions!"

## *His Early Life*

Who was Tertullian? He was born in Carthage from heathen
parents. No one knows the date of his birth. The guesses range from
A.D. 145 to A.D. 160, although the earlier date is probably nearer
the truth. His father was a Roman centurion in the army of Africa,
something like an aide-de-camp to a higher officer. Because his father
had high aspirations for his son, Tertullian was prepared for civil
service in the empire through training in jurisprudence and the art of
forensic eloquence. His unusual intellectual abilities soon put him at
the head of his peers.

All this was abandoned when he was converted to Christianity.
Although he does not speak of his conversion in his writings, he

alludes to the fact that it was a sudden and dramatic event. He writes, "Christians are made, not born"—a reflection on God's sudden work which brought him from the darkness of paganism to the light of the gospel.

### *His Life's Work*

From the time of his conversion Tertullian became an unrelenting opponent of every enemy of the church and a vehement and forceful defender of the faith. He was a man of great ability, surpassed by few in the church's history. But he was also a man of sharp and vehement temper, quick of wit, and able to wield an often bitter and satirical pen against those who denied the faith. His writings remind one of Luther. He was not afraid to call his enemies anything within even the widest bounds of decency. He fought hard and long and fearlessly in defense of the faith.

Within ten years of his conversion, Tertullian became a presbyter in the church. This is rather surprising in light of the fact that he was married, for the church already at that early date tended to frown on married men holding special offices in the church. In two letters of great length to his wife, he extolled the blessedness of the marriage state and warned against adultery and immodesty. The thoughts expressed in those writings are pertinent to our own immoral age.

Tertullian was a fierce enemy of all who attacked Christianity. He despised pagan philosophy and defended the church against paganism. He fought against the heretic Marcion, the first higher critic of Scripture, who attacked the infallible inspiration of God's Word. He wrote at length against the Gnostics.

This latter is of no little importance. The Gnostic heresy, which caused the church so much grief in its early history, can very well be classified as the first attempt to establish a worldwide religion to which all men could subscribe. It fused together into one system elements of Christianity, Greek philosophy, and Oriental mysticism. It proposed a religion acceptable to all men because it kept what was supposed to be the best elements in every religion. It is like much of modern ecumenism, which also seeks to forge a system of doctrine which can be acceptable to Christians, Jews, Buddhists, Mohammedans, and pagans.

Against this fierce attack on the church Tertullian waged uncompromising war. He insisted that the Christian faith was unique among all the religions of the world because it had its origin in

Scripture, and Scripture was given by God. He said all other religions were apostate and deviations from the truth. It is not surprising that this stand did not win Tertullian friends. It was opposed then as it is now, for it is the enemy of all compromise and unholy toleration.

Tertullian did not only wield his fiery pen against heretics of every sort; he also devoted his energies to the development of the truth. This is beyond doubt his outstanding contribution to the history of Christ's church.

Two areas especially are notable in this respect.

Although his successor in North Africa, Augustine, was the one used by God to develop the doctrines of total depravity and sovereign and particular grace over against Pelagianism and Semi-Pelagianism, Tertullian anticipated Augustine in some respects. "He was the pioneer of orthodox anthropology and soteriology, the teacher of Cyprian [another North African theologian], and forerunner of Augustine, in the latter of whom his spirit was reproduced in twofold measure, though without its eccentricities and angularities."

One striking instance of Tertullian's ability to formulate ideas ahead of his time was his doctrine of traducianism. Traducianism teaches that the soul of a man is given him, along with his body, from his parents and is not specially created by God at the moment of conception. While the rightness or wrongness of this doctrine is not so important to us, it becomes important because Tertullian taught it in defense of the truth of original sin; in other words, that sin was transmitted through conception and birth to result in a depraved nature. We receive a corrupt body *and soul* from our parents because both body and soul come from our parents. Almost alone, Tertullian taught this important truth.

What gives Tertullian a place of lasting importance in the memory of the church is his teachings concerning the divinity of Christ and the doctrine of the Trinity.

To appreciate this, we must understand that the church did not have at this time any formulated doctrine of these important truths. They are, of course, the most profound in all the Christian faith. The early church struggled with them. How can God be both three and one? If God is three, it would seem as if the Christian religion taught a polytheism little different from paganism. If God is one, Christ cannot be God. How can these problems be solved?

Many answers were suggested, but every time an answer was given, the church looked at Scripture and condemned the answer as being contrary to the teaching of God's Word. It took a long time before the church was ready to say what Scripture in fact did teach on these important points. Partly, the problem was that the church had no adequate terminology to express this truth because the terms we use, such as "person," "essence," "nature," and "subsistence," are not biblical terms. The church had to develop and agree upon a terminology which it could use to express the teachings of Scripture. It was not until A.D. 324, and only after a long and bitter struggle, that these problems were solved and the great Creed of Nicea drawn up.

One notable feature of these controversies was the fact that they were almost exclusively limited to the Eastern church. The Western church never did have any trouble with these problems, was not bothered by these heresies, and had, almost from the outset, a correct understanding of these difficult questions. That this was true was due to the genius of Tertullian. He was the one who, a century before Nicea, understood the doctrine, taught it and wrote about it, and gave to the church terms which we still use today, terms such as "Trinity," "person," and "substance." He was the first to teach that God was one in essence and three in person.

I find this almost beyond understanding that one man could be used by God to do so much for the church. While storms of controversy tore the Eastern church apart over these difficult doctrines, the West went on its quiet way, undisturbed by the storms, firmly rooted in these truths, all because of the labors of Tertullian, who taught them a century before Nicea.

### *His Last Years*

But the story of Tertullian is not complete without its last, sad chapter.

Tertullian spent his last years (he died somewhere between 220 and 240) as a member of a sect, the sect of the Montanists.

The Montanists started a movement within the church which emphasized the mystical and subjective. It was an ascetic sect characterized by protests against worldliness and carnality in the church, but tending towards outward forms of self-denial, which Paul describes as having no profit. Montanism held to subjective revelation through the Spirit and special manifestations of the Spirit in those who were Spirit-filled. It has its modern manifestation in

Pentecostalism and the Charismatic movement. There is, indeed, nothing new under the sun.

Many students of church history debate the question why Tertullian joined this sect. Some ascribe it to his eccentricity, some to his radical nature, some to his ascetic bent. We cannot tell. What we do know is that Tertullian did protest vehemently against all forms of worldliness and spiritual carnality within the church. It may be that the ascetic character of the Montanists appealed to him. At any rate, in this sect he spent the last years of his life, and as a member of this sect he died. Augustine says that Tertullian returned to the church before his death, but there is no evidence that this is true. It is a sad ending to a gifted man, and we leave judgment to the Lord. The greatest of men in this world of sin have their faults. Our trust is not in men, but in the Lord.

Tertullian's membership with the Montanists is, however, an abiding warning that such movements as Montanism and Pentecostalism rush into the church as a mighty wind to fill a spiritual vacuum created by world-conformity and dead orthodoxy. Let us learn history's lessons and be wise.

## Chapter 4

# Anthony

## Ascetic among Ascetics

### Introduction

*Some men in God's church belong to the roster of the heroes of faith only because their witness, though in some respects wrong, is important.*

*Such were Anthony and the ascetics.*

*The strange conduct of the ascetics can be understood only in light of the theological thought of the age in which they lived. Already*

in the third century of the history of Christ's church, errors were present in the thinking of the church's theologians concerning salvation by grace. It was thought by some that salvation came, at least in part, through our own works. It must be remembered that the truths of sovereign grace in the work of salvation were not developed in the church until Augustine's controversy with the Pelagians and Semi-Pelagians in the fifth century. While generally the church held to the truth of salvation by grace, the place of works in salvation (a vexing problem which has troubled the church until the present) was not clearly understood.

The practice of asceticism was rooted in a wrong interpretation of the words of our Lord which commanded disciples to sell all that they had and give to the poor, and of the words of Paul that it is better not to marry. Taking these instructions as rules of conduct in the church, many recognized that it was impossible for every member of the church to follow these injunctions of Scripture lest the church cease to exist; nevertheless, they continued to consider them authoritative commandments.

To solve the problem, many began to think in terms of a "two-level morality."

The lower level was for the majority of God's people. They kept their possessions and married and brought forth children. But there was a higher level of morality as well. Those who chose to live on this level lived on a higher plane of holiness and, consequently, earned more favor with God. This higher level was the life of poverty and celibacy, to which many aspired.

Coupled with this was the notion that especially the Nazarites in Scripture had made an effective protest against apostasy and worldliness in the church by withdrawing from the life of the nation of Israel as a whole and by denying themselves many of life's comforts.

So, when the church in its early history, enjoying a measure of surcease from persecution, became worldly and carnal, men arose who attempted to protest this worldliness by withdrawing from the church and from society to live the life of an ascetic.

Two things were thought to be accomplished by such conduct: an effective protest against encroaching worldliness and the attainment of a higher morality which would win special favor with God.

The founder of asceticism was Anthony.

## His Early Life

Anthony was born in 251 in Egypt from wealthy parents who left all their possessions to him. Those possessions consisted of 300 acres of fertile land in the Nile Delta. But in keeping with the words of the Lord to the rich young ruler, Anthony sold all his possessions, gave the money to the poor, and retreated to the desert to live in solitude. The only exception he made in the distribution of the money to the poor was a small sum which was set aside for his sister, who had been entrusted by his parents to his care.

## His Ascetic Life

To conquer the temptations of the flesh, Anthony engaged in rigorous acts of self-denial. For a time he lived in a cave, then in a ruined house. The last years of his life were spent on a mountain about a seven-hour journey from the Red Sea. He wore only a hair robe and denied himself all but the basics of food and drink. His food consisted of bread and salt and some occasional dates. He ate but once a day, usually after sunset. He felt shame that he needed even this. Days of fasting completely were therefore interspersed among those of sparse diet. He slept on bare ground or a straw pallet, but often he slept not at all, spending his time instead in prayer through the night. His entire wardrobe consisted of a shirt, a sheepskin, and a belt. In later years he rarely bathed, thinking, perhaps, that filth was next to godliness. He spent his time in struggling with temptation through prayer and meditation on the Scriptures. Philip Schaff, leaning on the biography of Anthony by Athanasius, writes of these struggles:

> Conflicts with the devil and his hosts of demons were, as with other solitary saints, a prominent part of Anthony's experience, and continued through all his life. The devil appeared to him in visions and dreams, or even in daylight, in all possible forms, now as a friend, now as a fascinating woman, now as a dragon, tempting him by reminding him of his former wealth, of his noble family, of the care due to his sister, by promises of wealth, honor, and renown, by exhibitions of the difficulty of virtue and the facility of vice, by unchaste thoughts and images, by terrible threatenings of the dangers and punishments of the ascetic life. Once he [the devil] struck the hermit so violently, Athanasius says, that a friend, who brought him bread, found him on the ground apparently dead. At another time he [the devil] broke through the wall of his cave and filled the room with roaring lions, howling wolves, growling bears, fierce hyenas, crawling serpents and scorpions; but Anthony turned manfully toward the monsters, till a supernatural light broke in from the roof and dispersed them.

Only twice in Anthony's long ascetic life did he emerge from his isolation. Both times, by his ragged dress and emaciated and ghost-like appearance, he made a powerful impression upon Christians and heathen.

The first time Anthony emerged was during a time of persecution, when he appeared, almost like Elijah of old, to gain for himself the martyr's crown. He did everything he could to antagonize the persecutors. He visited Christians in the mines and in prisons; he argued with the judges in court; he accompanied martyrs to the scaffold to encourage them; he defended their cause at every opportunity. But no one dared lay a hand on him, and he was forced to retreat again to the desert.

The second time he emerged was during the Arian debate when he was 100 years old. He argued in support of his friend Athanasius and against the Arians, declaring that the Arian heresy was worse than the venom of the serpent and no better than heathenism, which worshiped the creature instead of the Creator.

When asked to remain in Alexandria, Anthony refused: "As a fish out of water, so a monk out of his solitude dies."

By his example, he attracted thousands to the monastic life. Many more thousands, while apparently unable to emulate his way of life, flocked to his cave to visit him and seek his prayers. To feed them in the howling wastes of the desert, he cultivated a large garden, from which he was said to have expelled wild beasts by the Word of the Lord. Miracles were ascribed to him, and his prayers were thought to have unusual efficacy. He spurned learning of every sort: "He who has a sound mind has no need of learning."

Anthony died in 356 at the age of 105, after retiring to his cave with two disciples whom he took along to bury him in an unknown place. Athanasius gives us his dying words:

> Do not let them carry my body into Egypt, lest they store it in their houses. One of my reasons for coming to this mountain was to hinder this. You know I have never reproved those who have done this, and charged them to cease from the custom. Bury, then, my body in the earth, in obedience to my word, so that no one may know the place, except yourselves. In the resurrection of the dead it will be restored to me incorruptible by the Savior. Distribute my garments as follows: Let Serapion, the bishop, have the other sheepskin. As to the hair shirt, keep it for yourselves. And now, my children, farewell; Anthony is going, and is no longer with you.

## Other Ascetics

Anthony's example was followed by thousands, some of whom went far beyond his excesses. Some, congregated in colonies, never spoke to each other except on Saturday and Sunday. Hilarion never ate before sunset. He cut his hair only once a year and engaged only in prayers, Psalm singing, Bible recitations, and basket weaving. Others refused to sit or lie, standing for days on end and sleeping by leaning against a rock. Others permitted themselves to be covered with stinging and biting ants in the desert sands. Still others drank only what water could be collected from the dew which occasionally fell.

Perhaps the most unusual of all were the Stylites, who lived on pillars. The sect was founded by Symeon, who himself lived for thirty-six years on a pillar sixty feet high. Yet another spent sixty-eight years on the top of a pillar, refusing to come down, having bits of food and drops of water raised to him from admiring throngs. In the blazing heat, under the cruel sun, soaked by cloudbursts, buffeted by the wind, enduring the bitter chill of the nights, these strange men found yet stranger paths to holiness.

The ascetics were the founders of monasticism, which spread rapidly into the northern Mediterranean world and then into Europe. This monasticism continues in the Roman Catholic Church today though harshly condemned by the reformers in the sixteenth century, who understood its evils. The way to holiness is not the strange way of the ascetics.

It is between two extremes that the faithful child of God must find his way. On the one side lurks the dangers of the monastic life; on the other, the ever-present threat of worldliness. Worldliness destroys the church, but asceticism destroys the soul.

Our Lord has specifically said that although His children are not of the world, they are nevertheless in the world. They are not called to unite with the world, but they are not faithful to their Lord by fleeing the world, either.

Ultimately, fleeing the world is impossible, for we carry the world in our flesh—whether we flee to a cave, a pillar, a cold and dank cell of a monastery, or a barren dune in some far-off desert. The struggle with the world is the most difficult on the battlefield of our flesh, as the hermits and monks learned. In fact, such world-flight, in disobedience to Christ, makes the battle with the world in our own natures the more difficult.

This world is God's world. It is destined to be redeemed and glorified. God loves His creatures, and "every creature of God is good, and nothing to be refused, if it be received with thanksgiving" (I Tim. 4:4). It is a grievous sin to spurn it, and a slap in God's face to despise it.

Being citizens of a heavenly land does not excuse our contempt for God's world; it rather urges us on in our calling to use God's world to seek the things which are above. The battle to attain holiness is born by the sanctifying power of the Holy Spirit, is carried on in the day-to-day struggle to attain obedience in our daily calling in life, and has its sure victory in faith; for faith is the victory that overcomes the world.

## Chapter 5

# Athanasius

## Against the World

### Introduction
*It pleases the Lord, the King of the church, in crucial times during the church's history, to raise men of fearless courage who are willing to sacrifice all for the cause of the truth. Such a man was Luther; such a man was Calvin; such men were the leaders of the "Secession" or "Separation" in the Netherlands in 1834; the Lord has blessed the Protestant Reformed Churches with such spiritual fathers.*

Such a man was Athanasius. At a most critical time, he was raised up by God to defend the truth of the divinity of our Lord Jesus Christ against almost all men in the church of his day. The epitaph attached to his name throughout all ages expresses the honored place Athanasius occupies: Athanasius *contra mundum*—Athanasius against the world. It is remarkable that at such times as these it is often just one man who stands in the gap in defense of Christ's cause. One man, *contra mundum*.

### Early Life

The birthplace of Athanasius was Alexandria in Egypt, the city in which was found one of the earliest seminaries of the early church, but also a city which was a seething cauldron of competing philosophies. Because of its strategic geographical position, Alexandria was a bustling center of trade and commerce where East and West met. Greek philosophy, Oriental mysticism, the Christian religion: all clashed and fought for supremacy in this port city of Egypt on the Nile Delta.

Not much is known of Athanasius' early life. He was born in 296 of parents of high rank and great wealth. In keeping with the

social status of his family, he received a classical and liberal education and became well-versed in Greek philosophy. At an early time in his life he had come to know and love the Christian faith.

The story, perhaps apocryphal, is told of a number of bishops of the Alexandrian church who, while meeting in the house of their chief bishop, saw through the window a group of boys on the street imitating certain rites of the church, as children are wont to do. Watching while one of the boys was going through the rite of the baptism of his playmates, the bishops decided that the game had gone too far. After calling the boys into the house and quizzing them, they learned that the "baptizing bishop" was the young Athanasius. The chief bishop of Alexandria, named Alexander after the name of the city, took Athanasius under his wing and instructed him more carefully in the Christian faith. This was the beginning of a long period of close friendship between Alexander and Athanasius, the latter soon becoming the spiritual and theological superior of his mentor. Athanasius was soon made the private secretary of Alexander and deacon in the church of Alexandria.

## The Great Controversy

The story of Athanasius is woven into the warp and woof of one of the greatest controversies that has ever troubled the Christian church, a controversy concerning the doctrine of Christ's divinity.

The great enemy of the church, Satan, the prince of devils, has several powerful weapons in his arsenal which he repeatedly uses to attack the stronghold of Christ's church. Persecution is one such weapon, but Satan had failed in his efforts to destroy the church with this weapon, for "the blood of the martyrs had become the seed of the church."

Now Satan turned to false doctrine. His weapon was aimed at the very heart of the Christian faith: the truth of Christ's divinity. If Satan could rob the church of that doctrine, the church would be destroyed forever. The Lord Himself had told His disciples that it was upon the rock of this confession that He would build His church, and the gates of hell would never prevail against it (Matt. 16:13–19). The apostle John had warned the church that everyone who denies that Jesus Christ is come into the flesh is of Antichrist (I John 4:3).

Because the church was still very young, no formulation of this doctrine had been made; indeed, there was much confusion over the

point. How could God be the only true and living God while at the same time, both the Father and the Son were God? This was the question with which the church struggled. Various solutions to the problem had been proposed, but all had been rejected by the church as being contrary to the clear statements of Scripture. But what exactly Scripture did teach on this subject, the church was not prepared to say.

In these circumstances a man by the name of Arius set forth his solutions. He was a man of no little ability, but he was also vain and arrogant. He proposed that the Son, just because He was the Son, could not be God. Though perhaps He was eternal, He nevertheless had to be created. And if He was created, there was a time when He was not. Thus Arius taught that our Lord Jesus Christ was not God but a creature, even though the highest of all creatures.

Because of Arius' influence in the church, his views were widely accepted, and many began to defend what he taught. The result was that the whole church was torn by confusion, controversy, schism, and bitterness. The unrest reached also into the city of Alexandria. Here Alexander and his bishops saw the evil of the views of Arius and resolved to do all in their power to combat them. Alexander's deacon and secretary Athanasius was God's man to help in this noble cause.

Constantine was the emperor of the Roman Empire. He had thought to give a decaying empire new life and unity by embracing and supporting the Christian faith and making it the faith of the empire. When he saw his fondest hopes about to be dashed to pieces by internal conflicts in the church, he resolved to attempt a settlement by calling an ecumenical council at which would be present delegates from the church in every part of the empire.

## *The Great Council*

The council is the famous and venerated Council of Nicea, which met in 325, the decisions of which are incorporated into the Nicene Creed.

The council met in the city of Nicea in the northwestern part of Asia Minor, near the Bosporus. Over 250 bishops from all parts of the Eastern church were there; the emperor was present; a delegation from the West, sent by the bishop of Rome, was present; and Alexander and his youthful secretary were also there. Some of the members of the council came with bodies scarred and broken by the persecution of Diocletian, which had ended only a little more than ten years earlier.

The council was divided roughly into three factions: a group of men who were determined to support Arius and establish his views in the church; an orthodox group to which Alexander and Athanasius belonged, very small, numbering only about twenty men, who were ready to fight long and hard for the truth of Christ's divinity; and the majority who stood somewhere between these two factions.

The orthodox group was, far and away, the most capable; and by their steady and biblical defense of the truth, they finally prevailed upon a majority to adopt the solid orthodox position: that Christ is "very God of very God, begotten, not made, being of one substance with the Father." In the formulation of this Creed, Athanasius played a leading role and emerged from the council as the most able defender of the truth of the divinity of Christ. He was recognized as a man of outstanding "zeal, intellect, and eloquence."

One would think that the decision of this council would have settled the matter; for the truth was set forth, Arius was condemned, and the position which he took was anathematized. But this was far from the case. The controversy continued unabated in the church; in fact, it became more bitter, more rancorous, and more divisive until the church was fairly torn to pieces by the struggle. While, generally speaking, the out-and-out Arians declined in influence, another party arose, basically Arian but taking the position that while Christ was truly divine, He was of a "like essence" with God and not of the "same essence." This difference was expressed by two key words. The orthodox held to the truth that Christ was *homo-ousios* (of the same essence) with the Father; the Semi-Arians, as they were known, held to the idea that Christ was *homoi-ousios* (or similar essence) with the Father. I am always a bit amused that people today can get excited about what they perceive to be useless hair-splitting in doctrinal controversies in the church when the great truths of the divinity of Christ hung, in this controversy, on whether or not the little letter "i" ought to be included in this key word.

### *His Sufferings for the Truth*

It was during this period of confusion and ecclesiastical chaos that the light of Athanasius shone brightly. In 328, after the death of Alexander, he became bishop of the church in Alexandria. While almost the whole world went chasing after the Arian heresy, Athanasius stood like a rock for the truth of Scripture and Nicene orthodoxy.

For his troubles, he was banished no fewer than five times. Of the forty-six years of his ministry as bishop of Alexandria, he spent twenty years in exile.

His first exile began with his condemnation at the synods of Tyre and Constantinople. He was banished to Treves, in faraway Gaul (now France) on the borders of the empire, where his enemies thought he could do no harm. He was banished by the emperor for refusing to permit Arian men to the table of the Lord. He was accused of being a disturber of the peace and a troubler in Israel. In fact, the hatred of his enemies was so intense that accusations of murder and fornication were hurled against him. The former accusation he proved false by presenting to the council the very man whom he was accused of murdering. His accusers were momentarily speechless, but they continued their bitter attacks, and Athanasius was severed from his beloved congregation.

The fortunes of the orthodox party rose and fell with the particular emperor who happened to occupy the throne of the empire. When a new emperor came to power, Athanasius was recalled from exile in 338 and returned to his congregation. His enemies remained fierce and bitter, however, and the following year he was exiled again. This time he fled to Rome to find safety with the bishop of Rome, Julius by name. The West was far more orthodox than the East, and Athanasius found a sympathetic audience for his views. The time of this exile was spent in rallying the West to the orthodox position.

In 346 he was recalled, but again his labors in his congregation were interrupted. After ten years, a new emperor attempted to accommodate the Arians, and the enemies of Athanasius saw another opportunity to get rid of their opponent. In 356, while Athanasius was conducting a service with his congregation, 5,000 armed soldiers stormed the church building. Calmly, he began reading Psalm 136 and asked his congregation to respond. It was a moving moment. When he read, "O give thanks unto the Lord; for he is good," his congregation responded, "For his mercy endureth forever."

This time he went into the desert to spend time with the monks who had retired from the church to find God in their own peculiar ways. The time in the desert was spent in writing, and the content of his writings was the defense of the great truth that Christ is fully God. The Arians were idolaters who worshiped strange gods and were no different from the heathen.

Again (in 362) Athanasius was recalled to his flock but was almost immediately driven away by those who were stung by his attacks against them. As he left his weeping congregation, he comforted them with the words: "Be of good cheer; it is only a cloud, which will soon pass on." He escaped hired assassins on an imperial ship on the Nile and found refuge once again in the desert.

Once more he was able to return. Once more he was driven from his flock, this last time to find refuge for four months in the tomb of his father. By this time he was an aged man and longed to spend the last years of his life with his beloved sheep. The Lord granted this prayer, and he was able to return and spend the few remaining years of his pilgrimage with those whom he had so long and faithfully served. He died either May 2 or May 3 in Alexandria in the year 373.

## *His Character*

This remarkable servant of God suffered as few are called to suffer, yet he never once deviated from his defense of the great truth of Christ's divinity. He was a man of small stature, somewhat stooped, emaciated by fasting and many troubles, but fair of countenance, possessing a piercing eye and great power of presence. Though in his old age he became increasingly weary of the battle and the cares of the church, he never wavered from his position. Nor did he live to see that position finally vindicated at the great Council of Constantinople in 381, which emphatically reaffirmed the Creed of Nicea.

Athanasius' love for the truth was not rooted in a mere love of doctrinal speculation. He was intent on maintaining his position because he believed that the salvation of the church rested on the truth of Christ's absolute divinity. As he expressed it: the divinity of Christ is necessary for redemption because only God can do the impossible; in other words, only God can save poor sinners such as we are.

Other major accomplishments marked Athanasius' troubled life. In 367, while temporarily at peace in his congregation, he wrote a pastoral letter to all the churches. This is an interesting footnote to history. The churches were, by this time, accustomed to celebrate Christ's resurrection on the first Sunday after the first full moon after the vernal equinox—as we do to this day. The bishop of Alexandria was instructed to determine the date each year and inform the churches of the date. This instruction was due to the fact that the best astronomers were to be found in Alexandria. The bishops of Alexandria also took these occasions to write a pastoral letter to all the churches on some important point of doctrine. When this duty fell on Athanasius in 367, he used the opportunity to instruct the churches in the canon of Scripture and to enumerate the books which rightly were the rule of the faith and life in the church. Athanasius' letter contained the sixty-six books of the Bible as we now have them, and excluded the apocryphal books.

Athanasius wrote extensively on many subjects, but he concentrated on a defense of the great truths of the divinity of our Lord. Added to his many books was one which contained a biography of the venerated monk Anthony. It remains to this day a classic of the solitary life. Athanasius himself lived an ascetic life and was much influenced by the desert monks who gave themselves to the isolation of the desert to live near to God.

Athanasius proved his greatness "in suffering, and through years of warfare against mighty errors and the imperial court." The expression "Athanasius *contra mundum*" best describes "his fearless independence and immovable fidelity to the Scriptures."

"It was the passion and the life-work of Athanasius to vindicate the deity of Christ, which he rightly regarded as the cornerstone of the edifice of the Christian faith, and without which he could conceive no redemption. For this truth he spent all his time and strength; for this he suffered deposition and twenty years of exile; for this he would have been at any moment glad to pour out his blood. For his vindication of this truth he was much hated, much loved, always respected or feared. In the unwavering conviction that he had the right and the protection of God on his side, he constantly disdained to call in the secular power for his ecclesiastical ends, and to degrade himself to an imperial courtier, as his antagonists often did."

Gregory of Nazianzus, a contemporary of Athanasius, spoke of him in these words:

> He was one that so governed himself that his life supplied the place of sermons...He was a patron to the widows, a father to orphans, a friend to the poor, a harbor to strangers, a brother to brethren, a physician to the sick, a keeper of the healthful, one who "became all things to all men, that, if not all, he might at least gain the more."

May God be pleased to raise up such men in His church today.

## Chapter 6

# John Chrysostom
### Golden-Tongued Preacher

**Introduction**
*"Almighty God, who hast given to us grace at this time with one accord to make our common supplications unto Thee; and dost promise, that when two or three are gathered together in Thy name Thou wilt grant their requests: fulfill now, O Lord, the desires and petitions of Thy servants, as may be most expedient for them; granting us in this world knowledge of Thy truth, and in the world to come life everlasting, Amen."*

This beautiful prayer, so appropriate for worship, is taken from the liturgy of Chrysostom. It was used in the worship services which he, as the most famous preacher in the early church, used in leading God's people to the worship of their Lord.

Preaching has always been the lifeblood of the church. From the preaching of the apostles in the early church to the pulpits of God's church today, preaching has always occupied a central and important place. Only when Rome introduced into the church meaningless and godless practices did preaching decline and all but disappear from the worship of the saints. The Reformation was, above all, brought about by preaching—simple, biblical, expository preaching. And so it has been in the 400 years since the Reformation. When the church was strong, the pulpit was strong. When the church was infiltrated with false doctrine and worldliness, it was because the pulpit had failed. When reformation came into the church, it came on the wings of preaching.

It is not amiss, therefore, to consider the greatest preacher of the ancient church, John Chrysostom. Not only has his name become synonymous with preaching, but the last part

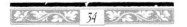

of his name, "Chrysostom," was given him because it means "golden-mouthed," and was indicative of the high respect granted him as a minister of the gospel.

## *His Early Life*

John was born in Syrian Antioch in 347 from Secundus, a pagan military officer, and Anthusa, a godly woman of great moral force and character. His mother had married young and was widowed at the age of twenty. When Secundus died, John was an infant, and his spiritual nurture came from his mother. So careful was she in John's religious instruction that a prominent heathen of the day said in astonishment at her devotion, "Bless me! What women these Christians have."

Antioch, where the believers were first called Christians, had become a worldly and godless city. One writer put it this way—and it gives us some idea of the environment in which John was reared:

> The warmth of the climate disposed the natives to the most intemperate enjoyment of tranquillity and opulence, and the lively licentiousness of the Greeks was blended with the hereditary softness of the Syrians. Fashion was the only law, pleasure the only pursuit, and the splendor of dress and furniture was the only distinction of the citizens of Antioch. The arts of luxury were honored, the serious and manly virtues were the subject of ridicule, and the contempt for female modesty and reverent age announced the universal corruption of the capital of the East.

John was given an excellent education in the best schools in Antioch, studying especially philosophy and rhetoric in preparation for a career in law. He was not immediately baptized by his mother, chiefly because of some erroneous views of baptism which prevailed in the church at that time. These views, held by some in the church, consisted mainly in the notion that baptism washed away all previous sins. It was considered wise, therefore, to postpone baptism so as to be free of as many sins as possible. At twenty-three years of age John was baptized by Miletus, the bishop of the church in his city. Later John himself would protest this practice of delaying baptism.

John marked his own conversion as happening in his twentieth year. After his conversion he abandoned his studies in law and a secular career and devoted himself exclusively to the work of the church. In preparation for this work, he studied under Diodore, who had founded a monastic school and was influential also in the establishment of a seminary in Antioch.

This is worthy of more than passing note, for the seminary in Antioch was devoted to the principle of biblical interpretation which insisted that the literal meaning of Scripture was the correct one. They took a position contrary to the seminary in Alexandria, Egypt, which promoted an allegorical method of interpretation. The tradition of the seminary at Antioch, however, was the tradition in the church during those periods when preaching was strong, and it is still the method taught today in all orthodox seminaries. God used this education to prepare John for his work as preacher. A fellow student was Theodore, later a bishop of the church in Mopsuesta, and himself a leading church father.

John had strong leanings towards the monastic life but refrained from entering a monastery because of his mother's wishes. Only after she died did he retire for ten years to live the life of a hermit in the hills outside Antioch. As a hermit he caused irreparable damage to his health, and he bore those bodily afflictions to his deathbed.

### His Service to the Church

God had more important work for John. He was summoned to return to Antioch where he first became a lector (reader of Scripture in the worship service), then a deacon in 381, then a minister in the church. It was during this period that he wrote a book on the nurture of children, and another on the ministry, entitled *The Priesthood*. Both gained for him a reputation of excellence, for they were filled with profound wisdom.

Above all, Chrysostom was a preacher. Already while he was studying for law, his oratorical gifts were noticed, but God put them to use in the service of the ministry of the Word.

For twelve years Chrysostom occupied the pulpit in the church of Antioch. It was his custom, as it has been in our own Reformed tradition, to preach series on a given book of the Bible or on one theme. Many of his sermons are still extant. He preached sixty-seven sermons on Genesis, ninety on Matthew, eighty-eight on John, thirty-two on Romans, seventy-four on I and II Corinthians, as well as series on other books. He preached not only on the Lord's day but also during the week, sometimes five days in succession. His auditorium was always packed with people, and sometimes the congregation, appreciative of his preaching, would break out in spontaneous applause—for which he severely reprimanded them.

One noteworthy incident demonstrates the power of Chrysostom's preaching. During the Lenten season of 387, the people of Antioch rioted over new taxes imposed upon them by the emperor Theodosius and burned a number of statues of the emperor and his family. Theodosius threatened to destroy the city in his anger and sent troops into the city to quell the rioting and judges to try the instigators. Chrysostom took the occasion to preach twenty sermons on the subject "On the Statutes" in which he reminded the people of their responsibilities to those whom God had put over them and reminded the emperor of the evils of undue cruelty. These sermons served to bring about a quietness in the city and an amnesty from the emperor. One writer of the time said of these sermons, "Though such a crowd had come together, the silence was as deep as though not a single person had been present." One is reminded of Luther's sermons which quelled the disorders in Wittenberg, brought on by the unruly Zwickau prophets.

Because of his great preaching powers, Chrysostom was appointed by the agent of the emperor to be minister in Constantinople. He had to be escorted out of Antioch by troops because of the great devotion of the people in whose midst he had labored for twelve years.

The pulpit in Constantinople was the most prestigious in the entire Eastern church, and perhaps in the entire church. The city was, after the time of Constantine the Great, the capital of the empire. Located on the shores of the Bosporus in Greece, the church was the most influential of its time.

But it was not long before Chrysostom was in trouble. Great preacher that he was, he feared no one and preached the Scriptures regardless of whom he offended. Because Constantinople was the imperial city, it was filled with luxury and corruption, intrigue and depravity. Against all these sins Chrysostom preached with vehemence and force, and his preaching earned him the undying hatred of the Empress Eudoxia. Conniving with the bishops of Alexandria, she secured his exile across the Bosporus, but it was to last only a short time. He returned in triumph to his pulpit and continued to condemn the evils in the city. From an earthly point of view, he probably made his fatal mistake when he called Eudoxia another Herodias who would not rest till she had obtained the head of John.

This time Chrysostom had gone too far. The emperor deposed him, but John refused to obey the command to abdicate his pulpit. The emperor sent troops into the cathedral during a baptism ceremony and mixed the blood of the worshipers with the water used for baptism. Chrysostom was exiled to Cucresus in the Taurus mountains of Armenia. In a letter he described his feelings upon being exiled:

> When I was driven from the city, I felt no anxiety, but said to myself: If the empress wishes to banish me, let her do so; "the earth is the Lord's." If she wants to have me sawn asunder, I have Isaiah for an example. If she wants me to be drowned in the ocean, I think of Jonah. If I am to be thrown into the fire, the three men in the furnace suffered the same. If cast before wild beasts, I remember Daniel in the lions' den. If she wants me to be stoned, I have before me Stephen, the first martyr. If she demands my head, let her do so; John the Baptist shines before me. Naked I came from my mother's womb, naked shall I leave this world. Paul reminds me, "If I still pleased men, I would not be the servant of Christ."

## In Exile

Even in exile Chrysostom's influence continued, for people from Antioch and other parts of the empire came to visit him, and he carried on correspondence with people in all parts of the empire—a total of 242 letters.

And so the empress had Chrysostom banished to another place, so far removed from the churches that he could have no influence at all: the remote northeast corner of the Black Sea, called Pitys. On the way, he was cruelly treated by the soldiers and died during the journey. The year was 407. He was buried in an obscure grave. Notwithstanding, the church honored him and several years later exhumed his body and moved it to a grave in Constantinople. He had died a martyr for the faith in a time when there was supposed to be no persecution.

"The personal appearance of the golden-mouthed orator was not imposing, but dignified and winning. He was of small stature (like David, Paul, Athanasius, Melanchthon, and others). He had an emaciated frame; a large, bald head; a lofty, wrinkled forehead; deep-set, bright, piercing eyes; pallid, hollow cheeks; and a short, gray beard."

Chrysostom was a preacher who emphasized the moral aspects of the Christian faith. He himself described his work in this way:

"My work is like that of a man who is trying to clean a piece of ground into which a muddy stream is constantly flowing."

In keeping with his times, Chrysostom held some views which were later considered erroneous by the church. Orthodox in all matters to which the church had addressed itself, he took a weak position on the depravity of man and the power of sin in man's nature, but these issues were not to be defined by the church until the work of the great church father Augustine.

John Chrysostom has gone down in history as one of the church's great preachers. Fearless, catering to no man, willing to suffer the consequences of his firm commitment to Scripture, he is an abiding testimony of the importance of the preaching in the church. May God give such preachers to the church today.

Chapter 7

# Augustine
## Theologian of Sovereign Grace

### Introduction

*There are times in the history of the church of Christ when God has such an important work for a man in the defense and development of the faith that in a special way God determines his life, almost from infancy, to prepare him for that calling. This was the case with Martin Luther, whose deep struggle with the assurance of his salvation was used by God to lead him to the great*

truth of justification by faith alone. This was also true of Augustine, whose wayward and sinful youth was used by God to prepare him for the development of the truths of sovereign and particular grace. Herman Hoeksema writes:

> God had prepared Augustine also spiritually for this battle (against Pelagianism). He had been forcibly drawn out of the forces of sin unto the redemption there is in Christ Jesus. He had tasted that, "It is not of him that willeth, nor of him that runneth, but of God that showeth mercy." It had become a fact of experience to him that only efficacious grace was sufficient to draw the sinner out of darkness into light, and the free-will moralism of Pelagius was an abomination to him because of that experience...We can understand that when...the refined but highly superficial Pelagius and his disciple began to make propaganda for a doctrine that was not only clearly in conflict with Scripture but also militated against all that Augustine had experienced of the grace of God, he threw himself into the battle with all his heart.

### His Life of Sin

Augustine was born on November 13, 354, in Tagaste, a part of North Africa which is known today as Algeria. One wonders what happened in

the days of the courtship and marriage of his parents, for his father, Patricius, was an unbeliever whose interest in his son was limited to preparing Augustine for a career which would lead to fame and fortune, and his mother, Monica, was a woman of exceptional piety and godliness whose great sorrow in life was her wayward son. So long and bitterly did she weep and pray for her son that he has become known as a "son of tears."

Although Augustine attended classes for catechumens, he early fell into the sins of idleness, dissipation, and immorality. When he was only seventeen years old, the same year his father died, he took a mistress, and a year later he fathered a son, Adeodatus.

All this time Augustine was pursuing his education, and he proved to be an able student. As is so often true, his very ability proved his downfall. He drifted, as a bumblebee looking for nectar, from one heresy to another. First it was the Manichaean error, which taught that there are two eternal and independent principles in the world: light and the good god, and darkness and the evil god. These two principles are in eternal conflict, with the outcome forever undetermined.

Then it was astrology with its vain and empty superstitions. From astrology Augustine drifted into skepticism, a philosophy which is nothing but an intellectual shrug of the shoulders: it is impossible ever to know what is true and what is false, what is right and what is wrong.

During this period of immorality and apostasy, Augustine began to develop a career. In 376 he taught grammar in his birthplace; a short time later he went to Carthage to teach rhetoric. In 382 (now twenty-eight years old) he determined to go to Italy but did not want his mother with him. He left without telling her of his departure or destination but took with him his mistress and son. He briefly taught rhetoric in Rome. From there he went to Milan where, by divine appointment, he came under the influence of the powerful preacher Ambrose, the godly and courageous bishop of the church in Milan.

## *His Conversion*

Although Augustine went to hear Ambrose preach only in order to learn more of Ambrose's skills as an orator and rhetorician, he soon came under the power of the gospel. Gradually his errors were stripped away, although he resisted with all his might, especially because of the lusts of his flesh. It was a time of struggle.

> Obstinate in seeking truth outside of her only sanctuary, agitated by the stings of his conscience, bound by habit, drawn by fear,

subjugated by passion, touched with the beauty of virtue, seduced by the charms of vice, victim of both, never satisfied in his false delights, struggling constantly against the errors of his sect and the mysteries of religion, an unfortunate running from rock to rock to escape shipwreck, he fled from the light which pursued him: such is the picture by which he himself describes his conflicts in his Confessions.

This fierce struggle finally brought Augustine to understand, with a profound awareness, that the grace of God delivering from sin is sovereign and irresistible, overcoming and defeating all our resistance, accomplishing a work the author of which is God alone.

Augustine himself tells us the story of his final conversion in his *Confessions*, and we can do no better than hear him tell it. One day, torn by violent struggles, he fled to a garden to attempt to find calm. While in the garden he heard a voice say, "Take up and read. Take up and read." Augustine tells us that he picked up "the volume of the Apostle."

> I seized it and opened it, and in silence I read the first passage on which my eyes fell. "Let us walk honestly, as in the day; not in rioting and drunkenness...But put ye on the Lord Jesus Christ, and make not provision for the flesh to fulfill the lusts thereof." I had no wish to read more and no need to do so. For in an instant, as I came to the end of the sentence, it was as though the light of faith flooded into my heart and all the darkness of doubt was dispelled.

Later, explaining it all, he wrote the following in a touching confession:

> I have loved Thee late, Thou Beauty, so old and so new; I have loved Thee late! And lo! Thou wast within, but I was without, and was seeking Thee there. And into Thy fair creation I plunged myself in my ugliness; for Thou wast with me, and I was not with Thee! Those things kept me away from Thee, which had not been, except they had been in Thee! Thou didst call, and didst cry aloud, and break through my deafness. Thou didst glimmer, Thou didst shine, and didst drive away my blindness. Thou didst breathe, and I drew breath, and breathed in Thee. I tasted Thee, and I hunger and thirst. Thou didst touch me, and I burn for Thy peace. If I, with all that is within me, may once live in Thee, then shall pain and trouble forsake me; entirely filled with Thee, all shall be life to me.

After a year of preparation, Augustine and his son Adeodatus were baptized by Ambrose. Augustine soon left Milan to return to Africa. His mother, who had followed him to Italy, now set out to travel

with him back to Africa, but she died at the port on the Tiber River in the arms of her son, with the joy of answered prayer in her heart, and after a profound and moving discussion with him of the glories of heaven.

## *Labors in the Church*

Augustine journeyed to Africa, revisited Rome, returned again to Africa, and began his work in the cause of Christ. In 389 he was, against his will, ordained presbyter in the North African city of Hippo Regius by Valerius, its bishop. In 395 he was ordained assistant bishop, and in 396, at the death of Valerius, he was ordained his successor. Augustine spent the rest of his life as pastor of the large flock in Hippo, as prolific writer, ardent defender of the faith, and faithful man of God in the service of the truth.

Augustine produced an enormous amount of work after his conversion, most of it of enduring value. Some of his better known works are these: *Confessions*, part of which every child of God ought to read at some time in his life; *City of God*, written to explain the fall of Rome before the barbarian hordes, but including a Christian philosophy of history, a clear exposition of the antithesis; and some of his teachings on sovereign predestination; a treatise on *The Trinity*, which is the clearest exposition of this doctrine prior to the writings of Calvin; *Retractions*, in which he corrected all his earlier writings and withdrew statements with which he disagreed after coming to maturity of thought; and many writings against the Pelagians and Semi-Pelagians.

Augustine did battle with the Manichaeans, a sect to which he had belonged prior to his conversion, and with the Donatists, a schismatic sect which he attempted to woo back into the church. But his greatest battles were waged against the Pelagians and Semi-Pelagians. About these battles we must speak.

It must be remembered that, prior to Augustine, the church had made no advances in the areas of such doctrines as the fall of Adam, the depravity of man, the work of salvation through grace, or the doctrine of predestination. In fact, it was generally held in the church that, although the salvation of man is rooted in the cross of Christ, it is dependent upon man's free will. Almost all the church fathers held to this.

Pelagius appeared on the scene with his superficial and God-denying teachings in which salvation was entirely rooted in the

natural ability of man to do good and to earn his own salvation by
good works. The Semi-Pelagianism which followed outright
Pelagianism was only an early form of Arminianism and a
modification of Pelagianism.

Against this sort of nonsense, Augustine fought. It is a never-
ceasing source of amazement to me how clearly Augustine saw the
issues and developed the doctrines involved. Not only did Augustine
take issue with the errors promoted by Pelagius and the Semi-
Pelagians, but he also developed the doctrine of sovereign and
particular grace. More specifically, he denied any kind of "free offer
of the gospel" and "common grace," even calling the so-called good
works of the heathen "splendid vices." He taught sovereign and
double predestination, limited atonement, total depravity, imputed
guilt, and salvation by the sovereign work of grace in the hearts of
the elect. Single-handedly he laid the whole foundation for a biblical
anthropology and soteriology.

Sad to say, Augustine's doctrines were never received in the
Romish church. Semi-Pelagianism won the day shortly after
Augustine's death, and a mighty defender of Augustine's views,
Gotteschalk by name, was martyred in the ninth century for teaching
them. In a way this was inevitable, for the church, even in
Augustine's day, had committed itself to a view at odds with
Augustine's teachings: the meritorious value of good works. To
embrace Augustine's teachings would have involved a repudiation of
a doctrine already held dear by much of the church.

For this reason, in the inscrutable wisdom of God, true
Augustinianism had to await the time of the Reformation for
acceptance in the church of Christ. One who has even a cursory
knowledge of Calvin's *Institutes of the Christian Religion* will know
how often Calvin appeals to Augustine in a conscious effort to point
out that he stands in the tradition of the great bishop of Hippo.

And so do we. Students and disciples of Calvin as we are, we know
that the truth we love and cherish is a truth which goes back all the
way to the fifth century and the teachings of the beloved Augustine,
bishop of Hippo. In holding to those teachings of Scripture which
were dear to Augustine, we can find his words echoing in our own
hearts: "Thou hast made us for Thyself, and our heart is restless till it
rests in Thee."

As he lay on his deathbed, Augustine asked to have the Penitential
Psalms written on the wall so that they might be constantly before

him to read at will. He died August 28, 430, at the age of seventy-five, just a short time before the Vandals (a barbarian tribe from Europe) sacked the city of Hippo and destroyed it.

### Chapter 8

# Patrick
## Missionary
## to Ireland

**Introduction**
*Our Lord assigned to the church its task when, just before His ascension into heaven, He said to His disciples, "But ye shall receive power, after that the Holy Ghost is come upon you: and ye shall be witnesses unto me both in Jerusalem, and in all Judea, and in Samaria, and unto the uttermost part of the earth" (Acts 1:8).*

*The early history of the church of Christ is an exciting and*
moving history of its missionary enterprise. Scripture itself records for us how the gospel was brought to Judea, Samaria, and the entire Mediterranean world, with the result that the church was established in every part of the Roman Empire. The early annals of the church provide us with information of courageous missionaries who moved beyond the Mediterranean world into darkest Europe to bring God's Word to the many barbarian tribes who had moved into Europe and settled there.

Through the labors of the church, the whole of Europe was Christianized, so that it was changed from darkest heathendom and paganism to become the cradle of modern Christianity. Although the work covered many centuries, it had its lowly beginnings in the lives of men who sacrificed all for the cause of the gospel.

This is the story of one such missionary: Patrick, missionary to Ireland.

### Early Life

Not a great deal is known of Patrick's life; indeed, many myths about his labors have grown over the years. What is certain is what he himself wrote in his *Confessions*. He was born in Britain somewhere around the year 389.

Although the precise place of his birth is not known, he was born in a small village somewhere on the western coast of Britain, across the Irish Sea from Ireland.

At the time of Patrick's birth, Christianity had already come to Britain, probably through Christian soldiers in the Roman army, for Britain formed the northernmost boundary of the Roman Empire. The Romans had succeeded in establishing in southern Britain a rather advanced civilization, and through the spread of Christianity many in Britain had become Christians. Within the sphere of the influence of Roman control, Patrick was born.

Patrick tells us in his *Confessions* that his father, Calpornus, was a deacon and a local magistrate, and his grandfather was a priest in the church of that time. He received some Christian instruction, although he leaves the impression that this instruction was meager and unsatisfactory. He learned the rudiments of the Christian faith, but true faith in God had not yet found a place in his heart.

Tragedy struck Patrick's home when he was sixteen years old. Raiders from across the Irish Sea—crude and illiterate barbarians— raided the coast where Patrick lived. We can only imagine the suffering and pain which was the lot of the inhabitants when thousands of young men, including Patrick, were captured and sold as slaves in Ireland.

In the providence of God, however, this captivity, which lasted about six years, was to be Patrick's preparation for his great work as missionary to the Irish. He was sold to a farmer who assigned him the task of taking care of cattle. It was during this time of loneliness and suffering that Patrick was converted. He speaks of it himself.

> After I arrived in Ireland, every day I fed cattle, and frequently during the day I prayed; more and more the love and fear of God burned, and my faith and my spirit were strengthened, so that in one day I said as many as a hundred prayers, and nearly as many in the night.

Although the time there, spent in loneliness and grief, was a time of suffering, it gave Patrick a knowledge of the Irish language then used, and it instilled within his heart a love for these crude and heathenish people among whom he was forced to live.

After six years of captivity, he escaped from his master and, after a perilous journey over land and sea, arrived safely in Britain. He speaks of his captivity as an interruption of his education, which he now pursued with some diligence.

### *Missionary Work*

Patrick could not escape the thoughts of the Irish from whom he had fled. He considered the Ireland in which he had been a slave to be as far west as one was able to go and on the very edge of the world. In his "Letter to Coroticus" he declared that he had been "predestinated to preach the Gospel even to the ends of the earth." He promised never to leave the people whom the Lord had "purchased in the farthest ends of the earth." Referring to Matthew 28:19, 20, Patrick saw "his work as culminating the expansion of the Faith begun by the Apostles, to be followed by the coming of the end. He gives thanks to God, who heard his prayer, so that...'in the last days' he undertook 'such a holy and wonderful work, imitating those who were sent to preach the Gospel for a testimony to all nations before the end of the world...The Gospel has been preached to where there is nobody beyond.'"

It was Patrick's burning desire to bring the gospel to the Irish, which probably accounts for the dream he claims to have had in which he saw a man who handed him some letters which included the plea, "Holy boy, we are asking you to come home and walk among us again." He considered this to be a call from God.

To this end Patrick entered the ministry of the church and was ordained bishop and apostle to Ireland in 432. He spent the next thirty years of his life working in the land of his captivity. He found an Ireland "untouched by the Roman culture that had helped to mold the British society into which Patrick was born. The Irish had no towns; their primary social order was the tribe, or extended family. They raised cattle, lived in wattle-and-turf houses, and repaired to forts, mostly wooden, during raids and wars. Their lives were full of superstition and magic presided over by Druid priests who were Christianity's chief Irish opponents."

It was difficult labor, filled with danger and hardship. Patrick's opponents were many and the people totally pagan. Yet the Lord was pleased to bless this work, and thousands were brought to the faith. Most of his work was done in Northern Ireland, that part of the island which is now called Ulster. The center of his labors was Armagh, and from it the gospel spread.

In his *Confessions* Patrick wrote,

> I am greatly a debtor to God, who has bestowed his grace so largely upon me, that multitudes were born again to God through me. The Irish, who never

had the knowledge of God and worshipped only idols and unclean things, have lately become the people of the Lord, and are called sons of God.

While undoubtedly Patrick's work was blessed richly by God, many strange traditions and stories have been woven into his life's story. He is said to have converted all the Irish chieftains and bards. He is supposed to have founded between 365 and 700 churches and consecrated 3,000 priests. Even miracles were ascribed to him: it is claimed that he healed the blind, raised nine persons from death, and expelled all the snakes and frogs in the island. But he himself makes no such claims. They are part of Romish mythology.

Nevertheless, Patrick's writings give evidence of the fact that he was a dedicated and humble child of God. A certain sweetness of character shines through his writings, and an unmistakable humility is evident in them. He never was a highly educated man, and he often bemoaned his lack of education. In fact, he was hesitant to write anything because his Latin was so inferior. But that very lack of education gave him a directness of speech which, even today, is moving. It was without affectation that he began his letter to Coroticus: "I Patrick, a sinner, very badly educated..." This letter, in which he speaks much of his calling and faith, was written to a certain king in Britain who, while professing to be a Christian, had captured many young boys and girls in Ireland. The letter was written to excommunicate King Coroticus until he repented and made restitution for his evil deed.

## *Results of His Labors*

Patrick established a Christianity in Ireland which was a far cry from the Christianity of Roman Catholicism. It was orthodox and biblical, the Bible being Patrick's only book. It was a Christianity that was completely independent of Rome and the influence of Rome's bishops. In fact, it was several centuries before Rome finally succeeded in bringing the Irish church under its papal rule. It was the beginning of the church in Ireland, which continues to the present, although only through great struggle and persecution.

The date of Patrick's death is not known, but he died peacefully somewhere between 461 and 493. He died a faithful servant of the Lord and was buried in an unknown grave in the Ireland which he loved.

Patrick was one of many such brave men who sacrificed all to bring the light of the gospel into the dark regions of paganism where only idolatry and superstition ruled. He is a noble figure in the annals of the church's missionary calling and an inspiration to all those who are called by God to bring the gospel to the ends of the earth.

## Chapter 9

# Columba
### Missionary to Scotland

*Introduction*
*Noah, after awaking from his drunken stupor, blessed his two sons, Shem and Japheth. Japheth's blessing was that the day would come when he would dwell in the tents of Shem. With the work of the apostle Paul, and in subsequent centuries, God brought Japheth into the tents of Shem as the church was established first*

in Antioch, Syria, Greece, and Italy, and then in the whole of Europe. Gradually Europe, where cruel and fierce barbarians lived, was brought the gospel, was Christianized, and in time became the center of the church.

At the time of the Reformation, when Rome had become apostate, Europe was split between Protestants and Roman Catholics. Only very few countries became completely Protestant, one of which was Lutheran (Sweden) and three Calvinistic: the Netherlands, England, and Scotland.

Some of the greatest heroes of the faith were to be found in Scotland. There the Covenanters shed their blood for the cause of the gospel as they fearlessly raised their voices in protest against all forms of papacy and prelacy. The purest of Presbyterian churches was established there. From them the great truths of Calvinism spread, especially into the United States. None fought so fiercely and bitterly against every corruption of the pure gospel as the Scots.

It is hard to imagine, then, that prior to the sixth century, Scotland was inhabited by some of the most fierce, warlike, superstitious, idol-serving, and reprehensible heathen among all the barbarian tribes: the Picts and the Scots. It was the gospel which subdued them; and it was the gospel which established in Scotland the church of Christ.

The story of the conversion of Scotland is the story of the great missionary Columba.

### *His Early Life*

Columba was born probably on December 7, 521, in County Donegal, in that part of Ireland which is known today as Ulster, or Northern Ireland. He was born a Celt from royal parents. The Celts were an ancient barbarian tribe in Western Europe who were supplanted by the Germanic tribes and who, after moving to the British Isles, were the ancestors of the Irish, Welsh, Scots, and Picts.

Columba is pictured by later biographers as a rather wild child, full of energy and mischief and always looking for a good fight. He was tall and strong, possessed a powerful and pleasing voice, and had a mischievous sense of humor. Raised from childhood in the Christian faith, he soon showed promise of intellectual achievement. He grew up in the company of a people who were quarrelsome and given to fighting; who, though they were in some superficial sense Christian, nevertheless retained many pagan customs and superstitions; who were fond of music and song; and who were characterized by a rough individualism. All these native characteristics were woven into the makeup of Columba.

Under the influence of his tutor, a priest named Cruithnechan, Columba soon became religiously inclined. His habit of spending a part of each day in a little church soon earned him the affectionate nickname "Columcile"—Colum of the church. Under the later tutelage of two teachers—both named Finian—he began a systematic study of Scripture and was instrumental in the establishment of several monasteries and churches in Northern Ireland.

### *His Life's Work*

About 561, two events took place which altered Columba's life forever.

The first arose out of his interest in the Scriptures. Eager to have his own copy of the Scriptures, he secretly copied the Psalms and the Gospels from a manuscript which Finian had taken with him from Rome. When Finian unexpectedly came upon Columba while he was copying, Finian demanded the copy. When Columba refused, the matter was submitted to the king, who ruled in Finian's favor.

But Columba was adamant in his refusal and was consequently branded a rebel.

The second incident arose out of the first. The king who ruled against Columba was Columba's cousin. A rift developed between them to the point where it led to open war. Columba, at the head of his clansmen, went to battle against the king and decisively defeated him. The slaughter was great, and at least 2,000 of the king's followers were killed.

After the slaughter, Columba was so smitten with remorse over the body-strewn battlefield that he determined to live the rest of his life in penance. Whether he was forced to flee Ireland because of these two events, or whether the choice to leave was his own, is not known. But shortly after these events, in 562 or 563, when Columba was over forty years old, he took with him twelve companions and sailed for the coast of Scotland. After a rough and perilous journey and a lengthy search for a good place to settle, he found the small island of Hy, now known as Iona, where he determined to live. The island was a treeless, barren piece of land measuring about three miles in length by one mile in width with a breath-taking view of the sea and of the coast of Scotland.

Here, on this small island, Columba built a monastery. It was not an imposing structure but a small group of huts which included a refectory, a library, a guesthouse, a kiln, a mill, two barns, and a small church. Here was organized around Columba a monastic life consisting of three groups of residents: the seniors, who were responsible for leading in worship, preserving manuscripts, and teaching the other residents; the workers, who performed the manual labor necessary to keep the monastery functioning; and the juniors, who were responsible for miscellaneous tasks. It was a hive of activity but was devoted especially to the training of missionaries who would be sent out to the inhabitants of what is now Scotland. Columba, in his own words, had now dedicated his life to bringing as many heathen to Christ as were killed in the battle with his cousin, the king.

Missionary work in those days was difficult. It required that the monks who were trained on Iona, and Columba himself, go to the mainland, where they were in constant peril of fierce people, wild animals, rugged terrain, an unforgiving climate, and the enmity of the Druids (the priests of pagan religion who hated with all their souls the arrival of Christianity). Here too lived the Picts and Scots, who—though Christianity had made some inroads into their land—were still basically the race of barbarians they had been long before our Lord was born in Bethlehem.

The stories that are told of the work of Columba are, in many instances, legendary. His biographers relate how he counteracted the magic of the Druids with miracles of healing; how he drowned out the chanting voices of the Druid priests with songs of praise to God sung in his own booming voice; how he gained the respect of Brude the king of the Picts who lived in a castle on the shores of Loch Ness; and how he labored with unrestrained zeal for the cause of the gospel. Stripped of all the legendary stories, the work of Columba shines as a light in the midst of the darkness of heathendom. His missionary labors were blessed by God in Scotland so that the true gospel was proclaimed there and the church of Jesus Christ was gathered. His missionary zeal is an example to all those whom God throughout the years calls to this difficult work.

Columba returned briefly to Ireland, the land of his birth, to attend various meetings of the church. His prestige and the respect in which he was held made all his past troubles in Ireland seem irrelevant. He used the opportunity to work towards the settlement of various disputes which had begun to trouble the church in Ireland, and his influence often led to a successful solution of these difficulties.

### *His Death*

Columba's heart remained in Scotland. To Scotland he returned, and in Scotland he died. On the last day of his life, at the age of seventy-five, he spent his time in transcribing a Psalter. In the late night, at midnight, he arose with difficulty from his hard bed to take part in the traditional midnight service. He arrived somewhat earlier than his fellow monks to kneel in prayer before God. Weakened by years of difficult labor, burdened with cares of the church, and bearing the ravages of many years, he suddenly collapsed. He revived briefly when his fellow monks arrived, took the few moments he had left to bestow on them his final blessing, and died peacefully in the early hours of Sunday, June 9, 597.

The character of Columba never changed throughout his life, for God gives to each man his character and personal characteristics at birth. His love of fighting, his robust constitution, and his tendency towards entering into every controversy were tempered, however, by

the grace of the Holy Spirit, and under the tempering power of sanctification, he became the powerful missionary that he was.

Columba possessed great leadership abilities. He was a man of impressive and attractive appearance. God had blessed him with a powerful voice. His singing—unusually beautiful—could be heard above any gathering. His melodious voice was eloquent as he brought the gospel to the heathen Picts and Scots. He was also forthright and uncompromising in the cause of the gospel. An old Gaelic eulogy speaks of him as "not a gentle hero." He had no patience with evildoers and could not abide duplicity. He was, and always remained, quick to reprimand sinners, and he would tolerate no shame upon the gospel which he loved and preached.

There was also another side of Columba's gifted personality. He was a man who showed great love for the poor and downtrodden. His deeds of mercy and compassion were known throughout the land. He possessed a deep love for the beauties of God's creation and reveled in the glories of God's handiwork in trees and moors, flowers and sunshine, heather and wildlife. All this was possible because he possessed a poetic soul. Some of his poetry has remained, and the reading of it is still enjoyable.

It is true that Columba lived in an age when the Romish church had already departed from the pure worship of God, but Columba was his own man more than he was a son of his church. That is, he was more Christ's man than a man in all things loyal to the Romish faith. This is especially evident in his deep devotion to the Scriptures. Although he loved the poetry of the Scriptures more than other parts, to the whole of the Scriptures he was faithful. He carried them with him wherever he went. He taught his fellow monks and others of God's people to honor and study the Scriptures and to meditate upon them. His preaching was simple, direct, and, above all, biblical. Always he expounded that great and glorious theme of the Scriptures: Christ crucified. If it could be said of Patrick, missionary to Ireland, that he "lived with the Bible," the same could be said of Columba.

Through the labors of Columba and others who braved the dangers of heathen lands to bring the gospel to barbarians—for Columba is only one example among many—God was pleased to begin to bring Japheth into the tents of Shem.

## Chapter 10

# Boniface
## Apostle to the Germans

**Introduction**
*When in the early history of the new dispensational church God was pleased to bring the gospel to Europe, the continent was overrun with many different barbarian tribes which were in darkest paganism and were constantly on the move. They were uncivilized, warlike, and worshipers of idols, and they were perpetually fighting with each other. They were a threat*

to the Roman Empire and finally destroyed the empire in the West in the fifth century. All the institutions of society in the Roman world were destroyed, except for the church. The church alone remained through all the turmoil and destruction of this terrible time.

The church was deeply conscious of its missionary calling and without interruption sent out its servants to bring the gospel to these barbarian tribes. It took men of self-sacrifice, courage, and conviction to venture into the lonely forests and mountains of Europe to fulfill the command of Christ. The dangers were many, not the least of which was the constant threat of vicious tribes who knew nothing of Christ and who despised all that belonged to Roman culture.

God was pleased to bring the gospel to these barbarian tribes in such a way that Europe was "Christianized." By this term I mean that the gospel, over the course of many centuries, so entered into the warp and woof of the life of these barbarians that not only were the barbarians brought into the church, but Christianity itself became woven into all the institutions of society. Society as a whole became Christian. The missionary work of the church produced Christian nations. We in America are heirs to this heritage.

This was not, of course, outside God's purpose. These very Christian nations of Europe and America have, over the course of the years, while retaining an external form of Christianity, become antichristian and will, in God's time, produce the great beast of Revelation 13. But from these nations the gospel has gone forth to the ends of the earth, by which gospel the church is gathered.

### Early Life

One of the great missionaries to bring the gospel to the barbarian tribes in Europe was a man by the name of Boniface. He was born in Craediton, near Exeter, in the little Saxon kingdom of Wessex in the land of England around 675. He was given the name of Winfrith by his parents, who belonged to the nobility. Because royal blood coursed through his veins, he had the opportunity to engage in studies, and he received the best education available. In his early years he proved to be an able scholar and soon advanced in his career. He entered a monastery and was busy there until the fortieth year of his life. In the monastery he was teacher, poet, grammarian, and theologian. So great were his grammatical skills that he prepared a Latin grammar for use in the school. It seemed as if a life of leisurely teaching and learning were to be his vocation.

### Preparation for His Mission Work

But God then called Winfrith to other labors. Reports reached the quietness of his monastery of a catastrophe that had taken place in the Lowlands, now the Netherlands. A missionary by the name of Willibrord had labored there. This faithful servant of Christ had had some success in his work among the barbarian tribes which inhabited the land on the far west of Europe, but his work had been completely destroyed by a fierce Frisian king named Radbob, who rooted all Christianity out of his lands.

When Winfrith (Boniface, as he was now called) heard these reports, he determined to travel to the Lowlands to attempt to restore the work. He forsook his life of ease, his home, and his homeland to travel to the dark forests and swamps of northwestern Europe to bring the gospel to the fierce Frisian barbarians. With two or three companions, he set sail and soon landed on the coast. But his work met with little success, and he determined to press on into the interior (into what is now Germany) to bring the gospel there.

Before traveling to Germany, however, Boniface decided that he would attempt to gain the endorsement of the most powerful man in Europe in the hopes that this would assist him in his missionary enterprise. Traveling first to what is now France, he secured the endorsement of Pepin, the ruler of the Franks, and then went on to Rome to secure the endorsement of the pope.

This latter endeavor was filled with important consequences for Boniface's work. In order to understand this, we must know a bit about the currents of history running through Europe at this time. The barbarian tribes themselves were constantly at war in efforts to expand their territories. Among the Franks a strong centralized government was gradually emerging, and the kings of the Franks were attempting to extend their empire into Germany by subduing the Saxons. An endorsement by the king of the Franks would, in the opinion of Boniface, aid him in the work. From another direction, the bishop of Rome was attempting to extend his influence and rule over the whole of Europe, and he saw missionary work as an instrument to accomplish this. Between the Franks and the pope an alliance had been formed which was to last for centuries. Boniface was, therefore, convinced that to receive credentials from both the Frankish king and the pope of Rome would advance his work greatly.

Having received commendation from the pope, Boniface became a loyal son of the church who fought with great energy to advance the cause of the papacy in Europe. He would tolerate no opposition to the church of Rome whatsoever. This involved him in struggles with other missionaries who had come to the continent from the British Isles and who wanted to establish a church far more independent from Rome than anything either the pope or Boniface wanted. These Scottish and Irish missionaries became Boniface's opponents.

### *His Successful Mission Work*

Germany itself was still under the sway of barbarianism. Some missionary work had been done there, but constant wars between the tribes and the general paganism and superstition of the people had resulted in an almost complete destruction of earlier missionary influence.

Into these streams and currents of life Boniface set out to preach the gospel. He had a rare gift for preaching and soon established churches and monasteries in many different locations as thousands

were turned to the church by his labors. The most famous monastery which he erected was in Fulda. He met with fierce opposition, and his life was constantly threatened.

Perhaps Boniface's greatest victory was scored early in his labors in Germany. The Saxons venerated a large oak tree as the sacred tree of their god Thor, the god of thunder. The people not only worshiped the huge and solid tree, but held their tribal meetings under the "divine" protection of its branches. When Boniface saw that the oak was an obstacle to his work and that it was a barrier to the reception of the gospel, he took an ax and, in the presence of a quivering throng of idol-worshipers, began to hack away at its trunk. While the gasping people were convinced that Thor would come in judgment upon this presumptuous missionary, the tree was felled without any interference from the heathen idol. Legend has it that a powerful wind from a thunderstorm arose as Boniface was chopping and assisted him by blowing the tree down and splitting the oak into four pieces of wood of equal length. At any rate, Boniface boldly used the wood of the oak to construct a chapel in the area for the worship of God.

As his success among the Saxons increased, Boniface rose in the estimation of the pope, who appointed him bishop in 722 and archbishop in 732. In the meantime, he applied his considerable abilities to the organization of the churches in Saxony and to the rooting out of evils. He traveled and preached, and he presided at synods called to rectify abuses and settle disputes. He was unsparing in his labors to root out the superstition and immorality which plagued these peoples, and he was totally intolerant of the Scottish and Irish missionaries who wished to labor with him, but who were not, in his judgment, as loyal to the church of Rome as they ought to be. He extirpated pagan customs, set rules for conduct, and punished heretics and wicked men.

When Boniface was an old man, the tug of the Lowlands came once again, and he resolved to return to the place of his earlier failures. He traveled there in 754, taking his burial shroud with him, apparently aware of the fact that in the Lowlands he would die and be buried. Here he labored with some success in the brakes and swamps of what is now Friesland in the Netherlands. But his work was early cut off. The enemies of the faith were aware of his work and determined to destroy it. While he was near the village of Dokkum to baptize a number of converts, a band of fierce Frisians fell upon the company. While the Christians wanted to resist and protect their leader, he admonished them, "My children, do not fight; let us follow the example of our Lord in Gethsemane. We shall soon see Him in His glory. I have longed to see Him, and to be with Him. Let us pray." As the Christians knelt in prayer, the mob, yelling and shrieking, fell upon them and killed Boniface and fifty-one of the people. He died on June 5, 754.

## Evaluation

We would surely want to criticize Boniface for his strenuous efforts to establish churches loyal to the papacy, and he must be criticized for this. Yet he was a faithful preacher of the gospel and was willing to live a life of hardship and self-denial in the cause of missions. In the course of his work he had himself defined his labors: "Let us die for the holy laws of our fathers. Let us not be dumb dogs, silent spectators, hirelings who flee from the world, but faithful shepherds, watchful for the flock of Christ. Let us preach the whole counsel of God to the high and to the low, to the rich and to the poor, to every rank and age, whether in season or out of season, as far as God gives us strength."

Boniface was surely an example of that mixture of holiness and weakness which characterizes all God's servants. One of his biographers says of him that "he had a restless, unsteady, complex nature, dangerously wracked by the black humours of despair, and he was extremely self-effacing and timid; although [he] accomplished an immense work, it was done almost reluctantly and without his ever having had the slightest desire to push himself to the forefront. The superior interests of the Church alone guided him, but when they were in play this timid man was carried away by his enthusiasm, and his boldness knew no bounds..."

Today a statue stands in the Frisian city of Dokkum commemorating the work of Boniface. The Netherlands became not only Christian but, after the Reformation, the cradle of the Reformed faith.

God uses weakest means to fulfill His will.

*Part Two*

# *Medieval Period*
## *750-1517*

# Part Two:

## Medieval Period (750-1517)

| | |
|---|---|
| | **700** |
| Battle of Tours 732.............. | **Alcuin** 735-804 |
| | **750** |
| Reign of Charlemagne | |
| 768-814........................ | **800** |
| | **Gotteschalk** 806-868 |
| | **900** |
| | **1000** |
| | **Anselm** 1033-1109 |
| | **1050** |
| First Crusade 1096-1099...... | **Bernard of Clairvaux** 1090-1153 |
| | **1100** |
| Second Crusade 1145-1153... | |
| | **1150** |
| | **Peter Waldo** b: unknown; d: 1218 |
| | **Francis of Assisi** 1182-1226 |
| | **1200** |
| | **1250** |
| Babylonian Captivity of the | **1300** |
| Church 1309-1377........... | **John Wycliffe** c.1324-1384 |
| Beginning of Black Death | **Catherine of Siena** c.1347-1378 |
| in Europe 1347............... | **1350** |
| Papal Schism 1378-1417....... | **John Hus** 1373-1415 |
| Council of Constance | **1400** |
| 1414-1418 .................... | |
| | **1450** |
| | **1500** |

## Chapter 11

# Alcuin
## Educator

**Introduction**
*In the eighth century, the time in which Alcuin lived, Europe was in a sorry state. In the fifth century the Roman Empire had fallen before the barbarian hordes that swept over Europe, and the old Graeco-Roman culture of the Roman Empire had been destroyed. In its place, the roving and militant tribes of uncivilized barbarians had inhabited Europe, and a great darkness had settled*

on the continent. Although by the eighth century a great deal of missionary work had been done, Europe remained for the most part under the control of illiterate and superstitious pagans who had obliterated all learning and reduced Europe to chaos.

It was not as if mission work had not been done in earlier years, but the constantly migrating and fighting barbarians had made the work ebb and flow like the tides of the sea.

Europe's most powerful kings were to be found in what is now France. The Merovingian Dynasty ruled there, not powerful by today's standards, but the strongest among all the barbarians. While national boundaries had not yet been formed, the power of France's kings was expanded throughout much of what is today France and into Germany. This dynasty had, however, been forced out of power by papal intrigue and the connivance of high officials in the realm. The Carolingian Dynasty had taken its place.

The greatest ruler of the Carolingians was Charles the Great, better known as Charlemagne. He was the founder and first ruler of the Holy Roman Empire, which some waggish historian has characterized as neither holy, nor Roman, nor an empire. Nevertheless, the Holy Roman Empire was important, for it was the realization of papal dreams: a political empire under the rule and control of the bishop of Rome, the pope.

Alcuin was the educator of this kingdom during the time of Charlemagne.

### *His Early Life*

Alcuin was born in England in the year 735, in the shire of York, now known as Yorkshire, and near the city of York, where now stands one of England's great cathedrals, Yorkminster. Born of royal blood, he was orphaned in infancy but remained heir to many possessions of his parents. Because of the untimely death of his parents, he was given over to the monastery in York, known then already as Yorkminster. Here he was well cared for by the abbot, Ethelbert, who was also his teacher.

Alcuin soon showed signs of great ability and became a favorite of the abbot, Ethelbert. He was given perhaps the best education available in England at the time, for the monastery in York possessed one of the greatest libraries in the whole kingdom. It contained manuscripts (books) from the church fathers and from ancient Roman authors, and it gave Alcuin access to classical Roman thought as well as church theology. Alcuin found himself in a literary paradise, and he eagerly devoured every scroll he could find.

Not only was the library the best in England, but Ethelbert was himself a great lover of books. Periodically he traveled to the monasteries of Europe and to other centers as far south as Italy to search for books. He had the financial resources available to him to spend vast sums of money in the acquisition of such books as, in his opinion, would enhance the value of his library in York. When Alcuin was a bit older, he accompanied his master on these trips, and Alcuin gained additional respect for Ethelbert's broad knowledge and learning and unerring instinct for good books.

In 766 Ethelbert became archbishop of York, and Alcuin became headmaster of the monastery school, responsible for the education offered there. He served with distinction in this capacity for fifteen years.

In 780 Ethelbert was awarded the "pallium," and Alcuin was sent to Rome to fetch it. The pallium was a yoke-like garment worn over the shoulders and indicated that the wearer had a share in the pontifical office. In more recent times, all archbishops petition for and receive it as a condition of office, but in the days of Alcuin it was a distinction of honor. Alcuin's errand was a high privilege. While in

Rome he met Charlemagne, a meeting which was to change his entire life.

## *Alcuin's Work in France*

Charlemagne was one of Europe's great kings. He was a monstrously large man, seven feet tall, and so huge that he needed a special horse to carry him. He was a mighty man of war who waged many campaigns against the Saxons of Germany and finally subdued them, forcing them to become Christians under penalty of death. He gave 2,000 Saxons the choice of being baptized or losing their heads. It is not difficult to surmise what option the Saxons preferred.

Charlemagne was a strange man of complex character. He was a friend of the church and, outwardly, a pious and faithful member. One of his "capitularies" reads, "It is necessary that every man should seek to the best of his strength and ability to serve God and walk in the ways of His precepts; for the Lord Emperor cannot watch over every man in personal discipline." Charlemagne's private life, though, left much to be desired. He combined in his character a generous disposition with murderous and brutal hatred of his enemies. He had four wives and numerous concubines and lived immoderately. He was himself never completely literate although he strove mightily to learn to read and write. In his kingdom he opened roads, gave his attention to the smallest details of the empire, introduced a settled order in the realm, and welded many different barbarian tribes into a political and economic unity. His main interest was in education. He gathered about him the ablest scholars of Europe and enjoined education on all males within his realm. It was in connection with this latter that he persuaded Alcuin to come to France and help him in his educational enterprises.

Charlemagne established what we can probably call a court school, over which Alcuin was the head. To this school came Charlemagne himself, plus the members of the royal family and court. Here Alcuin began his important work of bringing education to barbarian France.

The court of Charlemagne was a migratory court, moving about from place to place as Charlemagne waged his wars against the Saxons and sought to bring effective rule to his empire. This constant movement gave Alcuin the opportunity to work at the establishment of schools throughout France and parts of Germany, something at which he was very successful. From 781 to 790 he busied himself in this work. Because his interest had always been in books, he was instrumental in building libraries wherever he went and bringing to his schools valuable and important works from all over Europe.

In 790 Alcuin returned to England, but he returned to France in 796, settling in Tours, where he established a famous abbey school and built an extensive library. While heading this school, he not only developed educational theories but also supervised the copying of ancient manuscripts, including those of the Bible. These latter became part of the great body of manuscripts which form the basis for our King James Version of Scripture. Here Alcuin died peacefully in 804.

### His Character

Charlemagne so thoroughly trusted Alcuin that all kinds of difficult and wearisome responsibilities were laid upon him. Alcuin took part in various doctrinal controversies, was constantly sought for advice on all sorts of political questions, supervised various imperial enterprises, and was called upon to engage in almost constant preaching. All these activities were more than he could perform, and his health was severely undermined. This may very well have been one reason why he retreated to England and returned again to France only when he could enjoy the relatively peaceful life of the abbey in Tours.

Besides being the heir of his father's fortune, Alcuin received additional estates from Charlemagne in appreciation for all his labors. Most of his vast fortunes were used in the paying of the expenses of the schools he established and in the acquisition of manuscripts to fill the libraries. He was a moral reformer of no little ability and was instrumental in bringing morality and piety to the monasteries and churches of Charlemagne's empire.

Alcuin was a man of gentle disposition—willing, patient, and humble—and an unwearied student. He mastered Greek, Latin, and Hebrew as well as his native language and the barbaric "French" of Charlemagne's empire. He constantly protested Charlemagne's determination to force Christianity on the conquered but with little success. Charlemagne was too drunk with the notion that to Christianize the pagans (even at the point of the sword) was faithfulness to the church.

Many of Alcuin's works are extant. He wrote widely in the fields of exegesis, theology, liturgy, ethics, biography, and education. Nearly 300 of his letters are still available, letters which are

enormously important for an understanding of the times in which he lived.

## *His Influence in Education*

Alcuin's educational theories included a stress on the mastery of the ancient classics of Rome along with a study of the church fathers and various theological works. This labor was to have great influence on education in Europe. Alcuin is really the father of Europe's educational system. He began the famous monastery schools, schools which later developed into France's famous universities. His theories of education and his development of the curriculum were to be continued in Europe for hundreds of years, and even today much of education owes its ideas to Alcuin, the educator of France.

As Europe was gradually Christianized under the efforts of the Romish church, education became a part of this process. It is true that, after Charlemagne, the Renaissance of France disappeared and France sank into intellectual darkness. Charlemagne's empire was divided among his three grandsons, and the great work of Charlemagne did not long endure. Yet Alcuin's work was preserved in the monasteries, and the time of its full blossoming came when Europe emerged from the "Dark Ages."

As Rome worked its will on Europe, it was through education that Europe became Christian. The spread of the gospel brought the principles of Christianity to barbarians. Along with this gospel went the forces of education, for Christianity is always vitally interested in education and considers education an integral part of its calling. When Europe was civilized through education, it was also Christianized, and the principles of Christianity were woven into the warp and woof of all the institutions of society. Thus Europe (and America, settled by Europeans) became the Christian nations that they are. In God's eternal purpose, this was brought about through education. In this, Alcuin played a major role.

## Chapter 12

# Gotteschalk
## Martyr for Predestination

### Introduction

*In a series of radio sermons, broadcast in the 1940s, Rev. Herman Hoeksema called predestination "the heart of the gospel." This precious truth of predestination was first taught in the church in the fifth century by Augustine, the bishop of Hippo, who developed this doctrine of Scripture in his controversy with the Semi-Pelagians. The Roman Catholic Church, while claiming Augustine as one of its saints and while*

professing to be faithful to Augustine's teachings, rejected Augustine's doctrine of double predestination. The Roman Catholic Church committed itself to Semi-Pelagianism, and this became the dominant and official view of this church, a position which the Romish church still holds.

Not only did the Roman Catholic Church reject Augustine's doctrine of double predestination, but—far worse—it persecuted and killed an ardent defender of this doctrine about three hundred years after Augustine died. This is the story of a relatively obscure monk by the name of Gotteschalk, who gave his life in defense of a scriptural truth which has been the confession of every Reformed and Presbyterian church at some time in its history. It is still the confession of those who are faithful to the Word of God. That one man in the dark and dreary Middle Ages was willing to give his life for this truth is inspiration to all God's people who confess that God is sovereign also in election and reprobation.

### His Life

Gotteschalk was born in 806 in the home of a German count named Bruno. Gotteschalk's name appropriately means

"Servant of God." Little did his parents realize, when giving him that name, how appropriate it was. When he was still a young child, Gotteschalk's parents gave him to the Hessian monastery of Fulda as an *oblata*, in other words, as a gift to God.

When Gotteschalk was about twenty-three years old, he rebelled against a monastic life and asked permission to be released from the monastery. His appeal was made to the Synod of Mainz, which met in 829. This synod granted his request. However, Rabanus Maurus, the abbot of the monastery, disagreed with the decision of the synod and appealed to the emperor. He succeeded in his efforts to keep Gotteschalk in the monastery but became the lifelong enemy of this faithful servant of Christ. Gotteschalk was, however, transferred to the monastery in Orbais, France, in the diocese of Soissons in the province of Rheims. Here he was ordained to the priesthood.

Determined to make more of his life than remaining a mere monk, Gotteschalk applied himself to the study of the writings of Augustine. During this study, Gotteschalk was surprised to learn that the bishop of Hippo had taught a sovereign and double predestination (election and reprobation), a doctrine quite different from what was taught in the Romish church. After studying the Scriptures, Gotteschalk became convinced that Augustine had faithfully set forth the truth of predestination, and he became an ardent and vocal preacher of this doctrine. In his excitement over this discovery, he discussed the issue with his fellow monks and succeeded in persuading many of them of the truth of his position.

About this time (837–847), Gotteschalk began a series of lengthy travels throughout the Mediterranean world, visiting such places as Italy, Caesarea, Constantinople, and Alexandria. Wherever he went, he preached and taught his views on predestination. He was confident, though perhaps naively so, that the church, after hearing him out, would agree with him and alter its Semi-Pelagian position. He corresponded with scholars, debated with theologians, preached to people, and spoke of his views at every opportunity. He considered his views so essential to an understanding of Scripture and the true gospel that he could scarcely speak of anything else.

His interest in the doctrine of predestination was not, however, interest for its own sake. Gotteschalk believed with all his heart in the truths of sovereign and particular grace. He saw, as Augustine had seen, that sovereign and double predestination was the biblical foundation on which the truths of sovereign grace rested.

### *His Martyrdom*

In 846 and 847 Gotteschalk found a home with Bishop Noting of Veronica in Italy. This was the beginning of his troubles. He discussed predestination with Bishop Noting, pointing out how Augustine had taught sovereign and double predestination and how these views obviously agreed with the Scriptures. But Bishop Noting was alarmed. He wrote a rather lengthy letter to Rabanus Maurus, Gotteschalk's old enemy, to acquaint Maurus with what Gotteschalk was teaching and preaching. Maurus, who by this time had become archbishop of Mainz, decided to silence his monk once and for all. He called a synod in Mainz (or Mayence) to meet on October 1, 848, at which synod the German emperor was also present. Maurus himself presided. Gotteschalk was asked to present his views, which he did "in the joyous conviction that it was in accordance with the one doctrine of the church."

It is striking that Gotteschalk, in his defense of his views, not only boldly and courageously defended double predestination but insisted, too, that Christ died on the cross of Calvary only for the elect.

Under the heavy-handed influence of Maurus, Gotteschalk was condemned, and his views were branded as heresy. Maurus handed Gotteschalk over to Hincmar of Rheims, the metropolitan bishop of Gotteschalk. The accompanying letter read in part, "We send to you this vagabond monk, in order that you may shut him up in his convent, and prevent him from propagating his false, heretical, and scandalous doctrine."

Hincmar, though a learned man, was arrogant and cruel. He determined not only to keep Gotteschalk confined to the monastery but also to elicit from his monk a retraction. To accomplish this, Hincmar called a synod at Chiersy which met in 849. The results of this synod were fatal for Gotteschalk and his views. Gotteschalk steadfastly and courageously refused to recant, even in the face of the cruel threats of Hincmar. The synod condemned him. They adopted decisions which approved such heretical teachings as conditional reprobation, a universal atonement, and a desire on God's part to save all men. The synod deposed Gotteschalk from the priesthood, ordered his books to be burned, ordered him to be shut up in a monastery, and had him publicly whipped.

The cruel Hincmar was not yet finished with his "rebellious" monk. Evidently unable to tolerate any disagreement with his position, he was determined to force Gotteschalk to recant. Within

the walls of the monastery Gotteschalk was whipped so severely that he nearly died. But as he lay on the floor of his torture chamber, bloody and near death, he continued to refuse to retract his position. Even the rage of Hincmar could not elicit from this saint a denial of what he believed to be God's truth. The treatment of Gotteschalk was so cruel that it was protested by some leading clerics of his day.

Utterly defeated by the courage of Gotteschalk, Hincmar allowed the saint to languish in prison. While imprisoned, Gotteschalk, after recovering somewhat from the cruel treatment he received, composed two confessions in which he clearly stated his views. In these confessions, which have come down to us, he gave expression to his firm conviction that the truth of God would stand. He affirmed his faith in double predestination, in the particular atonement of his Savior, and in God's sovereign purpose and will to save in Christ only those who were ordained to eternal life; while at the same time he confessed his belief that the wicked are sovereignly reprobated to hell in the way of their sins against God.

After twenty years of imprisonment, Gotteschalk died at the age of sixty-two or sixty-three in the year 868. Hincmar forbade that he be buried in consecrated ground, and the last indignity of dying outside the church was heaped upon him. He died faithful to the end, a noble martyr for the cause of the truth. He died for a faith which was not again to be heard in the church until the time of Luther and Calvin some 700 years later.

## Conclusions

With the martyr's death of Gotteschalk, events took an ominous turn in the Roman Catholic Church. Since the church had officially condemned the truth of Scripture and had, on its highest ecclesiastical levels, condoned heresy, the result was that from that point on, the church gave official sanction to false doctrine and stretched the wings of its protection over those who opposed the truth, while it destroyed God's servants who defended the truth and fought for it with the courage and boldness of faith. The church set itself on a path which was to continue through the centuries until Europe ran red with the blood of countless martyrs. Crushed by the cruel and despicable Inquisition, the church of Christ could barely survive. When God brought Reformation in the sixteenth century, the pages of the history of the Reformation were written in the blood of the saints which still cries out for vengeance.

The Belgic Confession describes the false church as that institution which "persecutes those, who live holily according to the Word of God, and rebuke her for her errors, covetousness, and idolatry" (Art. 29). Nor has Rome changed its position in the least. It is prevented in our day from carrying out its wishes; it hides its cruelty behind a mask of benevolence as it speaks of "erring brothers"; but given the right circumstances, and they may very well come, its fangs shall once again be bared, and those who stand for the truth shall have to endure the full fury of its hatred of God.

Gotteschalk was a lonely voice in a barren wasteland. His courage was great and his death a martyrdom. Hans vonSchubert is correct when he writes concerning Gotteschalk, "It is not only our right but also our obligation to regard this German Calvin as one of the first heroes of the history of our faith."

## Chapter 13

# Anselm
## Archbishop of Canterbury

### Introduction

*The Middle Ages, from the time of Augustine, bishop of Hippo, to the time of the great Reformation, was a period of spiritual darkness. The Roman Catholic Church ruled supreme in Europe. It is difficult to find the true church during much of this troubled period. It is perhaps to this period, along with*

others, that the Belgic Confession refers in Article 27:

> And this holy Church is preserved or supported by God, against the rage of the whole world; though she sometimes (for a while) appears very small, and in the eyes of men, to be reduced to nothing: as during the perilous reign of Ahab, the Lord reserved unto him seven thousand men, who had not bowed their knees to Baal.

In our discussion of outstanding men in the church, it is difficult to find men in this period about whom to write, who were genuine men of God, in other words, men who held firmly to the truth and who represented the cause of God without the additions of erroneous Roman Catholic heresy and practice. In short, there were few, if any, who were in all respects faithful to the Word of God.

In treating men of this period, therefore, we have to deal with men who carried the freight of Romish error with them. In spite of this, they were men who were, for one reason or another, outstanding men in the history of the church, or who were representative of various currents of thought in the days in which they lived. We shall have to tolerate their mistakes. Anselm, archbishop of Canterbury, was one such man.

## His Early Life

Anselm was born in 1033 in Aosta of Northern Italy in the shadow of the towering Alps. His mother, Ermenberga, was a pious and godly woman who gave her son such spiritual education as was important for the religious upbringing of a child born in the church. His father was quite another matter. Gundulf by name, he was a thoroughly worldly and rude nobleman who attempted to dominate the lives of others and who was without compassion or sympathy in his dealings with his acquaintances. Ermenberga lived with the "Nabal" of her day. Gundulf's spiritual insensitivity changed when he lay on his deathbed and, just prior to dying, he became a monk to escape, if possible, the torments of hell.

It seems that Anselm, from his youth, was a sensitive and somewhat mystically inclined boy who delighted in contemplating the soaring pinnacles of the mountains in his backyard as means to bring him nearer to God. In his own words, when he was not yet fifteen, he sought "to shape his life according to God."

This soon brought him into such fierce conflict with his father that he left home, never to return, and fled to Normandy in France, far to the north and west. There he found his heart's desire and became a monk in the Dominican monastery at Bec. It was the gracious providence of God which led him there, for he came under the influence of the great Lanfranc, one of the most notable men of his age. Lanfranc was the prior, or governing head, of the monastery. He took Anselm under his wing to give him the education which was to prepare him for his life's calling.

## His Life As a Monk

When Lanfranc left France to become archbishop of Canterbury in England, Anselm was appointed prior in Lanfranc's place. Anselm's reputation as a scholar, a man of brilliant intellect, a theologian of considerable note, and yet a kind and gentle man, had already caught the attention of Europe's leaders. He served as prior in Bec from 1078–1092. During this period he did much of his writing.

In 1092 he, too, was called to England, where his reputation had preceded him. He went at the request of the earl of Chester, who wanted Anselm's help in his sickness. Anselm did not remain idle in England but spent his time organizing the monastery of St. Werburg

in Chester. After a year had expired, Lanfranc died, and Anselm was appointed to Lanfranc's place once again, this time as archbishop of Canterbury. He took this position with the greatest reluctance because the archbishopric of Canterbury was the highest ecclesiastical post in England, and all the responsibility for the welfare of the church fell upon his shoulders. He was ordained to this office on December 4, 1093, and served for sixteen years until his death on April 21, 1109. He served with distinction and has gone down in history as one of the great churchmen of the Middle Ages.

We must try to put some flesh on these bones of Anselm.

## *Teacher and Pastor*

There are many different facets to Anselm's character. He was a gentle man, apparently more like his mother than his father. This gentleness was shown in his love for animals. The story is told that, as archbishop of Canterbury, he was riding his horse from Windsor when a rabbit found refuge from its hunters beneath his horse. He dismounted with tears, picked up the quivering rabbit, and sharply reprimanded the hunters by comparing the plight of the rabbit to the plight of a dying man who fears the torment of punishment to come.

Anselm was not a great preacher; his strength lay in study, in teaching, and in guidance for those in distress. He could enter the minds of his students and anticipate and answer questions which they dared not ask. He maintained discipline that was wise and fair. When a fellow abbot complained that he could not improve his boys however much he beat them, Anselm responded, "Have you tried not beating them?" He was surely beyond his times in education and was one of the most popular teachers of his day. Since Anselm understood the problems of spiritual struggles with sin and doubt, he was able to counsel troubled souls who sought his help. To them he offered advice, compliments, consolation, reproof, and affection. He carried on an extensive correspondence in which he was always understanding and sympathetic yet firm, as well, when this was needed. To one troubled monk he wrote, "Of evil works we ought to repent, and forsake them before we die: lest the day find us in them. But of good works we ought to persevere till the end, that in them our soul may be taken out of life."

Anselm also was given to works of mercy. His greatest delight was in nursing the sick in the hospitals of his day and taking the poor under his care. About the only thing that angered him was the greediness and immoderation of his fellow monks.

He was an extremely mild man who suffered easily the follies of his fellow men. The story is told that at the Synod of Rockingham in 1095, during a period of bitter controversy among the delegates, Anselm was noticed sound asleep with a smile on his face.

## Man of the Church

Anselm found himself deeply involved in the investiture controversy in England. While this controversy was a complicated one spanning several centuries, its basic issues are easily understood. Many of the higher clergy in the Romish church were also feudal lords who ruled over vast estates. The pope wanted to control the clergy, something which he could do only if he possessed the right to ordain the clergy into office. On the other hand, the kings of Europe also wanted to ordain the clergy because these same clergy were secular rulers who ruled under the king. The kings claimed, therefore, that they should have the right to appoint to office since these bishops and archbishops were secular rulers under the king.

The bottom line, as is usually the case, was money. Both the popes and the kings wanted the taxes and revenues from these estates as their own. The pope wanted the money to flow into the coffers of Rome, and the kings wanted the money to come into the royal treasury. Then, as now, the love of money was the root of all evil.

As a loyal member of the church, Anselm did what he could to stymie the actions of William Rufus (wanton son of William the Conqueror) and Henry I, both of whom insisted on the right to ordain clergy. In his loyalty to the pope, he was forced to flee England two times to save his life. Part of his tenure as archbishop was spent in exile in France.

## Theologian

Anselm was also a thinker of great note. He is, in fact, often called the "father of the scholastics." While many in his day set reason before faith, Anselm himself followed this dictum: faith precedes knowledge. "I do not seek to understand," he wrote, "in order that I may believe, but I believe in order that I may understand, for of this I feel sure, that, if I did not believe, I would not understand." Certainly in this respect he was on the right track. But he was not always faithful to his own commitment.

Anselm is the father of the so-called ontological proof of God. In attempting to prove God's existence by reason, he argued that all men have an idea in their minds of "most perfect being." But, so he argued, that which is most perfect being must exist in fact as well as in thought. Since God is most perfect being, God must exist. Philosophers for centuries struggled with this "proof" of God's existence, and many efforts were made to show Anselm wrong. Apart from the whole question of whether Anselm's proof is sound or not, the fact is, as every child of God knows, that God is so great that He lies beyond the reach of human proof. He is God. He can be known and believed only by faith.

In all the Middle Ages, almost no advancement in the truth of Scripture was made. Anselm stands out as an exception. If he is worthy of our respect for no other reason, we ought to know about him for his doctrine of the atoning sacrifice of Christ. He carried this truth beyond anything the church had confessed prior to his time. He developed his views in an important book called *Cur Deus Homo?* (Why Did God Become Man?) He answered his own question by arguing that the incarnation and atonement of our Lord Jesus Christ was necessary because of the justice of God. We need not go into his argument here, for it was substantially taken over by our own Heidelberg Catechism in Lord's Days 5 and 6. To read these Lord's Days is to read a brief summary of Anselm's argument. His great insights into these truths have become part of the confessional heritage of the Reformed churches.

## *Troubled Saint*

Anselm wrote many meditations and prayers. It is enlightening to read them. Being a child of his times, he directed his prayers to Mary and many of the saints. They are filled with a profound understanding of sin, of the struggle which the Christian experiences in his battle against sin, and of his longing for forgiveness and holiness. They breathe a spirit of genuine piety and godliness.

And yet there is one characteristic of Anselm's prayers which cannot escape the attention of the reader: he never came to assurance. He never attained comfort and peace. Always reaching, never attaining, he continued lost in what is almost hopeless and black despair. We give here a few quotes from these writings. In a prayer to St. John the Evangelist, Anselm prayed this:

> Jesus, against whom I have grievously sinned,
>     Lord, whom I have wickedly despised.
> Omnipotent God, whose anger I have stirred up by pride;
>     You are the lover of John, your blessed apostle,

> And to him your terrified accused flees.
> Your sinner, your offender, however great his wickedness,
>> However great his disgrace,
>> Holds the name of your beloved
>> Between him and the threatening sentence
>> Of your just judgment.
> By that blessed love spare him who seeks John's protection.
> Lord, by what name will you have mercy upon sinners
>> If you condemn someone who prays
>> By the name of your beloved?
>> Lord, under what cover is there protection,
> If under the name of your beloved there is punishment?
> Where is there refuge if with your beloved there is peril?
> Lord, do not feel hatred for him who flees to your beloved.
> Lord, Lord, do not let my iniquity avail for damnation...

Or, again, he prayed to St. Nicholas,

> But if God looks down on me, who will look up to me?
> If God turns his face from me, who will look towards me?
> If God hates me, who will dare speak on my behalf
>> O God, "merciful and pitiful,"
> Do you indeed ward off one who would return to you,
> So that you cannot bear to have mercy upon one who cleaves to you?
> Will you curse one who has grieved you so much
>> that you will not hear any of your friends on his behalf?

This is instructive, and yet inevitable. Within the context of Romish thought, true comfort is beyond the reach of the sinner, for he must merit peace with God through his own good works. It is all reminiscent of Luther's great struggles. Within Roman Catholicism, comfort is impossible.

The hopelessness of these prayers underscores the greatness of the gospel of the Reformation which broke like a thunderclap over Europe. We have, the reformers insisted, a gospel which brings peace to God's people. We come with comfort. Can you imagine the mighty power, on Europe's despairing throngs, of that simple question and answer with which our Heidelberg Catechism begins?

> What is thy only comfort in life and death?
> That I belong...to my faithful Savior Jesus Christ.

That is all. That is enough. Anselm never knew it.

## Chapter 14

# Bernard of Clairvaux
## Monastic Reformer and Preacher

*Monasteries*
*It is impossible to understand the history of the church in the Middle Ages without having some idea of monasticism. Monasticism was so common, so much a part of medieval life, so influential in the history of the church in this period, that every aspect of the church's life was shaped and formed in the monasteries. Although monasticism began very early in the history of the church (it was already*

present in the third century), it reached the height of its influence in the Middle Ages. It was through the establishment of monasteries that the gospel was spread throughout barbarian Europe. Small groups of monks would enter the thick forests of Europe, establish a small monastic community, and make that community the center of missionary enterprise.

Monasteries were found by the hundreds throughout the continent. As the dreary ages of medieval history ran their course, these monasteries became centers of the life of the church. Thousands were attracted to them and entered them to find a true spiritual life. People from all classes of society took monastic vows: from the very poor to the rich and powerful, from the weak and insignificant to Europe's princes and rulers. Those who themselves did not join monasteries were often so influenced by them that enormous donations of land, money, gold, silver, and books were made to them. It is estimated that at one time monasteries owned one-fifth of the landed property in Europe.

Inevitably this vast accumulation of wealth led to spiritual and moral depravity. The result was that the monastic movement went

through periods of decay and reformation, which reformation was often brought about by the establishment of new monastic orders. Each new order grew rapidly until it often numbered hundreds of individual monasteries, some composed of men, others of women.

Each monastery had its own order or rule, although all were agreed that the vows of poverty, chastity, and celibacy were the principal vows which initiates had to take to become a part of the monastery.

In these monasteries was to be found the best and the worst of all that characterized the medieval church. Monasteries represented the worst of all ecclesiastical life when they declined spiritually and the inmates became guilty of every gross sin under heaven. They were sometimes cesspools of iniquity, filled with gluttony and drunkenness, with gross immorality of every kind, and with almost total ignorance and superstition. The monasteries produced a kind of quasi-clergy, men who were neither priests nor laity, but who often interfered with the ecclesiastical labors of members of the clergy. They were vagabonds who wandered Europe, preaching and administering the sacraments as they saw fit, mesmerizing the people with supposed miracles and filling the people with every sort of superstition. They were wealthy and indolent, influencing affairs in the church by the power of their wealth. Monks were also a sort of standing army of the papacy, for they were invariably loyal to the bishop of Rome and served him with fervor and extreme zeal. Evil popes could use these monks to impose their will upon recalcitrant clerics, kings, nations, and bishoprics. And, of course, monasticism was built upon a totally unbiblical basis: that true holiness could be attained only in world flight.

At the same time, monasticism represented what was also the best in the church. Monasteries which were not full of corruption were places of quietness and spiritual retreat in the confusion and turmoil of Europe as wild barbarians dominated throughout the continent. They were places where men and women gave themselves over to the cultivation of true godliness through prayer, meditation on Scripture, and the discipline of a life of self-denial. Monasteries were islands of safety and peace in the stormy seas of Europe's life. They provided shelter for the homeless, hospitals for the sick, schools for the uneducated, inns for travelers, and places of safety from marauding bands of brigands and warriors. They produced Europe's great universities and cathedrals. They developed the sciences of husbandry

and agriculture. They produced many of the arts and crafts which were later to become industries. In them, books were preserved and copied, especially the Scriptures. It is due to the painstaking work of scribal monks that we have today correct manuscripts of the original, inspired Scriptures. Their reformatory movement often served as dams against the tidal waves of corruption which all but engulfed the church.

## Bernard's Early Life

Into this situation Bernard was born. His birth in a castle of Fontaines-les-Dijon in Burgundy, France, in 1090, was into a family which belonged to the lesser nobility, a family characterized by an unpretentious life-style and what we would probably call an old-fashioned piety. His father, Tescelin, went on the first crusade and was one of the small minority who returned. His mother was to Bernard what Monica was to Augustine, for Alethea was a woman of rare piety.

Though trained as a nobleman, Bernard soon left this life and entered the newly organized Cistercian monastery. He was twenty-two years old. He entered the monastery with zest, taking with him his five brothers and thirty other men whom he persuaded to enter. He was a fanatic monk who gave himself so completely over to self-denial that he permanently ruined his health, something which, in later life, he came to regret. At the age of twenty-five he was sent by his superior to organize a new monastery in Clairvaux, which became the center of his activities till his death in 1153 at the age of sixty-three.

Devoting his life to the monastic ideal, he organized seventy additional monasteries and governed ninety more. His monasteries were not places of idleness, for all the monks under him were required to work hard from dawn till dark, all the while maintaining their monastic vows. His new movement became an instrument to reform monastic life in general and revitalize an institution which had fallen into disrepute.

## His Influence

From his monastery Bernard had tremendous influence upon the entire life of the church. Europe's nobility sought his advice, and the church's prelates, from the highest to the lowest, came to him for counsel. Nor did he fear the popes, one of whom was severely reprimanded by Bernard for his dissolute life.

One historian writes:

> Although he never sought high office, from his monastery he advised kings
> and popes and was virtually the uncrowned king of Europe. The fact that a
> monk who seldom left his monastery could exercise such an influence testifies
> to the tremendous respect in which spiritual leaders were held. The ability of
> one man without political office or power to change history solely by his
> teaching and example is without parallel until the sixteenth century, when
> Martin Luther would once again transform Europe from his pulpit and
> professor's chair in a small town in Saxony.

Bernard was a theologian of no little power. He not only opposed
heresy wherever he saw it, but he was also an enemy of several
Romish doctrines which have since been incorporated into Roman
Catholic thought. He opposed the doctrine of the immaculate
conception of Mary; he fought against justification by works in
addition to faith, against purgatory, against all works of supererogation,
and against the developing doctrine of transubstantiation.

## *Preacher*

Bernard was above all a preacher. His eighty-six sermons on the
Song of Solomon are extant. It was particularly his preaching which
had such impact on the church. So godly a man was he that Luther
said of him, "If there has ever been a pious monk who feared God, it
was St. Bernard; whom alone I hold in much higher esteem than all
other monks and priests throughout the globe." And of Bernard's
preaching Luther said, "Bernard is superior to all the doctors in his
sermons, even to Augustine himself, because he preaches Christ most
excellently." This is high praise indeed, coming as it did from one of
the church's greatest preachers and from one who despised monkery.
"Bernard," says Luther in another place, "loved Jesus as much as any
one can."

That the Song of Solomon appealed to Bernard is not surprising,
for he loved God's creation. "Thou wilt find," he wrote, "something
greater in the woods than in books. The trees and rocks will teach
thee what thou canst not hear from human teachers. And dost thou
not think thou canst suck honey from the rocks and oil from the
hardest stones!" A man who enjoys God's world cannot be all bad.
At other times, Bernard could be so lost in his meditations that he
could travel a whole day along the shores of the beautiful lake of
Geneva and be so oblivious to the scenery that at the end of the day
he had to ask what his companions had seen on their journey.

Perhaps one of the most interesting aspects of Bernard's life was his commission by the pope to preach the second crusade, one of those strange "holy wars" launched by the papacy in an effort to wrest the Holy Lands from the hands of the Seljuk Turks. While the first crusade had ended in victory for the church, some years later Edessa in Syria had fallen again to the Moslems. In attempting, through his preaching, to persuade people to go on the new crusade, he influenced so many people in Vitry to join the crusade that he had to cut his own robe into pieces to make crosses for the people. (To agree to go on a crusade was "to take the cross." This was literally done by sewing a piece of cloth in the shape of a cross on one's clothing.) Bernard's efforts were directed also towards Conrad III, Germany's powerful king. Conrad was reluctant to go but was finally moved to tears by Bernard's vivid descriptions of eternal torments and by his eloquent reminders to Conrad of all God's goodness to the king. In a passionate outburst, Conrad cried out, "I acknowledge the gifts of the divine mercy, and I will no longer remain ungrateful for them. I am ready for the service which He Himself hath exhorted me."

Bernard felt keenly the humiliation of the failure of this crusade but ascribed it to the sins of the crusaders and of the Christian world. "The judgments of the Lord are just," he wrote, "but this one is an abyss so deep that I dare to pronounce him blessed who is not scandalized by it."

Bernard was also a gifted hymn writer. The well-known hymn "Oh Sacred Head Now Wounded" is an adaptation of Bernard's original hymn. One of his better known hymns has this beautiful stanza:

> Jesus, Thou Joy of loving hearts,
>> Thou Fount of life,
>> Thou Light of men,
> From the best bliss which earth imparts
>> We turn unfilled to Thee again.

## Conclusion

Although Bernard's fanaticism for the monastic life led him to approve of the persecution of those who opposed the church, he represented, on the whole, the best in monasticism, which is evidence of the fact that God sometimes preserved His church during these troubled times behind the walls of Europe's monasteries. Bernard did not think it was possible to live a life pleasing to God in any other place than in the cold grayness of a monastic cell, but perhaps in his times this may have been close to the truth.

## Chapter 15

# Francis of Assisi

## Medieval Saint

### Introduction

*"The legends began the day Francis died. He was sainted (1228) by the medieval church; artists and poets added to this beatification by granting to Francis an almost unparalleled place in the history of Christianity. The painter Giotto depicted him as the one who most suffered the wounds of Christ. Dante placed him above*

the doctors and founders of medieval orders in his *Divine Comedy* (c. 1305). Francis was so celebrated as the perfect imitator of Christ that the Protestant Reformers believed memory of him usurped the place of Christ in popular piety."

The story of Francis of Assisi is one of those strange and troubling stories that create in one who reads it admiration mixed with perplexity. His life was in some respects what the Christian life ought to be; it was in other respects so contrary to genuine piety that one shrinks from it with some revulsion. It was the life of an unusual medieval saint.

### Early Life

Francis was born in 1182 to wealthy parents who lived in Assisi, an important town in central Italy. His father, Pietro de Barnadone, was a textile merchant who traveled extensively, mostly to France, to increase the family fortunes. His mother, Pica, an aristocrat by birth, enjoyed the society life of her city while having little, if any, significant influence on her eldest son's spiritual development. Francis was baptized Giovanni but renamed Francisco, apparently to express Pietro's love for France.

Francis received an education open to the wealthy and elite but profited little from it. He was much too involved in the gay life of a wealthy merchant's son and the youthful exploits of those who have little else to do with their time but to get into mischief.

Italy was by no means a unified nation, and the rivalry between various commercial cities was fierce. So bitter was the rivalry between Assisi and Perugia, a nearby commercial city, that war broke out. Francis quickly joined the forces of Assisi and rode forth to battle. He was captured and held hostage for a year but was released when a ransom was paid for him. He was about twenty-one at the time.

## His Conversion

It seems as if Francis entered a period of spiritual struggle and severe self-doubt at this time. While wanting to fight again, he was dissuaded by inner turmoil which made his past life seem empty and useless but which gave him no direction as to his future.

In 1205 Francis journeyed to Rome on a pilgrimage and spent some delightful hours among the holy shrines in the center of Christendom. But one incident disturbed him beyond reason. Meeting a begging leper in the streets, he was moved by the destitution of this despised member of society, and after steeling himself to kiss the leper's hand, he exchanged his own clothes for the rags of the leper to experience himself what destitution was.

Returning to Assisi, Francis was praying in the church of St. Damian when he heard Christ telling him to rebuild the house of God. This seemed to make some sense to him, for the small chapel of St. Damian was humble, rudely furnished, and in some disrepair. Later he was to realize that Christ was referring to the corrupt medieval church rather than the chapel in which he was praying, but for the time being he decided that he would devote himself to rebuilding that chapel and to ministering to the needs of the outcasts who lived on the edges of Assisi.

The trouble was that he needed money for this project; and so, to finance his work, he sold all his possessions and some of the textiles of his father. His father did not think very highly of this and was, in fact, disgusted with a son who seemed to him to be a lazy ne'er-do-well. Pietro brought the matter to the local bishop, accusing his son of theft. Francis was ordered by the bishop to restore the money that belonged to his father and make proper restitution. In what can only be interpreted as a gesture of defiance, Francis stripped every stitch of his clothing from his body, tossed everything he owned onto a pile, and told the bishop to give it to his father, while he left the house stark naked. His words as he left were, "Up to this time I have called Pietro Barnadone father, but now I desire to serve God and to say nothing else than 'Our Father which art in heaven.'" So far as we know, from that day on he had nothing more to do with his parents.

## *His Monastic Life*

The incident was, however, a turning point in his life. After spending some years with lepers in the nearby village of Gubbio, he returned to Assisi to rebuild some churches and live as a hermit. Poverty now became for him a way of life. In 1208 he was listening to a sermon on Matthew 10:7–19, which reads in part, "And as ye go, preach, saying, The kingdom of heaven is at hand. Heal the sick, cleanse the lepers, raise the dead, cast out devils: freely ye have received, freely give. Provide neither gold, nor silver, nor brass in your purses, nor scrip for your journey, neither two coats, neither shoes, nor yet staves: for the workman is worthy of his meat." Especially the call to preach and the call to live a life of poverty struck like fire into his soul.

From that day on, he was to be a traveling preacher who literally owned nothing. Others, attracted to him, soon began to accompany him. The first to join was an extremely wealthy town councilor called Bernard, who at first doubted Francis' sincerity. As the story goes, he invited Francis to his house to spend the night. He gave Francis his own room in a lavishly furnished villa and watched what Francis would do in the night hours. Francis arose from his luxurious bed as soon as the house was quiet and spent the rest of the night on his knees in prayer. Bernard was persuaded, and selling all his possessions, he joined Francis as a traveling preacher. When others joined, they called themselves "The Little Friars" and requested from Pope Innocent III permission to be recognized as a monastic order. The story is told that Pope Innocent III (the mightiest pope the world has ever seen and the clearest picture of Antichrist up to today), unimpressed with what appeared to him to be nothing but a group of beggars, told Francis to go wallow with the pigs and preach to them. Even though Innocent may have been expressing his contempt, Francis followed his instructions and returned with the same request, which then was granted.

So began one of the greatest of all monastic orders, the Franciscans. It became known as a "mendicant order" because of its vows of absolute poverty, which required its members to obtain their

daily needs by begging. The rules of the order were very simple. While like other orders with their vows of obedience and chastity, the Franciscans distinguished themselves by vows of absolute poverty. Francis insisted that no one in the order own anything at all. Personal property was absolutely forbidden. Even the clothes which they wore were to be given to others in greater need than themselves. They might not carry with them the smallest coin. They might not keep the least crumb of bread; if any food was left after their meal they had to give it to the poor. They might own no buildings or shelters. They even had to walk barefoot.

Francis was convinced that poverty was the great way of following the example of Christ and the lofty ideal of the imitation of Christ. Given the fact that the corruption in the church was due to its immense wealth, he sought reform through poverty.

Francis hated idleness. He insisted that his fellow monks be constantly busy. They were to be busy traveling, preaching, administering to the needs of the poor and outcasts of society, washing the dirty lepers, feeding the starving, and helping the downtrodden. They were to do their work cheerfully, and they were to treat every man, even their enemies, with courtesy. They were to avoid all pomp and outward show and be happily content with their poverty. This latter was demonstrated vividly when a well-known follower of Francis was greeted at the entrance of a city with a large and magnificent parade of clergy and prelates. He promptly went into a nearby field and played on a see-saw with some small boys until the entire parade disbanded in consternation.

Two other sub-orders were formed during Francis' lifetime. One was for women who wanted to practice the same ideals. It was organized by Clare Schiffi in 1212 and was called "The Poor Clares." The other was an order for laymen who wanted to live in poverty along with Francis and his brothers but who were not permitted to preach.

## His Importance

Francis himself was a very simple person. He feared education as a spiritual threat and discouraged his followers from pursuing it. Though often hungry and dressed in rags, and though living in a body wracked with pain, he was himself always cheerful. He had a deep appreciation and love for God's creation, and one could find him from time to time in the woods alone talking to the birds and the squirrels about the things of God. He once told the birds, "Brother birds, you ought to love and praise your Creator very

much. He has given you feathers for clothing, wings for flying, and all things that can be of use to you. You have neither to sow, nor to reap, and yet He takes care of you." Francis had the ability to laugh at himself, and he could recognize the foibles of human nature. He called his body "Brother Ass" and often gently chided it for its apparent weaknesses.

The brotherhood spread like wildfire throughout Europe and soon went beyond the control of Francis. While Francis was off to try to do mission work among the Mohammedans in Egypt, unscrupulous prelates in the Romish hierarchy gained control of the Franciscans and organized them into a much more rule-bound and controlled organization than Francis wanted. They also forced the movement to change its rules so that the members could own property—the one thing Francis feared the most. When he returned from Egypt, he found these alterations destroying all he had wanted for his movement. Unable to summon the energy necessary to fight the dark and powerful forces of the church, he lived in sadness the remaining days of his life and died of a broken heart at the age of forty-four.

One of his enduring masterpieces was his "Canticle to the Sun." Written when he was under severe temptation and going blind, it expressed his great love of God's world. A few lines will give us some sense of it:

> O most high, almighty, good Lord God, to Thee
> > belong praise, glory, honor, and all blessing!
> Praised be my Lord God with all His creatures,
> > and specially our brother the sun,
> > who brings us the day and who brings us the light;
> > fair is he and shines with a very great splendor:
> > O Lord he signifies to us Thee!
> Praised be my Lord for our brother the wind
> > and for air and cloud, calms and all weather
> > by the which Thou upholdest life in all creatures.
> Praise ye and bless the Lord, and give thanks unto Him
> > and serve Him with great humility.

This song was the inspiration for the well-known hymn "Praise to the Lord, the Almighty, the King of Creation."

## Conclusion

Francis himself was the closest one could come to the monastic ideal. I think sometimes such a life can conceivably appear to be attractive to those who are concerned about spirituality in the midst of carnality and worldliness. It may seem to be the way to piety; and, it may, because of its great difficulty, seem to be the path of godliness. In fact, this is not the case. God does not call us to express piety in poverty, and godliness in a denial of this earth's goods. Indeed, the way of Francis is not the hard way, but the easy way. The hard way to which we are called is the way of being in the world but not of it; of taking God's good gifts and with thanksgiving using them in God's service; of possessing a house and clothes, but seeking in all things, even with our earthly possessions, the kingdom of God and His righteousness. That is the hard way, but it is the way of obedience and the way approved by God.

# Chapter 16

# Catherine of Siena
## *Mystic*

*Mysticism*
*It is not possible to understand the strange times which we call the Middle Ages without understanding mysticism. Mysticism was a current running in the church of Christ which began in the third century and continues to the present.*

*That this should be so is not surprising. The pendulum in the spiritual life of the church of God swings from one*

extreme to the other. On the one extreme lies that lack of emotion that accompanies either cold formalism or dead orthodoxy, often characterized by rationalism; on the other extreme lies the fervency of mysticism. Between these two extremes the life of the church swings. It is difficult for the church to keep a proper spiritual balance. The swing is to be explained by the fact that neither extreme satisfies.

When the church falls into the spiritual graveyard of dead orthodoxy, the people of God want more from religion. They desire a spiritual life which is warm and fervent, filled with the personal experience of union with Christ, characterized by piety and godliness. If this desire is not met, the pendulum swings towards mysticism with all its emphasis on feeling, subjective experience, evidences of conversion, inner union with God, and piety. But because mysticism tends to denigrate the *knowledge* of faith, this too cannot long satisfy, and the life of the church swings back again on its weary course towards rationalism and an exclusive emphasis on knowledge for knowledge' sake.

In the Middle Ages, the Romish church developed rapidly towards outward forms of

worship. The worship of the church was filled with liturgy; the mass was said in Latin; the life of the people was regulated by law upon law and precept upon precept. The worst of this was that the salvation of the people of God was placed in the hands of the clergy so that nothing was required of the saints but outward conformity to the regulations of the establishment. It is not surprising that mysticism should flourish. It was an understandable reaction to the external form of religion. Mystics abounded. They were present in every decade of medieval times. They were present also at the time the Reformation burst over Europe.

## Early Life

As an example of mysticism, Catherine of Siena stands high above all the others. Of her such eulogies as these have been spoken:

> "She is the most eminent of the holy women of the Middle Ages whom the Church has canonized. Her fame depends upon her single-hearted piety and her efforts to advance the interests of the Church and her nation...Although the hysterical element may not be altogether wanting from her piety, she yet deserves and will have the admiration of all men who are moved by the sight of a noble enthusiasm..."

> "She is one of the most wonderful women that have ever lived."

> "Catherine's figure flits like that of an angel: through the darkness of her time, over which her gracious genius sheds a soft radiance."

Catherine Benincasa was born in Siena, Italy, around 1347. She was the twenty-third child and a twin in a family of twenty-five children. Her father, Jacobo, was a dyer who belonged to the lower middle class. Her mother, Lapa, was a housewife. Catherine received no schooling at all and learned to read and write only in later life.

Catherine was born in a time of upheaval throughout all Europe, but especially in Italy. The Renaissance—that great pagan revival of learning—was sweeping Europe and clashing with the darkness of preceding centuries. National, economic, social, and educational changes were in the wind. Under the influence of French cardinals in Rome, the papacy had been moved to Avignon, France, and had come completely under the domination of the French. This so-called "Babylonian captivity of the church" had resulted in the secularization and moral decay of the papacy. No longer was the church trusted. It had lost the prestige of its apostolic seat in Rome, and a general dissatisfaction with the church prevailed throughout Europe.

Catherine's mystical life began early. At the age of seven, she claimed to have seen a vision of Jesus with Peter, Paul, and John, which led her to resolve to devote her life to religion. While first her parents objected on the grounds that she suffered from delusions, they were persuaded at last of her claims and set aside a part of the house for her in which to pray, meditate, and receive visions and trances. In her own corner of the house she became something of a recluse. She refused to sleep, ate almost nothing, and beat herself three times a day with a whip or a chain. When she was fourteen and her parents arranged a marriage for her, she cut off her beautiful hair to dissuade her intended husband. When her face was pock-marked from an attack of smallpox, she accepted it as a special gift of God which would make her unattractive to men. Her biographer describes her vividly:

> Nature had not given her a face over fair, and her personal appearance was marred by the marks of smallpox. And yet she had a winning expression, a fund of good spirits, and sang and laughed heartily. Once devoted to a religious life, she practiced great austerities, flagellating herself three times a day—once for herself, once for the living, and once for the dead. She wore a hair undergarment and an iron chain (bound about her waist). During one Lenten season she lived on the bread taken in communion. These asceticisms were performed in a chamber in her father's house. She was never an inmate of a convent. Such extreme asceticisms as she practiced upon herself she disparaged at a later period.

### Her Service in the Church

At about the age of twenty, in obedience to what she considered a vision, Catherine joined the Sisters of Penitences, a Dominican order, although she refused to become a part of a convent, disdaining the restrictions which convent life required. Her life was an active involvement in the daily affairs of the people in Siena and in the problems of the church.

Her reputation is based in large measure on her many charitable works. She went among the poor to alleviate their suffering. She nursed the incurably ill, especially those with cancer and leprosy. She worked with prisoners, staying with them during their trials and executions. When a young nobleman was condemned to die for words of disrespect to the magistrates, she comforted him in his despair, taught him to be joyful in the face of death, and was present with him on the block when he was beheaded. She caught his head in her hands and was pleased to be splattered with his blood. She is said to have performed miracles of healing and raising the dead during a plague which ravaged the city. At every opportunity she preached to the people and soon gained a large following of men and women who were mostly from the laity and who wanted to imitate her piety.

It is not surprising that the fame of such a selfless woman spread rapidly, and she soon found herself involved in the affairs of the church at large. It was at this time that she began writing her famous "Letters," 400 of which are extant. They were written to family members, poor and distressed, sick and dying, princes and rulers, popes and cardinals, foreign kings and soldiers. They were filled with admonition, sharp reproof, comfort, advice, and details of her own mystical experiences.

Because she operated so freely outside the church's official authority, she was tried for heresy by a Dominican tribunal, but was cleared of all charges. The court did, however, appoint for her a spiritual adviser, Raymond of Capua, who became her friend, secretary, biographer, and confessor.

Her participation in church affairs involved her in efforts to organize another crusade, which she intended to be used to bring the gospel to the Moslem Turks. She worked hard to get the papacy out of Avignon and finally succeeded in restoring it to the ancient papal see in Rome. Her first trip to Avignon to speak with the pope resulted in bitter disappointment, for she found the papacy to be "a stench of infernal vices" rather than "a paradise of heavenly virtues," as she expected. But the return of the papacy to Rome resulted in a graver problem: the great papal schism in which two rival popes claimed the papal chair. To her despair, she failed to settle this problem, which was not resolved until the Council of Constance, the same council which burned John Hus at the stake.

Her efforts were not always welcomed. At Avignon the cardinals treated her with coolness, the influential women with disdain, and the bureaucrats with hatred. The niece of the pope, while kneeling at her side in prayer, ran a sharp knife through Catherine's foot, which gave her a permanent limp.

She died before reaching her thirty-third birthday, with final words to her companions which sharply underscore her mystical bent:

"Dear children, let not my death sadden you, rather rejoice to think that I am leaving a place of many sufferings to go to rest in the quiet sea, the eternal God, and to be united forever with my most sweet and loving bridegroom."

## Her Mysticism

The mysticism of Catherine is typical of many in the medieval period. Dreams, visions, and trances continued throughout her life. She claimed to have drunk the blood of Christ which flowed from His side and the milk of Mary, Christ's mother. At an early age she said that she had been married to Christ and that she wore His ring on her finger—although no one else could ever see it. Because she meditated too often and so intensely on the sufferings of Christ, she professed to have Christ's "stigmata" (the wounds of the nails and the spear-thrust) in her body, although these too were invisible to everyone but herself. Many of her "Letters" were written in a trance-like state.

The goal of medieval mysticism (as with all mysticism as it has appeared throughout the ages) was "union with God." This was the highest ideal of the saints. Such union with God could come about only through rigorous spiritual and physical exercises. It required of one that he or she meditate unceasingly on the suffering Christ, forsake the world with all its attractions, and rigorously suppress sin by fierce ascetic practices, for only in this way could one escape from what was called "the dark night of the soul." Emerging from this dark night, one awoke to glorious, unearthly, supremely blessed union with God Himself. This is what Catherine meant by her marriage to Christ.

Union with Christ is taught by Scripture as the blessedness of salvation. The joy and comfort of the assurance of salvation is the experience of God's people. Meditation and study of God's Word are held before us as obligatory for a godly life. Genuine piety and a life of fellowship with God are the portion of the righteous even here in the world.

Mystics go wrong when they reduce all religion to experience and feeling. Mediated by dreams and visions, trances and appearances of saints and angels, the Christian life for the mystic is defined in terms of subjective and indefinable inner states of feeling. Knowledge is spurned, and true knowledge is considered unessential. But this is terribly wrong. It is the knowledge of the truth that sets us free. To know God and His Son Jesus Christ is to have eternal life. After all, faith—the faith that unites us to Christ in the mystical union of His blessed body—is first of all knowledge. It is more than knowledge, but it is knowledge for all that. The spiritual experience of the child of God may and does ebb and flow, but we know whom we have believed. That is salvation.

*Chapter 17*

# The Waldensians
## Medieval
## Protestants

Earliest known
Waldensian symbol based
on Psalm 119:105

**On the Late Massacre in Piedmont (Sonnet 18)**
Avenge O Lord thy slaughter'd Saints, whose bones
    Lie scatter'd on the *Alpine* mountains cold,
    Ev'n them who kept thy truth so pure of old
    When all our Fathers worship't Stocks and Stones,
Forget not: in thy book record their groanes
    Who were thy Sheep and in their antient Fold
    Slayn by the bloody *Piemontese* that roll'd
    Mother with Infant down the Rocks. Their moans
The Vales redoubl'd to the Hills, and they
    To Heav'n. Their martyr'd blood and ashes sow
    O'er all th' *Italian* fields where still doth sway
The triple Tyrant [the pope]: that from these may grow
    A hunderd-fold, who having learnt thy way
    Early may fly the *Babylonian* wo.

    With the words of this sonnet the blind poet John Milton commemorated the terrible massacre of the Waldensians by the Romish church.

    Even in the Middle Ages, when the Roman Catholic Church ruled supreme and invincible over all Europe, it did not always have everything its own way. Almost always during these dark times individuals or groups raised voices of protest against the tyranny and corruption of Rome.

    The only explanation for the presence of such dissenters from Romish teachings is the great work of God in preserving His church.

One evidence of God's preservation of His church is the existence, throughout most of the Middle Ages, of a group called the Waldensians. They must be among the  most faithful of all the dissenters in the Middle Ages. They are one of my favorite groups of saints.

## *Origin*

Although there is some dispute over the origin of the Waldensians, most historians consider Peter Waldo, after whom they were named, to be the founder of the movement.

Although almost nothing is known of Peter's early life, it is known that he was the son of a rich merchant in Lyons, France, and that he inherited his father's wealth. No one knows the date of his birth, but his death was in 1218, which puts him very early in the Middle Ages, a child of the twelfth century.

Troubled by his wealth, the fact that it had been increased through usury, and the obvious worldliness of his life, Peter asked his priest concerning the best way to God. He was told, as was common in those days, that the way to God was to sell all that he had, give to the poor, and follow Christ.

Peter did not hesitate to follow what to him was a clear command of his Lord. Because he was married, he provided sufficient money for his wife; he placed his daughters in a convent to be cared for there; he paid back all those from whom he had taken usury; and he gave everything else he owned to the poor.

Peter Waldo gathered about him a small group of men who began to translate the Scriptures into the vernacular and began to assume the responsibilities of preaching. They were known by different names: the Brethren in Christ; the Poor in Christ; the Poor in Spirit; but finally they became known by the name of their founder, Peter Waldo. They lived lives of total poverty and dedication to God.

## *Teachings*

In 1179, Peter Waldo asked his archbishop for permission to be recognized as a separate and approved movement and asked for permission to be organized as a preaching fraternity. The request was passed on to the pope, Alexander III, who refused the request. The group appealed to the Third Lateran Council in 1179, but this council also refused their request. Convinced that they were only doing that which was biblical, they continued to preach anyway, and thus incurred the wrath of the church, which excommunicated them at the Council of Verona in 1184.

What is particularly interesting about the Waldensians is their views. I doubt whether any group of people in all Europe, prior to the Reformation, understood the truths of Scripture so clearly as these poor people. Philip Schaff even calls them "the strictly biblical sect of the Middle Ages." It is almost impossible to imagine how these simple folk could have come to such excellent knowledge of the truth in the times in which they lived. They were the lowly, the uneducated; they were despised and persecuted; they had been brought up in the chains of Roman Catholic heresy; yet they were so clear on such important points. So much were they forerunners of the Reformation that when the Calvin Reformation dawned, most of them were quick to join it; it was as if the Calvin Reformation was exactly what they had been waiting for all these centuries. Only the fact that God preserves His church can adequately explain their existence.

At the beginning of the movement, the Waldensians did not depart from Roman Catholic teachings. They did not reject the authority of the pope, the entire sacramental system of Roman Catholicism, or the church itself as the mother of believers. They were, in fact, very much like a religious order. They demanded vows of poverty, chastity, and obedience for full membership and insisted on a novitiate before allowing adherents to become full members.

From the outset their main emphasis was on preaching. It was preaching that got them into trouble with the church, for they preached without permission. They continued even in the face of excommunication because they were convinced that preaching is decisive for salvation, a Reformation doctrine that stood at the heart of both the Lutheran and Calvinistic reforms of the church. Rome taught that the sacraments were essential for salvation and that preaching was subordinate to the sacraments. The Waldensians saw the error of this and insisted that the Lord had added the sacraments to the preaching and that, therefore, God saved His people by the preaching of the Word. It was especially this doctrine which Rome hated, for the sacraments stood at the very heart of the entire papal-sacerdotal system of which Rome was so proud.

It really ought not to surprise us, in the light of the times, that the Waldensians went too far with their idea of preaching. They were opposed to Roman Catholic clericalism, and they soon came to see

the importance of what Luther later called the "office of all believers." With their emphasis on the office of all believers, and failing to distinguish between the special offices in the church and the general office of believers, they gave to the laity, including women, the right to preach. All God's people were preachers, and they were preachers not by virtue of ordination but by virtue of a godly and spiritual life which manifested that they were believers.

One benefit of this erroneous viewpoint, however, was the fact that they saw the need for all God's people to possess the Scriptures. They therefore translated the Scriptures into the vernacular, and even insisted on the final and absolute authority of the Scriptures for life, doctrine, and preaching. Preaching had to be exposition of God's Word.

After persecution and excommunication, their views developed. They saw inconsistencies with the position they had taken and the other teachings of Rome. Bit by bit, they rejected the oath, purgatory, prayers for the dead, the mass, and transubstantiation.

### *Persecution*

Such teachings as these attracted immense throngs to the Waldensians, and the movement spread rapidly into France, Italy, Switzerland, and even parts of Eastern Europe. It was exactly because of the threat to Romish power and the popularity of the movement that the fury of Rome was brought down upon the Waldensians. The full force of that cruel, unjust, and frightening institution for the suppression of heresy—the Inquisition—was brought to bear against them.

The stories of suffering and torture which these folk endured make one weep even today. Their fathers and mothers were torn apart on the rack and burned at the stake. Their children were burned with irons to force them to report evil deeds of their parents. Men, women, and children who had fled to a mountain cave to escape were suffocated by a huge fire built at its entrance and its smoke being forced into the cave. As Milton's poem points out, mothers with their infants clutched in their arms were hurled over the sides of cliffs.

Under the pressures of persecution, the Waldensians fled into the Alpine valleys and high plateaus of Switzerland, and there they survived.

Were they so cruelly treated for wrongdoing? An inquisitor himself said of them, "They are modest and well-behaved, taking no pride in their dress, which is neat but not extravagant. Avoiding commerce,

because of its inevitable lies and oaths and frauds, they live by working as artisans, with cobblers as their teachers. Content with bare necessities, they do not accumulate wealth. Chaste in their habits, temperate in eating and drinking, they keep away from taverns, dances and other vanities. They refrain from anger and are always active. They can be recognized by their modesty and precision of speech."

So widely was Waldensian piety recognized that one man, suspected of Waldensian error, was able to prove at his trial that he was not and could not be a Waldensian, but had to be a good Catholic, because he lied, swore, and drank.

These saints of God who stained the Alps with their blood eagerly embraced the Reformation. But did Rome? To this day Rome has not confessed any wrongdoing for shedding the blood of the saints, nor has Rome changed at heart. It would, I am convinced, do the same today, given the opportunity. But the souls of the Waldensians cry from under the altar, and the Lord will answer their prayer.

**Chapter 18**

# John Wycliffe

## Morning Star of the Reformation

*Introduction*
*The great*
*Protestant*
*Reformation of the*
*sixteenth century*
*did not burst upon*
*Europe as*
*something entirely*
*new and without*
*prior preparation.*
*The work of God*
*through Luther and*
*Calvin was built*
*upon God's work in*
*men who preceded*
*them and paved the*
*way. Two such men*
*were John Wycliffe*
*in England and*
*John Hus in*
*Bohemia.*

England was a difficult place in which to live during Wycliffe's life. Although a great deal of emphasis was placed on education, and the road to success was through the colleges, very few had the means to go to college, and the lot of the peasant was difficult and spiritually empty. One description is graphic:

> The peasant could not expect any preaching from the resident priest, but he would get it from the preaching friar, and from the traveling pardoner, with his wallet "bret full of pardons, come from Rome all hot." Besides these religious roundsmen there were others who would travel through the winding, muddy roads and green lanes of England: minstrels, tumblers, jugglers, beggars and charlatans of every kind, living off the poor peasants. The peasant knew something of the sayings of Christ and Bible stories, but they were so embellished by the friar's sensational and entertaining sermons that he would not know truth from error. He never saw a Bible in English, and if he could have seen one he would not have been able to read it.

Nor were the times peaceful and quiet. They were unusually turbulent. During Wycliffe's short lifetime the Black Death struck Europe and England and carried away one-third of the population. During his lifetime the Peasants' War left parts of

England devastated and brought about major economic upheaval. In the church as well, confusion and unrest reigned. It was the time when the papacy was not in Rome, the eternal city, but in Avignon under the control of the French. Although during Wycliffe's days the so-called "Babylonian Captivity of the Church" came to an end, the end was the papal schism during which there were two popes, and sometimes three, bellowing away at each other like mad bulls and hurling back and forth anathemas and excommunications.

### *Early Life and Education*

Very little is known of Wycliffe's early life, not even the date of his birth. Some argue for 1324; others for 1330. He was born near West Riding in Yorkshire in a small village called "Wycliffe," which would seem to indicate that his parents were lords of the manor in the area, wealthy and respectable. Little more is known of them, other than the possibility that they totally repudiated their son when he began to teach biblical ideas.

At about fifteen or sixteen he went off to Oxford to study. The years of study were long and difficult: under ordinary circumstances, one who went through the entire program could not expect to complete his studies until thirty-three years of age. Wycliffe spent much of his life in Oxford: he gained his B.A. in 1356, his B.D. in 1369, and his D.D. in 1372—although his studies were interrupted for two years by official business. Not much is known about these years. He was probably in Merton College; was master of Balliol College from 1359–1360; and had some dealings with Christ's College.

### *Preacher and Oxford Don*

Oxford was composed at this time of six colleges. It had about seventy-five members, all of whom were of the clergy, and it served about fifteen hundred undergraduates. It was surrounded by priories and halls which were full of monks and friars who were a constant source of irritation to the members of the university. Yet it was the best university in all of Europe, surpassing even the great universities of France.

In 1361 Wycliffe became rector in the church of Fillingham, in Lincolnshire, which meant technically that he was its pastor, but which meant in fact (as was the custom in those days) that he received the income from that parish while he could continue his studies and work in Oxford. This did not mean that he totally neglected his parish, for he preached there from time to time; and it did make him an ordained minister in the Roman Catholic Church. In 1368 he was transferred to Lutterworth, a parish in which he spent the last years of his life.

Oxford was, however, the seat of his labors. During his studies, and for years after he had completed them, he was a teacher at Oxford. Much of his reformatory work was done within those halls. He was always and pre-eminently a professor and not, in the first place, a preacher.

The friars who lived on Oxford's premises, and who caused the university untold grief, were to become the first objects of Wycliffe's anger. He wrote a book, *Objections to the Friars,* which sounded the trumpet blast of reform.

### *Wycliffe the Patriot*

The crucial issues came up in Wycliffe's life in connection with political problems. As is so often true of the affairs of men and nations, the bottom line was money. The trouble was that much of England's wealth was flowing out of the country and to the papacy. While this had been more or less true from the time that England had come under Roman Catholic control, it was most emphatically true after King John, more than 200 years earlier, delivered England to the pope as the pope's kingdom and had received it back as a papal fief. This was humiliating and intolerable to good Englishmen. The tax levied by the pope was 1,000 marks a year, an almost impossible burden. But money moved out of England in other ways as well. Ecclesiastical offices were sold to the highest bidder, with the money going to the pope. Many offices in England were held by foreigners who never saw the land in which they held office. Some of those officers were nothing but children, but they reaped the income of the offices—after the pope had been paid off. The pope often moved bishops from one see to another and received one year's salary as his part of the transaction. Much money for the forgiveness of sins was funneled out of England to the papal coffers. In fact, the pope received five times more money than the king. To add insult to injury, the money was going to a French pope and eventually found its way into French hands, and France was at war with England. England was thus supporting its enemy in the wars.

So intolerable did this become that Parliament passed a Bill of Indictment against the pope which read, in part,

God hath given his sheep to the Pope to be pastored and not shorn and shaven...therefore it would be good to renew all the statutes against provisions from Rome...No papal collector should remain in England upon pain of life and limb, and no Englishman, on the like pain, should become such collector or remain at the court of Rome.

Into this issue Wycliffe was thrust. He not only became involved in the problem as a writer of pamphlets and treatises, but he also served on a committee of the king to meet in Bruges of the Lowlands with papal representatives to arbitrate the issues, if possible. With patriotic zeal, he defended the rights of England against the papacy.

It was in Bruges that two important things took place which were to have influence on Wycliffe's later life. The first was the fact that in dealing with papal representatives, he learned that they were a treacherous and deceitful lot and that they represented a papacy which was wholly secular, covetous, immoral, corrupt, and a tool of French kings. He so completely lost his confidence in the papacy and hierarchy of the church that he had nothing but contempt and scorn for it from that day on. The second event of importance was that he met the duke of Gaunt, who was in Bruges for other business, and who was probably the most powerful man in England after the king. The two became friends, and it was due only to the friendship of the duke of Gaunt that Wycliffe was not in later years killed by the Romish church.

## *Wycliffe the Critic of Rome*

Wycliffe's defense of England's rights to keep its revenues within its own borders was courageous and bold. The deeper he entered into this defense, the more clearly he wrote against the corruptions of the Romish hierarchy. He was the first to call the pope Antichrist—a name later echoed by the Westminster divines and incorporated into the Westminster Confession. He denied the pope supreme power in the church, denied the temporal rule of the pope in the nations, denied the power of the pope to forgive sins, and, in fact, denied that anyone but a godly pope had any authority whatsoever. An old chronicler speaks of Wycliffe as running about from place to place barking against the church. The pope, in Wycliffe's own words, was "the antichrist, the proud, worldly priest of Rome, and the most cursed of clippers and cut-purses." It is no wonder that the church did not take too kindly to all this. From the

pope on down, notice was taken of Wycliffe, and the orders went out from the highest levels of ecclesiastical hierarchy to silence the blasphemer.

The first effort made to silence him was a summons from the archbishop of Canterbury to appear before this highest ecclesiastic in England for trial. It was an interesting meeting. The duke of Gaunt was there with some of his soldiers, as well as a large number of people from the monied classes, many of whom supported Wycliffe. Before the archbishop could get on with any kind of a trial, he got involved in a heated discussion with the duke over the question whether Wycliffe should sit down: the archbishop insisting he ought to stand as a measure of respect, the duke insisting he should sit down since the archbishop did not really amount to that much. The whole meeting ended in a brawl, and nothing could be done against Wycliffe. This was on February 19, 1377.

In April of 1378 Wycliffe was once again summoned to the courts of the church, but this time to an assembly of bishops. The bishops were confident that this time they would succeed in sentencing Wycliffe to the stake and be rid, once and for all, of his critical writings and preaching, which were such an embarrassment to the church. But this effort also proved unsuccessful, for not only did Wycliffe enjoy the favor of the people, but the queen mother sent word to the bishops that although they could try Wycliffe as much as they pleased, they had better not condemn him, on peril of their lives. This so filled them with fear and consternation that they immediately disbanded the meeting. God used strange ways and strange people to protect His servant.

### Wycliffe the Reformer

The year 1378 proved to be a turning point in Wycliffe's life. Shortly after the convocation of the bishops, Wycliffe underwent what was almost a conversion. He was no longer interested in the politics of the realm, nor in helping promote the cause of the king and the landowners in their battle with the papacy. It seems as if, under God's leading through the Spirit of Christ, he began to see that the evils in the Romish church were, after all, not primarily evils in practice, but evils rooted in the false doctrines which Rome had adopted over the years. He began to concentrate his labors on the investigation of Scripture and the development of the truths of Scripture. Through strange and remarkable ways, God had preserved him from the fury of the Romish church and from almost certain death at its hands.

It may be also that another incident in his life was used by God to bring about this conversion. About this same time, Wycliffe became desperately ill, ill unto death. The friars and monks were sure he was going to die. They sent a delegation to him under a hypocritical pretense of seeking his spiritual welfare, while nothing would have delighted them more than his death. They attempted to force him to recant all he had written and to make peace with the church. Though desperately ill, in sheer exasperation Wycliffe finally managed, with some help from a servant, to raise himself upon the bed. Glaring at the assorted friars and monks gathered about him, he assured them not only that he was going to recover from his illness, but that the Lord would spare him to do yet more harm to their evil cause. With these words he drove them from the room.

God did spare him—for yet greater things.

To turn his attention to doctrinal matters was no easy thing for Wycliffe to do, for there was a large price to pay for it. Because he refused to involve himself any longer in the affairs of the realm and in the battle to keep England's wealth from flowing into papal coffers, those who were only interested in this aspect of the controversy with Rome lost interest in Wycliffe. First he lost the popularity of the people. Then the duke of Gaunt was no longer interested in protecting him. Finally, even his colleagues in Oxford refused to rise to his defense.

In 1381 the Peasants' Uprising occupied the attention of the nation, and very little effort was made to silence Wycliffe, but on May 17, 1382, a council of bishops met in London under the prodding of the pope to consider what to do with the pestilential teachings of John Wycliffe. Just as the council was beginning its meeting, a rare and unusual earthquake struck London, causing many walls to collapse and stones from buildings to rain down on the streets. Wycliffe interpreted this to mean that the judgment of God was upon the council met together to condemn him; but the archbishop assured the assembly that they should continue with their deliberations because the earthquake was proof that the awful teaching of Wycliffe had seeped into the ground and that now the earth had belched to rid itself of these foul doctrines. This council was, from that time on, known as the Earthquake Council. It succeeded in condemning Wycliffe but did not dare to execute him. It prevailed

upon Oxford to expel him, which Oxford did, though reluctantly. John Wycliffe retired to his parish in Lutterworth, where he spent the rest of his days preaching, teaching, and developing his theology.

## Wycliffe's Teachings

It is really quite amazing how clearly John Wycliffe saw the truth almost 200 years before the Reformation.

One great advantage which he had in Oxford was access to a Bible which, more and more with the passing of the years, attracted his attention and study. Another great advantage was two excellent teachers in his early years of study.

One of these teachers was a man by the name of Grosseteste, who hated and fought bitterly against the corruption of the church. At one time he wrote prophetically, "To follow a pope who rebels against the will of Christ is to separate from Christ and his body; and if ever the time should come when all men follow an erring pontiff, then will be the great apostasy...and Rome will be the cause of an unprecedented schism." When the powerful Pope Innocent ordered Grosseteste to make his infant nephew a canon of Lincoln cathedral, Grosseteste flatly refused with words which ought to ring today in every church: "After the sin of Lucifer there is none more opposed to the gospel than that which ruins souls by giving them a faithless minister. Bad pastors are the cause of unbelief, heresy and disorder."

Another excellent teacher whom Wycliffe was given was Thomas Bradwardine. Because of his brilliance, he was called "Doctor Profundus." While able in philosophy and mathematics, he was above all a student of the Scriptures. It was Bradwardine who led Wycliffe to know the truth of the absolute sovereignty of God in grace over against all the Pelagianism in the Romish church. Bradwardine taught his students the grace of God as determinative in salvation, and he opposed fiercely the doctrine of the free will of man. In fact, he taught these doctrines as they applied also to election and predestination.

As Wycliffe developed his theology, he saw clearly many truths which were not to become fully the possession of the church until the days of Luther and Calvin. Some of the more important ones are worthwhile to list. Wycliffe was the first in centuries to teach the absolute authority of the Scriptures, over against the Romish error of the authority of the church. Wycliffe did battle, too, with Rome's doctrine that the church was the Romish hierarchy and institute. He taught instead (in a major breakthrough) that the church was the body of Christ and was composed only of the elect. It was in this connection that he also taught the truths of sovereign election and reprobation. Wycliffe opposed the doctrine of transubstantiation (an opposition which particularly aroused the fury of Rome). He taught a spiritual presence of Christ in the sacrament of the Lord's Supper, although he was not very clear on what this meant. He repudiated the practices of Rome such as indulgences, the merit of pilgrimages, penance, etc. He denied that the church had the power to forgive sins and insisted that forgiveness came only from Christ. These were doctrines which, almost 200 years later, became the central teachings of the Reformation.

## *Bible Translator*

Wycliffe also put his teachings into practice. First at Oxford, but continuing especially after he left Oxford for Lutterworth, Wycliffe began a translation of Scripture, which he completed before his death. Although he did not know Scripture in its original languages and translated Scripture from the Latin Vulgate, he gave a remarkably accurate translation which enabled the common people to hear the Scriptures in their language for the first time. We include here a few verses of his translation of Genesis 1, in the old English which he used:

> In the firste made God of nougt heuene and erthe. The erthe forsothe was veyn with ynee and void, and derknessis weren vpon the face of the see; and the Spiryt of God was born vpon the watrys. And God seide, Be maad ligt; and maad is ligt. And God sawg ligt, that it was good, and deuydid [divided] ligt fro derknessis; an clepide [called] ligt day and derknessis, nygt. And maad is euen and moru [morn], o day. Seide forsothe God, Be maad a firmament in the myddel of watres, and dyuyde it watres from watrys.

It is difficult for us to imagine how these simple and familiar words must have thrilled the hearts of thousands when they heard them for the first time.

The translating of the Scriptures was also extremely dangerous because the church had forbidden that the Scriptures be put into the language of the common people. Nevertheless, even though printing had not been invented, many copies must have been made laboriously by hand, for there are still nearly 170 hand-copied Wycliffe Bibles extant.

Wycliffe believed strongly in the importance of preaching, something almost unheard of in his times in the decay of the Romish church. He not only preached in his parish, but already in Oxford he

began to train preachers to go out among the people with the gospel. He continued this while in Lutterworth and, arming them with a copy of Scripture or a part of it, taught them to expound the Word of God to the people. These traveling preachers became known as Lollards. While they were severely persecuted, they continued after Wycliffe's death and preserved his teachings until the Reformation finally broke upon England in the mid-1500s.

### *His Importance*

Although Wycliffe suffered a stroke when about fifty years old, he partially recovered from it and continued his writing, preaching, teaching, and the training of his beloved Lollards.

Finally, because the prelates in England seemed unable to do anything about Wycliffe, the pope himself summoned Wycliffe to Rome for trial. But Wycliffe had suffered his stroke and wrote a letter of decline. He suffered two more strokes, the last one in the pulpit, and finally left this life December 31, 1384.

Schaff includes this description of Wycliffe in his *History of the Christian Church:*

> Wyclif was spare, and probably never of robust health, but he was not an ascetic. He was fond of a good meal. In temper he was quick, in mind clear, in moral character unblemished. Towards his enemies he was sharp, but never coarse or ribald. William Thorpe, a young contemporary standing in the court of Archbishop Arundel, bore testimony that "he was emaciated in body and well-nigh destitute of strength, and in conduct most innocent. Very many of the chief men in England conferred with him, loved him dearly, wrote down his sayings and followed his manner of life."

Chaucer wrote his famous "Canterbury Tales" about this time and included a section about Wycliffe. It is all the more forcible because Chaucer, a good Roman Catholic, had some biting words to say about friars and monks. We include this, again in Old English.

> A good man was ther of religioun
> And was a poure persoun of a toun
> But riche he was of holy thoght and werk.
> He was also a lerned man, a clerk
> The Cristes gospel trewly wolde preche:
> His parisshens devoutly wolde he teche.
> Benygne he was and wonder diligent
> And in adversitee ful pacient...
> Wyd was his parisshe and houses fer asonder,

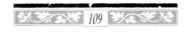

[the people to whom he ministered were widely scattered]
But he ne left nat for reyn ne thonder,
In siknesse nor in meschief to visite
the ferreste [furthest] in his parisshe,
muche and lite [rich and poor[,
Upon his feet, and in his hand a staf
This noble ensample to his sheep he yaf [gave]
That first he wroghte and afterward he taughte;
Out of the gospel he those wordes caughte [took].

John Wycliffe was a great man of God. In the all-wise providence of God the Reformation of the sixteenth century would have been impossible without his work. He is the "morning star of the Reformation" indeed.

So hated was he by Rome that, although Rome was restrained in his lifetime from harming him, the church could not let his bones rest in peace. On October 8, 1427, on order of the Council of Constance (the same council that burned John Hus at the stake), Wycliffe's body was exhumed, his bones burned, and the ashes strewn on the river Swift.

A later chronicler described this event in eloquent words:

> They burnt his bones to ashes and cast them into the Swift, a neighboring brook running hard by. Thus the brook conveyed his ashes into the Avon, the Avon into the Severn, the Severn into the narrow seas and they into the main ocean. And so the ashes of Wyclif are symbolic of his doctrine, which is now spread throughout the world.

## Chapter 19

# John Hus

## Bohemian Reformer

**Introduction**
*While we usually consider Luther's act of nailing his Ninety-five Theses on the chapel door of the church of Wittenberg to be the beginning of the Reformation, the fact remains that God began the work of reformation long before the days of Martin Luther.*

*Two men are called "pre-reformers" by historians: John Wycliffe of England and John Hus of Bohemia. Perhaps*

to call them pre-reformers does them no injustice, but they were more than pre-reformers. They were reformers in the truest sense of the word, Hus perhaps even more than Wycliffe. The reformation of the church in the sixteenth century would have been impossible without them.

The two men were different. Wycliffe was first of all a scholar for whom preaching was secondary. Hus was above all a preacher, and scholarly studies were subordinate to preaching. The dusty library was Wycliffe's home; the pulpit was Hus's. Wycliffe labored all his life for reform but left no movement that continued to the Reformation. Hus started a movement of reform that not only lasted to the Reformation, but has also come down to the present in almost pure form, primarily in the Moravians. Wycliffe's teachings were almost identical to those of Luther and Calvin; Hus, apparently, was never able to condemn the Roman Catholic corruption of the Lord's Supper. Wycliffe reflected all his life the middle class gentility of his upbringing; Hus, after the pattern of Luther, was of rough peasant stock. Wycliffe, it seems, did not know what it meant to laugh; Hus could banter and joke with his students even while lecturing. Wycliffe went

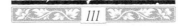

to the grave in peace; Hus was burned to death on a martyr's pyre. God used them both.

In Luther's famous debate with John Eck at Leipzig, Eck charged Martin Luther with being a Hussite because Luther appealed to the supreme authority of Scripture. Luther was not sure about this, but spent the noon break reading what Hus had written. At the beginning of the afternoon session he surprised everyone by loudly proclaiming, "Ich ben ein Hussite!" (I am a Hussite.)

### Early Life

John Hus was born in 1373 in the southern part of Bohemia (now Czechoslovakia) in the village of Husinec; hence his surname, Hus. The name Hus means "goose," a word which Hus often used in referring to himself. While he was imprisoned in Constance, he wrote his friends in Bohemia that he hoped the goose might be released from prison and that "if you love the goose, try to secure the king's aid in delivering him from prison."

Hus was born of poor peasant parents, and his early life was one of hardship and cruel poverty under the crushing heel of lords and princes. The difficulties of such a life were, amongst a peasant population, broken only by wild and riotous orgies of drinking and fornication. While it is clear from Hus's later letters that he was as riotous as his fellows, nevertheless, he earnestly insisted that he was never guilty of the immorality of his peers. From this the Lord saved him in preparation for greater work.

While his parents were not noted in any way for their piety, and apparently gave little thought to John's spiritual instruction, they did want him to go to school because they saw education as the only way for John and for them to escape their grinding poverty. In fact, they apparently considered an education for the priesthood to be the surest way to wealth, an irony that spoke volumes concerning the sad state of affairs in the Romish church.

Although John became a highly educated man, his peasant upbringing remained with him all his life, and his enemies repeatedly taunted him for his crude and rough origins.

In 1385, when thirteen years old, John began his formal education in elementary school at Prachatice. Finishing this part of his education in 1390, he went to the University of Prague, acquiring a B.A. degree in 1393 (at the age of twenty); an M.A. in 1396; and a B.D. (Bachelor of Divinity) in 1404. Until he earned his M.A., life

was financially difficult; and he earned a bit of money by singing and doing manual work. Upon gaining his M.A. degree, however, he was qualified to teach, which he did in the university. He was soon the most popular teacher in the university, partly because he broke old traditions by refusing to be the stern and unbending professor, preferring to laugh, joke, and socialize with his students.

## Hus the Preacher

In 1402 John was appointed rector and preacher at the Chapel of the Holy Infants of Bethlehem in Prague. Thus John occupied two of the most strategic positions in all Bohemia, although he was probably unaware of their importance. The city of Prague had a lengthy tradition of reform and could boast some outstanding preachers, who even preached from the Scriptures. To this tradition Hus fell heir. The University of Prague was in the very center of the reform movement and was a place of ferment as new ideas and programs for the church were constantly being discussed. The chapel to which Hus was appointed had been built in 1391 by a rich merchant as a center for reform preaching.

It was about the time that Hus began preaching that he also was converted. It seems as if his conversion was centered in his calling to preach. Prior to 1400, Hus had studied for the priesthood in the firm conviction that this was the way to escape from poverty. When actually confronted with the task of preaching, his life underwent a fundamental change, and he was overcome by the consciousness of the great task of preaching the gospel of Christ. He himself wrote of how important he considered preaching: "By the help of God I have preached, still am preaching, and if his grace will allow, shall continue to preach; if perchance I may be able to lead some poor, tired, or halting soul into the house of Christ to the King's supper."

## The Reformer

The teachings of John Wycliffe had come to Bohemia as early as 1390. A close alliance had been established between England and Bohemia because England's king, Richard II, had married Anne of Bohemia, the sister of Bohemia's king. Scholars had traveled between the countries, and one eminent scholar, Jerome of Prague, had spent some time in Oxford, Wycliffe's school, where he had absorbed the teachings of Wycliffe. On his return, he had spread Wycliffe's writings and teachings throughout Prague and the university.

Although reform had been in the air for many years, the spread of Wycliffe's teachings gave it direction and a doctrinal foundation. John Hus had become thoroughly familiar with the teachings of Wycliffe and, convinced of their truth, he had himself begun to teach them in the university and preach them in the pulpit. It is not surprising that the full fury of the Roman Catholic Church was soon turned against him. When general reform, especially of clerical corruption, was preached, even many Roman Catholics supported the reform movement. But when Hus and others began to preach doctrinal reform as well as moral reform, Rome turned in a rage against the reformers, and especially against Hus.

It seems as if from the time Hus began preaching, he was under suspicion. A curious document turned up near the end of Hus's life which was a collection of quotes from his preaching and teaching, taken secretly and obviously with the intent of using them to charge Hus with heresy. The more Hus emphasized that at the root of Rome's evils lay doctrinal error, the more he lost the support of the church, of the politicians, and of most of those in authority. The students Hus taught in school and the common people who loved his preaching continued to support him.

## *Opposition*

As the opposition to Hus grew, pressure of many kinds was put on him. First forty-five statements, purported to be Hus's teachings, were condemned. Then preaching was forbidden in all the chapels. When Hus refused to stop preaching, he was excommunicated by the archbishop. Soon he was summoned to Rome for trial, but knowing that he would never escape Rome alive, he refused to go and was excommunicated by the pope. Even this was not enough; Prague was put under the interdict so that no religious services could be performed in the entire city. Gradually the might of Rome was squeezing Hus into a corner.

In pity for the citizens of the city, and so that the interdict could be removed, Hus left and returned to the area of his hometown. His new residence soon became a center for preaching in all the surrounding countryside, and it gave him the quietness that he needed in order to write. Perhaps this move did not lessen his effectiveness but was God's means of spreading Hus's teaching beyond the confines of Prague.

At any rate, Rome could tolerate Hus no longer. He was summoned to the Council of Constance in 1414, a meeting that had been called to settle the papal schism. Three popes were all claiming to be the legitimate pope, and the outrageous situation was making a mockery of the claims of the church.

## Trial and Martyrdom

The Emperor Sigismund promised Hus a safe-conduct both to and from Constance, regardless of the outcome of Hus's trial. It was for this reason that Hus determined to go, although he was not at all certain that he would emerge from the trial alive. He told his friends, however, that a faithful testimony to his Lord and Savior required that he go.

Hus would have been safe in his hometown. He testified to this in Constance before his accusers when he told them, "I have stated that I came here of my own free will. If I had been unwilling to come, neither that king [Wenzel] nor this king [Sigismund] would have been able to force me to come, so numerous and so powerful are the Bohemian nobles who love me, and within whose castles I should have been able to lie concealed."

For one month, while in Constance, Hus was permitted to move about freely, even administering the Lord's Supper daily in his lodgings, the home of a widow whom he called his "widow of Zarephath." But Rome's godless and treacherous clerics could not permit Hus to remain free; he was imprisoned on the trumped-up charge that he had attempted to escape the city in a wagon.

Three months Hus was in a dungeon in a Dominican convent in a cell alongside the latrines. On March 24, 1414, he was chained and transferred to a castle dungeon at Gottelieven, where he was handcuffed and bound to a wall at night, though free to walk around in chains during the day. After seventy-three days, he was transferred to a Franciscan friary, where he was subjected to cruel and heartless hearings in efforts to make him recant. During all his imprisonment he was permitted no books, not even his Bible. He was nearly starved to death at times, and throughout he was so cruelly treated that he suffered from hemorrhage, headaches, vomiting, and fainting spells.

When finally he was brought before the council, he was permitted to say nothing, although repeatedly he made an effort to give the testimony to his faith he longed to give. God did not will that his

testimony be that of a confession of his mouth; his testimony was to be the far more powerful testimony of martyrdom.

The trial was a joke, a violation of every rule of justice, a farce of the worst sort. During its proceedings, Hus was repeatedly made the object of mockery, derision, humiliating treatment of the worst sort, and a cruel deposition when he was stripped of all his clerical clothing and publicly defrocked.

Finally he was sentenced to burning at the stake, and the council, afraid of spilling the blood of a man, turned him over to the secular authorities to carry out the sentence.

One interesting sidelight gives a glimpse into the magnificent wisdom of God. When Hus was sentenced to death, he appealed to the Emperor Sigismund, who was present, to rescue him, reminding Sigismund of his promise of a safe-conduct. While Sigismund did not have the courage to keep his promise, he did have the grace to blush a fiery red at Hus's rebuke. All this would not mean so much in itself. But just over 100 years later, Luther went to Worms under the safe conduct of Charles V, emperor of Germany, and made his courageous stand for Scripture. The Roman Catholic Church wanted Luther killed, but Charles insisted that the safe-conduct be enforced. When Charles was later asked why he permitted the dastardly heretic, Luther, to escape, Charles replied that he remembered all too well the blush of shame on the face of Sigismund when he treacherously went back on his promise. God used the blush of a shamed king to save Luther's life.

Several times on the way to the place of execution, Hus attempted to speak to the people but was in every case silenced. Finally, when the crowd arrived at the stake, Hus, with tears in his eyes, kneeled in prayer. Hus's hands were tied behind him and his neck bound to the stake with a sooty chain. The straw and wood were piled around him up to the chin, and rosin was sprinkled on the wood. When he was asked one last time to recant, his response was: "I shall die with joy today in the faith of the gospel which I have preached." As the flames arose around him, he sang twice, "Christ, thou Son of the living God, have mercy upon me." Praying and singing until the smoke began to choke him, he died a faithful martyr of Jesus Christ. To remove all possible opportunities for his relics to be preserved, his clothing was thrown into the fire and all the ashes were gathered and thrown into the Rhine River.

So died this faithful man of God, sealing his testimony with his blood.

## Importance

Hus was a godly man throughout his reformatory career, and he won the grudging praise of his enemies. A Jesuit testified, "John Hus was even more remarkable for his acuteness than his eloquence; but the modesty and severity of his conduct, his austere and irreproachable life, his pale and melancholy features, his gentleness and affability to all, even the most humble, persuaded more than the greatest eloquence." Another Roman Catholic, later a pope, wrote, "He was a powerful speaker, and distinguished for the reputation of a life of remarkable purity."

Hus was not the original thinker that Wycliffe was and, indeed, borrowed most of his thoughts from Wycliffe, especially Wycliffe's views of the church as the elect body of Christ and the sole authority of Scripture. But Hus became what Wycliffe never was, a powerful preacher of the gospel. By preaching he moved a nation. By preaching, he established a church in Bohemia which Rome could never destroy, but which joined the Reformation just over 100 years later.

Rome has the blood of countless people of God on its hands. It has never expressed one word of sorrow or regret for this. The blood of the martyrs still cries from under the altar against Rome: "How long, O Lord, holy and true, wilt thou not judge and avenge our blood on them that dwell on the earth?"

To Hus, along with the other martyrs of Christ, was given a white robe and the testimony that they should rest a little while until their brethren should be killed as they were.

*Part Three*

# Reformation Period
# on the Continent
# *1517-1600*

# Part Three:

## *Reformation Period on the Continent (1517-1600)*

Gutenberg's Printing Press
   1450...............................

**1460**

      **Frederick Wise** 1463-1525

**1480**

      **Martin Luther** 1483-1546
      **Ulrich Zwingli** 1484-1531
      **William Farel** c.1489-1565
      **Martin Bucer** 1491-1551

**1500**
      **Peter Vermigli** 1499-1562

      **Heinrich Bullinger** 1504-1575
      **John Calvin** 1509-1564

      **Fredrick the Pious** 1515-1576

Luther's 95 Theses 1517......
      **Theodore Beza** 1519-1605

**1520**

Diet of Worms 1521............
      **Guido deBres** 1522-1567
Inquisition brought to Netherlands by Charles V 1522..

Colloquy of Marburg 1529...
      **Peter Datheen** c.1531-1588
      **William the Silent** 1533-1584
First Edition of Calvin's
      **Zacharias Ursinus** 1534-1583
   *Institutes* 1536................
      **Caspar Olevianus** 1536-1587
First Helvetic Confession 1536

**1540**

Council of Trent 1545-1563..
Peace of Augsburg 1555.......

Belgic Confession 1562........
Heidelberg Catechism 1563..

Second Helvetic Confession
   1566...............................
**1565**
Diet of Augsburg 1566........

First Reformed Synod in
   the Netherlands 1571........
St. Bartholomew's Massacre
   of Huguenots 1572...........

**1580**

## Chapter 20

# Martin Luther
## German Reformer

### Introduction

*God had preserved His church throughout the dark and dreary Middle Ages when apostate Rome controlled the life and consciences of men. He had preserved His church through the Waldensians hiding in the valleys and caves of the Alps to escape the brutality of the Inquisition. He had preserved His church through*

faithful followers of the two Johns: John Wycliffe and John Hus.

But the institute of the church was corrupt, and the saints of God had no place to go with their children to be nourished by the Bread of Life. Gradually, under Rome's terrible pressures, the church became more difficult to find.

God has His own way and His own time of doing that which needs to be done to preserve His church. Applicable to the church, as well as to creation, is the old adage "It is always darkest just before dawn." Darkness grew deeper in Europe under Rome's heavy hand, but the dawn was about to break. It broke with the coming of an insignificant monk out of Saxony in Germany, when hope for reformation was gone. It broke from an unexpected source and in a surprising place. It is the story of one of the greatest works of God in the church since the time of the apostles. It is doubtful whether such a story shall again unfold before Christ returns at the end of time.

### The Reformation In Luther's Soul

From our earthly and human perspective it seems as if God is never in a hurry. He seems

to take His time about things which appear to us to be so crucial that any delay is disastrous. So it was at the time of Luther.

In the latter part of the fifteenth century, the situation in Europe seemed to be so bad that if God did not do something very shortly, it would be too late and the church would be forever gone from the earth. Reformation had to take place or reformation would never take place.

When reformation did come, it came as the mighty surge of a tidal wave which engulfed Europe; yet it began very slowly and was scarcely noticed. It came as a still, small voice in the soul of Martin Luther.

Luther was born November 10, 1483, in Eisleben, Prussia, in Saxony of Germany. His parents were rather poor, but honest, industrious, and pious members of the Romish church. Luther was brought up under the strict discipline and superstition of the church. He received his early education in Mansfeld, Magdeburg, and Eisenach. Because his parents were unable to support him, he sang to earn a bit of money and was helped by Ursula Cotta, wife of one of the wealthy merchants in Eisenach. His upbringing was the rough training of the peasantry, and he bore the indelible marks of his upbringing all his life. It made him a man of the people.

At eighteen, in 1501, he entered the University of Erfurt to study scholastic thought, logic, metaphysics, rhetoric, and physics—the traditional studies of his time. Because the Renaissance had entered German universities, he also studied the Latin classics and developed in poetry and music. At twenty years of age, he saw a complete Bible, probably for the first time. Thus began the struggle, created by God, in Luther's soul concerning his personal salvation. In 1502 he graduated from the university with an A.B. degree, and three years later he obtained an A.M., roughly equivalent to a Ph.D. Law was his main concern because it was his father's wish that he devote himself to what was one of the most promising careers in Roman Catholic Europe.

But God had other plans. Two events brought Luther into a monastery. One was the sudden death of a friend, either killed in a duel or struck by lightning; the other was a terrible thunderstorm in which he thought he would die and pleaded with St. Anne to spare him, promising, if spared, to become a monk. He was spared and became a monk July 16, 1505.

Luther wanted to be a monk because he thought of the convent as the way to bring some peace to his fear-filled soul. God put him in a monastery so that he could learn the utter uselessness of every prescription Rome offered to attain this peace. Rome's prescriptions were no help at all because they were based on what man had to do.

In the monastery Luther tried it all. As he himself put it, he out-monked all the monks. He mistreated himself so badly with various works of penance that he harmed his health. He confessed sins to his superior so often and in such detail that he was told finally either to commit some sin worth confessing or to quit bothering a busy man with silly little things.

God sent him some help in the monastery, perhaps sufficient to keep Luther sane, although not sufficient as yet to bring him peace. The help came from Johann von Staupitz, the vicar-general of the monastery, one who had mystical leanings and knew more about salvation than the whole Romish church but who never left Rome for all that. The vicar-general directed Luther to Scripture, turned Luther's thoughts to the forgiveness of sins in the cross, and planted the seeds of the priesthood in Luther's soul. During one of Luther's periods of black despair, von Staupitz, while sitting with Luther under a pear tree in the garden of the monastery, told him to prepare himself for preaching by becoming a doctor of theology. Luther's response was, "Your honor, Mr. Staupitz, you will deprive me of my life." Only half in jest, Staupitz replied, "Quite all right. God has plenty of work for clever men to do in heaven."

The time spent in the monastery was necessary for Luther to realize that the theology of the Romish church was wrong in its doctrine of salvation by works. The works which God required could never be performed by man. Luther himself was plagued with the thought that one either could not do enough good works, or that the works he did were not sufficiently good to earn his salvation. Because none of his imperfect and inadequate works could earn salvation, the peace and joy of salvation could not be his. But Luther needed to learn in the school of the Holy Spirit that salvation is not of the works by man, but by the grace of God.

### Luther's Conversion

Luther entered the priesthood and said his first mass May 2, 1507. He continued his studies towards a doctorate in theology which, when completed, opened the door for him to become professor in the University of Wittenberg. In the winter of 1512, the Reverend Doctor Martin Luther began his teaching with lecturing. He treated, in turn, the Psalms, Romans, Galatians, Hebrews, and, again, the Psalms. He saw studies of these books as crucial and later said, "In the course of this teaching, the papacy slipped away from me."

The breakthrough in understanding came with new insights into the phrase "the righteousness of God" as it appears in Romans 1:17: "For therein is the righteousness of God revealed from faith to faith: as it is written, The just shall live by faith." Luther had always thought of God's righteousness as God's essential perfection and His consequent hatred of sin. He had looked at God's righteousness as His burning wrath against anyone who did not keep His ways perfectly. In what later has become known as Luther's "tower experience," he suddenly came to understand that the phrase "the righteousness of God" did not refer to God's hatred of sin rooted in His own perfection, but meant that God imputed righteousness to the sinner without works and only because of the merits of Christ. It was a righteousness freely given to undeserving sinners by faith.

It seemed to him—Luther later said in describing this event—that the gates of heaven themselves were opened before him. Suddenly his awful sense of guilt and unworthiness fell away; his desperate attempts to achieve peace with God through his works seemed stupid and useless; all his monkish rituals had been exercises in futility. He was without any sin, not because he did not sin, but because Christ's righteousness was freely given. As he described it, he was righteous and a sinner at the same time. This brought him the peace he had been seeking, even in the struggle with sin.

The full implications of this theological "breakthrough" did not dawn immediately on Luther. Once having seen this great light, he now had to reread and restudy the Psalms and Paul, for understanding that salvation through imputed righteousness lay at the heart of Scripture, he had to look at it all again from the viewpoint of this "heart."

## *The Reformation*

A reformation had been, by God's grace, completed in Luther's soul. It was now time for reformation to begin in the church at large. God had readied the man He was to use, and even if Luther did not know it, the people of God were now to be led out of the Egypt

of Rome's church into the Canaan of the gospel . Luther was appointed the Moses.

The work began when the monk Tetzel decided to hawk his indulgences in Saxony of Germany, where the news of it came to Luther's attention. Convinced in his own soul of the evil of indulgences, Luther decided to open the subject to debate among the monks of the Augustinian order of which he was a part. To invite others to the debate, he attached Ninety-five Theses (propositions) to the chapel door of the church of Wittenberg on October 31, 1517, so that anyone wishing to participate would know the subjects of the debate.

It became evident from this time on that the Reformation was indeed the work of God, not the work of Luther. It was God's work in Luther's soul. Yet it continued to be God's work as it ran its course. In describing the progress of the Reformation, Luther was later to say,

> The first thing I ask is that people should not make use of my name, and should not call themselves Lutherans but Christians. What is Luther? The teaching is not mine. Nor was I crucified for anyone . . . How did I, poor stinking bag of maggots that I am, come to the point where people call the children of Christ by my evil name?

Later, in a sermon, he said,

> I simply taught, preached, wrote God's Word; otherwise I did nothing. And then, while I slept, or drank Wittenberg beer with my Philip and my Amsdorf, the Word so greatly weakened the papacy that never a prince or emperor did such damage to it. I did nothing. The Word did it all.

This conviction of Luther that what happened was God's work was apparent at the time of the posting of his theses. Luther, rather innocently, wanted a general discussion. God took the theses and, through the marvel of the printing press, caused them to be distributed through the whole of Europe, where they shook Europe to its foundations. The theses were the germ of the gospel of salvation in Christ alone, a truth for which Europe hungered.

We cannot, in this brief biographical sketch, give a detailed account of Luther's work. It is possible to mention, and then only in passing, some of the outstanding events.

## The Heidelberg Disputation

Although the upheavals in Europe over Luther's theses soon came to the attention of the pope, Rome was not immediately perturbed by these events and dismissed the whole matter as "a monks' quarrel." It was far more than that, and even Luther did not know the extent of it. But when the seriousness of it all became evident, some important events took place.

The Heidelberg Disputation, held in April of 1518 (less than a half year after the theses came to public attention), was a conference and debate within the Augustinian order over Luther's views. The Roman Catholic prelates appealed to papal authority and thought that would end the matter. Luther took the opportunity to get behind the indulgence question to expose various theological errors: the merit of good works and the free will of man. Nothing much came of it all except that Luther gained many for his views, including Martin Bucer, later a reformer of Strassburg.

## The Leipzig Disputation

Rome now began to take some interest in the matter and appointed Prierio, responsible for all that was taught in Christendom, to investigate. He wrote a tract attempting to refute the theses of Luther, but his chief appeal was to papal authority:

> Whoever does not rely on the teaching of the Roman Church and of the Roman Pontiff, as the infallible rule of faith, from which the Holy Scriptures themselves derive their strength and their authority, is a heretic.

Luther was ordered to appear in Rome to have his views examined, and Frederick, Elector of Saxony, was ordered to turn him over. Frederick refused and became Luther's protector throughout the Reformation.

The Leipzig Disputation, held from June 27 to July 15, 1519, was one of the great debates of all time. The main debaters were Martin Luther and John Eck, the latter a skilled orator and debater and a man devoted heart and soul to Romish orthodoxy. From a purely formal point of view, Luther lost the debate. He was charged with Hussitism and was forced to admit it because Eck proved to be the more skilled in debating techniques and drove Luther to positions he had not originally held.

But these positions were the ones where God wanted Luther to stand. Under the pressures of Eck's skillful attack, Luther was, step

by step, forced to deny the infallibility of church councils, the supreme authority of the papacy, the idea of priestly mediation, and the silly notion that the morality of monks in monasteries was superior to the morality of God's people. Finally, he stood where God wanted him to stand: on the sole authority of Scripture, on the truth that only that which is of faith is good in God's sight, and on the principle of the priesthood of all believers. Luther was forced to see the consequences of the position he had taken.

## *The Diet of Worms*

In June 1520 the bull of excommunication was issued in Rome at Eck's instigation. Because the German people were behind Luther, it was difficult to deliver the bull to Luther personally. When finally it was done, Luther publicly burned the bull in the street of Wittenberg in December of the same year. It was the complete break between him and an apostate church.

The next year (1521) Luther was summoned to appear on trial before the Diet in Worms. It was a meeting of the Reichstag—a convocation of all the princes ruling the different provinces of Germany—to settle, if possible, "the German problem" brought on by Luther's new teachings. Present were also high and mighty officials from the Romish church decked in all their splendid robes and miters, determined to force the will of the pope upon the Reichstag. Charles V, chosen by the princes to be ruler of the Holy Roman Empire, which included Germany, was there with his court.

At crucial times God arranges affairs in His church in such a way that just one man alone, among the multitudes, is called upon to stand for the cause of God and truth. So it was at Worms: Luther against the entire Romish church, Luther threatened by the cruelties of the Inquisition, Luther against the might of the empire, Luther alone.

He went, it is true, under a safe-conduct issued by the emperor Charles V himself, but Luther and his friends remembered all too well that a safe-conduct meant exactly nothing to Rome's charlatans, even though it was a sacred promise before God. When urged by his friends not to go, Luther responded that the cause of Christ required it and that if every roof tile in Worms were a devil, he would still need to go. Reflecting on those perilous days shortly before his death, he said, "I was fearless, I was afraid of nothing; God can make one so desperately bold, I know not whether I could be so cheerful now."

He was not given opportunity to defend his position but was asked whether the books lying before him on the table were his. When he acknowledged that they were, he was asked whether he would recant what he taught.

It was a solemn moment. Luther was awed by the assembly, nervous and excited, unprepared to be confronted with a question which could mean his life without any opportunity to defend himself. He asked for a day to consider his answer. After a brief consultation, the emperor granted it. Some thought Luther was about to collapse. His enemies were filled with glee.

The respite of a day brought Luther renewed strength and vigor. He wrote that night to a friend, "I shall not retract one iota, so Christ help me."

The next day had to be the most important day of Luther's life. On the way to the hall, an old warrior is said to have clapped him on the shoulder and said, "My poor monk, my poor monk, thou art going to make such a stand as neither I nor any of my companions in arms have ever done in our hottest battles. If thou art sure of the justice of thy cause, then forward in God's name, and be of good courage: God will not forsake thee."

After some preliminary discussion, and when finally instructed to make clear his position without equivocation, Luther uttered those words which have so many times moved the souls of the heirs of the Reformation, though they filled the enemies with consternation and dismay:

> Unless I am refuted and convicted by testimonies of the Scriptures or by clear arguments (since I believe neither the Pope nor the councils alone; it being evident that they have often erred and contradicted themselves), I am conquered by the Holy Scriptures quoted by me, and my conscience is bound in the word of God: I can not and will not recant anything, since it is unsafe and dangerous to do anything against the conscience. Here I stand. I can not do otherwise. God help me! Amen.

The Roman Catholics put a lot of pressure on Charles to break his safe-conduct promise and arrest Luther, but Charles refused. It has been said that Charles' refusal was because of his memory of the blush on the face of Sigismund when John Hus, as he was led away to be burned, reminded him of the safe-conduct he had issued. In any case, the Reichstag put Luther under the ban of the empire.

## Stay in Wartburg

Frederick, Luther's elector—fearful that Luther would be captured after all—arranged for his "kidnapping" by friends who carried him to the castle at Wartburg. Here Luther stayed for eleven months, writing constantly. His chief work was his translation of the New Testament Scriptures into the German language. It was an amazing accomplishment, for by it Luther gave the Bible to God's people; the literary style he used also determined the course of the German language for centuries to follow.

Luther returned to Wittenberg only when he heard that the radical Zwickau prophets, with their dangerous mysticism, were disturbing the peace and tranquillity of his city. If one wonders how important a role preaching played in the Reformation, one need only be reminded of the fact that Luther stopped the radicals in their tracks and sent them scurrying out of the city by means of a series of eight sermons which he preached from Wittenberg's pulpit.

From the time Luther returned to Wittenberg to the end of his life, Germany tottered on the brink of war between the armies of the Protestant princes and the armies of the princes who were determined to keep Germany Roman Catholic. It was a time of danger and struggle, but only after Luther's death did the Thirty Years War break out, a war which left Germany devastated.

## Luther the Preacher

Above all else, Luther was a preacher. This ought not to surprise us, for preaching is the one and only power of the church. No reformation can be brought about in any other way than through preaching.

Luther's preaching was characterized by exposition of Scripture and extremely down-to-earth imagery by which Luther made God's truth come alive in the minds and hearts of the simplest of God's people. The sermons reflected Luther's rapport with his own countrymen.

Luther always brought the congregation to the cross in his preaching. It is hard to find a sermon in which he did not do this. He himself had found the peace that passes understanding at the foot of the cross, and to that suffering and dying Savior, Luther was intent on bringing God's people.

His sermons are extant. They ought to be read. Nothing tells us of the struggles of the Reformation more clearly than these sermons, and nothing shows us the power of the Spirit in Christ-centered preaching more vividly than to read what Luther preached.

### Luther the Writer

Luther's writings are voluminous. In an edition in the library of the Protestant Reformed Seminary, his collected writings take up fifty-four volumes. Several of his works are so outstanding that sooner or later they ought to be read by God's people—as, indeed, they were read by God's people in Luther's day. In his *Bondage of the Will* Luther refuted the heresy of the freedom of the will taught by the "Prince of the Humanists," Desiderius Erasmus. It was Luther's break from humanism and is one of the great books of the Reformation.

Luther's three most influential pamphlets defined the basic truths of the Lutheran Reformation: "Address to the German Nobility," in which the doctrine of the priesthood of all believers was developed; "Babylonian Captivity of the Church," in which Luther made his case against Rome's sacramental system; and "Freedom of the Christian Man," a clear discussion of Christian freedom.

If anyone wishes to know Luther at his most down-to-earth and rugged character, he needs only to read the *Table Talks*. Here is Luther commenting on almost everything in life with simple expressions, biblical insights, humorous comments, and talk that would delight the soul of the rough-hewn peasant.

### Luther the Husband and Father

One could write a book on the family aspect of the Lutheran Reformation alone. Luther not only laid aside his monastic vows; he also married Catherine von Bora, a former nun with a mind of her own and a force in her own right in the home. He married her, he said, "to please my father, tease the pope, and vex the devil." She was affectionately called by her husband, "Kitty, my rib." She managed, sometimes with exasperation, the tumultuous household which always had visitors and never had enough money. To them were born six children, three daughters, two of whom died young, and three sons. Especially the death of Lena (Magdalen) touched Luther with great sorrow. Philip Schaff describes Luther's prayer at her bedside:

> "I love her very much," he prayed; "but, dear God, if it is thy holy will to take her hence, I would gladly leave her with Thee." And to her he said, "Lena

dear, my little daughter, thou wouldst love to remain here with thy father: art thou willing to go to that other Father?"

"Yes, dear father," she replied, "just as God wills." And when she was dying, he fell on his knees beside her bed, wept bitterly, and prayed for her redemption. As she lay in her coffin, he exclaimed, "Ah! my darling Lena, thou wilt rise again, and shine like a star—yea, as a sun. I am happy in the spirit, but very sorrowful in the flesh."

Luther wrote extensively on education because the education of the children of the church was crucial to him. In writing on this important subject, from which we can learn today, Luther was far ahead of his times.

Instruction in the home occupied a crucial part of Luther's life. The home of Martin and Katie was filled with prayer, Bible study, theological discussion, and the example of godly people. One prayer of Luther lives in my memory in a special way because it shows his intimate life of fellowship with God, his dependence upon divine grace, and his love for the church. It was a prayer at the end of a busy day.

My dear God, now I lie down and turn your affairs back to you; you may do better with them. If you can do no better than I, you will ruin them entirely. When I awake, I will gladly try again. Amen.

By his own home life, Luther brought true reformation into home and family, something sorely needed after the corruption of Rome. The effects of Luther's own example linger to the present in covenant homes.

## Luther the Warrior

Luther fought courageously and unflinchingly in the battles for the truth. Whatever was necessary in his mighty blasts against Rome to show its evils, he did. By his work he threw the entire church into confusion.

It must be remembered that he had to fight on two fronts: Rome on the one side, and on the other side, the miserable Anabaptist radicals, the so-called "right wing" of the Reformation. That he could maintain his balance between these two extremes is evidence in itself of the power of grace in Luther's life.

By means of his theology, Luther battered and destroyed the imposing and seemingly indestructible walls of the Roman citadel of

heresy. While Calvin was the one to rebuild Jerusalem's walls, Calvin could not have done his work without Luther's fierce cannonades against Rome. Luther also laid the foundations of the doctrines of sovereign grace so that the truths of salvation by grace alone could be more beautifully and fully set forth by those who were to follow.

It is always reason for sorrow that, on his doctrine of the sacraments, Luther should also have felt it necessary to do battle with his fellow reformers. While Luther's reasons for changing to consubstantiation are understandable, he never succeeded in freeing his views from Roman Catholic error.

## *Luther's Death*

Luther made a trip to Eisleben, Germany, the city of his birth and baptism, to handle some difficult negotiations. There, far from his beloved Katie and Wittenberg, at the age of sixty-three, he went to be with his Lord, whom he loved and served. The date was February 17, 1546. Luther had for a long time suffered severely from various ailments. As death neared, in characteristic fashion he committed his soul to God with the words of Psalm 31:5 and with the request to those at his bedside that they would pray "for our Lord God and His gospel, that all might be well with Him, because the Council of Trent and the accursed pope are very angry with Him." He died with the words of Simeon on his lips: "Lord, now lettest thou thy servant depart in peace. Amen."

The reformer had gone to join the church triumphant. His work lives on.

## Chapter 21

# Ulrich Zwingli
### Reformer of Zurich

### Introduction

*In the work of God's kingdom and covenant, no one man can do all the work which God needs done. Moses could deliver the Israelites from Egypt and lead them through the wilderness, but Joshua had to be called to bring them into Canaan. David could fight the battles of Jehovah on behalf of God's chosen people, but he could not build*

the temple. Solomon had to do that. Only Christ can do all the work that needs doing.

Many different men engaged in the work of the Reformation, some of great importance, some of lesser. Yet each had his place. Luther could not do it all; it took also Calvin in Geneva and Knox in Scotland. Even Calvin could not do all the work that needed doing in Switzerland. Zwingli had a role to play, and he is counted among these four great reformers.

### Zwingli's Pre-conversion Life

In the midst of stunning Alpine beauty, in the Toggenburg Valley at Wildhaus, Switzerland, Ulrich Zwingli was born in a lowly shepherd's cottage to the mayor of this small hamlet. He belonged to a large family: seven brothers (he was the third son) and two sisters. He was born seven weeks after Martin Luther, on January 1, 1484.

Zwingli received his education in the leading universities of Switzerland and Austria and was, throughout, instructed in the humanism of the Renaissance. This is important, for Zwingli's humanism was to be an influence in his theology even after his conversion and during the years of his reformatory work. The Renaissance was a movement which had begun in Italy a couple of centuries earlier and was characterized by a revival of learning, a return to the study of ancient Greek and Roman classics, and a humanistic exaltation of man.

In Basel, Zwingli studied Latin grammar, music, and dialectics. In Bern he studied under Lupulus, the greatest classical scholar and poet in Switzerland and a leading humanist. In Vienna he studied scholastic philosophy, astronomy, physics, and the ancient classics. His education differed somewhat from that of Luther and was more nearly like the education which Calvin received, but all three reformers were highly educated men. Moses also was "learned in all the wisdom of the Egyptians."

Returning to Basel, Zwingli studied and taught, acquiring his Master of Arts degree in 1506. Two events in Basel helped to shape his life. He was taught by Thomas Wyttenback, a man deeply interested in the reform of the church; and he met Leo Judd, who was to remain his friend and co-reformer for the rest of his life. Both these men turned Zwingli's thoughts toward need for reform in the corrupt church of Rome.

Zwingli early showed remarkable ability as a musician, and in the course of his studies he learned to play with skill the lute, harp, violin, flute, dulcimer, and hunting horn. He made good use of this gift throughout his career and wrote a number of beautiful poems and songs.

### *His Early Ministry*

In 1506 Zwingli's work as minister began. He was ordained to the priesthood in Glaurus but had to buy off a rival candidate for the sum of 100 guilders.

Some interesting things happened while Zwingli was in Glaurus. For one thing, he immersed himself in the pastoral ministry, preaching, teaching, doing pastoral work, and caring for the spiritual needs of his flock in so far as he could do this as an unconverted man. For another thing, he spent a great deal of time in personal study, reading avidly the old Greek and Roman authors. In order to read the Greek authors, he taught himself Greek and became proficient in this language. His admiration for classical writers grew with his reading, and he developed the idea that the Holy Spirit must have operated beyond the boundaries of Palestine among the heathen philosophers, for their writings could be explained only in

terms of the work of the Holy Spirit. In this respect he anticipated later mistaken views of the general and gracious operations of the Holy Spirit among the heathen, taught by the defenders of common grace. Because of his vast learning and ability, he supervised the education of two of his brothers and of several of the noblest young men of Glaurus, who became firm friends and remained such through his years of reformatory work.

During this period of study, Zwingli also made three trips with Swiss mercenaries into Italy and came to hate this Swiss practice, which played an important enough part in Zwingli's life to say a few things about it.

It was common in Switzerland for the men to hire themselves out as soldiers to foreign armies. The effects of accepting the post of a mercenary were spiritually demoralizing: the fathers were away from home for long periods of time and fell into all the immorality attendant on such a practice; and the mercenaries became accustomed to cruelty and hardness, which was a way of life on the battlefields. The practice later became an issue in the struggles with Roman Catholicism because the Roman Church supported the mercenary system, seeing in it a source of vast revenues. Some estimate the revenues for the church in Switzerland may have amounted to over $3,000,000 a year. From this practice of mercenaries dates the papal custom of having Swiss guards in the Vatican.

In 1515 Zwingli moved to Einsiedeln, where he continued about three years. During his stay in Einsiedeln he gradually came to understand the evil of many Romish practices. Especially the corrupt practice of indulgences came to his attention when a huckster by the name of Samson tried to sell his indulgences in Switzerland. It is interesting that at least two years before Luther's attack on indulgences, Zwingli was preaching against them and condemning them vehemently from the pulpit. In this matter, as well as in others, Zwingli anticipated Luther and taught many of the same things, although he developed his ideas independently.

It was also in Einsiedeln that Zwingli made the acquaintance of the famous humanist Erasmus, who about this time published his first edition of the Greek New Testament. Zwingli was deeply attracted to Erasmus, visited him, became his friend, and invited Erasmus to Zurich in 1522, which invitation Erasmus declined. It is to Zwingli's credit that, while he agreed with Erasmus on many points, he repudiated Erasmus' Semi-Pelagianism.

While Zwingli was in Glaurus and Einsiedeln, he fell into the sin of fornication. That this did not affect his standing in the church is only evidence of how common the practice was, but Zwingli later repented of it with great anguish of soul and lived with the burden of it all his life.

Zwingli never did free himself of his humanistic views, views which continued to influence his theology even when he became the reformer of Switzerland. All his studies had been from a humanistic viewpoint; he had read widely in classical literature; and his admiration for Erasmus all but guaranteed that humanism would play an important role in his thinking.

## Zwingli's Conversion

Zwingli's conversion was probably a gradual one which began while he was in Einsiedeln, but which came to full expression in Zurich, to which he was called in the latter part of 1518. God used several means to bring about his conversion. Increasingly, as he saw the need for reform in the church, he came to hate the Romish abuses which destroyed men's souls. As his studies turned more and more to Scripture, he—even before Luther—saw that Scripture alone had to be the authority for all the faith and life of the church. In fact, when he began his ministry in Zurich on January 1, 1519, on his thirty-fifth birthday, he began a systematic exposition of the Gospel according to Matthew. During the next four years of his ministry, he continued preaching systematically through the New Testament, going from Matthew to Acts, then to the Pauline and catholic epistles, and then on to the other books, with the exception of Revelation. During the week he preached from the Psalms. Such a study could not have left him untouched.

In 1520 the plague struck Zurich, carrying off 2,500 people, about one-third of the populace. Zwingli was untiring in ministering to the needs of his flock, until the plague struck him down. From it he almost died, but by it God made him a new man. A poem he wrote aptly depicts his faith:

> Help me, O Lord,
>     My strength and rock;
> Lo, at the door
>     I hear death's knock.

Uplift thine arm,
    Once pierced for me,
That conquered death,
    And set me free.

Yet, if thy voice
    In life's mid-day,
Recalls my soul,
    Then I obey.

In faith and hope
    Earth I resign,
Secure in heaven,
    For I am Thine.

## The Reformer

It was after Zwingli's recovery that reform began in earnest. Once having become persuaded that Scripture was to be the only norm and standard of our life and faith, and of the life and faith of the church, Zwingli could not rest until reform took place. In Switzerland, reforms came about in a unique way. The pattern was this: The reformers petitioned the magistracy in a given city or canton to implement certain reforms; the magistracy called a public meeting or disputation to which were invited Roman Catholic theologians and the reformers; both were required to defend their position on the matter at issue before the magistracy, which would then decide whether the reforms were to be implemented. In these disputations it was common for the councils to rule that the debate had to be conducted on the basis of Scripture alone.

The first disputation was held on January 29, 1523, in Zurich before a public audience of more than 600 people. As would almost always be the case in future disputations, it was also true in Zurich that the reformers easily won their point, partly because their position was the only one grounded on Scripture, but partly, too, because the Romish church had no significant and knowledgeable theologians who could hold their own in open debate with the reformers.

Victory followed upon victory, not only in Zurich, but also in other cantons of Switzerland where disputations were held. Lent was abandoned; clerical celibacy was declared unbiblical; the Bible was translated into the vernacular; images, pictures, and relics were removed from the churches; the churches were severed from the

control of the papacy; the monasteries were dissolved; fasting was prohibited; the mass was replaced; the Lord's Supper was held at regular intervals, usually four times a year; discipline was established under the control of officebearers in the churches; and biblical preaching was ordered in all the churches.

This first disputation, held in Zurich, ended in a complete victory for Zwingli and his fellow reformers, and the council instructed Zwingli "to continue to preach the holy gospel as heretofore, and to proclaim the true, divine Scriptures."

Just prior to the disputation, Zwingli had published sixty-seven articles of faith. This is an important historical document because it constitutes the earliest declaration of the Reformed faith. A few articles will indicate some of the basic beliefs of Zwingli:

> All who say that the gospel is nothing without the approbation of the Church, err and cast reproach upon God.
>
> The sum of the gospel is that our Lord Jesus Christ, the true Son of God, has made known to us the will of his heavenly Father, and redeemed us by his innocence from eternal death, and reconciled us to God.
>
> Therefore Christ is the only way to salvation to all who were, who are, who shall be.
>
> Christ is the Head of all believers who are his body; but without him the body is dead.
>
> All who live in this Head are his members and children of God. And this is the Church, the communion of saints, the bride of Christ, the *Ecclesia catholica*.
>
> Christ is our righteousness. From this it follows that our works are good so far as they are Christ's, but not good so far as they are our own.

These truths are now very familiar to us, but if one will only think of writing them in the context of 1000 years of papal error, it will give him a sense of how great a work of God was performed in the Reformation.

With the Reformation firmly established in Zurich, it quickly spread to other parts of Switzerland. From Zurich it spread to Glarus, Schaffhausen, Appenzell, and the city of St. Gall. The spread continued when the leading canton of Berne adopted Reformation principles and proceeded to introduce them into the cantons of Vaud, Neuchâtel, and Geneva—where Calvin was later to do his great work. In every case the Reformation came by way of a leading

reformer working closely with Zwingli and by a disputation ordered by the council. Of interest are the ten theses or conclusions adopted as a confession of faith in Berne. They read, in part,

> The holy Christian Church, whose only Head is Christ, is born of the Word of God, and abides in the same...

> The Church of Christ makes no laws and commandments without the Word of God...

> Christ is the only wisdom, righteousness, redemption, and satisfaction for the sins of the whole world...

> The mass as now in use, in which Christ is offered to God the Father for the sins of the living and the dead, is contrary to the Scripture...

> As Christ alone died for us, so he is also to be adored as the only Mediator and Advocate between God the Father and the believers.

> Scripture knows nothing of purgatory...

> The worship of images is contrary to Scripture.

> All to the glory of God and his holy Word.

The high-water mark of the Swiss Reformation was reached in 1530 when Zurich, Berne, Basel, and most of north and east Switzerland were Reformed and no longer Roman Catholic.

### *Three Important Events*

Three important events, in addition to his reformatory work, belong to this period in Zwingli's life.

The first is Zwingli's marriage.

It was not true, as Rome asserted, that the reformers married because they were consumed by uncontrollable lust. They married because they perceived marriage as natural for man and as a gift of God to be used and enjoyed. The practical benefit was that the reformers together reformed also the home and the family.

Because of the times, Zwingli married secretly. For two years only his friends knew of his marriage. In April 1524 he married publicly. His wife was Anna Reinhart, a widow with three children. From this marriage, four more children were added to the family. It is clear from Zwingli's letters that his home life was a happy one and that his wife was a faithful help to him in his years of work in the church.

The second important event in Zwingli's life was the controversy with the Anabaptists.

Anabaptism arose in Zurich during Zwingli's work there. It was a grievous threat to the well-being of the Reformation, for it was not only a doctrinal departure from the truth of Scripture, but it was, in some branches of the movement, a radical movement opposed to the authority of the magistrate and intent on setting up a kingdom of heaven upon earth. Zwingli and his followers were fiercely opposed to Anabaptism, as well they might be. The secular magistracy, in cooperation with the reformers, persecuted the Anabaptists severely, banishing them, imprisoning them, and in some instances drowning them. Anabaptism continued to be a threat to the Reformation throughout the rest of the sixteenth century.

As always, God uses the struggles and trials of the church for good. Though Anabaptism was a serious threat to the Reformation, it was the immediate occasion for the Swiss reformers to begin the development of covenant theology. In defense of the truth of infant baptism over against Anabaptism, the great truth of the covenant was set forth by Zwingli and later by other Swiss theologians. We, who so deeply cherish the truth of the covenant, do not look, in the first place, to Calvin as our spiritual father in this doctrine, but to Zwingli and the Swiss who worked with him.

The third event of note in Zwingli's life was the Marburg Colloquy, held in the German city of Marburg in 1529. Because of the threat of a united Roman Catholicism and the armies of Charles V, the Elector of Saxony and the Landgrave of Hesse wanted to unite all the Protestants in a common cause. To accomplish this, the differences between Lutheranism and the Swiss theologians had to be taken away. The Marburg Colloquy was called for this purpose.

Luther, Melanchthon, and other German theologians were there. Zwingli and his colleagues in the Swiss Reformation were there. Calvin could not come. It did not take very long to discover that the reformers from Germany and Switzerland were agreed on all matters except the doctrine of the presence of Christ in the Lord's Supper—the Lutherans maintaining their view of consubstantiation and the Swiss maintaining their position. Luther was harsh and unyielding. A story has it that he wrote in the dust on the table in front of him, "This is my body" so that he would not forget his insistence that the real body and blood of Christ were present in the sacramental elements.

When agreement proved impossible, the Swiss delegates wanted to extend the hand of fellowship to the German theologians but were rebuffed with the cold and cutting remark of Luther: "Your spirit is different from ours." Even Zwingli's tearful expression of respect and love for Luther could gain little more from the unbending reformer than a brief expression of regret that he had sometimes spoken too harshly.

Unity among Protestants proved impossible.

### Opposition, War, and Death

It is not difficult to understand that the Roman Catholics were not about to see Switzerland become entirely Protestant without some kind of opposition.

This opposition began by severe persecution of Protestants in those cantons that remained Roman Catholic. One Protestant was even burned alive. To relieve their oppressed and martyred brethren, the Protestant cantons were prepared to go to war with their Roman Catholic countrymen, forgetting the words of Jesus Himself: "They that fight with the sword, perish with the sword."

The story is quickly told. In 1529 the Roman Catholics were in no military shape to wage war and so sued for peace. Zwingli urged strongly against peace and gloomily predicted that if the Protestants did not take the opportunity to fight the Roman Catholics when victory was almost assured, they would eventually lose. He proved to be right.

The Roman Catholics used the peace given to strengthen themselves and prepare for war. A blockade, imposed on the Roman Catholic provinces by the Protestants, and which caused much suffering and even starvation, goaded the Roman Catholics to go to war in 1531. In the Battle of Cappel the Protestants were decisively defeated, and Zwingli, who had insisted on going along with the troops as their chaplain, was killed.

Zwingli was stooping to console a dying soldier when he was struck on the head with a stone. He managed to rise once more, but repeated blows and a thrust from a lance left him dying. Seeing his wounds, he cried out, "What matters this misfortune? They may kill the body, but they cannot kill the soul." For the rest of the day he lay under a pear tree, hands folded as in prayer and eyes fixed upon heaven. Towards evening a few stragglers of the victorious army asked him to confess his sins to a priest. He shook his head to

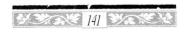

indicate his refusal. But after a bit, one of the men, in the light of his torch, recognized him and killed him with the sword, shouting, "Die, obstinate heretic!"

The soldiers, joyful at his death, quartered his body, burned the pieces for heresy, mixed the ashes with the ashes of pigs, and scattered them to the four winds.

So died one of God's faithful witnesses.

The spread of the Reformation in Switzerland was halted.

Zwingli was, in some respects, an anomaly. On the one hand, he was a reformer faithful to the Scriptures. He insisted on the sole authority of Scripture before Luther raised his voice in Scripture's defense. He taught emphatically salvation in Christ alone and in His perfect sacrifice. He emphasized strongly the truth of sovereign and eternal predestination and preached it from the pulpit. He correctly and vigorously opposed all the Romish practices contrary to Scripture. He was instrumental in laying the foundation for the beginnings of covenant theology.

On the other hand, he never quite shook free from his humanism. He held to the end his notion that heathen men of renown could be saved. He taught that all children in the world who die in infancy go to heaven. He continued to his last breath to admire Erasmus, that humanistic enemy of the Reformation.

In his opposition to the Romish mass, Zwingli went to the opposite extreme and taught that the Lord's Supper is nothing but a memorial feast and that Christ's presence in the bread and wine is not different from the presence of one we love whose portrait we cherish and by which portrait we remember our loved one, who has, nevertheless, gone on to heaven.

Ulrich Zwingli's place in the Reformation was to prepare the way for a purification of the Reformation in Switzerland, where Calvinism finally developed and flourished.

### Chapter 22

# John Calvin

## Genevan Reformer

*Introduction*
*When Karl Barth*
*was preparing a*
*series of lectures on*
*John Calvin, he*
*wrote to a friend,*
"Calvin is a cataract.
I lack completely the
means, the suction cups,
even to assimilate this
phenomenon, not to
speak of presenting it
adequately. What
I receive is only a thin
little stream and what
I can then give out again
is only a yet thinner
extract of this little
stream. I could gladly
and profitably set myself
down and spend all the
rest of my life just with
Calvin."

No one can possibly question the assertion that John Calvin is the greatest reformer of all time. More books have been written about him and his theology than about any other figure in the history of the church. All those who in the last 450 years have cherished the doctrines of sovereign grace have claimed Calvin as their spiritual father. All who confess a theology thoroughly biblical and embodied in all the great creeds of the sixteenth and seventeenth centuries call their theology Calvinism. Other than the Sacred Scriptures themselves, there are few if any books that have exerted the influence on subsequent centuries as Calvin's *Institutes of the Christian Religion*. Even to the present, the *Institutes,* in Reformed and Presbyterian circles, is often considered the final word on theological issues. Yet Calvin, after he began his life's work, never strayed far from Geneva, a relatively small city in French Switzerland. It was here he came on a stormy night; it was here he stayed, frightened by a threat of William Farel; it was here he did all his work. Now his writings have circled the globe. The only explanation for it can be that God, through Calvin, brought reformation to His beleaguered church.

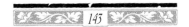

## *Background of the Reformation in Switzerland*

The part of Switzerland which is of interest to us was called French Switzerland because it bordered on France, and the French language was spoken there. It was composed of the cantons of Geneva, Vaud, and Neûchatel. In the canton of Geneva was the city by the same name, on the shore of a lake, also called Geneva.

The government of Geneva at that time requires a brief explanation because it was to play a major role in the Reformation there. The citizens of the city met annually in the General Assembly to choose four syndics and a treasurer. The citizens were, in turn, ruled by a Little Council of 25, which included the current syndics and those of the previous years. The Council of 60, appointed by the Little Council, decided matters of larger policy. In 1527 a Council of 200 was added which included the Little Council and 175 others chosen by the Little Council. It was especially this latter body which gave Calvin many of his problems.

The Reformation had not only come to Germany but had spread to other parts of Europe. In Switzerland, Zwingli had done the majority of the work, and in Geneva the way for Calvin had been prepared by the fiery and radical reformer William Farel.

Berne, to the north of Neûchatel, had joined the Reformation in 1528 and sent ministers into French Switzerland to preach the gospel there. Farel was the leader, and a more powerful figure could scarcely be found.

Farel's entire work was carried on with struggle and in turmoil, and in 1532 Farel was driven from the city. In 1534 he returned and through disputations and preaching won a bit of breathing room for the Protestants who were converted under his preaching. Working in his favor was the fact that, because Geneva was so small, it was technically under the rule of the city of Basel, and Basel supported the Reformation. Gradually the priests, monks, and nuns began to leave the city, and the Reformation was officially established in 1535 and 1536. Still, the city remained a place of frightening moral conditions, an inheritance of Roman Catholicism.

## *Calvin's Youth*

Calvin was born on July 10, 1509, in Noyon, France, twenty-six years after Luther's birth. While Luther was born in a part of the church where piety and religion were emphasized, Calvin was born into a part of the church which treasured education and culture.

Little is known of Calvin's mother; his father was apostolic secretary to the bishop of Noyon but fell into financial difficulties, became an embarrassment to the church, and was excommunicated.

Almost from the start Calvin was destined for the clergy, and in his twelfth year he received part of the revenue from a chaplaincy which supported him in his studies in various schools, mainly in Paris. Perhaps they can all best be summed up by the following description of his work in the Collège de Montaigu:

> ...a famous school known for its stern discipline and its bad food. Erasmus, who studied here a few years before Calvin, later complained of the spoiled eggs he was forced to eat in the refectory. Calvin's lifelong problems with indigestion and insomnia probably derived from the rigid fare and his penchant for burning the midnight oil at Montaigu. Later legend has it that during these years, his fellow students awarded Calvin the nickname of "the accusative case." While this is not true, Beza, in his adoring biography, acknowledged that the young scholar was indeed "a strict censor of every thing vicious in his companions." While his classmates were cavorting in the streets or running off to wild parties, Calvin was busied with the niceties of nominalist logic or the *quaestiones* of scholastic theology.

All in all, Calvin received one of the best educations in the humanities available at that time and emerged from his education a thorough-going humanist. He had made theology the object of his studies, switched to law, and then returned to theology. In 1532, still seemingly untouched by grace, he wrote a commentary on an essay by Seneca, the old pagan Roman, entitled "On Mercy."

## *Calvin's Conversion and Early Work*

Nevertheless, God had begun His work in Calvin. The first influences of any beneficial sort were from two professors, one named Cordier, who was later to become a Protestant, and the other Wolmar, a Lutheran in profession.

Unlike Luther, Calvin was always reticent about himself and his conversion. Beza tells us that Calvin's father persuaded him to study theology because Calvin "was naturally inclined [to theology]; because even at an early age, he was remarkably religious..." In an autobiographical note found in his letter to Cardinal Sadolet, Calvin wrote,

> When, however, I had performed all these things (satisfaction for offenses and fleeing to the saints), though I had some intervals of quiet, I was still far off from true peace of conscience; for, whenever I descended within myself, or

raised my mind to thee, extreme terror seized me—terror which no expiations nor satisfactions could cure.

That sounds a lot like Luther.

Calvin came to Paris at the very time when reformational ideas were altering the thinking of many. In 1533, Nicholas Cop became rector of the university in Paris and delivered a plea for reformation in his inaugural address, which some claim was prepared by Calvin. Persecution broke out when a paper, sharply critical of the mass, was widely distributed in Paris and a copy nailed to the palace door. Cop and Calvin were forced to flee for their lives. Thus Calvin was brought to the point where he repudiated the church of Rome and wrote his first theological work, a paper on, of all things, soul sleep.

For about three years Calvin wandered as an evangelist in southern France, Switzerland, and Italy. Part of the time he was under the protection of Queen Marguerite of Navarre, sister of the king of France; part of the time he was in Ferrara of Italy in the court of the duchess of Renee; and part of the time he visited Basel, where he came into contact with some of the Swiss reformers.

These must have been years of intense study in the Scriptures because Calvin began his work on the *Institutes* during this time, the first edition of which was published in 1536.

Whether Calvin liked it or not, Geneva was to be his home for the remainder of his life. It all started when Calvin, on his way to Basel, was forced to detour through Geneva. In this city he spent the night thinking that he would come and go unobserved, but his presence was noted and Farel was informed. Farel immediately visited Calvin and implored him to stay in Geneva and help with the work of reformation. Calvin was adamant in his refusal. Shy by nature and determined to devote his life to scholarship and study, Calvin wanted no part of the turmoil which would result from efforts to make Geneva a city devoted to the truth of Scripture. But after calling down from heaven curses upon Calvin should he refuse, Farel persuaded Calvin that his place was indeed in the city.

### First Stay In Geneva

So it was that Calvin's work in Geneva began. The date was September 5, 1536.

The city, with the effects of many centuries under Roman Catholicism woven into the fabric of its life, was filled with every vice and required great labor to bring its citizens under the yoke of the

gospel. To accomplish this, Calvin began teaching, convinced that instruction in the truth was the only road to reformation. He began expository lectures on Paul and the New Testament and a year later was ordained a pastor.

Together Farel and Calvin drew up a Confession of Faith and rules of discipline which were approved by the council. In fact, the council supported all the efforts for reform in doctrine, liturgy, and morals. That did not mean, however, that the opposition had been persuaded. Gradually Calvin's enemies were able to marshal their forces. Their opposition was especially against the Catechism and the laws which had been passed against prevalent sins. As they gained strength, they gained numbers on the council and were able to moderate the efforts towards reform.

Two issues especially brought things to a head. The Council of 200 decided to instruct the reformers to practice open communion so that no one could be barred from the Lord's table. This was a death blow to Calvin's discipline. The second issue was a decision by the council to make use of Bernese liturgy in the worship. Calvin did not object as such to the liturgy used in Berne, but he did object strenuously to the right of the council to decide such matters for the church. Neither would budge, and the result was that the council passed a decision to expel Farel and Calvin from the city.

## Calvin in Strassburg

After a brief stay in Basel, Calvin went to Strassburg, a city in southern Germany where the Swiss Reformation had already taken root. The three years he spent in this city were probably the happiest years of his life. He had no need to fight a council, no need to oppose a stubborn people at every turn of the way, no need to do battle with enemies on every side. He had peace and quiet, time for study and writing, and opportunity to do work in the fields of liturgy and church polity.

Calvin was appointed to the faculty of the university in the city and was called to be pastor of a church of French refugees. He had occasion to meet with Lutheran theologians and sharpen his own theological views. He worked on revisions of his *Institutes* and developed his views on church polity, the basic principles of which are incorporated in the Church Order of Dordrecht. He developed a liturgy for the church which included an order of worship (much like

the order of worship used today in Reformed churches), liturgical forms, and versions of Psalms.

These were productive years. Calvin engaged in a voluminous correspondence with all the leading figures of Europe. He wrote a number of his important works, one of which was his letter to Sadolet. Sadolet was a Roman Catholic cardinal who wrote a letter to the people of Geneva in an effort to win them back to Rome. From a certain human point of view, it was a masterful and persuasive piece of work. Calvin's response was without any bitterness or rancor against the Genevans but was instead the clearest and most helpful defense of the Reformation which could be found anywhere. It is "must" reading to anyone who wishes to know why reformation in the sixteenth century was necessary.

Calvin even married during his stay in Strassburg. His wife was Idelette de Bure, the widow of a prominent Anabaptist whom Calvin had converted to the true faith and who had died in a pestilence. Idelette was the mother of several children, but poor and in feeble health. Calvin took responsibility for her children as well as for her and brought them back to Geneva with him. He lived with her only nine years. Calvin remained single the rest of his life. With Idelette, Calvin had one son who died in infancy, a loss which Calvin bore the remainder of his life.

## Second Stay In Geneva

The happy years in Strassburg were soon to come to an end. The situation in Geneva steadily deteriorated. Three parties were vying for power, and the city was sinking into anarchy.

In 1541 Calvin was formally asked to return. Strassburg was reluctant to let him go. Calvin was even more reluctant to leave his happy life in Strassburg and take on the horrors of Geneva. But compelled by God, he returned to the whirlpool (Calvin's word) of struggle and controversy where he stayed until death took him to the church triumphant.

One evidence of the stature of the man was his conduct upon his return. The first Sunday he entered the pulpit of Saint Pierre before a huge crowd gathered, partly to hear him again, but partly to listen to him lambaste his opponents and smugly proclaim "I told you so." But in a letter to Farel, Calvin tells what he did. "After a preface, I took up the exposition where I had left off —by which I indicated that I had interrupted my office of preaching for the time rather than that

I had given it up entirely." Nothing could have been more prosaic and yet more effective. It was as if Calvin resumed his ministry with the words, "As I was saying,..."

The struggles with the council were not over for a very long time, and the efforts to subdue the city so that Christ's rule was present did not cease until many who opposed Calvin left for other places. His enemies were hateful and not afraid to show it. People called their dogs by Calvin's name, openly reviled him in the streets, sometimes threatened his life, disturbed him in his studies, and vowed to do harm to his family. Through it all Calvin endured: preaching, teaching, writing, and bearing the yoke of Christ's suffering for the cause of the gospel. Money and pleasure meant nothing to him. He repeatedly refused more money offered him by the council. He lived sparingly and without luxury. He was willing even to sell his beloved books when it became necessary. The pope himself was so impressed with Calvin's total lack of covetousness that he expressed his firm conviction that if he had in his retinue only a dozen men like Calvin, he could conquer the world.

Calvin preached regularly in the church in Geneva, sometimes as often as five times a week; his sermons were taken down in longhand, and many have been published. They make for some very fine reading. He established the famous academy in Geneva, which became a center of learning for students from all over Europe who, having received their education in Geneva, returned to their own lands to spread the gospel of the Reformation to their own people. John Knox studied in Geneva, and it was he who remarked that the most perfect school of Christ which could be found on earth since the days of the apostles was the city of Geneva. In the academy Calvin lectured, and his commentaries, still some of the best, were the results of these lectures. I rarely, if ever, prepare a sermon without checking what Calvin had to say on a given text.

## Calvin's Controversies

Within the city of Geneva itself, Calvin's struggles were with a party called Patriots. They were the descendants of the original citizens of the city, dyed-in-the-wool Roman Catholics when Calvin came, and much given to riotous living. As refugees streamed into Geneva from all over Europe to escape persecution, the Patriots resented the fact that the control of the city was passing into foreign hands. They hated Calvin and did all in their power to destroy him.

When the church was able finally to excommunicate the leaders for their licentiousness and the council approved, these men fled.

Calvin's theological controversies were most important. Calvin wrote against the papacy to show its evils and to demonstrate how far it had departed from the doctrines of Christ. He had to fight to defend the truths of the Trinity and the divinity of Christ against many who attacked these doctrines, not the least of whom was Servetus, burned at the stake in Geneva for blasphemy.

Especially his controversies swirled around his defense of the truths of sovereign and particular grace in the work of salvation. As is usually the case, the most vicious attacks were concentrated against the doctrine of sovereign predestination. Many hated this doctrine and sought to destroy it. Perhaps the most interesting controversy over this doctrine was with the heretic Bolsec. Bolsec interrupted the preaching of one of Geneva's pastors to get up in the middle of the sermon and make a speech against the truth of predestination. What Bolsec did not know was that Calvin had entered the sanctuary and was listening to Bolsec's tirade. After Bolsec finished, Calvin mounted the pulpit and, in a masterful sermon, extemporaneous but an hour long, explained the doctrine and proved it from Scripture.

Bolsec was not deterred, however, and continued to fight against this truth publicly in Geneva. He was arrested for his opposition to the church and council and was tried for heresy and public defamation of the ministers. The advice of the other Swiss reformers and churches was sought before Bolsec was condemned. To Calvin's bitter disappointment, not one church or reformer, with the exception of Farel, could be found to back Calvin's position completely and without compromise. Their caution or disagreement was concerning Calvin's doctrine of predestination.

Nevertheless, Calvin persevered, and Bolsec was condemned and banished from the city. From the controversy emerged one of Calvin's most important works, "A Treatise on the Eternal Predestination of God," a work which, along with another work on providence, has been published in the book *Calvin's Calvinism.*

## Calvin's Death and Importance

Calvin departed to be with his Lord on May 27, 1564. He had suffered many infirmities prior to his death, so many in fact that one wonders how he could surmount them all. One student of church

history claims that Calvin had no less than twelve major illnesses at the end of his life, many of which involved excruciating pain.

On May 19 Calvin summoned the pastors of Geneva and spoke his farewell to them. From that time he remained in bed, although he continued to dictate to a secretary. Farel, now an old man, came to see his friend although Calvin urged him not to come. Calvin spent his last days in almost continual prayer, and his prayers were mostly quotations from the Psalms. Although his voice was broken by asthma, his eyes and mind remained strong. He saw all who wished to come but asked that they pray for him. As the sun was going down around 8:00, he fell into a calm sleep from which he did not awake until he awoke in glory. He had lived fifty-four years, ten months, and seventeen days.

Calvin is the proof that God uses men according to His own good pleasure. Weak and shy by nature, Calvin was cast into the center of the maelstrom of the Reformation. It was a role he never wanted and which he called his daily cross. But he knew, as few men know, that discipleship is exactly characterized by denying oneself, taking up one's cross, and following the Lord.

And so God used Calvin as the key figure in the Reformation and in subsequent church history. Luther and Calvin agreed on all points of doctrine with the exception of the doctrine of the sacraments. Luther was ordained by God to smash the imposing and seemingly indestructible citadel of Roman Catholicism. Calvin was divinely appointed to build on the ruins a new house, a glorious temple, the church where God makes His dwelling.

Calvin was a man of iron will. Throughout almost his entire stay in Geneva he was ill, yet he surmounted all his ailments and never permitted sickness and pain to interfere with his work. He worked incessantly with little or no sleep until even his wife, in exasperation, asked for a bit of time to see him.

Calvin was, above all, a preacher and expositor of Holy Scripture. His preaching was his strength and remains of unparalleled influence to the present. His theology was rooted in exegesis because God's Word was the standard for him of all truth and right. His commentaries are still the very best available, and modern "scholarly" commentaries, so many of which are really sellouts to higher criticism, seem scarcely worthy of notice in comparison.

Calvin's influence spread throughout Europe and ultimately throughout the world. That influence was not only his theology, but

also his liturgy, his church polity, and his piety. The heritage of Calvin is also—let it never be forgotten—the heritage of genuinely Reformed piety. It would be well if a book were written only on that aspect of Calvin's life.

Calvin was not the dramatic personality that was Luther. Nor did Calvin "wear his heart on his sleeve," as Luther did. Especially in his old age, Luther became something of a crab and spoke far too vehemently in his opposition to those who did not agree with him on the doctrine of the Lord's Supper. Calvin always respected Luther for the great work Luther did in the work of reformation. He told others, who were not so generous towards Luther, that even if Luther would call him a devil, he would still honor him as God's chosen vessel.

Calvin could appreciate Luther for what Luther did because Calvin's life was consumed by the glory of God. His enemies called him a God-intoxicated man—drunk with God! What more wonderful thing could be said of a man? The deepest principle of his theology was God's glory, and the real essence of all he wrote was this great truth. The same was true for Calvin's life. He lived and died with God's glory his deepest desire. He is one in this cloud of witnesses whose voice shouts to us down the corridors of time.

## Chapter 23

# William Farel

### Fiery Evangelist of the Reformation

### Introduction

*We who are of the Calvin Reformation rightly honor John Calvin as the great reformer of Geneva and the spiritual father of Calvinistic churches throughout the world. Nevertheless, it is not an exaggeration to say that Calvin's work would not have been possible without the intrepid labors of another reformer, William Farel, who hacked away the*

undergrowth of Roman Catholic superstition and plowed the soil of Switzerland so that the seeds of Calvin could be sown and bear their fruit.

Schaff writes of him,

> Farel's work was destructive rather than constructive. He could pull down, but not build up. He was a conqueror, but not an organizer of his conquests; a man of action, not a man of letters; an intrepid preacher, not a theologian. He felt his defects, and handed his work over to the mighty genius of his young friend Calvin. In the spirit of genuine humility and self-denial, he was willing to decrease that Calvin might increase. This is the finest trait in his character.

The character which God gave him, forceful and belligerent, admirably suited Farel for the work of the Reformation and the unique place in it which he occupied. The work was important, for without it other reformers could not have accomplished what they did.

### Early Life

William Farel was born about 1489 near Gap in Dauphiny, in the mountainous regions of the Alps, in the southeastern part of France. This part of the country had at one time been under the influence of the

Waldensians, but they had been all but destroyed in France through the horrors of the Inquisition. Farel was the oldest of seven children, born from a family which belonged to the nobility but which had fallen on bad times and was very poor. He was baptized with the name Guillaume, the approximate French equivalent of William. He was born five years after Luther and Zwingli and twenty years before John Calvin. He belongs, therefore, to the first generation of reformers.

Paris, the center of Roman Catholic studies, beckoned him and, in his studies there, he concentrated on philosophy, theology, and the ancient languages, including Hebrew. He had, at this time, very little religious conviction, although he was zealous for Rome and was, in his own words, "more popish than popery."

But God used these very studies to bring him to faith in the truths of Scripture as set forth by the Reformation. Even in Paris, Luther's thoughts were being circulated and discussed, and Farel was brought under the influence of Jacques Lefèvre d' Étaples. Lefèvre was one of those shadowy figures in the Reformation who himself was convinced of the great truth of justification by faith but who never could summon the courage to break with Rome and join the Protestant cause. It was Lefèvre who said to the young Farel, "My son, God will renew the world, and you will witness it."

From that point on, Farel immersed himself in the Scriptures and was soon (1521) sent to Meaux in France, where he received authority to preach. It was in his preaching that his character began to become apparent.

We are told by his contemporaries that he was rather short, always carrying about a gaunt look, and possessing a red and somewhat unkempt beard. He reminded those who saw him of the rough appearance of an Elijah. He was fiery and forceful, not given to the use of tact, impulsive in his actions and preaching, and one who roared against papal abuses. As zealous as he had once been for Romish practices, so zealous and fierce did he become as a promoter of Reformation causes. He was a man who prepared the way for others, for he could break down but lacked the gifts to build up. He was no theologian, and he left no significant works which contributed to Reformation thought; rather, he was the man who with mighty blows tore down the imposing structure of Roman Catholicism.

Farel was a man of unsurpassed energy who traveled incessantly until, old and worn, he died; he was always on the move, full of fire and courage, as fearless as Luther but even more radical than the Wittenberg reformer. His close friend and fellow reformer, Oecolampadius, wrote to him, "Your mission is to evangelize, not to curse. Prove yourself to be an evangelist, not a tyrannical legislator." Zwingli, shortly before his death, admonished Farel not to labor rashly but to keep himself for God's work.

Farel hated the pope and despised all papal ceremonies. His mission in life, as he conceived it, was to destroy every remnant of popery in images, ceremonies, and rituals, which were the standard diet of those held in Rome's chains.

His strength was in his preaching. It was not so much in his careful preparation of sermons, for he mostly preached without preparation, and none of his sermons have come down to us. His strength was in his powerful delivery. Schaff writes,

> He turned every stump and stone into a pulpit, every house, street, and market-place into a church; provoked the wrath of monks, priests, and bigoted women; was abused, called 'heretic' and 'devil,' insulted, spit upon, and more than once threatened with death...Wherever he went he stirred up all the forces of the people, and made them take sides for or against the new gospel.

But Schaff also writes, "No one could hear his thunder without trembling, or listen to his most fervent prayers without being almost carried up to heaven."

## Evangelist

To understand this part of Farel's labors, we must try to put him in the setting of his times.

Although the views of Luther (as also those of the Swiss theologians) were being circulated, read, and studied in many places, the common people had not as yet heard them. Darkness still covered the land where Farel worked. The Reformation was just beginning in France, southern Germany, and Switzerland. The people were hypnotized as yet by the priests, bishops, and monks who promoted with zeal the superstitions of Rome. The darkness of corrupt Roman Catholic domination held the people in slavery.

Influenced by Lefèvre, Farel had come to love the truths of the Reformation and had devoted his life to promoting them through his fiery preaching. He was never officially ordained to the ministry although he had been licensed to preach when he first came to Meaux, France. He believed that his call came from God as that call had come to the prophets in the old dispensation. Nor did he ever stay long in one place, but he traveled about in Switzerland, eastern France, and southern Germany, bringing his powerful word. No one has been able to compute the miles he traveled. In all kinds of weather, through the dangers of robbers, brigands, and Romish clerics who hated him, he rode his horse or traveled on foot to areas where the true gospel had not yet been heard.

Farel aroused the hatred of Romish prelates wherever he went but drew huge crowds by the fire of his oratory.

To trace Farel's frequent travels would involve us in lengthy lessons in geography. But everywhere he went, his preaching did not permit that town or village or city to remain the same. We can only tell of some of his work and recall with amazement the troubles from which, by God's providential hand, he escaped.

Already in Meaux, where Farel began his preaching, he was soon in trouble for his zealous proclamation of biblical doctrine. It was a time in France when persecution of Protestants was beginning, and those who had given him permission to preach were nonplused by his sudden proclamation of biblical truth. He was soon forced to flee for his life, narrowly escaping those who hated him.

In Basel, Switzerland, Farel was instrumental in the conversion of the great Pelikan, who later was professor of Greek and Hebrew in the University of Zurich and became a brilliant Reformation scholar. It was in this city that he visited the great Swiss reformers: Oecolampadius, Myconius, Haller, and Zwingli.

It was also in Basel that he ran afoul of the humanist Erasmus, who still had sufficient influence to run Farel out of the city. It seems that Farel, in rather typical fashion, called Erasmus "a Balaam," something the learned Erasmus could not forgive. Erasmus wrote the council, "You have in your neighborhood the new evangelist Farel, than whom I never saw a man more false, more virulent, more seditious."

After a short sojourn in Strassburg, where he made the acquaintance of Martin Bucer, Farel was found in 1525 back in France in Montéliard, where he preached in his usual violent manner. On a procession day he pulled the image of St. Anthony out of a priest's hand and threw it from a bridge into a river. He barely escaped being pulled to pieces by a mob.

Not only was Farel fearless, but he refused to be swayed by the approval of men. In Neuchâtel of Switzerland he publicly rebuked a noble woman who had left her husband. When she refused to return to him, Farel roared against her and her supporters from the pulpit and created such a riot that he was saved only by a vote of the council, which was moved by his vast energy. Farel once interrupted a priest who was urging the people to worship Mary more zealously and became the victim of a mob of women who were bent on tearing him to shreds. In Metz he preached in a Dominican cemetery, booming out his message over the ringing of the convent bells, which were rung furiously in an attempt to drown his voice. While celebrating the Lord's Supper on Easter, he and those with him were attacked by an armed band. Many were killed or wounded. Farel himself, though wounded, found refuge in a castle and escaped the city by leaving in disguise. At seventy-two years old, still preaching, he was thrown into prison, rescued by friends, and, like Paul, saved in a basket let down from the walls.

Into the darkness of popery Farel burst, roaring like a bull, flinging about, without regard for his own personal safety, the great truths of Scripture which he had learned to love. He appeared on the scene as a meteor, smashing by his oratory and preaching all the carefully fashioned practices of the false church with which he had broken.

While we can, if we choose, criticize Farel for his vehemence and tactlessness (as his contemporaries often did), one wonders sometimes whether the times in which we live do not require preachers of equal courage. His trust was in His God, and he was intent on doing the Lord's work with no regard for himself.

### Contact with the Waldensians

Farel's greatest labors were the work he performed as a co-worker of Calvin.

Before we begin to describe his work in what was to become the center of Calvinism, it is appropriate to mention that Farel, more than any other reformer, was instrumental in leading many of the Waldensians, those God-fearing and horribly persecuted pre-reformers, into the fold of Calvinism.

We noted earlier that Farel was born in a region which had once been the stronghold of Waldensian thought. His contact with the Waldensians must have left its mark on him, for he maintained contact with them throughout his ministry. In fact, in 1531 Farel was sent with A. Saunier to the Waldensian Synod which was being held in Chanforans. There he explained to these people the Reformation truths, and there he persuaded many of the great work of God which was being done on behalf of the pure gospel. This influence with the Waldensians he was never to lose. If Farel is remembered for nothing more than for his work among these people, it would be enough to engrave forever his name in the memories of all those who love the Reformation.

## Work with Calvin

We must now turn to Geneva.

At this time Geneva was under the rule of Berne, a neighboring canton in Switzerland. It was a thoroughly Roman Catholic city where every vice was openly practiced and where the foul rituals of Rome were a staple in the spiritual diet of the citizens.

Farel's first stay in Geneva was not a long one. He came in 1532, when he was about forty-three years old. The city was full of religious strife and tottered at the brink of chaos. Within that city, however, were a few who had been touched by the truths of the Reformation, and Farel limited his preaching to private worship in the homes of these few faithful. But his preaching was too successful to be kept secret, and soon he was forced by circumstances to begin public proclamation of the gospel.

This practice could not last long in this citadel of Romish thought. He was soon summoned before a furious episcopal council which saw his preaching as a threat to Rome's authority. Farel produced his credentials from Berne; and although they made some impression, he was treated with insolence. One of the clerics present shouted to him, "Come, thou filthy devil. Art thou baptized? Who invited you hither? Who gave you authority to preach?"

Farel's response was, "I have been baptized in the name of the Father, the Son, and the Holy Ghost, and am not a devil. I go about preaching Christ, who died for our sins and rose for our justification. Whoever believes in him will be saved; unbelievers will be lost. I am sent by God as a messenger of Christ, and am bound to preach him to all who will hear me. I am ready to dispute with you, and to give an account of my faith and ministry. Elijah said to King Ahab, 'It is thou, and not I, who disturbest Israel.' So I say, it is you and yours, who trouble the world by your traditions, your human inventions, and your dissolute lives."

When another shouted, "He has blasphemed; we need no further evidence; he deserves to die," Farel responded, "Speak the words of God, and not of Caiaphas."

In response to this, the council could no longer contain its rage. It taunted him, spit on him, chased him with clubs, and as he was leaving, one member shot at him. Even that could not frighten the dauntless reformer. He turned to the one who attempted his murder with the words, "Your shots do not frighten me." It was only with difficulty that he escaped, and his first labors in Geneva came to an end.

Farel sent Froment and Olivetan, two fellow reformers, to continue the work which he had begun; he himself returned in 1533. Still under the protection of Berne, he labored with courage and zeal in times of great peril and danger.

Gradually the city was turned from its superstitions, and many were brought by God to the faith. Gradually the Roman Catholics began to leave, and on August 27, 1535, the Great Council of 200 in Geneva passed a formal decision that Geneva was to become Protestant.

The mass was abolished and forbidden. The people took the images and relics from the churches. The citizens pledged to live according to the gospel and established a school which became the forerunner of Calvin's famous academy. A hospital was built, financed by the revenues from older hospitals. The palace of the bishop, with fine irony, became a prison. Ministers, elders, and deacons were appointed. Sermons were preached daily. The sacraments were administered according to the Scriptures. All shops were closed on the Lord's day. Nevertheless, the city was far from a Reformed city. Troubles continued, and the work of reformation was far from over.

It was into this situation that Calvin came one evening. He had no intention of staying in the city but sought a night's lodging in his travels. When Farel heard that Calvin was in the city, he immediately sought out this man, whom he had never met, to implore him to stay in Geneva and help with the work. Calvin was of no mind to do this. Calvin, as he tells us himself, was shy and retiring by nature and yearned for a life of quiet and peaceful study in some sanctuary far from the rumble of the storms created by the Reformation. He steadfastly and strenuously resisted every overture of Farel until, in exasperation, Farel bellowed, "I declare, in the name of God, that if you do not assist us in this work of the Lord, the Lord will punish you for following your own interest rather than this call."

Calvin was overwhelmed by this threat of God's judgment and, in resignation to God's will, agreed to work with Farel in the difficult task of reformation in Geneva.

Thrown into the hurly-burly of the life of the city, Farel and Calvin worked day and night to bring about a thorough reformation, until the city, weary of the stringent discipline imposed on them, rose against them and expelled them. Calvin retired to Strassburg, where he spent some of the happiest moments of his life, only to return a few years later when he was summoned by a council alarmed at the chaotic conditions in the city. Farel went on with his work, especially in Neuchâtel, a city where also disorder and confusion reigned.

Farel's association with Calvin was close from the time of their labors in Geneva. In fact, during Calvin's stay in Strassburg, Farel was the one who urged Calvin to marry. In a letter to Farel, sent May 19, 1539, Calvin wrote, "I am none of those insane lovers who, when once smitten with the fine figure of a woman, embrace also her faults. This only is the beauty that allures me, if she be chaste, obliging, not fastidious, economical, patient, and careful for my health. Therefore, if you think well of it, set out immediately, lest some one else gets the start of you. But if you think otherwise, we will let it pass."

Although Farel did not return to Geneva when Calvin was called back, the two remained close friends, and the correspondence between them continued. Calvin spent the rest of his days in Geneva; Farel continued his evangelistic labors. When Calvin was near death, Farel, though nearly seventy-five years old, traveled to see his old friend and co-reformer for the last time. Aware of Farel's age and the difficulties of travel, Calvin begged Farel not to come. But Farel could not be kept away. Part of Calvin's letter reads, "Farewell, my best and truest brother! And since it is God's will that you remain behind me in the world, live mindful of our friendship, which as it was useful to the church of God, so the fruit of it awaits us in heaven. Pray do not fatigue yourself on my account. It is with difficulty that I draw my breath, and I expect that every moment will be the last. It is enough that I live and die for Christ, who is the reward of his followers both in life and in death. Again, farewell with the brethren."

Ten days after Calvin died, Farel wrote to a friend,

> Oh, why was not I taken away in his place, while he might have been spared for many years of health to the service of the Church of our Lord Jesus Christ! Thanks be to Him who gave me the exceeding grace to meet this man and to hold him against his will in Geneva, where he has labored and accomplished more than tongue can tell. In the name of God, I then pressed him and pressed him again to take upon himself a burden which appeared to him harder than death, so that he at times asked me for God's sake to have pity on him and to allow him to serve God in a manner which suited his nature. But when he recognized the will of God, he sacrificed his own will and accomplished more than was expected from him, and surpassed not only others, but even himself. Oh, what a glorious course has he happily finished!

Farel did marry but at the age of sixty-nine, much to Calvin's disgust. But Calvin did have the grace to write the preachers of the city in which Farel was working to "bear with patience the folly of the old bachelor."

Still traveling and preaching very shortly before his death, he returned to Neuchâtel to die. There, worn with his many labors, weary with the sufferings which came with the reproach of Christ, he died quietly in his sleep on September 13, 1565.

Wild and fiery as he was, he served an important place in God's work of bringing reformation to the church. Though his methods could surely be scrutinized and criticized, no one ever questioned his integrity, his courage, and his faithfulness to his God. His was the work of the plowman who was called to hack down the trees, clear away the underbrush, and do the hard work of plowing; others would come, more gentle than he, and sow the seed.

Neither Calvin nor Farel alone could do that which had to be done for reformation to come; God used both—first Farel to break down, then Calvin to build up. So it always is in the church of Christ; each member has his place and calling, and all together are called to labor in the cause of Christ.

Especially in his association with Calvin, a deeper and profoundly spiritual aspect of Farel's character came to the fore. With a sincere humility he was content to stand in the shadow of Calvin, to retire to the background when events required it, and to decrease in order that Calvin might increase. This was his most endearing quality, and it is a virtue registered in the books of heaven.

## Chapter 24

# Martin Bucer

### Ecumenist of the Reformation

### Introduction

*One of the charges which Rome leveled against the reformers was the serious accusation that the Reformation tore the fabric of the church and destroyed the unity of the body of Christ. Very shortly after the Reformation began, it split into various branches, chiefly the Lutheran, Calvinistic, and Anabaptistic groups. While there were good reasons for this, and while*

God in His inscrutable wisdom had His own purpose in this, it remained a serious problem with which the reformers had to deal.

While all fervently sought the unity of the churches of the Reformation, no one pursued this goal with as much vigor and effort as Martin Bucer, the reformer of Strassburg, Germany. His entire ministry can be characterized as a pursuit of unity. In his zeal to bring unity to the church of Christ, however, he often sought unacceptable compromises which made true unity impossible. Not only did he wish to bring Lutherans and Calvinists together; he did not even rest in his efforts to unite Protestantism and Roman Catholicism. In his burning zeal for unity, he forgot that unity is essentially a unity of the truth as it is in Christ and revealed in the Holy Gospel.

In spite of this, Bucer was a reformer of no little importance whose work had its own value for the church of Christ.

### Bucer's Early Life and Conversion

Martin Bucer was born in 1491 in Selestat, South Germany, not far from Strassburg, where he was to spend twenty-five years in the pastoral ministry. He was,

therefore, eight years younger than Luther and eighteen years older than Calvin. Although his father was a poor cobbler, Bucer received a good education from his youth, and at the age of fifteen entered the Dominican monastery. He did this not so much because he was enamored with a monastic life but rather because he desired a thorough education for which the Dominican order was famous. For further studies he was sent to Heidelberg, where perhaps the most important event of his life took place. Martin Luther had come to Heidelberg very shortly after the Reformation began, to discuss theological matters with members of the Augustinian order to which he belonged. Bucer heard Luther speak and was fully persuaded of the truth of Luther's reformation doctrines. In private, over supper, he discussed these questions with Luther and became fully committed to the Reformation.

When Luther was summoned to appear before the Diet of Worms for trial by the emperor, Charles V, he knew at the time of his going that he might never leave that city alive. Many tried to dissuade him from going, for the memories of the burning of John Hus by the Council of Constance lingered in the minds of Luther's associates. Among those who attempted to dissuade Luther was Martin Bucer, who warned him of the terrible dangers that awaited him. But when Luther insisted on going, even "if all the tiles on the houses in Worms were devils," Bucer accompanied him and heard Luther's stirring appeal to Scripture: "Here I stand. I can do naught else. So help me God."

## Bucer's Pastorate in Strassburg

In 1522, at the age of thirty-one, Bucer began his work in earnest. He labored in the city of Wissembourg and tried to make it a Protestant city. Despite Bucer's efforts at reformation, the Roman Catholics were successful in keeping the city faithful to Rome, and Bucer was forced to flee for his life. He went to the nearby city of Strassburg, where his parents were citizens.

While in Wissembourg, Bucer married Elizabeth Silbereisen, sometimes known as Elizabeth Palast. She was a former nun and bore thirteen children. Bucer was one of the first reformers to marry, and it was his marriage that prompted Erasmus to remark that the Reformation was not so much a tragedy as a comedy because it always ended in a wedding.

The busy household of Bucer was a godly one, an example to all of what a covenant home is, although the spiritual character of the home was in large measure due to Elizabeth, for Martin traveled extensively in the cause of the Reformation.

Elizabeth died before Martin, who married again, this time to a woman by the name of Wilibrandis Rosenblatt. She had previously been married to no fewer than three other reformers: Ludwig Cellarius, Oecolampadius, and Wolfgang Capito. Later she would go with Bucer to England and also outlive him. A woman married to four such great men must have been unusually attractive.

Strassburg was blessed with great preachers. Although Bucer himself labored there for twenty-five years, Zell, Capito, Hedio, Johann Sturm, and even Calvin during the years of his banishment from Geneva, were preachers in that same city. Seldom has one city been blessed with such a gallery of gifted and able ministers.

In Strassburg Bucer gave himself over to the work of the ministry. He preached faithfully, labored mightily in pastoral work, established Christian schools and a seminary, lodged refugees from persecution, wrote extensively (including correspondence with all Europe's reformers), traveled throughout Germany and Switzerland, and attended conferences.

When Calvin, after his brief stay in Strassburg, was called back to Geneva, Bucer, though loathe to see Calvin go, wrote a letter to the Syndic and Council of Geneva in which he said, "Now he comes at last, Calvin, that elect and incomparable instrument of God, to whom no other in our age may be compared, if at all there can be the question of another alongside of him." This letter is a fine illustration of the relationships which existed among the reformers. They were never hesitant to recognize the good gifts God had given to others, to praise their colleagues for the work, and to encourage one another in their calling. Would to God that this were also true in the difficult days in which the church today is called to live.

In 1549 the Interim of the Diet of Augsburg was imposed on Germany, and the Protestants were given almost no rights, only that the cup of the Lord's Supper could be given to the laity and ministers were allowed to marry. The seeming victory of the Romish church threatened Strassburg. Refusing to accept the Interim, Bucer was forced to flee his beloved city and congregation.

Although Bucer had an invitation from Calvin to come to Geneva, he decided instead to accept the invitation of Thomas Cranmer and

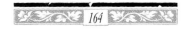

go to England. In England his enormous gifts were recognized. He was appointed Regius Professor of Divinity at Cambridge, met personally King Edward VI, received an honorary doctorate from Cambridge, and made a lasting impact on the English Reformation.

Martin Bucer died in England on March 1, 1551, not even attaining his threescore and ten years. His body was followed by 3,000 people on the way to the grave, and he was buried with honors. But Rome would not let him rest in peace. When Queen Mary Tudor, better known as Bloody Mary, came to the throne, she not only burned Ridley, Latimer, and Cranmer at the stake, but she would not rest until Bucer's body had been exhumed, tied with chains to a post, and burned. God, in grace towards England, made Mary's reign brief. When Elizabeth came to the throne, she took what was left of Bucer's ashes and gave them a decent burial.

## *Bucer's Work*

Bucer fought long and hard for the cause of the Reformation. When that miserable humanist Erasmus came out with his defense of free will, Bucer broke with Erasmus, even though Erasmus was a close friend. Bucer asked Luther to answer that "pestiferous pamphlet" of an "unhappy slave of glory, who pushes forward to prefer the spit of his own opinion to Scripture." When Anabaptists streamed into Strassburg, Bucer condemned them as opponents of the pure gospel. While Calvin labored in Strassburg as a colleague of Bucer, Bucer had considerable influence on Calvin and the development of his views.

Bucer wrote extensively. His works number about one hundred fifty volumes. As is the case with many theologians, he was extremely long-winded. Luther called him a chatterbox; Charles V said he was a windbag; and Calvin, more charitably, said, "Bucer is too verbose to be read quickly by those who have other matters to deal with...He does not know how to stop writing." His writing was so illegible that the English bishop Edmund Grindal said that a conjurer was needed to decipher it.

In all his striving for the cause of the Reformation, Bucer was moved by too great a zeal for union, not only between the various branches of Protestantism, but also between Protestantism and Rome if possible. He labored long and hard to achieve these ends. While indeed such labor is commendable, his desire for union made him choose unacceptable compromises of the truth.

Although Bucer attended many conferences in his pursuit of ecclesiastical unity, two illustrations will suffice to demonstrate his tendency to compromise.

Bucer was the chief author of the Tetrapolitan Confession, a document drawn up to achieve unity on the burning issue of the presence of Christ in the elements of the Lord's Supper. Without spelling out in detail the contents of this Confession (it is worth reading), we may note that Bucer made major concessions to the truth of Scripture in the hopes that especially Lutheranism and Calvinism would be brought together on this one issue which divided them.

This willingness to compromise on the doctrine of the presence of Christ in the sacraments became especially evident in the Colloquy of Marburg. This was a conference called by Philip of Hesse to discuss union between the Lutherans and the Reformed. It was attended by the leading theologians of Germany and Switzerland, including Bucer, although Calvin was not present.

As we noticed earlier, Bucer was an ardent follower of Luther. However, in his lifetime he gradually drifted into the Calvinistic camp, most probably under the influence of Calvin while the two were in Strassburg. It was for this reason that when Luther and Bucer met at Marburg, Luther said to Bucer, though with a smile on his face, "You are a good-for-nothing knave."

The conference was opened by a beautiful prayer by Zwingli: "Fill us, O Lord and Father of us all, we beseech Thee, with Thy gentle Spirit, and dispel on both sides all the clouds of misunderstanding and passion. Make an end to the strife of blind fury. Arise, O Christ, Thou Sun of righteousness, and shine upon us. Alas! while we contend, we only too often forget to strive after holiness which Thou requirest from us all. Guard us against abusing our powers, and enable us to employ them with all earnestness for the promotion of holiness."

It soon became evident at the conference that the reformers could reach agreement on all matters of the faith with the exception of the doctrine of the Lord's Supper. Though the Swiss pleaded with Luther for understanding and compassion, Luther remained adamant, and agreement was never reached.

Here, too, Bucer was willing to compromise for the sake of unity. We may be thankful that his pleas for compromise went unheard and that the Reformed position was maintained within the Calvinistic churches.

Unity of the church is an eminently desirable thing. To compromise for the sake of unity leads not to unity but to further trouble. Bucer made important contributions to the Reformation, but his zeal for unity remains an abiding warning against compromise of the truth of the gospel for purposes of attaining mere outward unity.

## Chapter 25

# V Peter Martyr Vermigli

### Italian Reformer

### Introduction

*Some of the men whom God used to bring reformation to the church in the sixteenth century are widely known, and even our children are acquainted with them and the work they did. Other reformers are not so well-known. They stand, as it were, in the shadows of Luther, Calvin, Knox, and Zwingli. If one knows them at all, they seem vague figures in the darker corners of the*

stage of church history when the great drama of the Reformation was taking place. Because of this, we might conclude that they are of little or no importance to an understanding of the Reformation. Such a conclusion would be a sad mistake.

It is my purpose in this chapter to bring one such reformer out of the shadows to stand for a few moments in the spotlight so that we can see him clearly and the great work he did on behalf of the cause of God in those remarkable times. His name is Peter Martyr Vermigli.

### Vermigli's Early Life

Vermigli's background has two very strange aspects to it, both of which point to the inscrutable ways of God. They have to do with the fact that, although the Reformation swept through nearly the whole of Europe, from the Balkans to the Atlantic, two countries were left almost untouched: Italy and Spain. Both countries played a role in Vermigli's early life.

The first is Vermigli's birth in Italy. It was, of course, the country in which was found Rome, the seat of the papacy. Yet it would not be correct to say that Italy was the most Roman Catholic of all Europe's countries. It

was almost totally unaffected by the Reformation because it was almost totally worldly. It was the country of the Renaissance at its worst. It was wholly apostate. It was corrupt and depraved. It cared not for God or man, for church or state. It was Jerusalem become Sodom. An Italian by birth, Vermigli thus became a "brand plucked out of the burning."

This must not be construed as meaning that Peter Martyr was the only one saved from Italy's apostates. Other men and women, though few, were saved, some through Vermigli's influence. Notable among these were Jerome Zanchius, the author of a still popular book entitled *Predestination,* and Ochino, an influential reformer who later was charged with Arian views. Peter Martyr was also to marry a God-fearing woman from Italy.

Vermigli was born in the city of Florence on September 8, 1499. He was born of parents who were part of the royalty of the city, moderately wealthy, capable of enjoying the pleasures of what was the largest and most influential city in all Italy. The family name was Vermigli, but Peter was called "Martyr" after a martyr by the name of Peter, whose shrine was near the family home. Many more children were born into the family, but they all died in infancy except one sister. This was probably why Vermigli's father disowned him when he joined a monastery. It is understandable that the father wanted someone to carry on the family name, something impossible for a monk.

Peter was a gifted student and dedicated man. His progress in his education and in the hierarchy of Italian monastic life was swift and sure. He began his monastic career at the age of sixteen as a canon regular of the order of St. Augustine, the strictest monastic order in Italy, and he spent the early years of his monastic life in the convent of Fiesole near Florence. In 1519 Vermigli transferred to the University of Padua. He was soon ordained a preacher and proved to be powerful and effective. He became abbot of Spoleto and later, principal of the college of St. Peter ad Aram in Naples.

## Vermigli's Conversion

It is not possible to pinpoint the moment in time when God worked His great work of grace in Vermigli's heart. He himself did not speak of it in all his writings—and his writings were many. We do know of certain influences under which Vermigli came and which God undoubtedly used in forming him as a servant of Christ.

I spoke above of two strange events in Vermigli's life. The second unusual event was the influence of a Spaniard, whose name was Juan de Valdéz. If Italy was almost untouched by the Reformation because of its awful worldliness, Spain was untouched by the Reformation because of its total loyalty to Rome and the papacy. From Spain came the terrible Inquisition, which was responsible for thousands upon thousands of deaths of God's beloved people. Spain was the one country in Europe which had as its unofficial motto, "My church, right or wrong." The pope's most loyal supporters were the Spanish. From Spain God brought a man to Italy, Juan de Valdéz, not a Protestant really, but one who almost believed the truth of justification by faith, who was serenely mystical in his life, and who taught and preached the literal meaning of Scripture. All three of these traits seem to have been combined in their influences on Vermigli.

The latter especially—so obvious to us—was a major breakthrough for Vermigli because it led him to a more careful study of Scripture, to a form of preaching and teaching which was expository, and finally to trouble with Roman Catholic authorities when his obedience to Scripture led him to refute certain doctrines held by the church. He was lecturing on I Corinthians 3:12–15 and denied that this passage taught the doctrine of purgatory, a position held by the Romish church.

A close reading of the writings of Luther, Zwingli, and Martin Bucer convinced him of the truths of the Reformation. As soon as Vermigli began publicly to propagate his views, his life was in danger. Even though every heresy under heaven was rampant in Italy, the papacy would not tolerate any teachings of the Reformation.

### *Vermigli's Reformatory Work*

Though by no means a coward, Vermigli fled Italy to seek refuge in Switzerland and Germany. In 1542 he found asylum in Strassburg, the city where Calvin had spent several happy years during his banishment from Geneva. Because of Vermigli's vast learning, he was soon appointed to the theological chair in Strassburg and became the ministerial colleague of Martin Bucer, the chief reformer of the city. In 1546 he married a converted nun, Catherine Wampmartin. These years were happy and productive and gave Vermigli opportunity to develop in Reformation thought.

In 1547 he received and accepted an invitation from Cranmer to come to England and work there. Henry VIII had died and his son Edward VI was on the throne, though he was only a boy. Edward was favorable to reform, and Vermigli found a congenial home as professor of divinity in Oxford University. Here, too, he could enjoy the fellowship of other English reformers.

Even in England, however, Roman Catholic opposition remained. Richard Smith, a fierce supporter of the papacy, was not reluctant to stir up mobs against Vermigli which interrupted his classroom lectures and created confusion in the class. Smith challenged Vermigli to public debate but fled in a funk to Scotland before the debate could be held. Edward died after a few years, and Bloody Mary, a daughter of Henry VIII and an ardent Roman Catholic, came to the throne. Under her reign Protestantism was harassed, reformers were burned at the stake, and many were forced to flee to the continent. Among those who fled was Vermigli himself, aided in his flight by a godly sea captain who secretly brought him across the Straits of Dover and landed him in Antwerp.

One incident of interest occurred in England. Vermigli's wife of eight years had died without leaving him any children. She had been a virtuous woman, grave and pious, who spent her time caring for the needs of the poor. Though she was buried in England, when Roman Catholicism once more gained the ascendancy in England, Cardinal Pole ordered her body dug up and thrown on a manure pile to rot. It was an act of cruel spite, indicative of the irrational hatred of Rome towards anything that belonged to reform. She was, however, held in such high esteem that when Mary died and Queen Elizabeth came to the throne, what was left of her body was dug out from the pile of manure and given an honorable burial in a cathedral.

After his escape from England, Vermigli resumed his professorial labors in Strassburg, but soon (1556) moved to Zurich in Switzerland to occupy the chair of theology in the university in that city. The call which had come from the Senate in Zurich was urgent and pressing, and he could not refuse.

Here in Zurich, Vermigli married again. His second wife was an Italian, Catherine Merenda by name. With her he had three children. Two died in infancy, and his wife was pregnant with his third child when he himself died.

An outstanding event of these years was Vermigli's presence at the Colloquy of Poissy in France. The colloquy was called because of the

great struggle which was going on between Catholics and Protestants in France, in the hope that the two parties could reach some accommodation. Vermigli was invited to attend by outstanding leaders in France: Margaret, the queen of France; the king of Navarre; the prince of Condé; and other French Protestant leaders. It is a measure of the respect with which Vermigli was held throughout Europe that he was—apart from Theodore Beza, the successor of Calvin in Geneva—the only theologian outside France invited to attend.

The colloquy accomplished nothing. After many days of fruitless debate, the Roman Catholic prelates ruined the conference by their arrogance, intransigence, and determination to rid France of Protestant heretics. But Vermigli displayed all those spiritual gifts which made him respected and loved throughout Europe: his enormous learning, his wisdom and moderation, and his irenic spirit.

## *Vermigli's Death*

Peter Martyr Vermigli died in Zurich on November 12, 1562, at sixty-three years of age, worn and old with the cares and work of a busy and eventful life. He was described by his contemporaries as

> ...a man of an able, healthy, big-boned, and well-limbed body, and of a countenance which expressed an inwardly grave and settled turn of mind. His learning was very uncommon; as was also his skill in disputation, which made him as much admired by the Protestants as hated by the Papists. He was very sincere and indefatigable in promoting a reformation in the Church, yet his zeal was never known to get the better of his judgment. He was always moderate and prudent in his outward behavior, nor even in the conflict of a dispute did he suffer himself to be transported into intemperate warmth or allow unguarded expressions ever to escape him.

Friend and foe alike acknowledged that Vermigli was one of the most learned writers of the Reformed churches.

Vermigli's greatest contribution was his development of the doctrine of the Lord's Supper. It is a never-ending source of amazement to me that the Swiss reformers could be so completely biblical in this doctrine. One would expect that they would react against the horrors of Rome's transubstantiation (along with Luther's consubstantiation) and adopt some kind of Zwinglian view which reduced the sacrament to a mere memorial service. They did not. Much of the credit for this goes to Vermigli's work. Some are even of the opinion that John Calvin was, at least in part, indebted to

Vermigli for his views on the Lord's Supper. Whether this is true or not, Calvin himself expressed complete satisfaction with the work of Vermigli in this important field of Reformation thought. The fact remains that the pure doctrine of the Lord's Supper as taught by the reformers can be explained only in terms of the work of the Holy Spirit of Christ who leads the church into all truth. Vermigli was one of those so blessed with the Spirit.

It is partly Vermigli's heritage which we have in those stirring words in our Belgic Confession:

> In the meantime we err not, when we say, that what is eaten and drunk by us is the proper and natural body, and the proper blood of Christ. But the manner of our partaking of the same, is not by the mouth, but by the spirit through faith (Article 35).

## Chapter 26

# Heinrich Bullinger
## Covenant Theologian

## Introduction

*The truth of God's covenant is part of the precious heritage of Reformed churches. We are not always aware of the fact that this truth goes back to the time of the Reformation. Prior to the Reformation this truth was unknown; it has its roots and origin in the Reformation in Switzerland, particularly in the work of Zwingli and Bullinger. Having already talked of Zwingli's contri-*

bution to covenant theology, we now turn to Bullinger.

## Early Life

Heinrich Bullinger was born on July 18, 1504, the youngest of five sons, to a parish priest in Bremgarten, Switzerland, near Zurich. Bullinger's father, though a priest, was married—apparently because of the loose enforcement of vows of celibacy in Switzerland. Although not much is known of Bullinger's parents, his father, when a very old man, came to believe and confess the doctrines of the Reformation, probably under the influence of his gifted son.

Bullinger began his formal education in the school of the Brethren of the Common Life in Cleves. His father gave him no money, believing that poverty was necessary for his son to develop good habits in life. Bullinger, like Hus and Luther, was required to sing to earn money to support himself.

During his studies, Bullinger wanted to enter a Carthusian monastery but was dissuaded by his brother. Instead, in 1519 he went to Cologne, Germany, where he earned a B.A. in 1520. At Cologne, Bullinger studied the scholastic theologians of the Middle Ages but soon became so disgusted

with them that he turned to the church fathers, particularly Chrysostom and Augustine. The one point which impressed him in the writings of these church fathers was their copious use of Scripture. Spurred on by their apparent determination to ground all their doctrine in God's Word, Bullinger turned to a study of the Scriptures. It was this study of Scripture which enabled Bullinger to read the writings of Martin Luther with pleasure, as they were then being circulated throughout Germany. During these years of study in Germany, the winds of reform let loose by Luther were blowing through Bullinger's life as well.

After earning his master's degree in 1522, Bullinger returned to his beloved Switzerland. Although already influenced by Reformation thought, he accepted a call by Wolfgung Rüpli, abbot of a monastery in Cappel, to teach in the cloister school. He taught the monks from the New Testament and from Philip Melanchthon's *Loci Communes,* which was the first systematic theology of the Reformation. Sent to Zurich, where Zwingli preached, Bullinger spent five months listening to Zwingli, perfecting his Greek, and beginning his studies in Hebrew. It was here that he became more thoroughly acquainted with Reformation distinctives. The result was that when he returned to the cloister school in Cappel, he persuaded the abbot and all the monks to accept the teachings of the Reformation.

In 1529 Bullinger was called to be minister in the church at Bremgarten, where he succeeded his father as pastor. Here he preached until the battle of Cappel, when Zwingli was killed and the Reformation in Switzerland was brought to a temporary standstill. In these years at Bremgarten, he developed his skills as a preacher and pastor, and served the congregation well. When Zwingli was killed in 1531, Bullinger was forced to leave his congregation and stop preaching. His absence from the pulpit was brief, however, for he was soon called to be Zwingli's successor in the prestigious congregation of Zurich. Here he remained till the end of his life, wrapped up in the ministry of the Word. Here, in the early years of his ministry, he preached six or seven times a week, later only on Friday and on the Lord's day.

### His Work

The death of Zwingli seemed to be a deathblow to the Reformation in Switzerland, but God provided for the churches there a man who could keep a steady hand on the tiller.

Bullinger was a devoted pastor, not only as a powerful preacher, but also as a faithful shepherd who visited his sheep day and night, opened his house to all who needed help, exposed himself to dangers when he visited those who were struck down by the plague that several times visited Zurich, and brought comfort and strength to the dying.

Although he lived on a very meager salary, his charity was known throughout the country. He freely distributed money, food, and clothing. He refused any gifts and gave anything beyond his salary to hospitals and institutions of mercy. He nearly always had in his home strangers and exiles for whom he provided shelter and food. He secured a pension for Zwingli's widow, took her under his roof, and assumed responsibility for the education of Zwingli's two children. His Christian love and charity brought him the respect and devotion of all his parishioners.

Bullinger was deeply committed to Christian education. He served as superintendent of the schools in Zurich and was instrumental in the staffing of the seminary with able theologians. He actively participated in the regulation of the schools according to the Word of God.

Bullinger was a devoted family man. In 1529 he married Ann Adlischweiter, a former nun from Zurich, and with her had several children. His biographers speak of the fact that his home was a happy place in spite of the fact that almost always strangers were lodging with them. He romped with his children and grandchildren and was deeply conscious of his covenant calling to teach them the ways of the Lord. When his parents could no longer care for themselves, Bullinger and his wife cared for them in their own home.

### Bullinger the Theologian

After Zwingli's death, Bullinger became the theologian of the Swiss churches other than the church of Geneva where Calvin labored.

The Swiss Reformation, outside Geneva, produced two remarkable and beautiful confessions, the First and the Second Helvetic Confessions. The First Helvetic Confession was the work of Bullinger, along with several other theologians: Megander, Grynaeus, Myconius, and Leo Judd. The Second Helvetic Confession was Bullinger's personal work, written as a personal confession of faith. It

was adopted by the Swiss churches in 1566. In many respects it is a beautiful confession and worth the time it takes to read and study it.

When controversy rose in Switzerland over the doctrine of the Lord's Supper, Bullinger not only defended the Reformed view against Lutheranism, but he also worked with John Calvin to bring uniformity among the Swiss. The result of their cooperative effort was the *Consensus Trigurinus,* an important Reformation document on the doctrine of the Lord's Supper.

Bullinger's influence extended throughout Europe, even though he never traveled beyond Switzerland. When exiles from England sought refuge in Zurich during the reign of Bloody Mary, Bullinger took them into his home and taught them more carefully the truths of Scripture. Through an astonishing correspondence Bullinger exerted influence on theologians everywhere. He corresponded with Swiss, German, and English theologians; he wrote to kings, princes, and queens. When he died, the English mourned his passing as a calamity and repeatedly expressed their great debt to this preacher of Zurich.

In one controversy, however, he showed a weakness. When Calvin in Geneva was struggling with the heresies of Bolsec, the consistory of Geneva sought the advice of the other Swiss theologians. Although in general these theologians agreed with Calvin in his doctrine of predestination (Bolsec denied sovereign predestination), they cautioned Geneva to proceed with care and questioned Calvin's strong statements on God's predestination of sin and sovereign, unconditional reprobation. Bullinger was among them. When Calvin drew up his *Consensus Genevensis,* Bullinger refused to sign it. This document is extremely important. It has been translated into English under the title "A Treatise on the Eternal Predestination of God" in *Calvin's Calvinism.*

Of great value to us is a controversy which Bullinger carried on in his debates with the Anabaptists. Against them he wrote no fewer than six books. In his defense of the biblical position on the doctrine of infant baptism, Bullinger developed his ideas of God's covenant of grace. It is in these writings of Bullinger, along with Zwingli's, that we have the first development of this doctrine which has meant so much to the cause of the truth. All subsequent covenant theologians, in both Reformed and Presbyterian circles, owe a great debt to Heinrich Bullinger.

## Bullinger's Death

Bullinger's last days were filled with suffering. The great burden of the work undermined his health. In 1562 he wrote to a friend, "I almost sink under the load of business and care, and feel so tired that I would ask the Lord to give me rest if it were not against his will." In 1564 and 1565 he nearly died from the plague, which took from him his wife, three daughters, and a brother-in-law. In all his sufferings he bore his burdens with great patience and submission to the will of God. Though often lonely and heartsick, he continued his labors until death overtook him.

Bullinger died on September 17, 1575, after suffering intensely from calculus, a disease which was probably what we would now call kidney and bladder stones, for which there was no cure in the sixteenth century. His youngest daughter, Dorthea, cared for him in his last years. When near death, he assembled the pastors of Zurich about him and exhorted them to purity of life, unity among the brethren, and faithfulness in doctrine. He warned them against temptation, assured them of his love, thanked them for their kindness towards him, and closed with a prayer of thanksgiving. After shaking hands with all of them with tears, he bade them farewell—as Paul did with the elders at Ephesus. He died reciting Psalms 51, 16, and 42, the Apostles' Creed, and the Lord's Prayer. His son-in-law preached the funeral sermon.

Bullinger was the man chosen by God to maintain the Swiss Reformation after the death of Zwingli. He was equipped by God with extraordinary spiritual gifts for this task. He was a man of patience, firm faith, courage, moderation, and endurance who "proved that the Reformation was a work of God" when, by his work, the Reformation in Switzerland survived Zwingli's death at the battle of Cappel.

To him, we who love the truth of God's covenant owe a great debt under God.

## Chapter 27

# Theodore Beza
### Calvin's Successor

*Introduction*
*Few reformers have been as much maligned as Theodore Beza, Calvin's successor in Geneva. The slanders against him came in his own lifetime from his Roman Catholic opponents, who evidently feared the power of his pen. Though of a different kind, these*

slanders have been found in the writings of modern-day "Calvinists" who charge Beza with corrupting Calvin's pure doctrine and giving his teachings new twists which Calvin would have repudiated. Specifically, Beza is charged with altering in significant ways Calvin's teachings on predestination and the atonement of Christ. While we may dismiss with scorn the Romish charges which were leveled against him in his lifetime, the accusations that Beza altered Calvin's doctrines of predestination and the atonement are more serious. It is maintained, for example, that pure Calvinism has been lost since Calvin's time because the Reformed fathers in Germany, the Netherlands, and America have followed Beza in teaching a view of predestination and the atonement which Calvin never taught. It is said that Gomarus, the Synod of Dordt, the Westminster divines, Perkins and Owen in England, Turretin, Abraham Kuyper, and Herman Hoeksema have followed Beza and not Calvin. It is time, so these critics opine, that today's Calvinistic churches return to pure Calvinism and repudiate Beza's corruptions of what Calvin taught.

## Beza's Early Life

Who is this Beza who is so widely criticized?

Theodore Beza was born in Vézeley in Burgundy of France on June 24, 1519. He was the son of Pierre de Besze and Marie Burderot, both from the lesser nobility. His mother, an intelligent and charitable woman, bore seven children, of whom Theodore was the last. She died when Beza was only three years old.

Beza never knew his family home. At a very young age his uncle Nicholas, a member of the parliament in Paris and one who was impressed with Theodore's intelligence, took him into his own home in Paris to supervise his education. Perhaps part of the reason why Theodore's father consented to this was the death of his beloved wife.

Protestantism had come into France with the first writings of Luther, which were widely circulated and read. As early as 1520, many Protestants could be found in the land, although they were isolated from each other and unorganized. It was to be the lot of Calvin and Beza to provide leadership in France and a haven in Geneva for the refugees who fled the fierce persecutions of Protestants in that Roman Catholic land.

Beza's formal education began in 1528 when, scarcely nine years old, he was sent to Orléans to study under Melchior Wolmar. Wolmar will be remembered in history as a man of Protestant convictions who had the privilege of teaching both Beza and Calvin. In fact, it is quite possible that the two knew each other already then, for they were students of Wolmar at the same time. Wolmar took Beza into his own family, and Beza stayed with Wolmar for seven years.

Although Wolmar made every effort to convert Beza to Protestantism, the young boy resisted strenuously and refused to forsake the Roman Catholicism of his family. As Beza himself later wrote, it was not until much later that God caused the seeds of Wolmar's teaching to grow and mature in his life. Nevertheless, the affection between Wolmar and Beza never diminished, and Beza followed Wolmar to Bourges.

In 1534 Wolmar fled to his native Germany during an incident regarding placards. Some Protestants had distributed placards in Paris which condemned the mass, and this brought upon them the fierce

persecutions which were to be so much a part of the life of the faithful in France.

Following the wishes of his father, Beza (much like Calvin) turned to the study of law in Orléans. His heart was not in it, though; he far preferred the study of ancient Greek and Roman literature, especially old Latin poets. He was a literary man above all, and he reveled in the writings of these Roman pagans.

Although he did set up a law practice with his uncle in Paris after he completed his studies, Beza spent more time in reading literature and writing Latin poetry than he did in practicing law. He even had many of his poems published in a book entitled *Juvenalia,* which made a huge sensation in the literary world in Paris. His mastery of the Latin and his elegant style in Latin were so impressive that all his contemporaries agreed that his Latin writings were stylistically more beautiful than later writings in his native French. The poems, however, were indecent and were to be a source of many regrets in his later life.

Beza was able to enjoy a life of comparative leisure because two benefices were arranged for him, which provided him with the steady income of 700 golden crowns a year. Such a handsome income enabled him to live luxuriously in the highest circles of Parisian society, where he wined and dined with the famous literary people of his day. While Beza, in reflecting on this period of his life, admitted sadly to many indiscretions and sins, he steadfastly maintained that he had never fallen into immorality or the more cardinal sins which were so openly practiced in the higher circles of society.

In 1544 Beza was secretly engaged to Claudine Denosse, a girl of the lower class. He insisted on keeping the engagement secret, for to make his engagement public would not only be an embarrassment to his literary friends, but it would also rob him of the income from his benefices. Yet his moral principles left him uneasy even then, and he promised his fiancée that at a proper time he would marry her publicly.

## *Beza's Conversion and Early Work*

God prepared Beza during these years for greater work in His kingdom. Much like Calvin, who was educated as a humanist scholar, Beza too, though he did not know it, was being fashioned and formed by his God for crucial labors in the Reformation by drinking deeply at the well of humanist thought.

Like Zwingli, Beza was brought to conversion by a serious illness during which he had much time to ponder the inscrutable ways of providence and to remember the faithful instruction of his old tutor, Melchior Wolmar. Humbled and chastised, he recovered from his illness a sound Protestant who now committed his life to the propagation of the gospel.

Because persecution continued in France, he took his fiancée and fled to Calvin in Geneva. Here he was warmly welcomed by his old fellow student, and here he kept his promise to Claudine by marrying her publicly in the church of Geneva.

By means of the influence of Peter Viret, Beza was appointed professor of Greek at the University of Lausanne. Calvin already then showed his high esteem for Beza when he wrote to Farel during a time when Beza was ill with the plague:

> I would not be a man if I did not return his [Beza's] love who loves me more than a brother and reveres me as a father: but I am still more concerned at the loss the church would suffer if in the midst of his career he should be suddenly removed by death, for I saw in him a man whose lovely spirit, noble, pure manners, and open-mindedness endeared him to all the righteous.
> I hope, however, that he will be given back to us in answer to our prayers.

### *Beza's work in Geneva and France*

Geneva needed Beza, and so in 1549 he was called to become professor of theology in the academy which Calvin had founded. Lausanne was reluctant to see him leave, but Beza felt the urge to work with his beloved Calvin. Beza served as professor in the academy from 1559–1599 and as rector from 1559–1563, when Calvin refused the position. He was pastor of the church in Geneva from 1559–1605, retiring only when old age forced him to do so. From 1564–1580, Beza served as moderator of the company of pastors after Calvin's death.

The academy in Geneva became the one most important school in all Calvinistic Europe. Students from every part of Europe came there to study and went forth from the academy to spread the truths of Calvinism to every part of the continent. Among those who studied there was John Knox, who returned to his native Scotland to fight for the Reformation in that land; and Jacobus Arminius, who, although he studied under Beza, never imbibed Beza's teachings and returned to the Netherlands to spread his own poisonous doctrines.

Beza will be loved especially by those whose ancestry dates back to the Huguenots (as Calvinists in France were called). It is impossible to relate here how many trips he took to France, how many years he spent among the Huguenots, and what services he rendered for them. When not receiving warmly their refugees in Geneva, he endangered his life by preaching to them, marching with their armies, writing on their behalf and in their defense, and attending their synods. He presided over the last French Reformed synod in La Rochelle before the horrible massacre of Protestants by the Roman Catholics on St. Bartholomew's eve made further synods impossible. While engaged in peaceful worship in a barn at Vassy, these hapless Protestants were set upon by the duke of Guise, who butchered hundreds of them.

Beza's greatest service to French Protestants was his attendance at the Colloquy of Poissy on July 31, 1561. This colloquy was called in an effort to bring peace between Protestants and Roman Catholics. Attending this notable conference were eleven Reformed pastors from France, delegates from Switzerland, French Roman Catholic bishops, the king of France (though he was a child), and the queen mother, Catherine de Medici. It was a notable assembly. The discussions, however, went nowhere. As Beza was speaking in defense of the Protestant cause, he was rudely interrupted by the bishops of Rome who were determined not to allow the Protestants to propagate their views. After fruitless efforts to continue the discussion, the assembly was adjourned. Yet the result was that the king and queen mother were exposed to Protestant teaching, Catherine de Medici was impressed with the clarity and boldness of Beza's presentation, and Protestantism was given some recognition and a measure of freedom. This, however, lasted but a short time. Cardinal Lorraine, the chief opponent of Protestantism, said of Beza, "I could well have wished either that this man had been dumb or that we had been deaf."

In a confrontation with the cruel and bloodthirsty duke of Guise, Beza made his memorable statement: "Sire, it belongs, in truth, to the church of God, in the name of which I address you, to *suffer* blows, not to *strike* them. But at the same time let it be your pleasure to remember that the church is an anvil which has worn out many a hammer."

## *Beza's Last Days*

The last days of Beza were spent continuing Calvin's doctrines, quietly teaching, attending meetings, writing, and corresponding with reformers and saints throughout Europe. His wife, Claudine, died in 1588 and Beza married again: a refugee from Genoa, Geneviève del Piano. When Calvin died in 1564, Beza preached his funeral sermon, and shortly after wrote a biography of his mentor and dear friend.

Weary of his many labors on behalf of the cause of Christ, he died peacefully on Sunday, October 23, 1605, at the age of 86. At his request, written in his will, he was buried in the common cemetery where Calvin was buried and near the grave of his wife. He had fought the good fight and had kept the faith, and he then received the reward of the crown of life.

## *Concluding Thoughts*

Though not the original thinker that Calvin was, Beza was nevertheless a man of great learning, vast intellect, and deep devotion. His labors and writings are staggeringly great. He wrote dramas, satires, polemical treatises, Greek and French grammars, biographies, political treatises, and theological works. He edited an annotated text of the Greek New Testament which he bequeathed to Cambridge University in England, which text received his name: *Codex Bezae*. He edited the publication of Calvin's letters and wrote a defense of the killing of Servetus, the heretic who denied the Trinity and was burned at the stake in Geneva by the order of the council. He defended Presbyterian church polity against the hierarchism of the Church of England. He refuted the Lutheran doctrine of the Lord's Supper, defended predestination against the heretic Castellio, and defended the doctrine of the Trinity against the Italian heretic Ochino. His pen was sharp and often filled with the ink of satire; his enemies feared him.

He attended countless meetings, not the least of which was a meeting with German, French, and Swiss Protestants in an effort to bridge the chasm between Lutherans and Calvinists, in the hopes that German Protestants would aid in helping the beleaguered French Huguenots.

Beza's enemies, showing their fear of him, did everything to discredit him. He was charged with immorality and with the gravest

of moral faults. Repeatedly the rumors of his return to the bosom of Rome were spread far and wide. In fact, specific efforts were made to persuade him to return to the Romish church. On one occasion, when Beza was an old man (1597), a certain Francois came to Geneva to do this. Francois was only thirty, young, zealous, skillful in debate, and the winner of countless encounters with adversaries. But all his skill failed to move Beza. When argumentation failed, he tried bribery and offered Beza in the name of the pope a yearly pension of 4000 gold crowns and a sum equal to twice as much as the value of his personal effects. This Beza could not tolerate. Politely but emphatically Beza told him, "Go, sir; I am too old and too deaf to be able to hear such words!"

Beza made explicit some of the key doctrines of Calvinism which were more or less implied in Calvin's writings: the truths of the particular atonement of Christ, the federal imputation of Adam's guilt, and supralapsarianism. It is for this that he is charged with altering Calvin's theology.

That Beza significantly altered Calvin's teachings is nonsense. The two men worked together in peace and harmony for many years in Geneva and the academy. Beza read what Calvin wrote, and Calvin read what Beza wrote. Who can know the many discussions they had between them on all matters of the truth? Not one word can be found in all the records that Calvin disagreed with Beza on any one point.

Yet the slander goes on. Some even call Beza the father of Hyper-Calvinism. If Beza was a Hyper-Calvinist, then so was Calvin himself. It is a slander which is easily refuted. Sovereign, unconditional, and particular grace, which Beza so ardently taught, is the truth of Scripture.

## Chapter 28

# The Story of Two Fredericks

**Fredrick the Wise**

**Fredrick the Pious**

## Introduction

*One cannot study the history of the Reformation of the sixteenth century without being impressed with God's all-wise and gracious providence over the affairs of men and nations which made the Reformation possible. History is replete with such examples, which only the blind are unable to see, and the Reformation provides some* startling instances of this. One example is God's use of earthly magistrates to protect and advance the cause of the Reformation. Although many powerful rulers in Europe were deeply involved in the history of the Reformation, two outstanding figures illustrate how God uses men to accomplish His purpose. These two men both bore the name Frederick.

They had much in common. Both were given the same name; both were born devoted Roman Catholics; both had the title Frederick III; both ruled over part of Germany; both were deeply involved in the Lutheran Reformation; both dared to oppose the might of Rome and to stand firm against papal threats and promises; both have received from history names which reflect the high esteem in which they were held: the first was called Frederick the Wise, and the second, Frederick the Pious; and both were used by God on behalf of the Reformation so that, humanly speaking, without them the Reformation would never have succeeded.

Yet, there the similarities end. One never left the Roman Catholic Church; the other became an ardent Calvinist. One remained single all his life; the other married twice and begat eleven children. One was quite old at the time the Reformation began; the other was involved in the terrible struggles in Germany which followed upon the Reformation. One was elector of the poorest province in Germany; the other, elector of the wealthiest. The roles they played in the Reformation, however, were equally crucial.

## Frederick the Wise

### *His Early Life*

At the time of the Reformation, Germany had no strong central government. It was divided into seven provinces, over each of which ruled an elector. When the need arose, these electors met in a Reichstag to choose an emperor who would rule in the name of the electors over the whole of Germany. Papal interference was common.

Frederick the Wise was born in 1463, twenty years before Luther. He was born of royal blood, for his father was elector of Saxony before him, and he inherited the electoral dignity upon his father's death.

Frederick was a model ruler whose outstanding characteristics were piety (in the Roman Catholic sense) and a deep love of justice. In keeping with his piety, he made a pilgrimage to the Holy Land in 1493 and purchased there many relics which he paid for out of his own purse. Carefully and lovingly he moved them to Wittenberg, where they were installed in the castle chapel—the very chapel on which Luther later nailed his Ninety-five Theses.

An old catalogue of the period lists the relics, 5005 in number. They were considered so impressive that the pope granted Frederick the right to give indulgences to anyone visiting them. Each such visit shortened the stay of the visitor in purgatory by 100 years. Nor would the indulgences be soon exhausted, for the total merit of the indulgences, ordered by the pope, was no less than 1,902,202 days.

The town of Wittenberg was not a place in which one would care to live. It was a small village of about 3,000 inhabitants on the banks of the river Elbe and situated in poor, sandy soil. Its buildings were made of rough wood plastered with mud. Its inhabitants were poor, crude, unlettered, and vulgar.

It was in this village that Frederick decided to build a university, probably in part because a castle of the elector was here but also because, the finances of the elector being limited, he could make use of the monks of the local Augustinian convent to teach, with little or no expense for salaries. While only about 415 students first attended this university, during Luther's day it became so popular that thousands of students were enrolled, and Melanchthon said that he heard no fewer than thirty-three languages spoken on campus by the students. But these glory days were yet to come.

It was probably at the suggestion of Johann von Staupitz, chaplain of Frederick and vicar of the Augustinian order to which Luther also belonged, that Frederick invited Luther to become professor there. Little did he know what events this appointment would trigger. Luther himself thought little of the town. He said it was on the extreme boundary of civilization and only a few steps away was barbarism. Repeatedly he wanted to leave it. Melanchthon, who came from the fertile Palatinate, often complained that he could get nothing fit to eat in the whole village.

### *Frederick and the Reformation*

Frederick's love for his university, coupled with the fact that Luther's presence on the faculty gave the university the prestige that Frederick wanted for it, prompted him to become the protector of the Reformation.

We believe in the truth of election and reprobation. We also believe that in God's eternal purpose, reprobation must serve election. Surely this implies that the rule of earthly kings and magistrates serves the purpose of the salvation of the church. We do not pass judgment on Frederick himself. Only God knows whether Frederick was one of His own. But this much we can say: the protection of Luther and of the Reformation by the state made the Reformation possible.

Meanwhile, Frederick remained loyal to his saints and relics. In fact, by 1520, three years after the Reformation began, the number of Frederick's relics had increased to 19,013.

Frederick's confidence in Luther was confirmed after the Heidelberg Disputation. Less than one year after the Reformation began, Luther went to Heidelberg to defend his theses among those of his own Augustinian order. His enemies refused to argue the issue of indulgences. They insisted simply that because the pope had approved indulgences, and because the pope was the supreme authority in Christendom, Luther had no choice but to submit to papal decrees. One Wolfgang, present at the Heidelberg Disputation, wrote Frederick, "Luther has shown so much skill in the disputation as greatly to contribute to the renown of the University of Wittenberg."

Shortly after Luther's theses spread throughout Europe, when the pope began to take notice of what he first thought was nothing but a monk's quarrel, Frederick was ordered to send Luther, that "child of the devil," to Rome to recant. Frederick refused this order from the pope on the grounds that Luther had not received a fair trial up till then and would not receive one in Rome, either. Instead, Luther went to Augsburg to defend his theses, but it was only after a safe-conduct had been promised Luther that Frederick permitted him to go.

Frederick's confidence in Luther was further confirmed when he asked Erasmus what he should do about Luther. Erasmus responded that Luther's only crime had been to touch the triple crown of the pope and the stomachs of the monks.

In 1520, upon the death of Maximilian, emperor of the Holy Roman Empire, the pope offered the crown of the Holy Roman Empire to Frederick. Frederick had the good sense and humility to decline, an act which Wylie, a church historian of note, described as "inexcusable timidity." Charles V from Spain, a bitter enemy of the Reformation, became emperor instead.

Frederick never openly espoused Luther's theology, always claiming that as a layman he knew nothing of these matters. As cordial as he was to Luther personally, he refused to come publicly to the defense of the Reformation. He always insisted that Luther had to fight out his own convictions, and he would continue to protect Luther until Luther was given a fair trial based on principles of justice.

Still, Frederick remained Luther's protector. He invited the theologian Melanchthon to Wittenberg when Melanchthon joined the Reformation. He never prevented Luther from preaching his convictions in the castle church. He continued to encourage Luther in his vast publishing ventures when the truths of the gospel were spread far and wide through the printed page. When Luther and his colleagues burned the papal bull of excommunication in the streets of Wittenberg in June of 1520, Frederick did not interfere. When Luther was summoned to the Diet of Worms, where he made his heroic stand on the basis of Scripture—"Here I stand. I can do naught else. God help me."—Frederick was there. In fact, it was

Frederick who insisted that Luther be given a safe-conduct from the emperor. Frederick saw all that happened; not once did he criticize Luther for what he was doing.

But his greatest contribution to the Reformation was his "kidnapping" of Luther after the Diet. He ordered Luther spirited away to his castle in Wartburg, deep in the Thuringian Forest. There, for nearly a year, he protected Luther from all his enemies who sought his life. It was in the peace and quiet of the castle that Luther wrote some of his important works and made the first translation of the New Testament into German.

Although Luther finally left the castle without Frederick's permission because of the uprisings in Wittenberg brought on by the Anabaptist prophets, Frederick did not interfere with what Luther considered his solemn calling before God. Luther's explanation to the elector of his return is worth quoting.

> Grace and peace from God our Father and our Lord Jesus Christ, and my most humble service.
>
> Most illustrious, high-born Elector, most gracious Lord! I received the letter and warning of your Electoral Grace on Friday evening, before my departure. That your Electoral Grace is moved by the best intention, needs no assurance from me. I also mean well, but this is of no account...If I were not certain that we have the pure gospel on our side, I would despair...Your Grace knows, if not, I make known to you, that I have the gospel, not from men, but from heaven through our Lord Jesus Christ...I write this to apprise you that I am on my way to Wittenberg under a far higher protection than that of the Elector; and I have no intention of asking your Grace's support. Nay, I believe that I can offer your Highness better protection than your Highness can offer me. Did I think that I had to trust in the Elector, I should not come at all. The sword is powerless here. God alone must act without man's interference. He who has the most faith will be the most powerful protector. As I feel your Grace's faith to be still weak, I can by no means recognize in you the man who is to protect and save me. Your Electoral Grace asks me, what you are to do under these circumstances? I answer, with all submission, Do nothing at all, but trust in God alone...If your Grace had faith, you would behold the glory of God; but as you do not yet believe, you have not seen it. Let us love and glorify God forever. Amen.

When the peasants revolted against the electors of Germany after suffering intolerable injustices, Frederick was the only elector who urged his colleagues to show mercy when between 100,000 and 150,000 peasants were slaughtered.

When in 1525 Frederick lay dying, he urgently called Luther to come to his bedside; but Luther was so far distant that by the time he arrived, the elector had died. Before he died, he partook of the Lord's Supper in both kinds, an act which some church historians claim is evidence of his embracing of Protestantism at the moment of death.

Whether we shall see Frederick in heaven I do not know. I hope so. But that God used him in mysterious ways for the good of the Reformation is a truth which no one can deny.

## Frederick the Pious

### *His Early Life*

The second Frederick we speak of was born in 1515 in Simmern Castle, for his father was Count John II, elector of the Palatinate. His mother, Beatrix, was a very beautiful woman, pious and upright in her life, a godly mother and one who gave lavishly to the poor. Frederick was the oldest of eleven children, of whom two became priests and five, nuns.

Frederick's father was a Renaissance man and wanted his eldest son to have the best education available. He also opened the doors of Europe's courts and chancelleries to his son. Frederick's father was a close friend of Charles V, emperor of the Holy Roman Empire. Charles was ruler of Spain, Germany, and the Lowlands. In his court, Frederick learned the skills of knighthood. In Europe's royal courts, he learned the life of royalty.

The glitter of royalty, however, never appealed to him, and Frederick soon left to test his skills in battle. When eighteen years old, he fought the Turks and earned knighthood for bravery and skill in battle.

An intriguing story of these early years makes one wonder whether his thoughts were not then already turned to the Reformation. While still in the court of Charles, he had a private meeting with John á Lasco, the renowned Polish reformer, whose work meant so much to the hard-pressed Protestants in the Netherlands. What came from that meeting only God, who brought them together, knows.

Frederick's courtship years were filled with disappointment. For two years he wooed Elenora, the sister of Charles V, but lost her to the old king of Portugal. In despair he returned to Heidelberg in the Palatinate. When the old king died, he once again pressed his suit

with Elenora, but lost her a second time to Francis I of France. He tried to persuade Maria, another sister of Charles V, to marry him but failed also in this endeavor. In 1537 he married another Maria, of royal blood and a Lutheran.

Although of royal blood himself, Frederick's years were spent in fighting poverty. With his wife he lived in an old castle of Berkenfeld, where together they had eleven children, only seven of whom reached maturity. He once complained, "I am like a sooty kitchen maid sitting behind the stove, concerning whom no one asked because she was so poor and dirty."

## *His Commitment to Lutheranism*

A bit of background is necessary to understand the important role which Frederick played in the Reformation in Heidelberg.

Germany itself was torn by war, which before it was over was to leave much of Germany in ruins. The Protestant Lutheran princes had formed a league to defend themselves against Roman Catholic attempts to destroy them by the sword. Between Protestants and Roman Catholics war periodically broke out.

Calvinism, born in Switzerland, had made inroads in Germany, especially in those parts bordering on the Swiss cantons. It is not an exaggeration to say that many Lutherans hated the Calvinists as much as or even more than the Roman Catholics, and they fought bitterly to preserve Germany for Lutheranism. The electors of Germany were under constant pressure to join one side or the other or, perhaps, the Roman Catholic forces.

After Luther's death, Lutheranism itself was divided. Radical Lutherans out-Luthered Luther, while some Lutherans, including Melanchthon, moved in the direction of the Calvinistic view of the Lord's Supper.

In the midst of all this confusion and distress, Heidelberg itself remained, under its elector, solidly Roman Catholic. Yet the people were far ahead of their ruler and wanted the Reformation introduced into their city. While the elector hesitated, the people themselves, in a mighty burst of enthusiasm, brought its beginnings about. On Sunday, December 20, 1545, the citizens were gathered for the worship of God in the Church of the Holy Spirit. As the priest was making preparations for the celebration of the mass, a member of the congregation began singing the Reformation hymn "Es ist das Heil Uns Kommen Her" (Salvation Has Come To Us). The first stanza is:

Salvation unto us has come
　　By God's free grace and favor;
Good works cannot avert our doom,
　　They help and save us never.
Faith looks to Jesus Christ alone,
　　Who did for all the world atone;
He is our one Redeemer.

Suddenly the whole congregation joined in singing the hymn, and the Reformation began.

In the meantime, under the influence of his Lutheran wife, Frederick became wholly committed to the Lutheran faith. One incident in Frederick's life in Berkenfeld showed his steadfastness and courage. After Roman Catholic successes on the field of battle, Frederick was asked to sign the Regensburg Interim, which had as its goal the complete suppression of the Reformation. This he refused to do, and he wrote the emperor, "Rather than do this, I will by God's help suffer anything; and if I am not safe in this country on account of my faith, I may be able to live at some other place with God."

In 1556, after his appointment as governor of the Upper Palatinate, Frederick made every effort to bring about reform in his province. He moved his castle to Amsberg and brought about reforms by appointing Protestant ministers, rooting out such Romish practices as masses, indulgences, and worship of images, and curbing such sins as immorality, drunkenness, ignorance, and superstition.

Frederick and Maria suffered great tragedies during this period. All the divisions of Protestantism were in their families: some were ardent Lutherans, some Melanchthonians, some Zwinglians, and some Calvinists. One of his sons was drowned and another was killed in battle defending Protestants in the Netherlands. Two of his children turned against him as he moved away from Lutheranism towards Calvinism.

## His Conversion to Calvinism

In 1559, about four years before Calvin's death, Frederick became elector of the entire Palatinate. From that moment on he knew not a moment of peace.

Four individual factors played their part in bringing Frederick to a Calvinistic position—in spite of the opposition of his Lutheran wife. Men who were Calvinists were appointed to offices in the church and the state. Continued reforms gradually eliminated both Romish and

Lutheran practices and brought about reform in church government and worship. A flood of refugees came into the Palatinate and Heidelberg from France, England, and the Netherlands—all of them Calvinists and all of them helped by Frederick's generosity.

The most important factor in bringing Frederick to Calvinism was the eruption in Heidelberg of the so-called Hesshus-Klebitz controversy over the presence of Christ's body and blood in the Lord's Supper. Hesshus was an arrogant and outspoken Lutheran; Klebitz was a Calvinist. Frederick devoted days and nights to a study of the question, searching the Scriptures to come to his own conclusions. He was pressured towards Lutheranism by his wife and some of his children. He was pressured towards Calvinism by many gifted professors in the university. When he finally made up his mind, he was convinced that the Calvinistic position was in keeping with the Word of God. To its defense he now dedicated himself. We may add, by way of parenthesis, that before Maria died, she also embraced Calvinism.

It was this bitter controversy, which nearly tore Heidelberg apart, that was the immediate occasion for Frederick to order the writing of a new Catechism. From the preface to it, which Frederick himself drew up, we learn that his reasons for it were to have a document which would serve the spiritual welfare of his realm, aid in reaching doctrinal unity among the people, and serve as a guide for preaching and the instruction of the youth.

Although they were assisted in their work by others, Caspar Olevianus, whom Frederick rescued from a prison in Trier, and Zacharias Ursinus bore the major responsibility for composing it.

From the pens of these two gifted men emerged the glorious confession of faith which has meant so much to the church of Christ over the years.

Its beauty and worth lie especially in the fact that its motif is "comfort." One cannot, I think, appreciate this motif unless he is aware of its tremendous significance in the times in which it was written. Roman Catholicism, with its doctrine of salvation by meritorious works, is a comfortless doctrine—as is all Pelagianism and Arminianism which bases salvation on human works. Luther experienced that fully in his own life, until he came to the truth of justification by faith alone. The Roman Catholic Church had written, as it were, above the doors of its churches and cathedrals, "Abandon all comfort, ye who enter here."

When the glorious truths of the Reformation began to be preached, the reformers, with one voice, shouted to all the world, "We come to you with a gospel of *comfort!* That comfort is in the full and free grace of God in Jesus Christ our Lord, and justification by faith alone without works!"

No wonder that that gospel spread like wildfire through Europe, for it alone could bring peace to the troubled souls of God's people.

The Heidelberg Catechism picked up that theme.

> Q: What is thy only comfort in life and death?
> A: That I with body and soul, both in life and death, am not my own, but belong unto my faithful Savior Jesus Christ; who, with his precious blood, hath fully satisfied for all my sins, and delivered me from all the power of the devil; and so preserves me that without the will of my heavenly Father, not a hair can fall from my head; yea, that all things must be subservient to my salvation, and therefore, by his Holy Spirit, he also assures me of eternal life, and makes me sincerely willing and ready, henceforth, to live unto him.

Frederick III, known as the Pious, has gone down in history as the father of the Heidelberg Catechism. This alone is sufficient to secure for him a cherished place in the memory of God's people.

## The Diet of Augsburg

The first publication of the Heidelberg Catechism in 1563 was not yet the spiritual high point of Frederick's life. Although he had ordered the Catechism to be written, Frederick did not compose it himself. Probably the clearest touch of his finger on the Catechism is Question & Answer 80, dealing with the popish mass, which Frederick ordered inserted into the original edition. The high-water mark of Frederick's own commitment to the Reformation came at the Diet of Augsburg in 1566. To the story of that stirring event we now turn.

A few brief statements about the background will help to put this important meeting in perspective.

The attacks made against the Heidelberg Catechism were many and fierce. They came from almost all quarters. The Roman Catholics hated it for its sharp condemnation of their many sins. The Lutherans were no less affronted by it, both because it constituted a threat to their domination in Germany and because the attacks made against their position on the sacrament of the Lord's Supper were no less sharp than those made against Rome. But, clearly, the more popular it became and the more widely it was hailed for its quiet beauty and deep comfort, the more vicious became the attacks.

Maximilian II was emperor of Germany. He was deeply devoted to the cause of Roman Catholicism but was prevented from exterminating either Lutheranism or Calvinism by events which continued to crowd in on his life and distract his attention. Notably, the Turks were knocking on the eastern door of Europe and were threatening to overrun the continent and to engulf Europe in a tidal wave of Mohammedanism. He was, therefore, content to abide by the provisions of the Peace of Augsburg (1555) in which Lutherans and Roman Catholics had come to a tenuous agreement that the ruler of each province would decide the religion of that province. The difficulty was that the Peace of Augsburg made no provision for Calvinism; it was an agreement between Lutherans and Roman Catholics. Frederick III was now a Calvinist.

Maximilian summoned a Diet to decide on various problems confronting Germany, including the problem of the Turkish threat. On the agenda was also an item ominous for Frederick: "How to check the destructive and corrupting sects." By virtue of his sponsorship of the Heidelberg Catechism, Frederick had been specifically charged with violating the Peace of Augsburg.

Considered a heretic by Roman Catholics and Lutherans, Frederick was in danger of losing everything at the Diet, including his life. Because of the danger, his closest friends urged him not to go but, as with Luther before the Diet of Worms, so Frederick was convinced that a faithful testimony to the truth required his presence. He responded to one friend,

> I find consolation in the hope that the Almighty power of my dear and faithful Heavenly Father will use me as an instrument for the confession of His name in these days in the holy empire of the German nation, not only by word of mouth, but also by act...I know...that the same God who kept [Duke John Frederick] in the true knowledge of the holy Gospel is still living, and is well able to preserve me, a poor, simple man, and, by the power of the Holy Ghost, will certainly do it, even if it should come to this that blood must be spilt. And should it please my God and Father in heaven thus to honor me, I should never be able to thank Him sufficiently for it, either in time or in eternity.

His own family bade him farewell with tears, certain that they would never again see him on earth.

At the Diet, almost all were against him, including the emperor. When the business of "destructive and corrupting sects" came up, Frederick was summoned before the emperor, by whom he was given this choice: either retract your position or suffer deposition. Lutherans and Roman Catholics alike eagerly nodded agreement. Only the small huddled group of Calvinists wondered what would happen and even half-seriously wished Frederick would capitulate.

We cannot quote here the speech Frederick made in his own defense although it has come down through the ages preserved for us. Only a few scattered quotes of a speech, which could not have lasted more than five minutes, will have to suffice.

> ...I promise myself...that his Imperial Majesty...will graciously hear and weigh the defense I shall make; which, if it were required, I would be ready to make undaunted in the center of the market place in this town. So far as matters of a religious nature are involved, I confess freely that in those things which concern the conscience, I acknowledge as Master, only Him, who is Lord of lords and King of kings. For the question here is not in regard to a cap of flesh, but it pertains to the soul and its salvation, for which I am indebted alone to my Lord and Savior Jesus Christ, and which, as his gift, I will sacredly preserve. Therefore I cannot grant your Imperial Majesty the right of standing in the place of my God and Savior...
>
> That my Catechism, word for word, is drawn, not from human, but from divine sources the references that stand in the margin will show. For this reason also certain theologians have in vain wearied themselves in attacking it, since it has been shown them by the open Scriptures how baseless is their opposition. What I have elsewhere publicly declared to your Majesty in a full assembly of princes; namely, that if any one of whatever age, station or class he may be, even the humblest, can teach me something better from the Holy Scriptures, I will thank him from the bottom of my heart and be readily obedient to the divine truth...Should it please your Imperial Majesty to undertake this task, I would regard it as the greatest favor...With this, my explanation, I hope your Imperial Majesty will be satisfied...Should contrary to my expectations, my defense...not be regarded of any account, I shall comfort myself in this that my Lord and Savior Jesus Christ has promised to me and to all who believe that whatsoever we lose on earth for His name's sake, we shall receive an hundred fold in the life to come.

It was a courageous defense. Everything hung in the balance, even the future of Calvinism in Germany. Elector August of Saxony, the only one among the princes to support Frederick, tapped him on the

shoulder in full view of the entire assembly and said, "Fritz, you are more pious than all of us."

Although the minds of few, if any, were changed, the godliness of Frederick was so obvious that no one dared to press the accusation brought against him. He was able to leave the Diet in peace and continue his work.

The victory at Augsburg was significant, for it saved Calvinism in Germany from Lutheran and Roman Catholic domination.

## *The Last Years*

Frederick really never knew any peace, even within his beloved Palatinate. Although the controversy over the question of the presence of Christ in the sacrament of the Lord's Supper was settled by the adoption of the Heidelberg Catechism, other controversies plagued the province. One of the most serious was a controversy over discipline, particularly whether the church or the state would exercise discipline in the Palatinate. Calvin had settled the problem in Geneva after a long struggle with the authorities in that city; but Lutheranism, with Luther's encouragement, had always tended towards giving ecclesiastical discipline to the civil magistrate. The struggle between Calvinism and Lutheranism in the Palatinate brought about this controversy over discipline. Unfortunately, Frederick, a civil ruler himself, favored the position that the state exercised key power in the church as well as sword power in the state.

Shortly after the triumph of Augsburg, Maria, Frederick's devoted wife of thirty years, died. After two years of deep mourning, Frederick married Amelia, a countess of Neuenahr and a widow from the Netherlands. She was related to various French Huguenots and, as a result of this marriage, Frederick's attention was more and more drawn to the sad plight of the persecuted Huguenots in France.

Frederick began, in these years, to send his armies to the aid of French and Dutch Protestants. The French Protestants were being butchered by the Roman Catholic king under the prodding of his Roman Catholic advisers; the Dutch Protestants were being slaughtered by the cruel and merciless Margaret of Parma and the duke of Alva. Unable to bear the suffering of his fellow saints, and out of sympathy for his agonizing wife, he ordered his troops into France and the Netherlands. Ursinus was opposed to this decision and urged upon Frederick the biblical truth that the cause of Christ

in the world was not advanced by the sword and that "they that fight with the sword shall perish with the sword."

Frederick's days were swiftly drawing to a close. His piety in his death was as great as in his life. Just a few days before he died, he said to his chaplain,

> I have lived long enough, both for you and the church. Now I shall be called to a better life. I have done for the church the best I possibly could, but have not accomplished a great deal. God who can do all things and who cared for his servants before my day, still lives and reigns in heaven. He will not leave you orphan, nor will he leave without fruit the prayers and tears which I have brought to him on my knees in this room for my successors and for the church.

A bit later he was speaking to Olevianus:

> The Lord may call me whenever it pleases him. I have a clear conscience in Christ Jesus my Lord, whom I have served with all my heart, and I have lived to see that in my churches and schools the people are directed away from men to him alone.

Just before Frederick died, he murmured to those about him, "I have been detained long enough by the prayers of pious Christians. It is time that my earthly life should close, and that I should go to my Savior into heavenly rest."

After asking that Psalm 31 and John 17 be read for him, and after hearing them read, he prayed, in a voice heard by all, a very brief prayer and quietly departed this life to be with Christ in glory. It was October 1576.

Calvin thought so highly of Frederick that he dedicated his commentary on Jeremiah to him. In the concluding paragraph of the dedication Calvin says,

> Though I can add nothing to the character of your Highness, either by my praise or by the dedication of this work, yet I could not restrain myself from doing what I thought to be my duty. Farewell, Most Illustrious Prince. May God enrich you more and more with His spiritual gifts, keep you long in safety, and render your dignified station prosperous to you and yours (Geneva, July 23, 1563).

No one who loves and cherishes the Heidelberg Catechism ought to forget to breathe a quiet prayer of thanksgiving to God for the gift of Frederick, whom God used to give this blessed creed to us. And no one can read of his courage before kings and rulers

without resolving in his own heart, by God's grace, to stand for truth and right with equal dependence upon Christ, in whom we have the victory through faith.

## Chapter 29

# Zacharias Ursinus & Caspar Olevianus

Zacharias Ursinus

## Authors of the Heidelberg Catechism

Caspar Olevianus

**Introduction**
*Without question, the Heidelberg Catechism is one of the most, if not the most, beloved confessions of all time. Those who cherish the heritage of the truth and turn to the confessions of the church to learn it will rejoice in the Heidelberger as a precious gift of God through the Spirit of truth whom Christ promised the church.*

Not only those who belong to churches which have made the Catechism their theological basis, but God's people from any tradition and from all ecclesiastical backgrounds love and cherish this glorious creed.

Its attractiveness lies in two characteristics. The first is its warm and personal style. It speaks to the experience of the child of God. It tells him what the truth means to him personally in his own life and calling in the world. The second is its dominating theme of comfort. The personal and experiential aspect of the Catechism looks at the truth in all our life as a truth which brings comfort. It echoes the words of God in Isaiah 40:1: "Comfort ye, comfort ye my people, saith your God."

In the last chapter we described the role that Frederick the Pious played in the writing of the Heidelberg Catechism. In this chapter we will let the authors themselves step out of the obscure past and take their place momentarily on the stage of history to tell us of what God worked in them.

# Zacharias Ursinus

### *Ursinus' Early Life*

Zacharias Ursinus was born on July 18, 1534, in the town of Breslau of Silesia, a province of Austria. He was born of a family by the name of Baer, or Bear. Those who know the Big Dipper as Ursa Major will also know that Ursinus is the Latin word for bear.

Ursinus' parents were poor, for the wages of a tutor were meager and his father was a tutor. Two advantages, however, were his, brought up as he was in a tutor's home. The first was that he was surrounded from infancy with learning, and the second was that he had an opportunity to meet many of the rich and famous in the course of his early years.

Ursinus studied in Breslau until his fifteenth year, when he went to Wittenberg. Four years after Luther's body had been laid to rest in the cathedral in Wittenberg, and while Philip Melanchthon, Luther's colleague and close friend, was still teaching, Ursinus came to this notable and famous school. Because his parents could not support him, his expenses were underwritten by the Senate of Breslau with the understanding that he would return to his native town to teach after he had completed his education.

Although he was a very able and gifted student, Ursinus was shy and retiring, tending somewhat to be moody, and not at all inclined to participate in the intellectual rough and tumble of classroom life in a university. Nor did he eagerly seek the companionship of his fellow students who, oftentimes with excessive gaiety, would celebrate the freedom of an academic life. He preferred to compose Greek and Latin verses in the solitude of his study.

He would probably have passed through the halls of the university scarcely noticed if it were not for the fact that Melanchthon observed his ability, took Ursinus into his own home, and became a friend and companion as well as teacher to the shy student. It was a strange but rich friendship, a fifty-three-year-old gifted theologian with a poor student of sixteen.

The Lutheran Reformation had penetrated Breslau prior to Ursinus' birth and had influenced his parents. Wittenberg was the

center of Lutheran studies. It is not surprising that Ursinus became an ardent Lutheran. Nevertheless, already Melanchthon was having second thoughts about Luther's view of the Lord's Supper and was more inclined to agree with the Swiss theologians regarding the presence of Christ in the bread and wine. Ursinus was influenced by Melanchthon and developed his own views, which were more like those of his mentor.

Ursinus spent seven years with Melanchthon and even accompanied him to Worms and Heidelberg in 1557. Heidelberg was the city in which Ursinus would do his most important work. He saw it for the first time in the golden autumn of October. On the hillside covered with trees stood the imposing castle in which the elector lived. The city was in the narrow valley of the Neckar River which flowed through the Black Forest to the Rhine just a few miles away. The Church of the Holy Spirit dominated the city with its spires soaring above the roofs of the houses. Almost at the feet of the spires was the most famous and oldest university in Germany, the University of Heidelberg. It had been Roman Catholic; it was now Protestant. Whether it would be Lutheran or Reformed had yet to be decided. It was Melanchthon's home, the land for which he longed. But Melanchthon had not come back to Heidelberg to stay; his life's work was on the sandy and dusty soil of Wittenberg.

After traveling together to Heidelberg, Ursinus and Melanchthon parted ways, Ursinus to travel for a year throughout Europe visiting the Protestant centers of learning in Germany, France, and Switzerland. He could read the Hebrew lectures of Jean Mercier in Paris, sit at the feet of Bullinger in Zurich, and talk with Calvin in Geneva. In fact, Calvin presented him with a gift of a complete set of Calvin's works, signed by their illustrious author.

For a few short years Ursinus fulfilled his obligations to Breslau by teaching there, but the Lutherans suspected him of being more Reformed than Lutheran in his views of the Lord's Supper. They were right; but it was a whispering campaign against him, finally exploding into public debate, which persuaded Ursinus to resign his position and leave the city. He never did enjoy controversy, and the bitterness of the hatred in Breslau was more than he could bear.

From Breslau, Ursinus went to Zurich. For a short time he found peace and quietness. Here he became a close friend of Peter Martyr Vermigli, the reformer from Italy who had made such a notable contribution to the Reformed doctrine of the Lord's Supper. Ursinus found companionship and fellowship with men with whom he was in complete agreement. Ursinus' decision to go to Zurich had been a difficult one. He told his uncle,

> Not unwillingly do I leave my fatherland, since it does not permit the confession of the truth, which I can not with good conscience give up. If my teacher Melanchthon still lived, I would go nowhere else but to him. But as he is dead, I will go to Zurich where there are pious, great and learned men. As for the rest, God will care.

Frederick the Pious wanted a Reformed professor in Heidelberg and called Peter Martyr. Martyr declined the call on the grounds of old age but recommended Ursinus. When Ursinus received the call from Frederick, he was most reluctant to go. He as well as anyone knew the tensions and controversies which were tearing apart that city. To a friend he wrote, "Oh that I could remain hidden in a corner. I would give anything for shelter in some quiet village."

But God has a way of calling a person to a work from which he shrinks. So it was with Moses. So it was when Calvin, at the threats of the fiery Farel, was persuaded to stay in Geneva. So God called Ursinus, shy and retiring, to the swirling ecclesiastical and doctrinal hubbub of Heidelberg.

## *Years in Heidelberg*

Times in Heidelberg were trying. Although through the wise and godly rule of Frederick the Pious Roman Catholicism had been mostly rooted out of the city, Lutheranism and the Reformed faith were vying for dominance. The differences were almost exclusively over the doctrine of the Lord's Supper, but violent and radical Lutherans were doing everything they could to rid the city of any man who disagreed with their position.

Ursinus was appointed head of the Collegium Sapientiae, the College of Wisdom, as it was called. But not long afterwards, he was appointed to occupy the chair of dogmatics, in which position every imaginable chore and obligation were thrust upon him as Frederick and others sought to make use of his enormous abilities and clear understanding of the truth.

It was not as a joke that Ursinus put on the door to his office in the university a sign on which was written a bit of Latin doggerel which, translated, read, "Friend who enters here: be quick, or go; or help me with my work."

Yet the work for which Ursinus is renowned is his authorship of the Heidelberg Catechism. With Caspar Olevianus, he was instructed to draw up a confession which could be used for the instruction of the people of the Palatinate and could serve as a basis of unity.

Ursinus had earlier written a small Catechism in Latin, which also had proceeded from the idea of comfort. It had suggested to Ursinus the theme of this Catechism, and much of this earlier work was absorbed into the Heidelberger. It is hard for us to believe that Ursinus was only twenty-eight years old at the time, but he had been steeped from infancy in reformational theology, and he was a man of brilliant gifts with which God had endowed him. The work began in 1562 and took nearly a year. It was a great time for confessions: the Thirty-nine Articles had been adopted by the Church of England; Bullinger had written his beautiful Second Helvetic Confession; and Spanish persecutors in the Lowlands were hunting the author of the Belgic Confession, Guido de Brès.

Frederick pressed the work forward at the swiftest possible rate. When the Catechism was nearly ready in early 1563, he summoned a large company of ministers and teachers from throughout the Palatinate to meet in solemn assembly to discuss and, if possible, approve the work. After solemn worship services and lengthy discussion, the assembled group was so moved by the genius of the work that they unanimously recommended to Frederick that it be adopted without change. And so it was.

In the second edition, Frederick ordered Question and Answer 80 to be added, though without the sharp language concerning the mass; but when the attacks of Roman Catholics increased in bitterness and intensity, Frederick made another change in this same question and answer which included the words which have ever afterward vexed the souls of Roman Catholics, words which branded the mass as "an accursed idolatry." Frederick also ordered that it be divided into fifty-two sections, or Lord's Days, so that it could be preached from beginning to end in one year.

The Catechism quickly ran through many editions and was soon translated into different languages, including the Dutch, where it became a treasured confession of the Dutch Reformed churches.

## Ursinus' Post-Heidelberg Years

The rest of Ursinus' years in Heidelberg were busy and relatively unhappy. Not only did his duties continue in the university, but he was now also asked to preach each Lord's Day on the Heidelberg Catechism. Furthermore, he became the chief defender of the Catechism against the many and vicious attacks made against it by Roman Catholics and Lutherans alike. They so wearied him who loved peace, so physically exhausted him, and so impaired his health, that in 1566 he ceased writing and two years later resigned his chair of dogmatics. The chair went to the esteemed Italian reformer, Hieronymous Zanchius, whose work *Predestination* is still widely read.

Disputes in Heidelberg continued, now over church government. Did the discipline of the impenitent rest with the state or with the church? The controversy was sharp and bitter. The main defender of Presbyterianism was an Englishman named George Withers. Bullinger and Beza were called in to give advice. Finally, annoyed by the silence of Ursinus, Frederick ordered him to express his views. He did so in a public assembly and in such a candid and kindly way that his views carried the day, and Presbyteries were established with discipline safely in the hands of the church.

All these years Ursinus had remained unmarried and had lived with the students in the dorms of the university. But in 1572, at the age of thirty-eight, he began to consider the possibility of marriage. He had noticed a quiet and friendly woman only a block away from the university, and one day, summoning up his courage, he took time out from his studies to propose to her. She accepted and they were married—perhaps one of the shortest courtships on record. They lived together nine years and brought forth one son.

Things were soon to change in Heidelberg. Frederick died, worn out by the cares of his kingdom. The elector Louis (Ludwig) came to the electorate. Louis was an ardent Lutheran and was determined to force Lutheranism on the Palatinate. Within one year he succeeded in doing this, and the Reformed faculty at the university, including Ursinus, were dismissed. Over 600 teachers and preachers left the Palatinate during this unhappy time.

Although Ursinus was invited to teach at Lausanne in Switzerland, he chose instead to go to Neustadt, where he set up a school in a nunnery with the help of his good friend Casimir, son of Frederick the Pious. The school obtained a good faculty and soon attracted many students from throughout Europe.

Ursinus taught only briefly in the school. He was asked by a reformed convention which met in Frankfurt in 1577 to draw up a

confession which could serve as a basis for unity of all Reformed churches in Europe, but he declined on the grounds of ill health.

The great work of these years was the writing of his well-known commentary on the Heidelberg Catechism, a volume which all who love this creed ought to purchase. The volume was put together from his lectures on the Catechism in Neustadt, lectures which he edited and prepared for publication, although this latter work he never finished. The book was published in 1584 after his death.

Ursinus' health continued to decline, and his teaching became increasingly sporadic. Finally on March 6, 1583, at the age of forty-nine, he died in Neustadt, leaving his wife a widow and his child without a father.

### Summary

Ursinus was not a very good preacher; his gifts lay in the classroom, where his lectures were learned, incisive, instructive, and delivered in a most interesting way. He was ever the cautious man, so much so that when questions were asked of him in class, he almost always postponed the answers to the following day so that he could have time to formulate a careful answer. His strength was in his penetrating mind and his deep commitment to the truth. The truth was not for him an intellectual matter, however; it was his "comfort," that which alone could sustain him through the grueling years of his work in Heidelberg.

God thrust this shrinking man into the maelstrom of Heidelberg. God knows what to do with His appointed servants even when His way seems all wrong to them and others. We are the beneficiaries, for to us has been given the time-honored treasure of the Heidelberg Catechism.

## Caspar Olevianus

### Introduction

God used more than one man to write the Heidelberg Catechism. Frederick III, elector of the Palatinate, ordered it written and supported the project, even offering suggestions from time to time. Zacharias Ursinus was its theologian. But Caspar Olevianus left his own indelible mark on it as well.

History has not recorded for us what precise part each of the two authors of the Catechism played in its formation, and speculations on

the subject by historians have proved fruitless. But it does seem to be a manifestation of God's great wisdom when, in the formulation of this marvelous creed, God used both the theologian Ursinus and the preacher Olevianus. Not only is the Catechism an unsurpassed summary of the Christian faith with the touch of a theologian, but it is also a confession eminently suitable to preach; it has the touch of a man who was himself a gifted and eloquent preacher and pastor.

## Early Life and Training

Caspar Olevianus was born on August 10, 1536, two years after the birth of his colleague Ursinus. He was born in one of the most famous cities in Trans-Alpine Europe, the city of Trier, or, as it was sometimes called, Treves. The city was built on the banks of the Moselle River on the border of Germany and Luxembourg. It boasted of the fact that its history went back to the days before the birth of Christ, and it claimed to be one of the oldest, if not the oldest city north of the Alps. The emperor Caesar Augustus had founded the city in 15 B.C. and had made it an important city in an ocean of barbarians.

The city had the distinction of being briefly the home of the great church father Athanasius when, because of his uncompromising defense of the truth of Christ's divinity, he had been banished from his church in Alexandria in Egypt. That was back in the first half of the fourth century.

The prominence of Trier in the Middle Ages was due in large measure to the fact that the cathedral in the city claimed to have in its possession the seamless robe of Christ over which the soldiers gambled at the cross. (This robe is still put on public display at twenty-five-year intervals, and hundreds of thousands crowd the city to look at it.) Further, the abbey church in the city claimed to be the burial place of the apostle Matthew, the only apostle, so tradition said, to be buried north of the Alps.

Olevianus was born of Gerhard von der Olewig and Anna Sinzig. The name "Olewig," which means "olive," actually refers to a part of the city, perhaps even a small village annexed to the city, known by that name. "Olevianus" is the Latinized form of it.

Caspar's father was a merchant, relatively wealthy, and a prominent citizen of this historic place. He was a baker, a president of the Bakers' Guild, a member of the city council, and treasurer of the city. He followed a family tradition of service to the city, for Caspar's

grandfather was president of the Butchers' Guild and also a member of the council. These positions in the city were important, for Trier, because of its ancient and illustrious past, was a "free" city in Germany.

Caspar's mother was a pious and godly woman who exerted great influence on her family and son. It is striking, if I may make here a somewhat parenthetical remark, that so many of those men who occupied places of great importance in the cause of God and of His church had very godly and pious mothers. It is a fact of history that ought to give all covenant mothers pause: they never know what the effect of their piety and humble service of God will be upon their children and how God will use their godliness for His cause.

Trier was a Roman Catholic city. It remained such even though the Lutheran Reformation spread through much of Germany. It remained immune to Lutheran teachings. Caspar was brought up, therefore, in a Roman Catholic home and was taught in a Roman Catholic school in Trier the first fourteen years of his life.

Offsetting this Roman Catholic influence was one incident which made a deep impression on Caspar during these years, an incident of which he himself later spoke. While Caspar was at school, an aged but kindly and saintly priest planted a seed in his heart which was eventually to bear fruit. It was nothing more than a remark which the old priest made to him in the corridors of the school. Recognizing the abilities of the young boy, the priest put his arm over Caspar's shoulder and said to him, "Never forget that salvation and comfort are to be found only in Christ's perfect work." Again and again, through those dark and dreary centuries when Roman Catholicism held sway over the minds and consciences of men, we find isolated individuals who, in spite of Rome's denial of Christ's perfect sacrifice for sin, held to the truth that all our salvation is only in Christ. It must have been these lonely and scattered men who enabled the church of Christ to stay alive during those perilous times.

In 1550, at the age of fourteen, Caspar completed his studies in Trier. His grandfather stepped in and offered to support Caspar's further education in France provided he would study law. This was somewhat strange, for Trier had its own university; it becomes a bit understandable when we remember that Trier was solidly Roman Catholic, and its schools were steadily losing students while the universities of other parts of Europe were becoming very popular because of openness to Renaissance and Reformation teachings.

It was in France that Caspar's life took an extraordinary turn.

## Conversion and Early Work

The years Olevianus spent in France were profitable, if for no other reason than that they led to his conversion to the Reformed faith.

Caspar attended the universities of Paris, Orlèans, and Bourges, the same universities in which Calvin had received his training. Although he studied law, he came under the influence of leading thinkers in the universities who were more or less committed to Lutheranism; more importantly, he came under the influence of Huguenot teaching. The Huguenots were French Calvinists who had been delivered from Roman Catholicism but who were forced to meet secretly because they were severely persecuted by the king and the church. The shadow of the stake, the hangman's noose, and the sword constantly fell upon them and their families. Not only did Caspar come in contact with them, but he became persuaded of their position and even attended their secret meetings.

Especially one experience changed his life. While walking with a friend, a prince from Germany, along the river which ran by Bourges, Caspar and this friend were invited to cross the river in a boat in which were other students. Caspar refused because the students in the boat were drunk, but his friend took up the offer. In midstream the students began rocking the boat, and it overturned. Caspar dived into the water to save his friend but was unable to do so because of the swift current. He was himself in danger of drowning. At that crucial point, Caspar promised that if God would spare his life, he would preach the gospel in Trier. His friend's valet, mistaking Caspar for his master, hauled Caspar from the water, while the friend drowned. Although Caspar continued his studies in law, that promise made in the cold waters of the river Auron was not forgotten.

After completing his studies in France, Olevianus returned to Trier, not yet to preach (he was untrained for this), but to practice law. His promise, however, sat heavily upon his soul, and he found no satisfaction in the legal niceties of a sixteenth century law practice. In disgust and restlessness, Caspar traveled to Geneva for the express purpose of talking with Calvin.

The two years Olevianus spent in Switzerland were important ones. He not only met with and talked to Calvin, but he also had opportunity to spend many hours with Theodore Beza, Henry Bullinger, Peter Martyr, William Farel, and Peter Viret, all luminous stars in the Reformation heavens. The years were not spent, though, in idle chatter; he studied in Geneva under Calvin, learned Hebrew, mastered theology, was instructed in the art of preaching, and prepared himself for the ministry.

It must have been good instruction which he received in preaching because, along with the development of his native gifts, this instruction made Olevianus one of the outstanding and most eloquent preachers of the times—and the times were blessed with many gifted preachers!

The year 1559 was an important one in the history of the Reformation. During this year French Protestants held their first synod in Paris; John Knox returned to Scotland to establish the Presbyterian Church there; William the Silent made his vow to drive "the Spanish vermin" from the Netherlands; Elector Frederick III, the Pious, began his reign in Heidelberg; and Calvin opened his academy in Geneva and published the last edition of his *Institutes*.

In June of this important year, at the urging of Farel—that firebrand of a reformer who had been instrumental in keeping Calvin in Geneva—Olevianus returned to Trier.

## Work in Trier

Trier was still a Roman Catholic city, and Olevianus' presence as a minister of the truth of the Calvin Reformation would not have gone over very well there. But two influential men in the city, Otto Seele and Peter Sierk, were known in Geneva to have some Calvinistic leanings. To them Calvin wrote to try to encourage them to work towards reformation, and especially to bring Caspar Olevianus to Trier to help them.

It seems as if Caspar went to Trier without revealing his position on reformational matters. For the time being he must have concealed his true purposes. Because of the reputation of his parents and grandparents, he had no difficulty obtaining an appointment to teach philosophy in the school in solidly Roman Catholic Trier. He chose to teach Melanchthon's dialectics. The instruction was in Latin, and dialectics was rather boring to any but the most ardent students; therefore, Olevianus could be of little influence. In a sense he was flying under false colors, eager to keep a vow he had made long before, but hiding in a philosophy class in a dying school.

Because few people in Trier could understand Latin (even most of the students were not very proficient in the language), Olevianus

could scarcely be an effective teacher of the truths he had learned to love.

In his discomfort over his vow that he would preach, and determined to reach the common people, Olevianus decided to hold a public lecture in German, the language of the people. The lecture was announced. A large crowd assembled. The success of the lecture was the beginning of a series of lectures in the German tongue, which became expositions of a Reformation catechism.

Because the people received what he had to say eagerly, and because the crowds continued to grow, Olevianus asked permission of the council to preach to the people, which permission was reluctantly given. He chose for this sermon the subject of justification by faith, which he ably set forth in a crowded room, and which became an occasion for him to attack various Romish practices. At last he was beginning to keep the vow he had made to God in the river of Bourges.

Although the town clerk supported this public proclamation of the gospel, Olevianus was brought before the city council, which was less receptive to the idea. Somewhat reluctantly, but probably because the city council did not really understand what was at stake, the men of the council voted to permit him to preach.

The crowds grew rapidly and soon a Protestant and Calvinistic congregation was organized. But Archbishop John, a cleric in the church of Rome as well as elector of that region, heard reports of what was going on. He knew the significance of it, and soon, marching with a number of soldiers to the gates of the city, he demanded that such "nonsense" stop. When the city refused to open the gates to him, he took up headquarters near the city and began to harass the citizens by taking away their status as a free city, burning their crops, seizing and attacking citizens as they traveled to and from the city, threatening the city with many fierce threats, cutting off their water supply, preventing supplies of food from entering the city, and summoning more soldiers to make a determined march on the city.

Finally John attacked the city, threw Olevianus into jail, banished all who upheld Protestant practices, and restored Roman Catholicism. It was a total triumph for Rome. To add insult to injury, the archbishop instituted an annual "Olevian Procession" to celebrate the punishment of this man of God. It was nearly 250 years before any worship services other than Romish were held there again.

Olevianus was held in prison for ten weeks and was finally released only at the insistence of the elector Frederick the Pious, who paid an enormous ransom for the release. Olevianus never again returned to the city of his birth.

He had thought (and promised) to preach the gospel in Trier. He kept his promise, though only for a short time; God had need of him elsewhere. The year was 1560. Olevianus was only twenty-four years old.

## Work in Heidelberg

Although Olevianus had many offers to work elsewhere, he chose to go to Heidelberg at the invitation of Frederick. In Heidelberg he became leader and director at the college. There he completed his doctoral studies in theology and was appointed to the chair of dogmatics. For use in his lectures, he made a summary of Calvin's *Institutes,* which book was the major textbook in the class.

The abilities of Olevianus were not, however, primarily the gifts of a professor; he was above all a preacher. And so, when Zacharias Ursinus came to the university, Olevianus moved out of the chair of dogmatics to make room for Ursinus, and Olevianus became chief pastor in St. Peter's Church and later in the Church of the Holy Spirit. Here, on the pulpit, expounding God's Word, he felt at home. Here God used his gifts to the advantage of the church.

So it was that both a professor gifted in theology and a preacher, eloquent and faithful in the pulpit, were under God's providence chosen to write the Heidelberg Catechism. Ursinus was twenty-eight years old; Olevianus was twenty-six. It is hard to believe that they were so young. The Catechism gives evidence of authorship by spiritually and theologically mature men. And so they were. Maturity before their thirties—that was the measure of their God-given abilities.

The Catechism is a teacher's book and a preacher's book. It is a systematically arranged treatise covering the whole of the Christian faith; but it is not the doctrine of the classroom or lecture hall; it is the doctrine of the pulpit and the faith of the people of God. The systematic theology of the creed reflects the gifts of Ursinus; the passionately pastoral approach of the application of comfort to doctrine is the delicate touch of the preacher.

Olevianus' work on the Catechism was by no means all he did in Heidelberg. His congregational responsibilities were enough to keep him busy, but he was also deeply involved in continuing reform in the Palatinate. He was instrumental in bringing into the Palatinate hundreds of Reformed teachers to teach in the schools and preachers to preach in the pulpits. He was deeply involved in the defense of the Reformed faith over against Lutheran and Roman Catholic attacks. He was especially instrumental in solidifying genuine biblical church government in the Palatinate, although not without a bitter battle with those who wanted the state to rule the church.

### The Last Years

Even such good things as Olevianus' work in Heidelberg had to come to an end.

There are so many things in God's eternal purpose that seem all wrong to us. Just at that point when so many battles seemed to be won and when Heidelberg was becoming a center for Reformational studies, God stopped it all.

The cruelty which Ursinus suffered came also to Olevianus. Ludwig came to the throne. The pulpits and schools were the first objects of Ludwig's attacks. Olevianus was fired from his post and put under house arrest. When this arrest was lifted, it was only to banish from the entire Palatinate anyone who breathed a Reformed word. Over 600 preachers and teachers, including Olevianus, fled, and the Calvin Reformation came to an abrupt halt.

Olevianus went for a short time to a castle of a friend in central Germany to tutor his son and help in the reformation work which was being done in that area. After his expulsion from Heidelberg, he went to Herborn, another city in Germany, as the chief preacher of the church there and as promoter of the Reformation. The result was that, although Lutheranism was the dominant faith in Germany, there were various places where Calvinism flourished and a Reformed church grew strong.

In the same year that Olevianus came to Herborn he started a seminary, more properly an academy, for the school taught also the subjects which were necessary for pre-theological studies. Olevianus once again occupied the chair of dogmatics. Under his labors and leadership the seminary expanded and grew with incredible speed. A year after it had been started, the famed Piscator came to the school along with twelve other teachers of prominence in the Reformed movement. The student body was a cross-section of Europe's Calvinists.

But we near the end of the story.

Though only fifty-one, Olevianus was worn with labor and toil in the cause of the gospel. As he lay dying, he confessed, "I have only learned to know in this sickness what sin is, and how great is the majesty of God." He spoke of a dream he had had: "Yesterday I was filled for more than an hour with unspeakable joy. It appeared to me that I was walking in a meadow resplendent with light, and while I was moving about, heavenly dew fell on me, not in drops but in streams. Both my body and soul were filled with exceeding great joy." Hearing this confession, Piscator said, "So the good Shepherd has led you into His green pastures." Olevianus replied, "Yes, he has led me to the fountain of living water." Olevianus requested that Psalm 42 and Isaiah 53 be read to him. He asked that those at his bedside sing a Reformation hymn, and he joined with them in a weak voice. He died shortly after telling those around him, "I would no longer postpone my journey to the Lord. I desire to depart and be with Christ." He said his farewells to his wife, his aged mother, his children, and his friends, taking the time to bless each of them. And so, living and dying in that "only comfort in life and in death," he went to be with the Lord.

Olevianus' power was in his preaching. Nevertheless, one more accomplishment, and that in the field of theology, must be mentioned. He wrote a book, undoubtedly the best of all his writings, entitled *The Covenant of Grace*. What is so striking about this book is that although Olevianus often spoke of the covenant as a pact or an agreement (an idea in keeping with his times), he also, amazingly, spoke of the covenant as a bond of friendship and fellowship, an idea which was not to be fully developed in all its beauty until the theology of Herman Hoeksema in the twentieth century.

Such is a measure of the stature of this eminent man of God through whose hands God gave us the Heidelberg Catechism. No wonder that in that very Catechism should appear a profoundly covenantal truth: "Are infants also to be baptized? Yes: for since they, as well as the adult, are included in the covenant and church of God; and since redemption from sin by the blood of Christ, and the Holy Ghost, the author of faith, is promised to them no less than to the adult; they must therefore by baptism, as a sign of the covenant, be also admitted into the Christian church..." (Q & A 74).

Chapter 30

# Guido de Brès
## Author of the Belgic Confession

**Introduction**

*Part of the power and enduring value of our confessions is the fact that they arose out of the life of the church. They were not drawn up by men sitting in ivory towers, contemplating the truth of Scripture, far removed from the battle for the faith. They breathe the life of the church's struggles.*

*The Heidelberg Catechism was written in the struggles between Calvinism on the one hand and*

Lutheranism and Romanism on the other hand, as these struggles were bitterly fought out in Frederick's Palatinate. The Canons of Dordt arose out of the fierce battle with Arminianism, which all but engulfed the churches in the Netherlands in the first part of the seventeenth century. The Confession of Faith (sometimes called the Belgic or Netherlands Confession) was written during and reflects the bitter persecution of the saints in the Lowlands in the early years of the Reformation.

It is the Christian life in the midst of this persecution that gives to the Confession of Faith its moving power. The affirmations of the Confession ("We all believe..."; "We confess..."; "We believe and profess...") take on new meaning when we understand that they are shouts that arise from scaffolds, burning piles of tinder, dark prison cells, and cruel torture chambers.

Its author, Guido de Brès, died on the scaffold for his faith. To his story we now turn.

### Early Life and Conversion

Guido de Brès was born in Mons in 1522, the fourth child of a family of glass painters. In Mons the art of glass painting had been highly developed, and Mons deservedly had an international reputation for the skill of its artists. Guido himself was trained for this work.

Guido's family carried on the traditions of the guilds in Mons. But the children were split regarding Reformation doctrine. John, the oldest, while remaining Roman Catholic all his life, helped Protestants in times of persecution. Christophe was a seller of glassware but also spent his entire life distributing Bibles and Protestant literature, often at great risk to his life. Jerome became a cloth dyer and remained within the Romish church. Marlette, the only girl, married a Protestant in Valenciennes and, with her husband, was deeply involved in Protestant affairs.

The city of Mons was on the border of France and that part of the Lowlands which is now Belgium. Here Lutheranism had first come and had been eagerly studied by the citizens, but the Huguenots from France soon followed with the purer doctrines of John Calvin.

Guido, already in his teens, heard these Reformation truths and could not help but listen to the stories of those who, already then, were being killed for the sake of the gospel. He was only fourteen when the news reached him of Tyndale's cruel martyrdom. It may have been Tyndale's willingness to die for the sake of translating the Bible into the language of the people that led Guido to study the Scriptures. But it was through this study that God led him to true faith in Jesus Christ.

Guido decided, perhaps because of persecution in the Lowlands, to go to London and join a refugee church in East London, a haven for refugees from many different countries in Europe who had been forced to flee because of persecution. In that part of London could also be found a Walloon congregation, composed of French-speaking citizens of the Lowlands, to which Guido joined himself. The refugees had peace in England because of the benign rule of young Edward VI, who favored Protestantism. Here Guido studied for the ministry and listened to the powerful preaching of the great reformers á Lasco and Martin Bucer.

## *Work in the Lowlands*

Guido's love was for his native land, however, and in 1552, at the age of thirty, he returned as an evangelist and traveling preacher. From that moment on, his life was in almost constant danger.

His first field of labor was the city of Lille, in which a large, secret Protestant community had been established under the name "the Church of the Rose." From Lille he went to Ghent, where he published a tract entitled "Le Baton de la Foi" (The Staff of the Faith), a stirring defense of the Reformed faith.

Guido enjoyed a brief interlude at this time. Traveling to Frankfurt in Germany, he met Calvin and was persuaded to come to Geneva. In the three years he spent in Geneva, Guido learned the Reformed faith more perfectly, mastered Greek and Hebrew under Beza and Calvin, and more fully equipped himself for the gospel ministry. During this period he also married Catherine Ramon and with her had four or five children.

While Guido was in Geneva, Charles V retired, weary and careworn, to a monastery in Spain. His cruel son Philip II came to the throne. Philip was determined to stamp out all "heresy," especially in the Lowlands. Therefore, while up to this time persecution had been sporadic and relatively light, it now became more severe and bitter.

After returning again to the Lowlands, de Brès was forced to travel in disguise and under the pseudonym of Jerome. Although the cities in southern Belgium and northern France (Lille, Antwerp, Mons) were the area of his labor, his headquarters was in Doornik, where he ministered to the congregation which had chosen as its name "the Church of the Palm." Here two ministers had been burned at the stake for their faith; here the congregation knew de Brès only as "Jerome"; here the meetings of the congregation were always held in secret and at night, with small groups of not more than twelve attending at one time. In spite of the problems which the congregation faced, de Brès organized the church with elders and deacons and faithfully administered the sacraments.

Even this situation did not remain, for a more radical group of the believers, under the leadership of Robert du Four, thought it cowardly and unfaithful to Christ to keep their faith secret. The group, several hundred strong, moved in public procession through the city, singing Psalms in open defiance of the authorities. The next night (September 30, 1561) 500 Protestants gathered for the same purpose. The result was that Roman Catholic investigators were sent with orders to suppress Protestantism in the city. Although Guido managed to hide until December and flee in safety, all the information of the secret congregation was discovered, Guido's true identity was found out, and the people of the church were forced to flee or be killed. Guido's rooms were ransacked, and his papers (including letters from Calvin) were burned. Guido was hanged in effigy.

Guido concentrated his work for several years after that in northern France, perhaps some of the quietest years of his ministerial career. Although elsewhere in France persecution raged against the Huguenots, in Guido's area the church had peace. He worked in Amiens, Montdidier, Dieppe, and Sedan, building up the congregations and preaching the gospel faithfully.

Still Guido could not refrain from making periodic trips into his own country, a "lion's den" of danger. He traveled three times to his old congregation in Doornik, once to Brussels to meet with William of Orange concerning matters of union between Calvinists and Lutherans, and once to a secret synod of the Reformed churches held in Antwerp (the password for entry was "vineyard") where de Brès' Confession was adopted as the official confession of the Reformed churches.

In 1566, de Brès went to Valenciennes to become a preacher in the church there, a congregation which called itself the Church of the Eagle. While the Protestant faith grew so rapidly that the Roman Catholic authorities dared not interfere in the religion of God's people, certain radical elements once again stepped forward and created trouble. Stirring up large mobs, they went through all the cathedrals, smashing and burning, destroying anything that in the least smelled like popery. Philip II, infuriated at this, sent troops to lay siege to the city, which surrendered on Palm Sunday, 1567. Although de Brès escaped with four companions, he was soon captured and imprisoned.

### *His Martyrdom and Importance*

de Brès spent the first part of his captivity in a prison in Doornik, where he could receive visitors. Many of his visitors, however, were enemies who came to taunt him. Just as was the case with the apostle Paul (Phil. 1:12–14), Guido's imprisonment became an occasion for him to witness to the truth. When a princess, along with many young court ladies, came to mock, and the princess said in horror at Guido's heavy chains, "My God, Mr. de Brès, I don't see how you can eat, drink, or sleep that way. I think I would die of fear, if I were in your place." Guido responded, "My lady, the good cause for which I suffer and the good conscience God has given me make my bread sweeter and my sleep sounder than those of my persecutors." Then, still responding to the princess, he added, "It is guilt that makes a chain heavy. Innocence makes my chains light. I glory in them as my badges of honor."

Soon Guido was transferred to Valenciennes and thrown into a dark, cold, damp, rat-infested dungeon known as the Black Hole. In spite of the cold, the hunger, and the horror of this hole, he wrote a tract on the Lord's Supper and letters to his friends, his aged mother, and his wife. The following letter to his wife is an especially moving testimony of his faith.

> My dear and well-beloved wife in our Lord Jesus,
>     Your grief and anguish are the cause of my writing you this letter. I most earnestly pray you not to be grieved beyond measure...We knew when we married that we might not have many years together, and the Lord has graciously given us seven. If the Lord had wished us to live together longer, he could easily have caused it to be so. But such was not his pleasure. Let his good will be done...Moreover, consider that I have not fallen into the hands of my enemies by chance, but by the providence of God...All these considerations have made my heart glad and peaceful, and I pray you, my dear and faithful companion, to be glad with me, and to thank the good God for what he is doing, for he does nothing but what is altogether good and right...I pray you then to be comforted in the Lord, to commit yourself and your affairs to him, he is the husband of the widow and the father of the fatherless, and he will never leave nor forsake you...
>     Good-bye, Catherine, my well-beloved! I pray my God to comfort you, and give you resignation to his holy will.
>                                     Your faithful husband, Guido de Brès.

Guido was publicly hanged May 31, 1567, at the age of forty-seven. He was pushed off the ladder while comforting the crowd which had gathered, urging them to faithfulness to the Scriptures. His body was left hanging the rest of the day and buried in a shallow grave where dogs and wild animals dug it up and consumed it.

Guido de Brès was the primary author of the Confession of Faith. He was assisted by Adrien de Saravia (professor of theology in Leyden), H. Modetus (chaplain of William of Orange), and G. Wingen. The Confession was written in the vain hope that it would persuade the cruel Philip II to see that the views of the Calvinists were truly biblical and to stop persecution against them. Roman Catholics had lumped the Calvinists with the radical and wild-eyed Anabaptists who rejected the authority of magistrates, and the Confession sets the Reformed faith over against Anabaptism.

The Confession was thrown over the wall in Doornik and ultimately did reach the king, but it served only to arouse Philip to greater fury against the saints of God.

In a letter which was added to the Confession, Guido and his co-workers protested being called rebels. They solemnly averred that though they numbered over 100,000 and were cruelly oppressed by "excommunications, imprisonments, banishments, racks, and tortures, and other numberless oppressions which they had undergone," they obeyed their government in all things lawful, and that "having the fear of God before their eyes, and being terrified by the threatening of Christ, who had declared in the Gospel that he would deny them before God the Father, in case they denied him before men, they therefore offered their backs to stripes, their tongues to knives, their mouths to gags, and their whole bodies to the fire."

From this spilled blood God caused to emerge a Confession of Faith which has held a special place in the hearts of Reformed believers. It is as if, knowing that the confession was written in blood, the saints receive it as a sacred trust, precious and vibrating yet with the faith of their fathers.

Our fathers both knew what they believed and were faithful to it, even to death. We have received, by the Spirit of truth, the glorious fruit which God worked through them. It is entrusted to our care that we may be faithful to it and teach it to our children.

We ought earnestly to pray that we may know the faith as they did, and that we may be faithful to it as they were, for persecution shall soon also be our lot.

Chapter 31

# Peter Datheen

## Father of Reformed Liturgy

*Introduction*
*I have given this chapter the title "Peter Datheen: Father of Reformed Liturgy." This does not mean that Peter Datheen made contributions to the Reformation in the Netherlands only in the area of liturgy; he was a leading figure in the work of God in the Lowlands, some say the most influential of all from an ecclesiastical point of view. One of the earliest preachers of the Reformed faith, he was bold and*

brave in the face of persecution. He was a fugitive from persecution more times than one would care to count. Above all, he placed an indelible stamp on the liturgy of the Reformed churches, a stamp which remains to this day. Hence the title.

Being a fugitive and exile was so much Datheen's life that one biographer, B.J.W. DeGraaff, has given his book on Datheen, with an obvious allusion to Psalm 42, the title *Als Een Hert Gejaeght* (Hunted as a Hart). The old spelling of the last Dutch word in the title is due to the fact that it is taken from the Dutch versification of Psalm 42 as composed by Datheen.

Datheen's work was done within the context of the early years of the Reformation in the Netherlands, and it is impossible to understand his work without understanding the suffering of those saints. We shall, therefore, first describe that early Reformation.

## Reformation in the Netherlands

### The Work of Reformation

The area that is now the country of the Netherlands was part of a larger area known as "the Lowlands" at the time of the Reformation. The Lowlands comprised approximately what is now the Netherlands, Belgium, Luxembourg, and part of northern France. It was technically a part of the Holy Roman Empire over which Charles V ruled, a kingdom made up of Spain, Germany, the Lowlands, and Italy. This Charles V was the same Charles before whom Luther made his stirring defense at Worms.

People of the Lowlands were much more independent than those in other parts of Charles' domain. They had been, from the time when the people were still barbarian, a freedom-loving people who fought tenaciously for their personal rights and were ready to make huge sacrifices to protect themselves from outside interference. The Lowlands were composed of seventeen provinces, each of which was ruled by a prince, but the whole constituted a rather loose federation. They were also extremely prosperous and poured much money into Charles' coffers. Industry, trade, commerce, shipping, and agriculture all flourished. Europe's goods passed through the Lowlands on their way to the sea and to foreign ports. Ships daily docked in the harbors and unloaded their treasures from distant countries. All these things were facts which Charles kept in mind when he allowed the Lowlanders a great deal of autonomy.

Many "Protestant" influences were present in the Lowlands long before the Reformation proper started. Fugitive Waldensians had found a home there; Lollards (followers of John Wycliffe in England) had come across the channel from time to time to escape persecution in their homeland; and some of the better mystics, such as the Brethren of the Common Life, had settled at the mouth of the Rhine River which emptied into the North Sea near the province of Zeeland. The Latin Vulgate had been translated into the vernacular so that many people possessed a Bible in their own tongue.

Earliest Reformation influences were Lutheran. Lutheran teachings had been widely circulated, and Lutheran writings were openly peddled and sold in the markets of the cities. Some of the provincial rulers adopted Lutheran teachings and urged their people to become Lutheran. In 1522, five years after the Reformation began, Luther's Bible was printed and a Dutch translation of it prepared.

Some less than favorable influences were also present. Zwinglianism could be found, especially in East Friesland, and the Anabaptists, persecuted elsewhere in Europe, settled in the Lowlands and found a haven of safety. Many of these were the more radical Anabaptists who rebelled against constituted authority, attempted to set up their own kingdom, and caused true Protestantism no end of grief, for the Roman Catholics were delighted to lump Anabaptists with other reformers.

## The Spread of Calvinism

Calvinism actually came rather late to the Lowlands. Around 1535 it first appeared in the French-speaking Walloon provinces and gradually spread northward. Its spread was aided by converted Anabaptists who had been instructed in Strassburg by Martin Bucer, Capito, and Calvin. It was not long before Calvinism swept all other influences aside. Anabaptism, Lutheranism, and much of mysticism gave way before the rapid spread of what was to become in these Lowlands the Reformed faith.

God used many different means to promote the Reformed faith. In 1561 Guido de Brès published that magnificent creed, the Confession of Faith, in the Lowlands, a confession quickly adopted by the churches. In 1563 the Heidelberg Catechism was written, and within a couple of years of its publication was translated into Dutch. The Convention of Wezel began the work which was later to become the Church Order. The first Reformed synod in the Netherlands met in Emden in 1571 and the second synod in Dordrecht in 1578.

## Persecution in the Lowlands

The Reformed faith was not established without suffering. The persecution in the Lowlands was some of the worst the church had ever experienced. While it is impossible to determine accurately how many people of God were killed, the conservative estimates run as high as 100,000, while others claim that as many as 200,000 were killed. From 1523 to 1573, a period of only 50 years, more Protestants were killed than in all the years when the Roman Empire engaged in persecution. From Nero's first persecutions in the middle of the first century to the reign of Constantine the Great, when persecution ceased in 312 (a period of over 250 years), fewer of God's people suffered martyrdom at the hands of that pagan world power than in the Lowlands when God's people were butchered by the Roman Catholic Church. Rome has never expressed one single word of regret! Our fathers sealed their faith with their lives and gave to us a heritage of the truth written in blood. How much the more ought we to treasure it!

Although Charles V issued an order in 1521 that all heresy should be extinguished in the Lowlands, the persecution did not begin until 1523 when two Augustinian monks were burned at the stake in Brussels for Lutheran tendencies. While the fire was burning, the two recited together the Apostles' Creed and sang the "Te Deum Laudamus" (We Praise Thee, O God). Their suffering moved Luther to write a hymn, one stanza of which is:

> Quiet their ashes will not lie:
> But scattered far and near,
> Stream, dungeon, bolt, and grave defy,
> Their foeman's shame and fear.
> Those whom alive the tyrant's wrongs
> To silence could subdue,
> He must, when dead, let sing the songs
> Which in all languages and tongues,
> Resound the wide world through.

Persecution remained somewhat sporadic, however, and so Charles, expressing a deep regret that he had not burned Luther at Worms, ordered that the dreaded Inquisition be used as an instrument of persecution in the Lowlands. That awful Inquisition, which used the foulest means, trampled under foot every principle of justice, made use of the most exquisite tortures, and was answerable to no one, became the instrument for the suppression of heresy. Within Charles' lifetime, almost 50,000 were killed.

But the worst was yet to come.

Charles, weary of ruling, plagued by gout, and perhaps burdened in conscience, retired to a monkery, and the rule passed to his son, the cruel Philip II. Under Margaret of Parma, sister of Philip II, who was made regent in the Lowlands, Philip attempted ruthlessly to exterminate all heresy from that part of his domain by ordering that no books by Protestant authors be printed, sold, or read; that no images in Roman Catholic Churches be destroyed; that no meetings of Protestants be held; that no reading of Scripture take place anywhere; and that no discussion of disputed points of doctrine be allowed. Violators who recanted and confessed their disobedience to Rome were to be killed anyway: men were to be beheaded, women buried alive. If Protestants refused to recant, they were to be burned alive. All their property was to be confiscated, and large rewards from the proceeds of the property were to be given to informers.

It was a time of terrible cruelty and suffering. Because many noble and courageous Protestants made good confessions to the assembled crowds while the fires were burning their flesh, the Inquisition ordered that their tongues be screwed with metal screws to their jaw bones and the whole cauterized with a hot iron so that the swelling would make it impossible for them to speak. The persecution became all but unbearable: towns were emptied, factories were idled, market places were without buyers or sellers, homes were dark—almost all life came to a stop.

The stories of the courage and steadfastness of God's people under the tortures of apostate Rome bring tears to the eyes. One can read of them in Wylie's extremely worthwhile work, *The History of Protestantism*.

Under these conditions, the princes of the Lowlands and the burghers of various cities joined together in a pledge to withstand and resist all tyranny. It became known as the Compromise of 1566. It was the beginning of national and political resistance to Spanish rule.

## Survival of the Reformed Church

It is difficult to imagine life during such horrible times of persecution, but the fact is that, as has been true throughout the ages, God used persecution to advance His cause. "The blood of the martyrs," Tertullian had said more than a millennium earlier, "is the seed of the church."

So powerfully did the Reformed faith spread throughout all the Lowlands that the people were on the very verge of overt rebellion. So serious was the situation that even Philip II had to take notice. Persecution eased somewhat.

One factor in the sturdy faithfulness of the people was the growing practice of field preaching. "Field preachers," with their pulpits strapped to their backs, wandered the land and preached to the people in every place possible—in empty buildings, open fields, market places, deep forests. Most of the time the services were held in secret, with guards posted at crucial junctures to give warning in the event Spanish troops were spotted. Sometimes meetings were discovered and cruelly broken up. On occasion they were held in peace. A description of one such meeting will help us to appreciate them.

> Citizens and strangers now poured out in one vast stream, and took the road to Overeen [the place where services were to be held]. Last of all arrived Peter Gabriel the minister. Two stakes were driven perpendicularly into the ground,

and a bar was laid across, on which the minister might place his Bible, and rest his arms in speaking. Around this rude pulpit were gathered first the women, then the men, next those who had arms, forming an outer ring of defence, which however was scarcely needed, for there was then no force in Holland that would have dared to attack this multitude. The worship was commenced with the singing of a psalm. First were heard the clear soft notes of the females at the centre; next the men struck in with their deeper voices; last of all the martial forms in the outer circle joined the symphony, and gave completeness and strength to the music. When the Psalm was ended, prayer was offered, and the thrilling peals that a moment before had filled the vault overhead were now exchanged for a silence yet more thrilling. The minister, opening the Bible, next read out as his text the 8th, 9th, and 10th verses of the second chapter of the Epistle to the Ephesians: "For by grace are ye saved through faith; and that not of yourselves: it is the gift of God. Not of works lest any man should boast. For we are his workmanship, created in Christ Jesus unto good works, which God hath before ordained that we should walk in them." Here in a few verses, said the minister, was the essence of the whole Bible— the "marrow" of all true theology:—"the gift of God," salvation; its source, "the grace of God;" the way in which it is received, "through faith;" and the fruits ordained to follow, "good works."

It was a hot midsummer day; the audience was not fewer than 5,000; the preacher was weak and infirm in body, but his spirit was strong, and the lightning-power of his words held his audience captive. The sermon, which was commenced soon after noon, did not terminate till past four o'clock. Then again came prayer. The preacher made supplication "for all degrees of men, especially for the Government, in such a manner that there was hardly a dry eye to be seen." The worship was closed as it had been commenced, with the melodious thunder of 5,000 voices raised in praise.

The slight surcease of persecution did not last long. Philip's lying promises betrayed the people, for while promising delegates from the Lowlands some surcease from persecution, he secretly plotted to increase its intensity. The iconoclastic riots brought persecution with renewed force. They took place throughout most of the Lowlands as the Reformed people, goaded by persecution, took their frustration out on every evidence of Roman Catholicism which they could find: churches, stained-glass windows, images, altars, decorations. Smashing, wrecking, destroying, they laid the interiors of many churches in ruins.

Philip had his excuse. The cruel duke of Alva was appointed to carry out Philip's vengeance. Alva asked for troops. The pope sent 10,000 troops from Italy with instructions to destroy Geneva on the way as a "nest of devils and apostates." Alva did not obey, but marched in speed towards the Lowlands and began to carry out Philip's determination to root Protestantism from the land.

The executioners were busy from dawn till dark. Within three months 1,800 men were hanged. That is 600 a month, 20 a day. They were slaughtered for every conceivable reason, one for saying "We must obey God rather than man." On February 16, 1568, a decree was issued which declared all the inhabitants, with only a few listed exceptions, condemned to death as heretics. Trials were then no longer necessary. The burning, hanging, and torturing went on unabated until Alva himself, sated with blood, frustrated in every effort to wipe out heresy, crept back to Spain a defeated man.

### *Freedom at Last*

Gradually the opposition became more organized. It really began with the "Beggars of the Sea," a rough group of sea captains with their crews and boats, who used their maritime skills and reckless courage to raid Spanish shipping and harass Spanish land forces. Every Reformed school boy who has any love for his heritage should read the exploits of these men.

Briel fell to the "Beggars," and it was with their help that the dreadful siege of Leyden was lifted.

Armed insurrection against Spain now also began to take place under the leadership of William III of Orange (the Silent). Religious and political freedom were so inseparably connected that to strive for the former was to commit oneself to fight for the latter. It was the beginning of the Eighty Years' War between Spain and the Netherlands. The war was undeniably an effort to promote the cause of the truth with the sword, something forbidden by Scripture. It resulted in freedom for the Lowlands but also the establishment of a state church—something which proved to be the Achilles' heel of the church in years to come. As wrong as the use of the sword may seem to us, we must at least have the sympathy to understand that our fellow saints were driven to distraction as their families were tortured and burned, their homes confiscated, their brethren murdered, their friends, male and female, subjected to the cruelest tortures devised by the sadistic and cunning mind of men—men of the church!

Freedom came gradually. Not many major battles were fought; the ones that were, usually ended in the defeat of the Protestants. Not much of the time was spent in actual military maneuvers and attempts to defeat opposing forces. The chief problem was that William was unable to hold together an army of sufficient strength to have any hope of defeating Spanish forces.

Although the Eighty Years' War did not officially end until the Peace of Westphalia in 1648, a combination of forces gradually brought peace. Spain gradually lost heart when all her efforts to destroy the Reformed faith proved futile. This loss of heart was hastened by the gradual weakening of Spain as a military power in Europe. Her navy was gradually destroyed by the might of Holland and Britain. Her mighty armada was wrecked by fierce storms off the coasts of Britain, Scotland, and Ireland. Her armies were no longer feared throughout Europe.

In addition to these factors was also the growing movement of toleration in Europe. Religious wars had destroyed Germany as well as the Lowlands, and men began to see that if they did not learn to tolerate opposing viewpoints, they would follow a path which could lead only to continental suicide.

Finally the Lowlands settled the problems by some sort of division. Gradually Roman Catholics drifted into the south, where Spain was strongest; and Protestants drifted north, where the Reformed faith was strongest. Two countries emerged: Belgium, which to this day remains strongly Roman Catholic; and the Netherlands, the cradle of the Reformed faith.

Hardly had the Reformed faith been established in peace in the Netherlands than the country was once again in danger of being torn to pieces by the Arminian controversy.

That story will be taken up in other chapters.

It was into the turmoil of the struggle of the Reformed churches in the Netherlands that Peter Datheen entered.

# Peter Datheen

### *Introduction*

It is a popular pastime nowadays to attempt to find one's roots. No one can deny that this is indeed interesting—to learn of one's ancestors, their struggles and sorrows, their lives and callings. It is a more profitable pastime for people of God, who recognize the truth that God saves His church in the line of generations, to trace their spiritual roots. To know one's family roots can sometimes be embarrassing, for often skeletons are found in unexpected closets. To know one's spiritual roots is of great profit, for these roots are the stories of saints and martyrs who have now joined the company of just men made perfect.

The Reformed churches of the Netherlands were born in fierce persecution. Out of that fierce persecution arose a marvelous creed (our Belgic Confession), a strong, biblical church government which has served the Reformed churches well for over 400 years, and a beautiful liturgy, most of which is still in use today. Much of our liturgy was born out of persecution; it is well that when we use it, we appreciate this fact. Peter Datheen played a role in our confessional heritage, a significant part in our church government heritage, and was no less than the father of our liturgical heritage. He was Holland's greatest reformer.

## *Early Life*

Peter Datheen's early life is so hidden in obscurity that the date of his birth is not known and nothing has come down to us of his parents. He was born sometime during 1531 or 1532 in the town of Cassel, in Flanders, now a part of Belgium. Somehow someone forgot to include in the church records both the date of his birth and the date of his baptism. The records of that time are extant; Datheen's name is not to be found in them.

At an early age, for an unknown reason, Datheen was placed in a Carmelite monastery in Ypres. This, though a seeming tragedy, was part of a remarkable plan of God to prepare Datheen for his work.

Three things happened in this cold monastery.

The Carmelites were a monastic order which specialized in hospitals and healing. Perhaps the most advanced knowledge of illness and medicine could be found among these monks. Datheen received an education in medicine and healing, something which was going to serve him well in the distant future.

Persecution was raging in the Netherlands, and three converted monks were burned near the cloister where Datheen lived. The story of their martyrdom and their heroic confession moved him deeply. He wondered how his church could possibly be the agent of such terrible persecution, and doubts about his church filled his soul.

Within his own cloister many were sympathetic to Reformation teaching, and Datheen learned much Reformation doctrine from those who shared with him the monastic life.

But the cloister at Ypres was not the only hotbed of heresy, according to Roman persecutors; many such monasteries hid those who were persuaded of the biblical truth of Lutheranism and Calvinism. As the reports grew, a systematic search of such cloisters was undertaken, and one by one the monasteries which harbored heresy were dismantled and their inhabitants put to the flames.

When about eighteen or nineteen years old, Datheen fled; it was the beginning of a long life of being a fugitive for the faith. He went to London, where many refugees from the Lowlands had gone to escape the fire and sword of the Romish church.

In London a church had already been formed by merchants from the Lowlands who were in London for business purposes. To this church many joined themselves, among whom was a Polish reformer, one who himself was to leave an unmistakable stamp on the Dutch Reformation, John à Lasco. He had become superintendent of the church.

Peter Datheen secured work as a printer in London and attended the church of refugees. Edward VI, only son of Henry VIII, was on the throne, a staunch though young Protestant who did all he could to promote the Reformation in England. The church of refugees flourished and grew as the number of exiles swelled. At one time the church had no fewer than 4,000 members, the French-speaking people in one group and the Dutch-speaking refugees in another.

It was a church without creed or liturgy, and some of the early work in developing a Reformed liturgy was done in London by à Lasco and Utenhove. Particularly, the Scriptures were translated into the native tongue of the refugees, and a rhymed version of the Psalms was prepared. The government required a specific liturgy, and John à Lasco prepared one along with an order of worship. The beginnings of a church order were also prepared by Martinus Micronius, who wrote his "Christian Ordinances."

The congregation soon recognized that Datheen was a man of unusual ability and of deep conviction with gifts for the ministry. The leaders of the church prevailed upon Datheen to quit his job as printer and give himself over full time to study for the ministry of the gospel. This he did, and in these few years of peace and quiet Datheen was prepared for his life's work.

During this time he also married a former nun by the name of Benedicta, with whom he had one daughter, Christiana.

The peace and quiet of life in London was soon over. Edward died after ruling only a few years, and Henry's cruel and thoroughly

Roman Catholic daughter came to the throne. She has gone down in history as Bloody Mary, for at her hands persecution against Protestants in England broke out.

The church in London was scattered, and many refugees were now forced to flee England. But the work of liturgy and church government went along with the refugees and was transplanted to Frankfurt in Germany.

It is hard for us, who know no such persecution, to appreciate the suffering of these saints. Literally hounded from one country to another, they were hunted like wild dogs. Forced to flee from one place to another with wives and children, leaving behind all they possessed, they were truly pilgrims and strangers in the earth. It was the false church which sought their lives! So it will be when once again the same will be true for us.

### *Ministry in Germany*

Many refugees from England, France, and the Lowlands were now settling in Germany, in various Protestant provinces, in hopes of finding there some relief from suffering. Frankfurt in Germany was such a place. It had been a strongly Lutheran city, but Calvinistic refugees had made it also Reformed. John à Lasco had gone to Frankfurt earlier than Datheen and had begun to organize a Reformed church in that city. Under the leadership of à Lasco, the congregation called Datheen as it pastor. In September of 1555, when Datheen was twenty-three or twenty-four years old, he and his wife settled into the ministry in Frankfurt. He was installed into office by the reformer Micronius and became pastor of this Flemish congregation.

Here his one and only daughter Christiana was born.

This period did not last long, either.

The Lutherans in the city became alarmed at the growing influence of Reformed thought. The radical and fiery Joachim Westphal, with whom Calvin carried on a bitter controversy over the doctrine of the Lord's Supper, incited the Lutheran clergy and people against the Reformed congregation. On April 23, 1561, the magistrates of the city forbade the congregation of refugees to worship according to their convictions. Frederick III (the Pious) made a special plea to the magistrates for toleration, but none was given. The congregation was forced to break up if it refused to become Lutheran. The congregation refused, and again they were forced to flee.

Many returned to England, where Elizabeth now reigned, and under whose rule peace came to the refugees. Others went back to the Netherlands and perished in the flames of the Inquisition. Some went to Frankenthal in the Palatinate where Frederick III ruled. Datheen traveled with this last group.

## Years in the Palatinate

God gave Datheen good years in Frankenthal, years which Datheen did not waste. They were his most productive years as far as his work in liturgy was concerned. What we owe to Datheen today is what he accomplished under the benign hand of the father of the Heidelberg Catechism, Frederick III.

Soon after his arrival in the Palatinate, because of his reputation he was summoned to the court of the prince, where he served as court pastor. During this time he was entrusted with various diplomatic responsibilities and missions. He continued to minister to the needs of the exiles as well. With four other pastors, Datheen engaged in a debate with five Lutheran ministers under the supervision of the elector.

These were busy years, but happy ones. Datheen was full of zeal for the cause of the church; he labored hard for the organization of the church and spent himself in the cause of the gospel.

Above all, Datheen did marvelous work to develop a distinctively Reformed liturgy for the churches in the Lowlands. Aware that persecution was still so severe that a normal life for the church was impossible, he believed that God would send a better day. His faith was expressed in his introduction to a church order he wrote "for the Netherlands Churches, if they should, by the grace of God, arrive at a public and free exercise of their religion."

His heart was really in the Lowlands and with his suffering fellow saints.

## Work in Liturgy

The liturgy, in use in the denomination of which I am a member and until a few years ago used in many Reformed churches, is old. It goes all the way back to the Reformation in the Netherlands.

In many Reformed churches this ancient liturgy has been abandoned. In its place has come a tidal wave of innovations which have so restructured the liturgy that it is no longer recognizable as Reformed. This is a great loss to the church. In the interests of making liturgy appealing and attractive to modern, twentieth-century man, the soul of the liturgy has been cut out, and what is left is meaningless (in some instances, downright wicked) exercises in futility.

All this is not to say that we should never change anything, that tradition is sacred, that what was once done is perfect for all time. No, a Reformed church is indeed a reforming church.

But before a Reformed church makes changes, it ought to be very sure that the changes are improvements, in other words, that they bring worship more closely in conformity with the Word of God, and that they are not merely changes for the sake of change.

The liturgy handed down to us from Reformation times is hard to improve. Before we begin to tamper with it, we ought to spend a bit of time pondering the fact that our liturgy was born out of the fire of persecution; that it was woven into the very warp and woof of the Dutch Reformation in the Netherlands; that for it our forebears bled and died; that it has stood the test of over four centuries; and that it is doubtful, to say the least, that a spiritually wishy-washy age and doctrinally illiterate church are capable of improving it.

At any rate, we owe a debt of gratitude to Peter Datheen, the great reformer of the Netherlands, for this part of our heritage.

It must be understood that none of Datheen's work was wholly original. Already in London, Utenhove and à Lasco had done significant work in liturgy for the refugee congregation there. That work Datheen had taken with him wherever he went. It must also be remembered that the Palatinate, where Datheen did his work, was strongly under the influence of the Calvin Reformation, and that Calvin and his fellow reformers had also done significant and important work in liturgy and church government. To all this, as well as other work, Datheen was heir, but his stamp upon it marks our liturgy in so many ways.

Another contribution Datheen made was to prepare a translation in Dutch of the Heidelberg Catechism, a confession that had been completed in the Palatinate in 1563. From the beginning, Datheen intended it to be used for a confession in the churches of the Lowlands. It was, indeed, soon adopted there. Thus, Datheen was responsible for incorporating that beautiful creed into our creedal heritage.

Datheen's influence was also felt in the area of church government. He used the work of Micronius in London, modifying it in some respects to fit the situation in the Netherlands. Datheen was present at several of the early Dutch synods which began the work of preparing a church order, an order which was put into its present form by the Synod of Dordrecht (Dordt), 1618–19. Datheen presided at the Convention of Wezel (1568); he was also present as a delegate from Ghent and presided at the Synod of Dordt in 1578 which did so much work in the development of the present Church Order.

This is not all. Reformed churches have two of the most beautiful liturgical forms in existence in their "Form for the Administration of Holy Baptism" and their "Form for the Administration of the Lord's Supper." Especially the former is a crown jewel among all liturgical forms in any tradition. Its beauty lies in its pure teachings concerning God's covenant of grace. In its precision, in the rolling cadence of its language, in the soaring beauty of its prose, in the concise statement of its doctrine, it is unexcelled. Both are forms written in large measure by Datheen. The form we use in the Lord's Supper is very much similar to the form prepared by Datheen. The form we use in baptism came also from his hand, although the Synod of Dordt in 1618–19 added the section for the baptism of adults and made some minor changes in it, as well as in all the others. One's memories cannot he restrained from floating back to the horrors of the persecution of our fathers, out of which this liturgy was born, whenever these forms are read.

In singing, it is somewhat different. Our heritage, for the most part, does not go back to Datheen. That is not because Datheen did not do work in this area too. He did sterling work. His gifts were many and great. Although he used tunes from the Genevan Psalter of Louis Bourgeois, and although he relied on the Book of Psalms from the French versions of Beza and Marot, still he prepared a Psalter for the Dutch churches which was so popular that it was used in the churches until 1773, when only relatively minor changes were made in it. That book is still in use in some Dutch churches today. I myself well remember the church during Dutch worship services ringing with those words so loved by Dutch fathers and grandfathers: "Geloofd Zij God met diepst ontzag..." (Ps. 68) or "'t Heigend hert, der jaagt ontkomen..." (Ps. 42). A few of those tunes are left in the back of a Psalter used by my denomination, but this part of church heritage should be included in the liturgy as well, insofar as possible.

Finally, but also importantly, much of the present Order of Worship, though patterned after Calvin's liturgy, was given its present form by Datheen. This is why we have almost the same Order of Worship as is used in the Dutch churches which have not fallen prey to liturgical innovation.

One wonders sometimes what the church would have been like without Datheen. God used him in a marvelous way to give that which has become so precious to us.

## Datheen's Last Years

In a way, Datheen's years in Frankenthal, brief though they were, were the climax of his work. Although he did some important work in the following years, tragedy and great sadness also touched his life. These years are not easy to write about.

In 1566 Datheen returned to the Netherlands. A sort of compromise between the rulers of the Lowlands held forth something of a promise of relief from persecution, and Datheen could not possibly be restrained from returning to his beloved fatherland.

Datheen became a field preacher. Carrying his pulpit on his back, preaching wherever possible, he ministered to throngs of people wherever he went. Sometimes the crowds that flocked to hear him numbered as many as 15,000, for the "Word of God was scarce in those days" (I Sam. 3:1), and the people had a great thirst for the gospel.

Datheen's lack of extensive training made him somewhat crude in his preaching, but his intensity and captivating eloquence revealed his deep love for the Reformed faith. It was his love of the Reformed faith which also got him in trouble.

Datheen hated compromise. He hated compromise with Rome and with Spain. He distrusted the princes' compromise and firmly believed that concessions had been made to Spain which would, in time, destroy the Reformed faith.

And so he preached vehemently and eloquently against such compromises, and he earned the enmity of William of Orange, the leader in the fight against Spain. William of Orange, in fact, was convinced that Datheen was in large measure responsible for the iconoclastic riots in the Lowlands, when frenzied crowds, intolerably oppressed by Rome, vented their fury on the Romish churches. Smashing, destroying, burning wherever they went, they tried to purge the Lowlands once and for all of anything Romish. But their fury only brought against them the princes who sought to suppress the riots, which succeeded in giving Rome the excuse it needed to renew persecution.

Whether Datheen was responsible for the riots is hard to judge. Surely, his refusal to compromise in any way with Rome was contrary to the policy of the princes at this time. His fiery preaching moved the people deeply. But he himself always pleaded innocent to the charges that he had incited the crowds.

The breach between him and William was to remain to the end of his life.

Once again Datheen was forced to flee to the Palatinate. He became minister of a congregation composed of Dutch, French, and Walloon exiles, and later, court preacher for John Casimir.

The rest of the story is quickly told.

In 1578 Datheen served as minister of the congregation in Ghent in his beloved homeland and was a delegate to the Synod of Dordt. During that same year he traveled throughout Holland and preached in many places while the shortage of pastors was acute. But here he was also imprisoned for eight months and finally sent into exile.

Returning to Frankenthal, Datheen resumed a ministry there, but nearly died of the pestilence. He was relieved of his pulpit because he was no longer able to do the work.

Datheen was embittered by his treatment at the hands of William of Orange and by his dismissal in Frankenthal. He became a wanderer and to support himself and his wife, took up the work of a physician, putting into practice skills he had learned as a youth in the cloister. He wandered through Husum, Slade, Danzig, and Elbing in Germany, where his bitterness led him to join, for a short time, a heretical and revolutionary sect. The report of this foolish act came back to the Netherlands, and he was barred from the Dutch churches.

To the credit of these churches, however, they sent a delegation to Datheen. To these brethren, who had come to express the love of the churches and their concern for his soul, Datheen confessed his sin of joining a heretical sect (from which he had already parted before the delegation came), and he was reconciled and restored to the fellowship of the church. However, because of wars in Germany and in his own land, and because of the great infirmities of age and a life of fleeing persecution, he could not return to the church and land he loved. He died an exile on March 17, 1588, far from home, from friends, from church, and from his fatherland.

But it is better to suffer death in the fellowship of the church than to lose that fellowship which is so important to keep us faithful to our God.

Datheen died in peace. Although he could not possibly have known what his work would mean to the church, God knew and knows, and we are blessed by God through this servant who suffered so much.

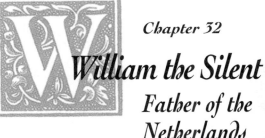

**Chapter 32**

# William the Silent
## Father of the Netherlands

### Introduction

*William of Orange, also known as William the Silent, is to the citizens of the Netherlands what George Washington is to Americans. If anyone at all can claim to be the father of that country, it is William. Yet he is more than father; he is also the savior, under God, of Calvinism in the Lowlands. He occupies a crucial place in Dutch history, and he is honored in the* Dutch national anthem: "Wilhelmus van Nassau; ben ik van Duitschen bloed" (William of Nassau; I am of German blood).

That William could have been both father of his country and savior of Calvinism was due to the close relation between church and state in those times. But it was because God used him to be the savior of Calvinism that he is of interest to us. The Calvinism of Dordt, of the great theologians in Dutch Reformed theology, of the *Afscheiding*, of a robust, Calvinistic church in the Netherlands, and of Reformed churches in America is the fruit of the courageous work of William the Silent.

### Early Life and Youth

William was born in the last half of April, 1533, in Germany—hence the line in the national anthem. His family was of the nobility (of the House of Nassau) and lived in Dillenburg in Nassau. William was one of twelve children, and the family was brought up and educated in the principles of the Lutheran Reformation. From an early age, William was prepared to take over the family property of Orange in southern France. Thus, in later years, his official title was William I of Orange of the House of Nassau.

Charles the V, a Spaniard, had been chosen shortly after the Reformation in Germany to be emperor of the Holy Roman Empire, an empire which included Spain, Germany, parts of Italy, and the Lowlands. The Lowlands, though belonging to the empire from earlier times, had always been granted a great deal of autonomy and had become, under the hard-working and thrifty Lowlanders, far and away the most prosperous part of the emperor's domain. The Lowlanders loved their independence and would be loyal to the king and emperor only as long as he did not interfere unduly in their affairs. Each province had its own "stadholder," the principal magistrate who had effective rule.

Because they were nobility, William's family had contact with the emperor, and Charles V became interested in William's career. Charles took him to court to learn the ways of imperial policy.

It was while in the court of Charles that William learned the art of ruling, but the price that had to be paid was training in and commitment to Roman Catholicism and a loss of his Reformation heritage, for Charles was a bitter enemy of the Reformation and was determined to stop the spread of Lutheranism in his realm.

The king took a special liking to William, and he became Charles' closest intimate. William was the only one present with the king when Charles met foreign ambassadors on important official business. He became a confidant of the king in the most secret matters of the empire. He even could give advice to the king, which the king acknowledged was useful to him. No one was more influential. Although some dispute exists over the question, most historians claim that William received the name "the Silent" because of his complete discretion in matters of the realm.

God prepares His servants in ways in which they themselves are not conscious of being prepared. William's education in the court included a study of languages, which made him fluent in Flemish, German, Spanish, French, and Latin. William's family possessions in Orange gave him entry into French political circles. His appointments and assignments as a servant of Charles brought him into contact with and gave him knowledge of the Lowlanders. All these were to be used at a later date in William's important work.

### Conversion to Protestantism

William was on his way to fame, fortune, honor—and a life in the Romish church—when suddenly God intervened in a strange way.

Charles V, weary of the cares of empire and the struggles with the problems confronting Europe when the whole continent was in turmoil because of the Reformation, decided to abdicate and to spend the rest of his life wearing a hair shirt in an obscure monastery in Spain. Announcing his abdication while leaning on William's arm, Charles gave Spain and the Lowlands to his son, the cold Philip, who hated the Reformation with an implacable hatred.

From that time, William occupied a rather anomalous position in the court. He continued to be used in various diplomatic tasks, although Philip was distrustful of him for his close association with Charles V.

It was during this time that William's sympathies began to change to concern for and interest in the battered and beleaguered Calvinists in the Lowlands.

It is not entirely clear what events God used to bring about this change, for God often works in mysterious ways, and perhaps William himself was not altogether sure of what was happening to him or of how to give account of the changes taking place in his soul. But several things are clear. William had been brought up in Lutheranism, and one never forgets what one learns as a youth. He may forsake it, as many do, but he cannot forget it. Sometimes God is merciful and will use that early instruction for good, even after a terrible period of apostasy.

William saw Roman Catholicism at its cruelest under Philip. Philip was determined to eradicate Calvinism from the Lowlands, and he used the Spanish Inquisition at its cruelest to accomplish this task. William, often in the Netherlands, saw firsthand the blood and heard the screams of thousands who died for their faith. It made an indelible impression on him.

William hated tyranny of every kind and in every land. He hated the tyranny of the Spaniards. His heart went out to those who suffered under Philip's relentless blows.

One event brought the whole matter to a head. A diplomatic mission brought William to France while Henry II, a dedicated Roman Catholic, ruled. Here in France William learned of the secret plot which Henry and Philip had hatched to destroy Protestantism. Henry thought William occupied the same confidential position in the court of Philip that he had occupied in the court of Charles; and so, in the woods on a hunt, in a moment when no one else was

around, Henry told William of the plan to destroy "that cursed vermin, the Protestants," even though it would require treachery.

Appalled at such an outrage, William managed to keep an outward demeanor which did not reveal his true feelings. But as soon as he was able, he informed the Protestant leaders in Brussels of the foul plan. It did not take long for Philip to learn that the secret was out, but he did not suspect William.

## *Savior of the Calvinists*

William's work in the Lowlands increased in importance. He served as a representative of Philip; he was a member of the council of state which was to assist the Spanish regent in ruling in Philip's name. The regent was first Margaret of Parma, who had some sympathy for the Protestants. She was replaced by the duke of Alva, one of history's more cruel men. The regent was responsible to carry out Philip's plans to destroy Calvinism. William was also stadholder of the provinces of Holland, Zeeland, and Utrecht. In these positions he did what he could to help the Protestants, ease the horrors of persecution, and restore political power to the stadholders of the provinces in the Lowlands.

All of Williams' efforts proved unsuccessful, and Philip multiplied his cruelties and continued his treacherous conduct. At last William could take it no more; he increasingly considered himself responsible for what was happening. He retired briefly to his home in Nassau in 1568 where he evaluated his life, scrutinized his loyalties, brought his dilemma before the Lord, and decided to cast his lot, for better or for worse, with the persecuted people in the Lowlands.

The whole story of William's long and difficult struggle for freedom in the Lowlands is too complicated to tell here. It is a story of victories and defeats, of courage and sacrifice, of suffering and grief, of losses and gains, but finally of victory, which came more through stalemate than success on the battlefield.

Three different times William raised an army in Germany or France or in the Lowlands. Every time his efforts failed, sometimes because of changing political fortunes, sometimes because his armies were insufficiently equipped to fight the skilled and well-equipped Spaniards, sometimes because of a lack of financial resources, sometimes because the horror of persecution overwhelmed the people.

Several events helped gradually to turn the tide. The Dutch navy, manned by men called "Beggars of the Sea," was successful in raiding

Spanish shipping, seizing Spanish armed boats, and harassing Spanish troops in lightning raids on the mainland. Noted for their skills in seamanship, their unmatched courage, their knowledge of the canals, dikes, bayous, marshes, and swamps of the Lowlands, they kept the Spaniards from overcoming the country and were the main reason why many cities in the Lowlands declared themselves independent from Spanish rule.

The siege of Leyden is a remarkable instance of the courage and skill with which the Lowlanders fought. Surrounded by Spanish forces who were unable to breach the thick walls of the city, the inhabitants were nearly starved into submission. Seeing their families and children dying from the famine, many spoke of capitulation until the burgomaster stirred their failing spirits with the words "Here is my sword; plunge it, if you will, into my heart, and divide my flesh among you to appease your hunger; but expect no surrender as long as I am alive."

The Beggars of the Sea had breached the dikes in an effort to sail to Leyden's rescue, but contrary winds prevented the waters from moving sufficiently far inland to sail the boats over the land. But on October 3, 1574, God turned the winds about so that the tidal waters rushed inland, carrying the boats with them and bringing supplies to the beleaguered garrison. The Spaniards were routed, the siege lifted, and the city spared.

For the courage of the citizens, William proposed the establishment of a university within the city, and the University of Leyden became one of the great schools in subsequent Dutch history.

Although the Lowlanders never could whip the Spaniards in pitched battle, the Spaniards never got close to subduing the nation and overcoming the Dutch. What was to the advantage of the Dutch was the possession of key cities which Spain could not recapture as well as total supremacy at sea.

In 1576 seven Dutch provinces (Holland, Zeeland, Utrecht, Friesland, Groningen, Overijsel, and Gelderland), under the leadership of William, signed the Union of Utrecht by which these provinces became a republic. William became the king, and the Netherlands was formed. The country has often been referred to as "Holland" after its largest and most prosperous province.

The Spanish were not defeated but were gradually driven from the north and pushed to the south so that two nations emerged:

Belgium, primarily Roman Catholic to this day, and the Netherlands, a strong, independent country which was Calvinistic throughout. Although fighting ceased, the war was not officially over until the Peace of Westphalia was signed in 1648, which brought to an end all the religious wars in Europe.

William was something of an enigma through it all. He suffered greatly, for he lost all his possessions in the interests of helping the persecuted people of God. His motives for coming to their rescue have never been completely clear. No doubt he hated tyranny of all kinds and in all lands. He hated the Spanish for their persecution of the Lowlanders and the presence of Spanish troops on Dutch soil, but he sought the formation of new Roman Catholic bishoprics in a land in which the people had chosen for the Reformation. He wept because of the persecution of those whose only crime was a determination to worship God as they believed right but was willing to grant Roman Catholics the right to worship according to Roman liturgy as well.

William was a man of deep religious convictions, though he cared little for the forms of religion. He was a man of faith, resolution, and unbending tenacity of purpose. But his motives were political as well as religious.

He had to have been moved by love for His God and for the faith of Calvin, or he would never have sacrificed all that he possessed for a cause which often seemed hopeless. Out of his untiring efforts was born not only the land of Dutch Reformed theology, but also a bastion of Calvinism which was to influence thousands upon thousands in that land and abroad.

Above all, William was a man who, before the times were ripe for it, wanted nothing so much as freedom of religion. When he marched with his army into the Netherlands, he issued a proclamation which read, in part, "My taking up of arms is because of 'the security of the rights and privileges of the country, and the freedom of conscience.'"

In instructions issued to his deputy, William required this of him:

> First of all, to deliver the towns of that Province from Spanish slavery, and to restore them to their ancient liberties, rights and privileges, and to take care that the Word of God be preached and published there, but yet by no means to suffer that those of the Romish church should be in any sort prejudiced, or that any impediment should be offered to them in the exercise of their religion.

When the Union of Utrecht was formed, William insisted absolutely that freedom of religion be practiced in the land.

## *His Death*

Philip hated William and offered 25,000 crowns and nobility to anyone who would kill him. Many tried, lured by such promises, and one succeeded. He was a down-in-the-heel scoundrel by the name of Balthazar Gerard, who obtained an audience with William on the pretense of having important business. Mad with covetousness, Gerard shot him through the body in Delft on July 10, 1584. William died shortly thereafter with the prayer: "My God, have mercy on my soul and on these poor people."

God delivered His people in the Netherlands from oppression at the hands of the Romish church, as He always delivers His people from their oppressors. More importantly, God made the Netherlands the cradle of the Reformed faith. It did not remain that, but it was such for a sufficiently long period of time to be the means for the Reformed faith to be brought to many places around the world. Of that faith we are the heirs.

# *Reformation in Britain*
## *1525-1600*

# Part Four:

## Reformation in Britain *(1525-1600)*

| | |
|---|---|
| | **1475**    **Hugh Latimer** <br> b: c.1475-1490; d: 1555 |
| | **Thomas Cranmer** 1489-1556 <br> **William Tyndale** c.1490-1536 |
| Reign of Henry VIII <br> 1509-1547...................... | **1500**    **John Knox** 1505-1570 |
| Tyndale's English Translation <br> of N.T. 1525.................... | **1525** |
| Reign of Mary Queen of <br> Scots 1542-1567.............. | **Andrew Melville** c.1545-1622 |
| Reign of Edward VI of <br> England 1547-1553.......... | **1550** |
| Reign of "Bloody" Mary <br> (Mary I Eng.) 1553-1558... | |
| Reign of Elizabeth I of <br> England 1558-1603.......... <br> First Scottish General <br> Assembly 1560................. | **1560** |
| Scottish Confession of Faith <br> 1560............................. | |
| Act of Uniformity 1571........ | |
| Reign of James VI of Scotland <br> 1578-1603....................... | **1575** |
| | **1600** |

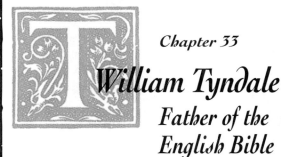

*Chapter 33*

# William Tyndale
## Father of the English Bible

### Introduction
*We all have many Bibles in our homes: our own Bibles and our children's Bibles, as well as Bibles used for family devotions. Most of us have the King James Version of the Bible, sometimes called the Authorized Version, prepared under the aegis of James I in 1611. It is a sad fact that our Bibles often lie unused, taken for*

granted, a somewhat peripheral part of our life. Yet behind them stands a story of great heroism, towering faith in God, and drops of martyr's blood. The story is that of William Tyndale, father of the English Bible.

### Tyndale's Early Life

William Tyndale was born sometime in the early 1490s on the Welsh border into the home of a well-to-do farmer. He went to Magdalen Hall, Oxford, where he received his M.A. degree in 1515 and was ordained into the Roman Catholic clergy. In that same year, he transferred to Cambridge University, probably because he had heard that the Greek New Testament of Erasmus was available there, and he was interested in reading Scripture in its original language.

One must understand the situation in England at this time. Henry VIII, husband of many wives, was on the throne. Dedicated Roman Catholic, but bitter enemy of the pope's rule in England, Henry persecuted Protestants on the one hand, but separated the church of England from papal control on the other hand. The church itself was rife with evil, wickedness in high places, and fornication of every sort. One of the chroniclers of the age characterized the priests as running from the houses of prostitutes to the altar to perform mass; mumbling their liturgies in a Latin they were incapable of understanding; superstitiously worshiping such relics as a gown of the virgin Mary, a piece of the burning bush of Moses, straw from the manger at Bethlehem, and a complete skeleton of one of the babies murdered by Herod the Great; and becoming drunkards and gluttons whose wicked lives were supported by the blood, sweat and tears of the common working folk.

Meanwhile, the universities were seething with the new learning of the Renaissance, the discoveries of Columbus and Cabot, and the teachings of Luther, the reformer of Germany.

It was in Cambridge that Tyndale was converted from his Romanism to Lutheranism. In these ancient halls Tyndale first became acquainted with Scripture in its original Greek, and not in the fusty Latin of the Vulgate.

### *Preparation for His Work*

It was in 1521 that Tyndale joined the household of Sir John Walsh at Little Sudbury Manor, a few miles north of Bath. Here he functioned as chaplain, tutor, and secretary, and preached occasionally at Bristol, where he expounded the Lutheran doctrines of justification by faith alone and the free gift of forgiveness of sins through repentance. He was also a frequent guest at the table of Sir John Walsh, where notable clerics from all over England often assembled. Their sophistries and hypocrisies were exposed by Tyndale's bold appeals to scriptural teachings so that, along with his sermons, Tyndale's views aroused the hatred and fury of friars, abbots, and prelates.

It was at one of these meals that Tyndale spoke to a visiting cleric those words for which he remains beloved by all succeeding generations of those who cherish Scripture: "If God spare my life, ere many years pass, I will cause a boy that driveth the plough shall know more of the Scriptures than thou dost." (These words were an echo of the famous wish of Erasmus, who in the preface of his *Greek New Testament* wrote, "I would to God that the ploughman would sing a text of the Scripture at his plough and that the weaver would hum them to the tune of his shuttle.")

Warned by his superiors to desist in his teachings, and resolved to begin the great work of making the Bible available to the people of his beloved country, Tyndale set out for London to secure permission from the authorities in the church to translate the Scriptures. This permission he sought from Cuthbert Tunstall, bishop of London, a scholarly man and close friend of Erasmus. But Tunstall, loyal to Rome and afraid of the new Lutheranism, refused permission to Tyndale and became, in later years, one of Tyndale's most vicious opponents.

During his stay in London, Tyndale lived with Lord Monmouth, to whose house God graciously and providentially brought the reformer. Lord Monmouth was an influential Lutheran, but more importantly, a friend of the merchants who operated the docks in London over which poured a steady stream of Lutheran literature. Tyndale was convinced that his endeavors to translate Scripture would never be successful in England. "Not only was there no room in my lord of London's palace to translate the New Testament," Tyndale wrote, "but also that there was no place to do it in all England." London merchants agreed to support the endeavor, and Tyndale left the country for Germany, never to return. The year was 1524. Tyndale performed his work abroad, and the merchants smuggled the translations into the country in bales of cloth.

### The Work of Translating

It might be well to pause for a moment and consider what Tyndale was doing. The Romish church in England had forbidden the Bible to be translated into the common tongue. The church was adamant about this and did everything in its power to enforce this rule. There is no question about it that the reason was simply that the Bible in the hands of the common people would reveal how totally corrupt the Romish church had become. The church did not want people to know this. One cleric with whom Tyndale spoke about translating the Scriptures raged, "We had better be without God's laws than the pope's."

Tyndale saw the absolute need for reform in England. He saw, too, that no reform could possibly come about without the Bible as the standard of truth and life. Undoubtedly persuaded by Luther's doctrine of the priesthood of all believers, he understood that the Bible had to be in the hands of every believer in a language which they understood.

All of this is obvious. What is so amazing is that Tyndale's convictions were so strong that he determined to devote his life to accomplish that goal. And he determined to devote his life to that goal in spite of the fact that it would mean exile, poverty, suffering, and finally a martyr's death. Though it was clear to Tyndale from the outset that he would eventually be killed for what he determined to do, he went ahead with the work anyway.

Tyndale's time in Europe was not pleasant. He probably stayed briefly in Wittenberg, where he almost certainly met Luther. But the main work of publishing was done in Cologne. The New Testament was ready for printing in 1525—only a year after Tyndale fled England. While the printing was in progress, an assistant spoke too freely over his wine about the work, and the news came to Johannes Dobneck, alias Cochlaeus, a bitter enemy of the Reformation. A raid was arranged, but Tyndale was forewarned and succeeded in fleeing with the printed pages and manuscripts.

Tyndale settled in Wörms, and in 1526 published the first complete edition of the English New Testament. It was smuggled into England through the London merchants in bales of cloth, boxes of food, and other goods of trade. Many of the copies were confiscated and burned by the Roman authorities, and many were bought up by the church and burned in St. Paul's by Cuthbert Tunstall. In God's irony, the money gained by the sale of these volumes was sent to Tyndale to be used for an edited and improved edition.

Tunstall hated the Bible and almost exhausted himself in denigrating it:

> [It is] intermingled with certain articles of heretical depravity and pernicious erroneous opinions, pestilent, scandalous, and seductive of simple minds...of which translation many books, containing the pestilent and pernicious poison in the vulgar tongue, have been dispersed in great numbers throughout our diocese; which truly, unless it be speedily foreseen will without doubt infect and contaminate the flock committed to us, with the pestilent poison and the deadly disease of heretical depravity.

This was the opinion which the church had of God's Word!

New and improved editions of the New Testament were constantly being prepared by Tyndale, many containing marginal notes, some of which were directed against the papacy. Tyndale also began work on the Old Testament. For this he had to learn Hebrew, which he did in the course of his wanderings in Europe. In 1530 the Pentateuch was completed and printed in Antwerp, Belgium, although Tyndale had to do the work twice because in traveling by boat, he suffered shipwreck, and the first manuscripts were lost. Because the volumes continued to be smuggled into England and because the authorities in England could not stop the steady flow and wide distribution, their fury increased and their determination to kill Tyndale became an obsession. It was decided to send men to Europe to catch Tyndale and arrest him. These efforts were, for the most part, unsuccessful. It is hard to know why. The spies were many and clever, and Tyndale made no great efforts to keep his whereabouts secret. It is true that Tyndale had many friends, also in Antwerp, but it seems that we finally must come to the conclusion that God watched over His servant in a special way because God was bringing reformation, through His holy Word, to England.

## *Tyndale's Martyrdom*

When God's work for Tyndale was completed, God took Tyndale out of this life, giving his faithful servant the privilege of leaving this life through a martyr's death. A worthless no-good by the name of Henry Philips thought to ingratiate himself with the authorities of the church, and perhaps win fame and fortune, by trapping Tyndale. He was successful. He posed as a friend, established a close relationship of trust with Tyndale, wormed his way into the home of Poyntz (with whom Tyndale was staying in Antwerp—although Poyntz never really trusted Philips) and when Poyntz was out of town, Philips persuaded Tyndale to go with him for a walk. Leading Tyndale down a dark alley, he pushed the reformer into the grasp of some scoundrels no less evil than himself, who seized him and turned him over to the authorities.

Tyndale was imprisoned in the castle of Vilvorde near Brussels. Here he lived for one year and 135 days without heat or light from candles or lamps, without sufficient clothing to keep him warm or food to sustain his weak frame, without friends and books. His only visitors were tormentors who bombarded him incessantly with demands that he recant. While Poyntz and friends in England did everything in their power to secure his release, the Romish authorities, thirsty for his blood, were not about to let their quarry go, now that they had him in their grasp.

Tyndale was tried, defrocked, and sentenced to death. In the early dawn, he was bound to a stake; an iron chain was fastened around his neck, a hemp noose was placed at his throat, and brush was heaped about him. The executioner, with all his might, snapped down on the noose and within seconds Tyndale was strangled. His limp body was then burned as the pile of brush was lit. His last words were, "Lord, open the king of England's eyes." With that he fell asleep.

## *Our Heritage*

The lasting monument to Tyndale's martyrdom is our King James Version of the Bible.

Two centuries earlier, John Wycliffe had translated the Bible into English, but Wycliffe's translation was from the Latin Vulgate, and it had never been printed. Tyndale's was from the Hebrew and Greek. One incomplete copy of Tyndale's Cologne edition survives, and two copies of the 6,000 that were printed in Wörms are extant. The 1534 edition, printed in Antwerp, is the last and the best. It formed the basis for the famous Coverdale Bible. Though Thomas More, an English Roman Catholic and humanist, called Tyndale's Bible "The Testament of Antichrist," it survived first in Coverdale's Bible. In 1537 (one year after Tyndale's death) the king of England ordered that Tyndale's Bible be placed in every parish church in the realm and made available to every man, woman, and child within the kingdom.

Ninety percent of Tyndale's Bible passed into the Authorized Version and seventy-five percent into the Revised Standard Version. It is basically Tyndale's Bible which we use today. A brief quotation from his Bible will show the similarity, although the quotation is in the English of Tyndale's day. The passage is Romans 12:1, 2:

> I beseeche you therefore brethren by the mercifulness of God, that ye make youre bodyes a quicke sacrifise, holy and acceptable unto God which is youre reasonable servynge off God. And fassion note youre selves lyke unto this worlde. But be ye chaunged (in your shape) by the renuynge of youre wittes that ye may fele what thynge that good, that acceptable and perfaicte will of God is.

Not only ought the story of Tyndale give us renewed appreciation for our Bibles; it ought also to fill our hearts with thanksgiving to God that He has given the church such men of courage and conviction that we can have God's Word today to read, to study, to enjoy, and to believe. When we read the beloved words of our King James Version, we ought never to forget that these words were written with the ink of martyr's blood.

## Chapter 34

# John Knox

### The Reformer of Scotland

*Introduction*
*God not only calls men to particular tasks in His kingdom; He also suits the man He calls with the personality, gifts, and strength to do the work.*

*So it was with John Knox, the reformer of Scotland.*

*Born and raised in a harsh land, he emerged from his years of preparation a harsh and unbending defender*

of the faith. With roots deeply sunk into the soil of his motherland, he was fed with the sturdiness of Scotland's gloomy heaths. Heir of the dour, unbending individualism which so characterized Scotland's populace, he was tempered to stand alone against queens and princes, unmoved by their threats or tears. He was, in God's wisdom, the only one who could bring the Reformation to Scotland.

### Youth and Education

It is quite amazing, and a perpetual testimony of the power of grace, that the Reformation came at all to Scotland. Scotland was known throughout Europe as the most backward, the most superstitious, the most Roman Catholic of all countries. The church which had held sway here for centuries, unchallenged and unmolested, was a church in which corruption had reached depths found in few other places. One would think that reformation here would be impossible.

John Knox was born sometime during the year 1505 in the small village of Gifford in East Lotham. His parents were sufficiently wealthy, apparently, to provide him with a good education. He received his early training in Haddington and was then sent to the University of Glasgow. In the university he earned his M.A. degree and was sufficiently proficient in his studies to gain an assistant professorship.

Somewhere near 1530 Knox went to teach at St. Andrews on the east coast by the sea, just a bit north of the Firth of Forth. It may have been here that his studies included some of the old church fathers, particularly Jerome and Augustine, and that the first doubts concerning Roman Catholicism rose in his soul. At any rate, he remained a firm Roman Catholic for the present and was ordained into clerical orders.

### Early Reformation and Exile

It was not until 1542 that Knox became a Protestant, under what influences or by what means we do not know. So clearly did he begin to proclaim Protestant views that he was degraded from orders as a heretic, and he was compelled to go to the south part of Scotland to hide from those who hated him.

While in the southern part of his country, Knox tutored the sons of two nobles and occasionally preached. It was during this period that he met and became a close friend of George Wishart, a bold minister and teacher of Reformation doctrine. Wishart was soon apprehended by the Roman authorities and was taken away to be tried and condemned to burn at the stake. Here began Knox's commitment to the Reformation. Clinging to Wishart as he was led away, and hoping to die with him, Knox was told by his friend, "Nay, return to your bairns [children], and God bless you; one is sufficient for a sacrifice."

Wishart was burned to death by Cardinal Beaton of St. Andrews in March 1546. Nobles sympathetic to Protestantism stormed the cardinal's castle, killed Beaton, and invited other Protestants, including Knox, to take up residence in the castle.

Knox lived in the castle for awhile and engaged in preaching and teaching, but in July 1547 the castle was captured by a part of the French navy. Knox and others were made prisoners of the French, and after being sentenced in France, Knox was condemned to the galleys as a slave chained to an oar.

Who knows what agony he endured during the nineteen months of his slavery? Who knows how often he questioned the ways of God when, for example, he could glimpse the spires of St. Andrews Cathedral through the small oar opening in the hull of the ship as it

rode the waves off the coast of Scotland? He emerged from this ordeal with infirmities which were to remain with him all his life (his own "thorn in the flesh") but with a faith tempered in the fire of suffering and a stronger-than-ever determination to engage in the Lord's work.

Knox was released only because Edward VI, Protestant king of England, directly intervened on his behalf with the king of France. The date was February 1549, and Knox was forty-four years old. It was probably for this reason that Knox did not return to Scotland but took up residence in England. Here he spent about five years, married Marjory Bowes, often preached every day of the week, worked with the reformers in England, and was offered a bishopric. This offer he declined, partly, it seems, because he already had some misgivings about the hierarchical form of church government practiced in the Church of England but also partly because he foresaw "evil days to come."

These days came soon enough with the untimely death of Edward and the accession of Mary Tudor, Bloody Mary, as she was called, a loyal daughter of Rome and one determined to restore Roman Catholicism to England—even at the price of the blood of the Protestants.

Knox fled to Europe. The year was 1554. He had wanted to stay in England because, as he said with some understatement, "Never could I die in a more honest quarrel." His friends prevailed upon him to flee, however, and he began a new work on the continent in Frankfurt-on-the-Main in a church of English exiles. Things did not work out well there because a dispute rose over liturgy, particularly responsive readings, and Knox, with some disgust, resigned his work and took up residence in Geneva.

Calvin was at the height of his powers and influence, and the two spent much time together discussing theology and, more particularly, church polity. Knox pastored an English congregation on the shores of Lake Leman and spent the happiest time of his life there beneath the shadow of the Alps and, to use Knox's own words, "in the most perfect school of Christ that ever was since the days of the apostles."

Knox's stay in Geneva was interrupted by a rather hasty trip back to Scotland. It is not entirely clear why Knox went, nor is it clear why he returned to Geneva. During his stay, however, he preached, taught, and visited day and night. His influence was great, especially on some of the nobles. The result was that events began to favor the

Reformation, and the first National League and Covenant was sworn to in 1556.

Some have charged Knox with cowardice for not staying in his native land, but it is most likely true that if he had stayed, he would have been killed. Immediately after his flight, he was condemned *in absentia* and burned in effigy. Future events proved Knox was not a coward.

Two things resulted from Knox's stay in Geneva: he became thoroughly equipped to establish a complete reformation in Scotland, not only in doctrine, but also in church polity and liturgy; he also authored a pamphlet entitled, in language characteristic of him, "First Blast of the Trumpet Against the Monstrous Regime of Women." The pamphlet was written primarily against Bloody Mary, although no names were mentioned, but it got him into endless trouble with Elizabeth, queen of England, and with Mary, queen of Scotland.

In 1559 Knox returned to Scotland for good. With his return, the work of reformation advanced rapidly. It was evident that the common people hungered for the pure preaching of the gospel, a hunger created by a mighty work of the Spirit of Christ. Romanism was abandoned, superstition was condemned, the chains of Rome were broken, and the nation moved steadily in the direction of becoming a Protestant country. Knox's preaching led the way.

A few of the outstanding events and characteristics of the progressing Reformation are the following:

The Protestants began to be called "The Congregation" and their leaders "The lords of the Congregation." A Presbyterian system of church government was instituted, one which Knox had learned in Geneva and which was markedly different from England's.

As Protestantism advanced, especially in some areas in south and east Scotland and particularly in Perth, riots broke out during which images, Romish liturgical trappings, monasteries, and altars were smashed and burned by runaway multitudes of those who had come to see Rome's idolatry.

When war threatened by means of a possible invasion from France and because of the decision of England to send troops into Scotland, a compromise was reached which avoided war and called for the meeting of a free Parliament to settle religious questions. This Parliament, which met in August 1560, established the Reformed religion by adopting a confession (The Scottish Confession of Faith, which served as the confession of the church until it was superseded by the Westminster Confession), a Book of Discipline (a church order), and a Book of Common Order (a guide for ministers in their work and calling).

In that same year, in December, the first General Assembly of the Scottish Church met in Edinburgh in St. Magdalene's chapel.

In all of these activities, Knox assumed a leading role.

Perhaps there is nothing more interesting in all of Knox's reformatory work than his interviews with Queen Mary. Mary wanted nothing so much as to return Scotland to the papal fold. Knox stood in her way. In at least two interviews with him she tried by every means to dissuade him from his course. She argued, pleaded, cajoled, threatened, attempted to move him with her feminine wiles (of which she had plenty) and even wept in an effort to move John's heart to pity. Through it all Knox stood firm and unmovable, to the point where some of his contemporaries and subsequent historians have criticized him for failure to show proper respect to his queen and for a hard-heartedness which bordered on cruelty.

But this was Knox, a man of iron will and implacable purpose; a man who did not know that the word "tact" existed in the English language, or, if he did know, did not know what it meant. He spoke forthrightly and clearly and worried not an iota whom he offended if it was for the cause of the truth of God.

Knox triumphed over incredible odds. He was shot at, ambushed, and verbally abused beyond what many others had to endure. Of an archbishop's greed, he wryly said, "As he sought the world, it fled him not." His purpose he himself defined: "To me it is enough to say that black is not white, and man's tyranny and foolishness is not God's perfect ordinance."

As was true of the reformers throughout Europe, Knox was first of all a preacher. Every Lord's day he preached two times, and during the week three times in St. Giles Cathedral, Edinburgh. He had a distinction which few, if any, had: he was a priest in the Romish church, a clergyman in the Anglican church, and a minister of the gospel in the first Presbyterian Church of Scotland.

In 1563 he retired to relative privacy because his forcefulness and uncompromising attitude offended many, but his influence continued to be felt. When Mary was forced to abdicate the throne in 1567, reforms continued. It was decided, for example, that the ruler of

Scotland must henceforth be Protestant, and many provisions were made for the support of the clergy. Under Knox's influence, schools were established. He wanted schools in every parish, a college in every important town, and three universities to serve the nation.

In 1570 Knox was felled by a stroke, from which he partially recovered. He retired to St. Andrews, where his reformatory work had begun, and there preached even though he had to be carried to the pulpit. He spoke of the fact that he was "weary of the world" and "thirsting to depart." On November 24, 1570, at the age of sixty-five, he was taken home by the Lord.

Though Knox was small and weak, beset since his days in the galleys with many infirmities, he was of a vigorous mind and implacable will. His piety and zeal knew no bounds. He stamped his character on the church which he was instrumental in establishing. In Geneva, Switzerland, stands the Reformation Monument, on which appear figures of the great reformers. By Knox's figure are written the words *Un homme avec Dieu est toujours dans la majorite* (One man with God is always a majority). Such men the church needs today.

## Chapter 35

# Hugh Latimer
## English Reformer and Martyr

**Reformation in England**

*God works in mysterious ways, and the wonders of His providence sometimes leave us gasping in surprise. The Reformation in England is illustrative of this truth. In Germany and Switzerland God brought about the Reformation through the work of mighty men of God, such as Luther and Calvin. In England*

the Reformation turned on the lust and fornication of a king, Henry VIII, known throughout history as the man of many wives, some of whom he murdered.

About the lust of Henry we must say a few words because the work of the noble Hugh Latimer cannot be understood without the background of a fornicating king.

Henry, a Tudor king, was married to Catherine of Aragon. Henry wanted to be free of this marriage, partly because Catherine had not succeeded in giving him a male heir to sit on the throne and partly because Henry had his lustful eyes upon Anne of Boleyn, a girl of the palace who would not sleep with Henry unless he married her.

The pope would not release Henry from his marriage to Catherine, and Henry, in a fury against the pope, cut all ties between England and Rome, rejected the ecclesiastical and civil authority of the pope in England, made himself head of the church in England, and refused to allow any money to leave England's shores to find its way into papal coffers.

Under these circumstances, the Reformation came about in England. It was not as if Henry himself was interested in reforming doctrine; he hated it, remained all his life devoted to Romish heresy and superstition, persecuted and killed those who promoted reformation truths, and determined to keep his church in England loyal to the doctrine of the Roman church. But his determination to get rid of papal rule in order to marry Anne Boleyn opened the door to reformation efforts.

In Germany, Geneva, and other parts of Europe, reformation had come about through separation from the church of Rome. This was never to happen in England. In this country, reformation was attempted by efforts to change the church of Rome itself into a Protestant church. England still bears the effects of this today.

### Latimer's Early Life and Conversion

The date of Hugh Latimer's birth is not known, but it took place somewhere between 1475 and 1490. He was born of a prosperous farmer in Thurscaton in Leicestershire. Recognizing his great abilities, Hugh's father gave him every educational opportunity, and when Hugh was fourteen, he sent him to Cambridge. There he studied, became a fellow of Clare Hall, took a degree, entered into a study of theology with a view to devoting his life to the service of the church, and established ties with Cambridge which would last throughout much of his life.

Cambridge was in ferment for at least three reasons: the teachings of John Wycliffe had never been lost in England; the writings of Luther had come into the country and were avidly read, studied, and discussed in Cambridge's halls; and Erasmus had seen to it that his edition of the Greek New Testament was circulated in England's intellectual circles.

Although Latimer showed great intellectual abilities, profound insights into theology, and powerful oratorical gifts, he devoted his time and abilities to do all he could to combat anything that faintly resembled the Reformation. He was a bitter opponent of the Scriptures and ridiculed a colleague who expounded the Scriptures in his classroom. Latimer even used the opportunity of his dissertation for a divinity degree to attack the views and teachings of Philip Melanchthon.

God brought Hugh Latimer to the service of the Reformation, though in a rather remarkable and even humorous way. A group of men, one of whom was Thomas Bilney, was accustomed to meet to discuss ways of promoting the Reformation to which they were deeply committed. Bilney had seen Latimer's great potential and had long pondered ways to persuade Latimer to join the movement for reform. Finally he hit upon a clever way, though under God's blessing it was also successful. Pretending to desire to make confession and be absolved from sin by Latimer, he used Latimer's naiveté and pride (Hugh Latimer thought Bilney was about to make confession for his devotion to the Reformation and ask for forgiveness) to describe for Latimer his own conversion from the comfortless doctrine of work righteousness which Rome taught to the blessed peace of faith in the perfect sacrifice of the spotless Lamb of God. Latimer was moved as never before. Humbled before God, he cast his lot with the Reformation movement.

## *Latimer the Reformer*

Latimer's considerable gifts were now devoted to the cause of reform, and he became an ardent and eloquent preacher of reform. His life was, from that moment on, a life on an ecclesiastical roller coaster—sometimes full of success, sometimes loaded with heartbreak, apparent defeat, and suffering. As Latimer's preaching attracted more people, the bishop of Ely, Dr. West, began to take notice. While first rather tolerant of Hugh and inclined to be sympathetic, he was moved to anger when he heard Hugh preach against the great sins of bishops—a sermon which Latimer preached on the spur of the moment when, about ready to preach on another passage of Scripture, he saw the bishop of Ely with his retinue enter the building. Bishop Ely did not take kindly to such open criticism and forbade Latimer to preach in his diocese.

A sympathetic prior from the local Augustinian order, whose monastery was free from the supervision of the bishop, opened his pulpit to Latimer, and the crowds which came to hear him became larger than ever.

Greater triumphs awaited Latimer, but so did greater troubles. When Cardinal Wolsey looked favorably on Latimer, all the pulpits in England were opened to him. When Cardinal Wolsey (then England's most powerful man under the king) fell from favor, Latimer's enemies smelled blood. When King Henry became favorably inclined toward Latimer and took him under his protection, partly because Latimer, foolishly, approved the king's divorce from Catherine of Aragon, Latimer felt sufficiently free with the king to plead for some easing of the persecution of Protestants and received from the king the benefice of West Kingston, where he preached Reformed doctrine. But as soon as the king had his back turned, occupied with other matters, Latimer was summoned before the bishop of London, harshly and incessantly questioned over many days, and finally excommunicated and condemned. He was restored to favor only by appealing to the king and agreeing to fourteen points of Romish practice and worship, which included approval of Lent and the lawfulness of crucifixes and images in the churches.

This moment of weakness was, by his own admission, the low point in Hugh's life, a black day indeed, a sin which he confessed before his God, but a crucial point in his life: he resolved that, come what may, he would never do such foolishness again. It was a resolution which would be sorely tested.

Latimer's life of ups and downs continued. Through the favor of Anne Boleyn and Thomas Cranmer, Latimer received the bishopric of Worchester, where he spent several happy and fruitful years preaching reform, but sufficiently far from the public eye that he attracted little unfavorable attention. The Lord was not ready to leave Hugh in obscurity and, as his fame spread, he was summoned to preach at the opening of Parliament in 1536. In the same year a convocation was called to confirm Henry VIII as head of the church of England, at which Latimer was asked to preach. In both sermons, Latimer preached strongly in favor of reform and pleaded with the assembled dignitaries to bring about reform as swiftly as possible.

While it seemed as if his pleas were well received, an event of another kind spoiled it all. Lutheran theologians came from Germany to discuss union between the two countries and cooperation in the Reformation. When the Lutheran theologians were understandably unwilling to accept the Romish doctrine of transubstantiation, Henry became increasingly stubborn and not only insisted on the doctrine but threatened any who denied it with the direst punishments.

Latimer, fully aware that he could never teach the doctrine of transubstantiation, resigned his bishopric. He would probably have escaped punishment if it were not for the fact that a tree fell on him and caused injuries which brought him to London for medical help. He was immediately imprisoned, thrown into the Tower of London, and forced to remain there for six years until Henry, having exhausted himself with all his wives, died.

Edward VI, the son of Anne Boleyn and the only male heir, took the throne. Edward was strongly in favor of the Reformation and offered Latimer his bishopric once again, which offer Latimer refused on the grounds of his advanced age. But he did continue to preach, for he had always been and continued, above all, to be a preacher of the gospel.

## Latimer's Martyrdom

Edward soon died, and Mary came to the throne. This is the Mary who has rightly earned the name by which she has been known since her death: Bloody Mary. She hated all Protestants and had Latimer arrested and thrown again into the Tower of London, where he was deprived of even a semblance of creaturely comforts. He was tormented and questioned, threatened and mocked, while every effort was made to get him to recant. Though now past eighty years old, he remembered the shame and confusion of his earlier weakness and steadfastly maintained his confession of faith in his Savior Jesus Christ. His response to the taunts and ridicule of his tormentors was, "I thank God most heartily that he hath prolonged my life to this end, that I may in this case glorify God with this kind of death."

Hugh Latimer, with fellow reformers Ridley and Cranmer, was transferred to Oxford for trial and sentencing. All were found guilty of heresy and sentenced to be burned at the stake. On October 16, 1555, Ridley and Latimer were led from the Tower outside the north wall of the town, a stone's throw from Baliol College, with Latimer lagging a bit because of his feebleness. Kneeling together before the pile of faggots, they both prayed, and rising, submitted themselves to the will of God and their captors. They were tied to the same stake with a chain around their waists, leaving their hands and arms free. The faggots were piled around them, but prior to their being lit, a sympathetic onlooker tied bags of gun powder about their necks to speed their death. The faggots were lit and the pain began. It was then that Latimer uttered those immortal words which have rung down the centuries of time: "Be of good comfort, master Ridley, and play the man: we shall this day light such a candle, by God's grace, in England, as I trust shall never be put out."

The flames quickly reached the gunpowder tied about Latimer's neck, and he died with little suffering, but the case was not so with Ridley. The wood was wet and burned only around his legs. His agony was great and all but unbearable. His legs were completely burned away before an onlooker removed some of the higher faggots to permit the flames to rise and explode the gunpowder, ending his life.

The triumph was the victory of faith; the everlasting shame and reproach remains Rome's.

## *Latimer's Place in Church History*

All Latimer's contemporaries spoke highly of him. He was eloquent in speech, and was perhaps England's most powerful preacher. He was a man of impeccable moral conduct. He was kind, honest, enthusiastic about the work, given to many works of mercy, and wholly devoted to the cause of the spread of the gospel.

One writer says this of his sermons:

> The sermons of Hugh Latimer...although in style essentially medieval, belong in thought and intention to the days of reform. Racy, full of anecdote, reminiscence and humour, rich in homely English words like "ugsomeness," "dodipoles" and "belly-cheer," these sermons are an indication of the vigour and courage and outspokenness which belonged to the New Age. Latimer has hard words to say about the pope—"that Italian bishop yonder, the devil's chaplain"—and about the falseness of images and relics, of the Roman doctrine of the mass, and about the contemporaries, especially bishops and others who neglect the ministry of the Word and become "unpreaching prelates." Bishops, he says, "are so taken up with ruffling in their rents, dancing in their dominions...munching in their mangers and moiling in their gay manors and mansions" that they have no time for preaching, while the devil "the most diligent prelate and preacher in all England" is busy poisoning the hearts of men.

Hugh Latimer was "one of the most distinguished prelates of the Church of England, undoubtedly one of the ablest, if not the ablest ecclesiastic among the English reformers of the sixteenth century ...the John Knox of England, the bearer of a name that now shines over two hemispheres, and will blaze more and more till the last day."

Latimer, while dying, spoke of a light in England that would never go out. If today it has indeed not gone out, sadness fills the souls of those who must admit that it is now little more than a small and flickering flame.

## Chapter 36

# Thomas Cranmer
## Sinning Reformer

## Introduction

*God uses many different kinds of men in the work of the church. The differences are not only those of cultural background, abilities and gifts, personality and character; they are also differences in spiritual strength and weakness. Some of God's servants are of such noble moral character that one*

stands amazed at the power of grace in their lives. Some are very weak, to the point that they seem wholly unfitted for the work of the church. Some are Samuels and Gideons; others are Samsons and Jonahs. Some are Calvins and Luthers; others are Melanchthons and Bucers. Thomas Cranmer must be placed with the latter. There are so many blots on his life that one almost hesitates to include him among the heroes of faith, but the place he occupied in the Reformation was important, and his martyr's death is a tribute to a humble faith which inspires many of us who are weak as he was.

## Cranmer's Early Life

Already Cranmer's early life gave evidence of his genius. Born July 2, 1489, he soon entered Jesus College, Cambridge, and excelled in his studies. He mastered Greek, Hebrew, Latin, French, German, and Italian, and showed remarkable promise in theology. He was thoroughly acquainted with the ancient church fathers and the scholastic theology of the Middle Ages. When twenty-one years old he became a fellow at Cambridge, but forfeited his fellowship with an early marriage. His wife, however, died within a year and his fellowship was restored. Nothing is known of his wife.

Two things happened in the course of Cranmer's studies and teaching at Cambridge: Through his study of theology and his acquaintance with the writings of Martin Luther, he became persuaded of the truth of justification by faith alone. And through his work in the field of church history, he became convinced that the pope was not the head of the church. On these two pillars was to rest much of his reformational work.

## Cranmer's Weaknesses

Perhaps Cranmer's weaknesses can best be described as a certain lack of firmness and an unwillingness to stand for principle when the price that had to be paid was high. This weakness was to plague him to the end of his life.

It appeared first in his participation in and approval of the adulteries of Henry VIII.

In Chapter 35 we discussed Henry VIII's desire to free himself from his marriage to Catherine of Aragon because she failed to provide him with a male heir to the throne and because his lust for Anne Boleyn, a lady of the palace, burned white hot. Henry would easily have divorced Catherine and made short work of her if it had not been for the fact that the pope not only disapproved, but threatened Henry with all sorts of terrible things should Henry remarry.

It was into this sordid affair that Cranmer was drawn. In the course of a rather casual conversation, Cranmer expressed his opinion to two of the king's advisors that Henry's marriage to Catherine could easily be proved to be illegal. Cranmer's reason was that Catherine had been the wife of Henry VIII's brother, and that Leviticus 20:21 forbade the marriage in which Henry now found himself.

The views of Cranmer were quickly brought to Henry. In his pleasure, Henry appointed Cranmer to the position of chaplain to the king and sent Cranmer with a delegation to Italy to try to persuade Pope Clement of this idea. Clement was not persuaded and flatly refused to approve the divorce. Henry was no further ahead in his plans.

It is an interesting parenthesis in this part of Cranmer's life that, on his way back to England from Italy, he stopped in Germany to

confer with the Lutheran theologians. Two results followed from these meetings. Cranmer was more carefully and thoroughly instructed in the doctrines of Luther, and Cranmer married the niece of Osiander, Lutheran pastor of Nuremberg—even though clerical marriage was forbidden by the Church of England.

Upon Cranmer's return, he was appointed archbishop of Canterbury, the highest post in the Church of England. From this position of power, Cranmer engineered Henry's divorce and remarriage. On May 23, 1533, he declared Henry's marriage to Catherine void; five days later Cranmer married Henry and Anne Boleyn in a public ceremony. I say "public" because Henry could not wait to satisfy his lust and had secretly married Anne about five months earlier.

Cranmer's participation in these sordid events did not cease. Cranmer declared Henry's marriage to Anne void when, after only three short years, Henry wearied of her. If only by his silence, Cranmer approved also of Henry's cruel beheading of Anne. In the course of Henry's marital sins, Cranmer also had a hand in Henry's divorce of Anne of Cleves and in the execution of yet another wife, Catherine Howard.

It is impossible to justify all these activities of Cranmer, and there is no need for us to do that. This same weakness of character showed itself in other ways.

Because the threats of the pope thundered all the way across Europe and threatened Henry with excommunication and the lowest place in hell, Henry rescued himself by declaring that the pope was not the head of the church but that the king of England (namely himself) was head. Cranmer had come to this conclusion independently and assisted Henry in passing the necessary laws and decisions to make it effective. From a practical point of view, this meant that no money was henceforth to leave England for Rome without royal approval. The entire church was now under Henry's rule to do in the church as he pleased, and one of the things which he pleased was to shut down and raid the monasteries so that he could make himself heir of their enormous wealth.

We must bear in mind, however, that the reformational work in England was ambiguous and complicated. Henry wanted a church free from papal control, but he did not want a Protestant church; he was completely committed to Roman Catholicism, but many, including Cranmer, were pressing for reform. When the two were put together, reform gradually made progress in spite of the king, but it was a reform wholly different from the Reformation on the continent. In the reformations in Germany and Switzerland, the church was established by separation from the Roman Catholic Church. In England, reformation came about by changing the Roman Catholic Church into a Protestant denomination. This was no small task, and the efforts were never wholly successful. Especially in liturgy and church polity, the Church of England remained basically Roman Catholic—as does the Anglican church to this day.

Though strongly in favor of reform, Cranmer was hesitant and slow in pressing for needed change. When action was required, he shrank back. When Henry insisted on the mass and transubstantiation, other reformers in England resigned their posts in protest, but not Cranmer. Even Calvin, in a couple of letters to Cranmer, protested Cranmer's sloth in bringing about needed reform (See Calvin's letters of April 1552 and August 10, 1552). Undoubtedly Cranmer was interested in making the Romish church a Protestant church, but the goal was more difficult than he had anticipated. Part of his problem was his respect for tradition. He was willing to settle for a reformed Roman Catholic Church because he was of the opinion that the church had gone wrong in about the twelfth century, when, in fact, the evils of the Roman church began much earlier.

But our greatest source of grief is the weakness Cranmer showed when he was imprisoned under Bloody Mary. Under relentless pressure, he signed documents in which he recanted his Protestant position and begged forgiveness from the Romish church and from the pope. We shall say a bit more about this later.

### Cranmer's Strength

We have recounted only one side of Cranmer's character and life. Though Cranmer's efforts towards reform never went quite far enough and were never pushed with quite enough zeal (especially when the going became difficult), what he did in the work of reform was no small thing. He helped King Henry sever relations between England and Rome, making reform possible. When Tyndale died for translating the Bible and making it available in England, only a few short years later Cranmer had the Bible distributed in all the land and made it available in every parish church.

Though Cranmer remained content with an episcopal and Erastian form of church government in which the king was the head, he at least delivered the church from the worst of Rome's abuses. He made plans for the training of an effective and educated ministry to take the place of stupid, superstitious Roman prelates, and he succeeded in putting some of his plans into action. He attempted to compromise on matters of liturgy but was instrumental in producing the English Book of Common Prayer. Though it is written for the heavy and highly liturgical worship of the Anglican church and is, therefore, unacceptable to those who hold to Reformed principles of worship, anyone who wishes to learn the art of prayer can learn much from reading these liturgically beautiful, doctrinally sound, and biblical prayers. Some are rather odd, and we quote a couple of the more curious to give our readers a taste of them.

### For Rain

O God heavenly father, which by thy son Jesus Christ, hast promised to all them that seek thy kingdom, and the righteousness thereof, all things necessary to the bodily sustenance: send us (we beseech thee) in this our necessity, such moderate rain the showers, that we may receive the fruits of the earth, to our comfort and to thy honor: through Jesus Christ our Lord.

### For Fair Weather

Lord God, which for the sin of man didst once drown all the world, except eight persons, and afterward of thy great mercy, didst promise never to destroy it so again: we humbly beseech thee, that although we for our iniquities have worthily deserved this plague of rain and waters, yet upon our true repentance, thou wilt send us such wealth whereby we may receive the fruits of the earth in due season, and learn both by thy punishment to amend our lives, and by the granting of our petition, to give thee praise and glory: through Jesus Christ our Lord. (Taken from the Second Prayer Book of King Edward VI.)

In the area of doctrine Cranmer agreed with the continental reformers, particularly with Calvin. In his letters to Cranmer, Calvin did not scold Cranmer for holding to erroneous doctrines; his quarrel with Cranmer was the slowness with which Cranmer pressed for reformation in the church. Cranmer held to the Reformed view of the Lord's Supper, ordered both bread and wine to be dispensed (something forbidden by Rome), and was instrumental in the formulation of the Forty-two Articles (later to become the Thirty-

nine Articles, the official confession of the Anglican church). It was a truly Reformed confession in its doctrinal parts.

Cranmer took Martin Bucer, Peter Martyr, and other reformers from the continent into his home and confidence and helped some of them to secure teaching positions in the church. He had much correspondence with Calvin, Melanchthon, and other continental reformers who, without exception, showed him respect.

## Cranmer's Death

Cranmer's death showed the true character of his faith.

While Cranmer labored for reform with some hesitation during the time of Henry VIII, he worked with great boldness during the time of Edward VI. His work was brought to an end during the reign of Bloody Mary.

In 1553, along with Latimer and Ridley, Cranmer was consigned to the Tower of London for his views. Enormous pressures were put on him to recant. For a long time he held firm. During a debate over the doctrine of the Lord's Supper, he wrote, "From this your judgment and sentence I appeal to the just judgment of the Almighty, trusting to be present with him in heaven, for whose presence in the altar I am thus condemned." But, as we already said, he finally caved under the pressures and recanted in 1554. Because of his high position, he was sentenced to death in spite of his recantation.

Death came in 1556. He was expected by the authorities to read a public statement of his recantation. Imagine, then, the surprise of his murderers when, instead of publicly recanting, he made public confession of his sin of recanting:

> Now I come to the great thing that troubleth my conscience more than any other writings contrary to the truth which I thought in my heart, and writ for fear of death, and to save my life, if it might be; and that is all such bills which I have written or signed with mine own hand since my degradation, wherein I have written many things untrue. And forasmuch as my hand offended in writing contrary to my heart, therefore my hand shall first be punished, for, if I may come to the fire, it shall be first burned. And as for the pope, I refuse him as Christ's enemy and Antichrist, with all his false doctrine.

True to his word, when he was brought to the stake, he put his right hand in the fire first. As he was burning, he held up his right hand and said, "This unworthy hand! Lord Jesus, receive my spirit!"

It was his finest hour.

Powerful in the realm and in the church, holding the highest ecclesiastical office in the world under the pope; weak and vacillating when he should have been strong, altogether too much inclined to curry the favor of the crown rather than the favor of Christ, he nevertheless left a legacy which has been received by the church for centuries. Though later Puritans were to break with the Anglican church over matters of church polity and liturgy, they too acknowledged gratefully what Cranmer had done for the church in England—even though they were sure he had not gone far enough. His noble death sealed his witness to the truth insofar as that witness had been faithful.

## Chapter 37

# Andrew Melville
### Father of Presbyterianism

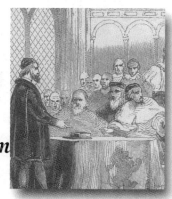

### Background

*As we noticed in the last chapter, the Reformation in the British Isles differed from that on the continent. While on the continent the Reformation churches left the Roman Catholic Church to form new denominations, in the British Isles the Reformation attempted to reform the Roman Catholic Church itself so as to create a Protestant church*

out of the old institution. This always made complete reformation very difficult; indeed, in England the Anglican church emerged as the Protestant church but retained a great deal of Romish liturgy and church government.

In Scotland this same method was followed; and the result was a gigantic struggle which lasted for over a century. The struggle was chiefly between a basically Roman Catholic church government and a genuine Presbyterian church government. It was in this struggle that Andrew Melville played an important role.

### Melville's Youth and Education

Andrew Melville was born in 1545, the youngest of the nine sons of Richard Melville. Richard Melville lived on a small estate on the banks of the South Esk near Montrose, a city on the east coast of Scotland about halfway between Edinburgh and Aberdeen.

Tragedy entered Andrew's life early. At the age of two he lost both parents. His father was killed in the battle of Pinkie, and his mother died later the same year. Because Andrew was now an orphan, his oldest brother, a minister in Maritoun, assumed responsibility for Andrew's education.

Though of a somewhat delicate constitution, Andrew proved to be an exceptionally good student. He was educated till the age of fourteen in the grammar school in his home town; after completing his work there, he went to St. Mary's College at St. Andrews for four more years of study.

Andrew proved to be such an excellent student that he soon gained a reputation for being the best philosopher, poet, and Greek scholar among all Scotland's university students. The rector of the school took a special interest in him and said to him when he left the college to pursue his studies elsewhere: "My silly [poor, meaning to be pitied] fatherless and motherless boy, it's ill to wit what God may make of thee yet."

At the age of nineteen, Andrew went abroad to study, first to Paris for two years and then to Poitiers, both cities of France. He determined to study law, not because he had any intention of entering the legal profession but because of the mental discipline which studies in law required. His reputation preceded him at Poitiers, and no sooner had he arrived than he was asked to take a professorship. After three years, troubles between the Protestants and the Roman Catholics made it advisable for him to go elsewhere. He chose Geneva and in 1567 began a seven-year stay which was perhaps the most happy and carefree time of his life. Beza, Calvin's successor and rector at the academy, offered him a professorship in the humanities, and in Geneva he enjoyed his work, his surroundings, his students, and his contacts with the great men of the Calvin Reformation. Here he would have liked to stay; but an urgent call from his friends in Scotland persuaded him that God had assigned him a place and a work in his homeland from which he could not turn away.

## The Beginning of the Struggle

The first General Assembly of the Scottish Churches had met in 1560 under the leadership of John Knox. That General Assembly had adopted a confession and prepared a book on church order. Knox spent all his later years struggling to establish a church in Scotland which would be Calvinistic in doctrine, liturgy, and church government, but the forces opposed to him, especially in the areas of liturgy and church government, were strong. The ruling monarch, Mary Stuart, queen of the Scots, was a perpetual obstacle.

By the time Melville returned to Scotland, Knox had been dead two years, James VI sat on the throne (later to become James I of England, after whom the Authorized Version of the Bible was named), and the church was governed by a sort of highbred polity composed of elements of Presbyterianism and prelacy, the latter a form of church government much like Rome's, though without the pope.

Melville's considerable ability was soon recognized, along with his devotion to Presbyterianism and his threat to prelacy. Morton, regent of the king, understood perhaps better than anyone else what a threat Melville could be. Upon Melville's arrival, Morton offered him a position of private tutor in the court of the regent, with promises of good wages and advancement. If Melville had accepted, he would probably have become an enemy of the church of Christ in his land, but he saw the danger and instead accepted the position of principal at Glasgow College, offered him by the General Assembly of the church. That began his active work in his homeland.

Soon he was deeply involved in the affairs of the church. He reorganized the college of which he was principal; was, as professor of divinity, present at ecclesiastical assemblies; and was involved in conferences within the church and conferences between the church and Parliament, or the church and the king.

Melville's stay in Geneva, where biblical principles of church polity had been developed and practiced by Calvin and the Company of Pastors, had convinced him that Presbyterianism was the only biblically sanctioned system of church government, and he began now to exert all his efforts to establish such a biblical system in Scotland. This brought him into direct conflict with the king and his court. Morton, who had originally offered Melville a lucrative place in the court, now became Melville's bitterest enemy.

Melville's courage was well known in the land. On one occasion, when Morton threatened Melville in an extraordinarily menacing way (Morton's threats had before made bold men quail), Melville responded: "Tush, man! threaten your courtiers so. It is the same to me whether I rot in the air or in the ground; and I have lived out of your country as well as in it. Let God be praised; you can neither hang nor exile his truth!"

It would carry us too far afield to describe in detail the long struggle between the king and the church, the latter with Melville at its head. The issue was not only whether prelacy or Presbyterianism

was to be the government of the church; the question was also whether James Stuart, king of Scotland and England, was to rule in the church of Christ. Just as in England the king (or queen) was the head of the church, so also James insisted that the king in Scotland be supreme in all matters of church government. That principle could not be tolerated by men concerned that Christ rule in the church as the church's only Head.

In their firm insistence that not King James but Christ is the Head of the church, they stood for a great truth. Melville was chosen as a leader of a delegation to bring to the king the protest of the Synod of Fife against royal encroachments on the church's autonomy. James was not impressed. After the king had expressed his displeasure, Melville himself set forth the principle in words that have become famous: "Sirrah, ye are God's silly vassal; there are two kings and two kingdoms in Scotland: there is King James, the head of the commonwealth; and there is Christ Jesus, the King of the church, whose subject James the Sixth is, and of whose kingdom he is not a king, not a lord, not a head, but a member."

In 1584 matters came to something of a head. Melville was summoned before the Privy Council for preaching a sermon at the General Assembly of the church in which he condemned the tyrannous measures of the court. He was cited for high treason and threatened with imprisonment. Although Melville appeared as directed, he denied the Privy Council the right to try him until he had been tried by an ecclesiastical court. This so infuriated the head of the Privy Council that he completely lost his temper. Melville, unmoved, took his Bible from his belt and put it on the table, telling his accusers: *"These* are my instructions: see if any of you can judge of them, or show that I have passed my injunctions."

Although in 1578 the Second Book of Discipline, which sanctioned a pure Presbyterianism, was adopted by the General Assembly, and although this became the standard in the Presbyterian churches and was sworn to in the National League and Covenant of 1581, James VI won the battle over Melville. The success of Presbyterianism had to wait for a better day.

When James was in London, he summoned Melville to London with guile and at the first opportunity had him imprisoned. Four years Melville was kept in the Tower of London, famous for the imprisonment and torture of reformers who suffered for the cause of the gospel. The first year was the worst, for he was deprived of all opportunities to communicate with others. Then the rigors of his confinement were relaxed a bit, and he was permitted to have visitors and to correspond from prison with his colleagues in the ministry. Men of prominence consulted him, and he used his imprisonment, as Paul did, for the extension of the gospel (Phil. 1:13, 14).

At the age of sixty-six Melville was released. Though his heart cried out for Scotland, and though he wanted to have his bones laid to rest in his homeland, the king adamantly refused, and Melville was forced to go to France to spend his last years in exile. There history lost him and, though he died somewhere around 1622 at approximately seventy-seven years old, nothing is known of his last days or the date of his death. He died alone, an exile in the cause of the gospel, with no family or friends to mourn his passing.

One of his biographers summed up the life of Andrew Melville. Though acknowledging that Melville was short of stature and physically somewhat frail, he said,

> As a preacher of God's Word, he was talented in a very high degree—zealous, untiring, instant in season and out of season, and eminently successful—and as a saint of God, he was a living epistle of the power of religion on the heart. Sound in faith, pure in morals, he recommended the Gospel in his life and conversation—he fought the good fight; and as a shock cometh in at its season, so he bade adieu to this mortal life, ripe for everlasting glory. If John Knox rid Scotland of the errors and superstitions of popery, Andrew Melville contributed materially, by his fortitude, example, and counsel, to resist, even to the death, the propagation of a form of worship uncongenial to the Scottish character.

Some noble men of God have died unknown and unrecognized in their own lifetime, especially when evil men came to power, but the legacy of their works has survived the centuries and has come down to us as a sacred trust.

# *Post-Reformation Period in Britain*
## *1600-1700*

# Part Five:

## Post-Reformation Period in Britain (1600-1700)

| | |
|---|---|
| Reign of James VI of Scotland 1578-1603......... | **1575** |
| | **1600**   **Alexander Henderson** 1583-1646 <br> **Samuel Rutherford** c.1600- c.1660 |
| Reign of Queen Elizabeth I of England ends 1603........ <br> Reign of James I of England and Ireland 1603-1625...... <br> Authorized "King James" Bible 1611.................... | **1610** |
| | **1625**   **Margaret MacLauchlan** <br> b: c.1622-1625; d: 1685 <br> **John Bunyan** 1628-1688 |
| National League and Covenant (Renewal) 1638... | **1640** |
| First Presbyterian Church in Ireland 1642................... <br> Westminster Assembly 1643-1552..................... <br> Rutherford's *Lex Rex* 1644.... | **1645** |
| Peace of Westphalia 1648...... <br> Charles I of England beheaded 1649................ | **1650** |
| Oliver Cromwell is Lord Protector 1653-1658......... <br> Reign of Charles II of England 1660-1685........... | **1660** |
| Conventicle Act passed vs Non-conformists 1664...... |   **Margaret Wilson** c.1667-1685 |
| | **1670** |
| Deposition of James II 1688.. <br> Battle of the Boyne 1690....... | **1690** |

### Chapter 38

# Alexander Henderson

## Covenanter

***Introduction***
*Presbyterianism was established in Scotland only after bitter struggle. If Andrew Melville, whose life we discussed in the last chapter, was the father of Presbyterianism, Alexander Henderson, more than any other, was responsible for fixing it firmly in the kirk of Scotland,*

although even after his life the struggle continued for some few years.

The Stuart kings were on the throne of Scotland, all of them strong proponents of the divine right of kings and eager to be the absolute monarchs which their predecessors had been. Specifically, after Melville died, James VI pressed the claims of an absolute monarch, and his policy was followed by Charles I.

The Stuarts were convinced, and correctly so, that Presbyterianism was a threat to their claims of absolute rule. They favored what was known as prelacy, the form of church government practiced in the Anglican church in England, a system of church government much like Rome's with archbishops, bishops, and lower clergy. The Scottish Presbyterians were just as convinced that such hierarchical forms of church government were contrary to all Scripture, and they were determined to resist, to the death if need be, any efforts by the Stuarts to impose prelacy on their land and in their church.

With Melville out of the way, the Stuarts, though still opposed by a few, were successful in nearly silencing Presbyterian ministers. They used the threats and punishments of imprisonment and banishment; they bribed wavering ministers with promises of bishoprics; and they sent recalcitrant men to remote parts of Scotland where their influence was nil.

The difficulty was that along with prelacy came other evils: the right of kings to rule in affairs of the church, episcopal liturgical practices in the worship services, and oftentimes the dreadful heresy of Arminianism. All these galled the soul of the Presbyterians, whose only desire was to worship God according to the commands of the Scriptures.

## Henderson's Early Life and Calling

Into this situation Alexander Henderson was born in Fifeshire around the year 1583. Nothing is known of his early life. He lived in obscurity until he began his studies in St. Andrews. He earned his M.A. degree in 1603, and because he soon acquired a reputation as a brilliant mind, he was given the chair of professor of philosophy at St. Andrews.

Here he might very well have lived a comfortable and settled life, enjoying the honor and income of a prestigious post and bothering very little about the life and death struggle going on in the church. He was a man who, without much thought, supported prelacy, and he really never considered that anyone could be so concerned about minute problems as to make a fuss over the question.

God had other designs for him, however. These plans began to become clear when in 1615 Henderson was made a minister of the gospel in the parish of Leuchars. Even this would not have amounted to all that much if it were not for the fact that the people in this parish were strong Presbyterians who had no intention of allowing an episcopal prelate on their pulpit. On the day of Henderson's ordination, they locked the doors and forced Henderson and his party to break into the church through a window.

There was fine divine irony in the events which followed. Robert Bruce, staunchly Presbyterian, attracted such large crowds to his ministry that Henderson was of a mind to go secretly to hear him, to learn if possible the secret of Bruce's popularity. After Bruce entered the pulpit, he read his text at the appropriate time, which text was, "Verily, verily, I say unto you, He that entereth not by the door into the sheepfold, but climbeth up some other way, the same is a thief and a robber" (John 10:1). Alexander Henderson could not help but recall how he had himself entered the church where he was pastor when first he came to Leuchars. He was so smitten in his conscience that he retreated from the service in shame, went to his own study to ponder what Bruce had said, and became convinced before God that Presbyterianism was the only form of church government and worship sanctioned by the Holy Scriptures.

With that remarkable conversion, Scotland gained one of its most ardent and passionate defenders of the cause of God.

## Henderson's Battle for Presbyterianism

From that time on, Henderson's life was devoted to the cause of Scottish Presbyterianism. We mention only a few outstanding events in a life of dedicated service.

At the General Assembly of 1618, the forces of prelacy in Scotland gained a victory of sorts when the assembly decided, under pressure of the king and his ministers, to impose upon the churches various episcopal practices which included kneeling at the sacrament of the Lord's Supper, private baptism in the homes or at the church outside worship services, private administration of the Lord's Supper, episcopal confirmation of clerics, and the celebration of various Christian holidays.

When the pastor of Leuchars opposed these episcopal innovations, he was summarily called to defend himself before the imposing High Commission of the king in St. Andrews. His defense of his position was so effective that the High Commission refused to do anything further to him in spite of his defiance of assembly decrees.

Something on the same order took place nearly twenty years later when efforts were made to force Henderson personally to make use of episcopal liturgy rather than the simple liturgy used by Presbyterians throughout the land who managed successfully to resist the king's best efforts.

On March 1, 1638, an event took place of momentous importance. This was the signing of the National League and Covenant in the Greyfriars churchyard in Edinburgh. This was actually the second National Covenant, sometimes called the Renewal of the Covenant. It included in it the First National Covenant or King's Covenant. It was a rather short document, signed and sworn to by large multitudes of people from all parts of Scotland and from all ranks and classes of the Scottish people. It was a solemn moment in Scotland's history, for the document bound the signers by oath to be true to the Reformed faith, to be loyal to the king and the liberties and laws of the kingdom, and to resist popery and every effort to impose prelacy upon them.

It was this National League and Covenant which gave to those signing it, and to subsequent Presbyterians, the name of "Covenanters." Alexander Henderson was chiefly responsible for the document and was one of its signatories.

Through the efforts of staunch Presbyterians, the faithful acquired a majority at the General Assembly of 1638, at which Henderson was chosen as moderator. Although the assembly was protested, resisted, and opposed by the bishops, and although it was officially dissolved by the king, it continued to meet until it had successfully excommunicated opposing bishops and adopted decisions favorable to strict Presbyterianism.

It was at this meeting that, in an eloquent speech, Mr. Henderson defined what, in the judgment of Presbyterians, was the responsibility of the king towards the church. We quote a few snatches from this speech to give some indication of the position which these men took on the sticky question of the relation between church and state.

> ...To a Christian king belongeth, 1. Inspection over the affairs of the church...2. The vindication of religion...he being the keeper of the *first* table of the law. 3...to confirm...the constitutions of the kirk...and give them the strength of law. 4. He both may and ought to compel kirk men in the performance of the duties which God requires of them. 5. The coercive power also belongs to the prince...6. The Christian magistrate hath power to convoke assemblies...and in assemblies...his power is great...

But the church also firmly believed that it had certain rights and responsibilities towards the king, which were put into practice by Henderson and the Presbyterians.

When Charles I flatly refused to give Presbyterians any leeway in their practices, war broke out in England against the king. The forces opposed to the king were directed by Parliament, in which the anti-Prelate or Puritan party had gained power. The men of Scotland were prepared to join with their brethren in England in the civil war which was sure to come. Henderson, in fact, became a chaplain in these forces, which scored several victories over the Royalist troops.

It is not our purpose to review all the events of that war. Any schoolboy knows how Oliver Cromwell and his Roundheads eventually defeated the king, who fled for safety to Scotland. And all know how he was turned over to the English, who promptly

beheaded him and established the Commonwealth with Cromwell as leader.

## Henderson's Last Years

Two more events can briefly be mentioned. As Parliament in London guided the war against Charles, so did Parliament take it upon itself to restore Presbyterianism to England and Scotland. The method used was to summon an assembly of divines to bring this about. The assembly of divines which came to London at Parliament's bidding has become known as the Westminster Assembly, that famous and illustrious group of Presbyterian divines. To that assembly Henderson was sent as delegate from Scotland, and on that assembly he labored diligently for Parliament's goals. More about the assembly is covered in the next chapter.

In 1645, before Charles' final defeat, Henderson spent time, at the king's personal request, in negotiations with the king in an effort to stop the civil war and bring peace to the commonwealth. Efforts proved fruitless, for the king would not surrender episcopacy. During the negotiations, although only after it became clear that they were fruitless, Henderson asked to be excused to return to his home in Edinburgh. His constitution was broken by overwork, and he was too weak to continue in these arduous struggles with England's king.

Henderson returned home but died eight days after his return, on August 19, 1646, in Edinburgh. He was buried in Greyfriars churchyard, where to this day a monument stands commemorating his faithful labors.

Henderson was among those who were tested to the limit in faithfulness to their calling to obey God rather than men. Their response puts them in the roll of the heroes of faith celebrated by Scripture.

**Chapter 39**

# Samuel Rutherford

## Westminster Divine

*Introduction*
*All students of*
*church history are*
*agreed that, from*
*the time of the*
*apostles to today,*
*the history of the*
*church of Christ has*
*never seen two*
*greater assemblies*
*than the Synod of*
*Dordt and the*
*Westminster*
*Assembly. It is a*
*surprising thing*
*that they were both*
*held in the first half*
*of the seventeenth*
*century—indeed*

that they were held within twenty-five years of each other. The times must have been particularly important or dangerous for the church of Christ for God to give to His people two assemblies such as the world had never known. It was a remarkable age.

In the last chapter we spoke of Alexander Henderson, a delegate to the assembly from Scotland. While God blessed the assembly with many great men, another Scottish minister played an outstanding part. We choose to tell something of the Westminster Assembly by a sketch of this towering man of God: Samuel Rutherford.

### His Early Life and Work

It is strange that more is known about the early life of some saints in the Middle Ages than about the early life of these men of God who were instrumental in the work of reformation in the church, but so it is with Samuel Rutherford. His early life is lost in the mists of forgotten centuries.

Rutherford was born around 1600 in a small farming community near Nesbit in the southern part of the Lowlands of Scotland, in the presbytery of Judburgh. His parents were farmers, and he was one of three sons.

How spiritually minded and God-fearing the family was remains a mystery. There is some reason to believe that Samuel did not receive much spiritual instruction and that his conversion took place at a later date. An old story, however, speaks of the fact that as a little boy he was barely saved from drowning in a well and that, in gratitude to God, his father dedicated Samuel to the service of Christ.

Even the details of Rutherford's early education are lost in the past. He probably received early training in an ancient abbey in Judburgh and went on, at the age of seventeen, to the College of Edinburgh. Three years later he graduated with a Master of Arts degree and was hired by the college in 1623 as regent of humanity. This post was about the lowest post one could hold in the faculty. The teacher was responsible for teaching Latin to the students who entered the college, for all the instruction was given in Latin, and the students, quite obviously, had to be thoroughly adept at Latin to gain an education.

There were four higher chairs of philosophy, and the professors in lower branches could apply for any of these four chairs when a vacancy occurred. At the first vacancy, four professors did apply, including Rutherford.

It is a measure of the emphasis placed on a classical education in those Reformation days that all four were required to talk for nearly an hour on a given ode of Horace, a Latin poet of the first century, and the one most able to do this was chosen. Rutherford won without difficulty. He was on his way to being a classicist without genuine religion, but he had, unknown to himself, work to do in God's kingdom.

Rutherford's tenure was not long at the College of Edinburgh, for in 1625 he was asked to resign for what was apparently a moral misdemeanor. This quite effectively put a stop to all his aspirations and hopes for a career in Scotland's universities. That he carried the burden of this lapse with him is evident from what he later wrote to a young man:

> The old ashes of the sins of my youth are new fire of sorrow to me...The devil...is much to be feared,... for in youth he findeth dry sticks, and dry coals, and a hot hearth-stone; and how soon can he with his flint cast fire, and with his bellows blow it up, and fire the house!

This lapse and dismissal must have made a profound impression upon Rutherford, and it appears as if the Lord used this folly to bring him to true repentance and conversion. He resolved to enter the pastoral ministry and set about studying for it in the University of Edinburgh.

## *Ministry in Anwoth*

In 1627 Rutherford assumed the pastorate of a small farming parish in the beautiful area of Anwoth in the southwest part of Scotland, where he ministered to a few farm families and a few nobility scattered throughout the area. John Welsh, a son-in-law of John Knox, had labored in this very parish up to 1600.

The story of John Welsh is itself a story of constant struggle between the faithful in Scotland and the Stuart kings. One incident, a kind of parenthesis in our story, will illustrate the whole matter. After Welsh had been imprisoned and later exiled to France, he was permitted to return to England. In 1621 his wife was admitted to the presence of James I. A chronicler of those days describes the interview.

> The king asked her who her father had been, and she replied, "John Knox."
>
> "Knox and Welsh!" he exclaimed; "the devil never made sic [such] a match as that!"
>
> "It's right like, sir," she said, "for we never speired [asked] his advice."
>
> He then asked how many of John Knox's children were still alive, and if they were lads or lasses. She told him that there were three, and that they were all lasses.
>
> "God be thanked," cried the King, lifting up both his hands, "for if they had been three lads, I had never buiked [enjoyed] my three Kingdoms in peace."
>
> She urged the King to let her husband return to Scotland and to give him his native air.
>
> "Give him his native air!" said James; "give him the devil!"
>
> But her wit flashed out with indignation as she rejoined: "Give that to your hungry courtiers!"
>
> The King at last said that he could return if he would first submit to the Bishops. She lifted her apron, held it out, and made reply in her father's spirit: "Please Your Majesty, I'd rather kep his head there."

Rutherford's ministry in Anwoth lasted nine years and was greatly blessed. His fame as a faithful preacher of the gospel spread, and people came from great distances to hear him preach. His ministry was also filled with great sorrows. His wife died after a long and painful illness. His mother, who had come to stay with him, also died in Anwoth. His two children were buried on the hillsides of Anwoth, and he himself was very ill for three months so that he had difficulty preaching even once on the Lord's day.

Many visitors from the land passed through, especially travelers between Scotland and Ireland, for Stranraer, not far distant from Anwoth, was Scotland's nearest port of travel to Ireland. The famous Bishop Ussher, bishop of Dublin, Ireland, was present incognito at a worship service, having heard the fame of Rutherford.

## Exile in Aberdeen

But Rutherford had yet greater sorrows to face. He was a bitter opponent of prelacy and of the Arminianism that almost always accompanied it. He was summoned to be tried by the Court of High Commission in 1636 for a book he wrote against Arminianism. Found guilty, he was forbidden to preach or teach and was banished to Aberdeen in the Scottish Highlands, a city which was a stronghold of prelacy.

In this exile in Aberdeen he was shunned by the good citizens of the city, who feared the wrath of the king and his minions. But he willingly bore this reproach as from Christ and wrote to a friend, "That honour that I have prayed for these sixteen years, with submission to my Lord's will, my kind Lord hath now bestowed upon me, even to suffer for my royal and princely King Jesus." The two years spent here were not idle years, however; during that time he wrote hundreds of letters, sent to all parts of the British Isles, now gathered into a single volume and containing some of his best writings.

## Professor at St. Andrews

After two years, with the resurgence of Presbyterianism in connection with the signing of the National League and Covenant, Rutherford felt free to leave Aberdeen and to return to his beloved congregation in Anwoth. After being there for only a short time, he was assigned the chair of Divinity at St. Mary's College in St. Andrews. He strenuously resisted, for his heart was not in teaching but in the pastoral ministry, but he had no choice in the matter. He consented to go only if he would be permitted to preach in St. Andrews in addition to his teaching responsibilities. He told the commissioners, "There is woe to me if I preach not the gospel, and I know no one who can go between me and that woe." This permission was granted him, and he moved to St. Andrews, an influential parish at the center of church life in Scotland.

Here he married again, Jean McMath, but this marriage also was filled with much grief. Although his wife outlived him, he lost his children through untimely deaths. The first two died while he was away in London attending the Westminster Assembly; only one of the five more children given him lived. God, however, uses even a man's sorrow for the comfort of others. To one who lost a son he wrote, "Your Lord may gather His roses and shake His apples at what season of the year He pleaseth." And to another he wrote, "I know there is a true sorrow that is without tears; and I know there is a real sorrow that is beyond tears."

Rutherford set about his new work in St. Andrews with vigor and favor. He was to remain in this position the rest of his life, although he was to be of service throughout Scotland.

### Work at Westminster

When the Puritans in England gained the ascendancy in Parliament in England, they determined to bring true Presbyterianism to the entire realm. In order to accomplish this noble goal they called together an assembly of divines from every part of Great Britain for this work. This assembly has become known throughout subsequent history as the Westminster Assembly.

It is not our purpose to give a detailed history of this assembly. We are particularly concerned with the role played here by Samuel Rutherford, and even that only briefly. Let it be clearly said, however, that with the possible exception of the Synod of Dordt, no greater assembly of orthodox theologians has ever been assembled; indeed, the assembly set the confession, liturgy, and government for all true Presbyterianism throughout the world in all following generations. Its shadow has been long and universal. To this assembly the Scottish Presbyterians were invited to send delegates. Samuel Rutherford was chosen, an indication of the high esteem in which he was held throughout the Scottish churches.

For four years the assembly met in the Jerusalem Room of Westminster Abbey in London. Here in London Rutherford remained throughout the entire time, separated from his family. It is some measure of the devotion to the cause of Christ which these men possessed that, during the four years' separation from his family, he did not return home when the two children he had with his second wife died; he returned to a home without children and to a wife who had grieved alone.

Sitting alongside his good friend and fellow Scotsman, George Gillespie, Rutherford rendered inestimable service to the assembly. The assembly had to determine the type of church government which would prevail in England. Represented at the assembly were not only Presbyterians, but also Independent Congregationalists and Erastians. The Congregationalists proposed a form of church government in which no federation of churches would have any authority at all, but each congregation would be something of a law unto itself. The Erastians, on the other hand, favored a state-controlled church in which ecclesiastical affairs would be regulated by the king. Rutherford fought long and hard for the Presbyterian form of church government, which ultimately prevailed.

The Westminster Confession was the doctrinal product of this assembly. Its sound and virile orthodoxy, however, did not come about easily. No doubt the greatest threat to a soundly orthodox position was represented by Amyraldianism, which taught a hypothetical universalism in the work of salvation and the atoning work of Christ, and which insisted on a universal love of God and a desire of God to save all who hear the gospel. Again, Rutherford was adamantly opposed to such a perversion of the gospel and fought in the vanguard for the clear and biblically sound statements of the Confession as we have it today.

It was not until 1646 that Rutherford was able to leave London. So impressed was the House of Lords with his work that it sent a letter to the Scottish churches at his departure which read, in part, "We cannot but restore him with ample testimony of his learning, godliness, faithfulness and diligence, and we humbly pray the Father of spirits to increase the number of such burning and shining lights among you."

## Declining Years

Upon his return to Scotland in 1648, Rutherford became principal of St. Mary's College in St. Andrews, and in 1651 rector of the university. His fame had by this time spread abroad, and in 1648 Rutherford declined an appointment to the chair of divinity in Hardewyck in the Netherlands. The Dutch would have liked very much to have had him, and in 1651 he twice received the appointment to the chair of divinity in Utrecht. But his heart was bound to his fatherland, and both appointments were declined.

In the years following, Rutherford's life was once again filled with sorrow. Charles I had been defeated by Cromwell's armies on English soil, and Charles had fled to Scotland. He was subsequently handed over to the English, who beheaded him. But Cromwell's successes did not solve Scotland's problems, and the Presbyterians in Scotland were bitterly divided over the question of the attitude which the Scottish churches thought they should take towards Cromwell's forces. Presbyterians were split, many friendships were broken, and bitter acrimony and fighting followed, in which Rutherford found himself in a minority position. It was no wonder that the Scottish were the first to welcome back to the throne Charles II, even though he was another Stuart.

Charles II came to the throne with solemn promises to observe the Solemn League and Covenant, but, as was true of the Stuarts in general, lying came easily to him. Just as soon as his position was secure, Charles turned in fury against the Presbyterians and did all in his power to force prelacy on Scotland once again.

During the days when Rutherford was at the Westminster Assembly, he had written a book entitled *Lex Rex* (The Law and the King). In it, he outlined carefully the position of Scottish Presbyterians towards tyrannical kings, and set forth the Presbyterian position on the relation between the people of Scotland, the church in Scotland, and Scotland's king.

Quite naturally, Charles II hated this book, for it argued forcibly against all for which kings stood. In September of 1660 the book was examined by the king's commissioners. It was condemned and the nation was ordered to turn in all copies by October 16. Those who refused to do so were declared enemies of the king. On October 16, collected copies were burned, with ominous implications, by the hangman in Edinburgh, and a few days later at the gate of Rutherford's own college in St. Andrews.

Rutherford was ordered to appear personally before the king's commissioners. This, however, he was unable to do because of his many infirmities and weaknesses. So he was tried, condemned, deposed from the ministry, and dismissed as professor *in absentia*. He was ordered to remain under guard in his own house until a further sentence could be executed.

It was indeed the "Killing Times." Rutherford's two colleagues were killed: Argyle was beheaded on the scaffold, and Guthrie was hanged. Rutherford was next in line, but by the time his turn came around he was dying.

In fact, according to his own confession, he preferred a martyr's death: "I would think it a more glorious way of going home to lay down my life for the cause,...but I submit to my Master's will." When he was ordered to appear in court to have the death sentence passed on him, he responded to the messengers, "Tell them I behove to answer my first summons, and ere your day come, I will be where few kings and great folk come."

It was the time when God's saints were called to "love not their lives unto death." Freely and joyfully they chose the way of obedience, though it led across the dark scaffold, for it was for them the only way home.

## *Rutherford's Character*

In many ways Rutherford was a man of strange paradoxes: paradoxes of character reflected in his writings. He was a man of easy anger and fiery temper, before whose fury bold men quailed, but he was also of infinite patience and kindness towards suffering parishioners, and they loved him for it. When Rutherford was exiled to Aberdeen from his humble parish church in Anwoth, many of his people went the entire distance with him, walking on foot 230 miles, only to have to return the same dreadful distance. When they left him at the gates of Aberdeen, they wept as those whose hearts were broken.

His writings could be, and often were, long, tedious, monotonously argued, and filled with extensive and heavy metaphors which all but crushed his thoughts beyond understanding. He could, however, write beautiful poetry that soared with the eagles. In our home library we have a small book of his poetry that stirs the soul.

In like manner, his writings could be, and often were, bitter, angry, intolerant, filled with seeming malice—especially when enemies of the gospel were the objects of his fury; but his letters, written from Aberdeen in the days of his exile, were warm, comforting to the sorrowful, encouraging to the discouraged, filled with the overflowing of a pastor's heart.

While often his writings sank beneath the weight of heavy and ponderous arguments and high-flown and over-blown rhetoric, sometimes his statements could come like a rapier. To a would-be professor in the university he said, "If you would be a deep divine [theologian], I recommend to you sanctification." On his deathbed he died with the words on his lips from which many preachers could profit mightily: "I betake myself to Christ for sanctification as well as justification."

Rutherford's forte remained his preaching. It is said of him that crowds were attracted to his preaching not so much by the persuasiveness of his argumentation, not because of the power of his oratory, not out of amazement at his exegetical skills, but because he preached Christ—and did so with passion.

He lived a faithful servant of Christ and died escaping a martyr's death by a hair's breadth. His legacy lives on in that towering monument of orthodoxy, the Westminster Confession.

### Chapter 40

# The Story of the Two Margarets

## The Wigtown Martyrs

**Monument overlooking Site of Martyrdom in Wigtown, Scotland**

*Introduction*

*In previous chapters we have noticed how a bitter struggle went on in Scotland after the Reformation to preserve the truth of Scripture and the biblical way of worshiping God. The Stuart kings were determined to impose prelacy on the realm; the Presbyterians were determined to resist it. With only a brief respite during the* days of Oliver Cromwell, the struggle went on from the time of James I to the deposition of James II in 1688. Our present story begins during the reign of Charles II.

While we have discussed the stories of leaders and theologians who bravely opposed prelacy but died "normal" deaths, the pages of Scotland's history are covered with the blood of many martyrs who suffered the cruelest of torments and finally were killed for the sake of their faith. They join a company of illustrious saints who, throughout the ages, "loved not their lives unto death."

As examples of the faith of many such martyrs, whose names are recorded in heaven, we turn to the lives and deaths of two women who shall serve as illustrations of those others whose stories we cannot tell here. They both bore the name of Margaret. One was an aged saint of seventy, and the other a young girl of eighteen, when they were cruelly put to death for their faith.

## *Their Early Lives*

The older woman, **Margaret MacLauchlan**, was the widow of John Mulligen, who had farmed about a mile west of the small village of Wigtown. Wigtown was at the head of the Firth of Solway in the Stewartry of Galloway. To the south were high moors and rugged mountains which gave beauty and remoteness to the area. Margaret was left to tend the farm herself and support her simple life from its products.

Margaret was a very plain woman, uneducated for the most part, early old with the rigors of farm life, but she was noted throughout the area as a woman of unusual intelligence and piety. She had become persuaded of the biblical character of Presbyterianism and of the wickedness of prelacy. Not one to believe one thing and live differently from what she believed, she refused to go to her church to worship when a curate led the services and the worship was according to Anglican rites, but she chose rather to worship with like-minded people on the Lord's day in her home. Only when Non-conformist ministers conducted the services would she attend. This was not simple stubbornness but a deep conviction that God was pleased only with worship which was according to His injunctions.

Margaret was not alone in her stand; many people throughout Scotland took the same unwavering stand; many were also forced to flee their homes and parishes to escape arrest and civil penalties. These became wanderers in their own country who sought refuge and food here and there. When they stopped at Margaret's home, her doors were always open, and shelter could always be found with her.

Such hospitality was a crime in the eyes of the law, and although Margaret was never caught in the act, the soldiers, who knew her absence from church and opposition to prelacy, took every opportunity to plunder her farm and rob her of her few possessions.

Before we proceed with her story, we have to tell of another Margaret: **Margaret Wilson**. Hers is a strange story indeed.

This Margaret was the oldest child of Gilbert Wilson, a farmer of Glenvernock in the parish of Penningham, Wigtownshire. She had one brother, Thomas, who was about sixteen, and one sister, Agnes, a girl of about thirteen at the time Margaret was martyred. They lived near, and knew well, Margaret McLauchlan.

The parents of these young people lived on a prosperous farm with good soil, abundant crops, and many sheep and cattle. Religious division characterized the family, and, strangely enough, it was division between parents and children. How this is to be explained is not known. Most probably the entire family was, in fact, sympathetic to the Presbyterian cause, but the parents, for one reason or another, were not prepared to stand for their principles and so worshiped in the local church under the curate and in the manner of prelacy.

The Wilson children were different, however, and apparently had stronger convictions than their parents. They refused to attend church when the curate presided, and they considered such unbiblical worship to be a denial of Christ their King.

Even though they were children, their absence from church did not go unnoticed. They were reported to the authorities, and when the government threatened punishment, they were forced to flee from their home to seek refuge with other wanderers in the caves of the rugged mountains of Galloway.

The parents did not escape suffering and were persecuted for their children's sake. They were forbidden to give their children food and shelter and were constantly harassed to reveal where the children were hiding. Soldiers (sometimes as many as 100) were quartered in their house and on their land, and the family was expected to support them. They were summoned repeatedly to the courts to give account of themselves. Their possessions were pillaged. They were soon reduced to abject poverty.

Such were the circumstances on the eve of the tragedy.

## *Their Martyrdom*

The cruel and heartless Charles II died. The wandering and homeless saints thought they would now have some surcease from danger. The two Wilson girls came out of their hiding to seek the comfort and encouragement of Margaret McLauchlan. Their brother Thomas stayed in the mountains and was lost to history.

The Wilson girls were permitted to spend only a few days with Margaret before a friend whom they trusted betrayed them, and soldiers were hastily sent to arrest them. Both girls, along with their host, were apprehended, and immediately the two girls were thrown into "the thieves' hole," while Margaret McLauchlan was put into the prison in Wigtown. Some time later the two girls were also put into the same prison, where they at least had each other's company.

During their imprisonment, the women were brutally treated. Deprived of warm fires and beds on which to sleep, given insufficient food to stave off the pangs of hunger, they were also mocked and

tormented. One weapon especially was used against them. Before his death, Charles II had given various commissions the power to require of anyone what was called an oath of abjuration. It was a kind of cruel tool which had a certain legitimacy about it. The Cameronians, a Scottish clan from the Highlands, had earlier drawn up a manifesto which vowed to resist the king if he continued his persecuting and God-defying ways. The oath of abjuration was an oath required randomly from people in which they would swear to renounce the manifesto of the Cameronians. To refuse was considered an act of treason subject to the penalties of death. Not only did commissions randomly require the oath of anyone who came their way, but soldiers, roaming the countryside, also took it upon themselves to require it of anyone they pleased. As often as not, if one refused to swear the oath, he was summarily shot in the open fields or in his own home.

The three women (two only girls) were required to swear this oath. They refused to do this, for it had become a shibboleth of orthodoxy.

On April 13, 1685, the three were summoned before the commission. Several formal charges were brought against them: they had been, so it was charged, on the battlefield of Bothwell Bridge, a charge false on the face of it. They had also been charged with attending field preaching and conventicles; this was almost certainly true.

However, since none of the charges could be proved, the three were once again required to take the oath of abjuration. Again they refused, and a jury found them guilty of treason. Sentence was pronounced, and all three were ordered drowned in the Solway Firth. The date of execution was set at May 11.

The frantic father of Agnes and Margaret hurried to Edinburgh to see if he could possibly stir up in the authorities some sense of mercy and clemency which would save his daughters. All he succeeded in doing was buying the freedom of his youngest daughter Agnes for £100; Margaret he could not save.

When the awful day came, the two Margarets were led by soldiers in chains to the banks of the firth. It was low tide, deliberately chosen as the time for execution. Although the townsfolk pleaded with the two Margarets to save their lives by taking the oath, they steadfastly refused.

Margaret McLauchlan was tied first to a stake pounded into the sandy soil far out in the firth where the waters of the incoming tide would cover her. Margaret Wilson was tied to a similar stake closer into shore so that she could witness the death of her aged friend and fellow saint before the waters would bury her.

It seems as if the older Margaret, spent with the sufferings of many years, said not a word. One of her tormentors shouted, "It is needless to speak to that damned old bitch; let her go to hell."

As the cold sea waters, gradually rising higher, engulfed the old saint, and as Margaret Wilson was forced to watch her drowning struggles, one of the soldiers mockingly said, "What do you think of her now?" Margaret responded, "Think! I see Christ wrestling there. Think ye that we are sufferers? No; it is Christ in us, for He sends none a warfare at their own charges [which they must fight alone]."

When the now limp form of the first Margaret was being tossed about by the swirling tide, the waters began to engulf Margaret Wilson. Her lips were not silent. First she sang the stirring words of Psalm 25:

> My sins and faults of youth
> Do thou, O Lord, forget:
> After thy mercy think on me,
> And for thy goodness great.
> God good and upright is:
> The way he'll sinners show;
> The meek in judgment he will guide
> And make his path to know.

Upon finishing this Psalm, she quoted the words of Romans 8: "Who shall separate us from the love of God...?"

When the waters had finally choked her, but she was not yet dead, the soldiers loosed her from her stake, dragged her to shore, revived her, and once again confronted her with the demand to pray for the king. All the villagers, eagerly wishing to see her spared, cried, "Pray for the king!" Her response was that she wished the salvation of all men and the damnation of none, and that, if God willed, He would save the king: "Lord, give him repentance, forgiveness, and salvation, if it be Thy holy will."

The soldiers were not content with that. "Damned bitch, we do not want such prayers," they said. So once again they attempted to force her to take the oath of abjuration. Her response was: "No! No! No sinful oaths for me. I am one of Christ's children. Let me go."

For this, they hurled her back into the waters of the firth, and there she drowned, to be brought through martyrdom into the company of just men made perfect.

The soldiers departed, congratulating themselves on a job well done; the townsfolk returned to their homes to try to pick up the threads of their lives; but two more saints had sealed their confession with their blood.

## Chapter 41

# John Bunyan

## Author of The Pilgrim's Progress

***Introduction***
*God has raised men in the history of the church who, though not orthodox in all their views, nevertheless have fashioned the thinking of subsequent generations. Such a man was John Bunyan, teacher of the doctrines of grace, but a Baptist in his covenant theology. His influence is due to the one book for which he is known*

by millions: *The Pilgrim's Progress*. Children and adults in succeeding generations who have read this fascinating allegory of the Christian life have come to appreciate and cherish it; people of God who have not read it do well to do so.

A brief description of the times in which John Bunyan lived is essential to understand his life.

After the Reformation in England, a struggle arose between those who were satisfied with the episcopacy of Anglicanism on the one hand and, on the other, those who desired a more profound reformation than Anglicans wanted. After all, Anglicanism retained many Roman Catholic elements, especially in liturgy and church polity.

Those who desired more complete reformation, after the order of Calvin's Reformation in Geneva, fought long and bitterly for their views. Becoming known as Puritans, they finally gained civil power in England after the royalist forces of Charles I were defeated by the Parliamentary forces under Oliver Cromwell. Their power lasted, however, only about as long as Cromwell himself, and shortly after Cromwell's death, the monarchy was restored in the person of

Charles II. Charles, a friend of Roman Catholics, did all in his power to restore that which was lost under Cromwell. The Puritans were defeated in their efforts.

The difficulty was that the Puritans themselves were divided. Some Puritans, while fighting for their views, were content to remain in the Anglican church and seek renewal of the church as a whole. They never succeeded, but they continue in that church until today. Others were convinced that the only way to purge Anglicanism was through instituting their reforms in their own parishes. For this they paid the price of ejection from the Anglican church, and many suffered greatly.

Many of this latter group did not favor a Reformed system of church government any more than Anglicans did; they opted instead for a congregational and independent form of church government which made each congregation self-governing, without any federative unity. These are the beginnings of Congregational-ism. Many became Baptist. Their influence is still felt today in the British Isles, which is filled with such independent Baptistic congregations.

In this political and ecclesiastical situation John Bunyan was born, raised, and did his work.

### Bunyan's Early Life

John Bunyan was born in 1628 in the village of Elston near the town of Bedford. His father was a tinker, a mender of kettles and pots. The class to which he belonged was, while not the most humble in England, still far from the nobility.

Tinkers in England were usually Bohemian gypsies, who were thought to be remnants of old Israel or ancient Egypt. Aware of this, Bunyan attempted, though unsuccessfully, to determine whether these Bohemian gypsies were his ancestors.

Because one of England's virtues was the nation-wide availability of education, Bunyan's father enrolled him in the Bedford Grammar School. But the school was so morally bad that his father, fearing for his son, took him out. That was the end of his education, and whatever he learned from that point was through his own efforts.

John Bunyan worked hard after leaving school, but he also played hard. He became known for his dissolute and profligate life. Especially his wild and blasphemous language made him a byword

among the local folk. Wearying of the discipline of the home, he ran away and joined the Parliamentary Army. He saw no action, distinguished himself in no way, and soon returned home as wild and wicked as ever.

After resuming his former labors and even spending a time in bell-ringing in the local parish church, he married a meek and poor, though exceptionally pious, young girl. She managed to curb his wild nature and to persuade him to engage in reading to advance his meager education.

While the godly influences of his wife can only be surmised, the local minister, Mr. Gifford, was instrumental in Bunyan's conversion. The year was 1653.

Mr. Gifford had come to the ministry in a rather strange way. He had been a royalist officer, an escaped prisoner, a gifted physician in Bedford, a licentious man, but finally a converted man of God who became pastor of the congregation in Bedford. This congregation was part of the Cromwellian state church during the days of the Cromwellian Republic. Now it was Baptist.

Bunyan came under the influence of Mr. Gifford and was instructed by him in the faith. Although Bunyan received no formal education for the ministry, he assumed this position after Mr. Gifford died.

Bunyan possessed a retentive, fierce, impatient, and energetic mind. While he was living in his sins, that mind made him a leader of the wicked young men in the area; under the power of divine grace, it became useful in a long and noble service in the gospel.

## Bunyan's Ministry

Through hard work and patient study, Bunyan became a powerful and beloved preacher whose congregation grew rapidly.

Tragedy came into his life at this point. His wife died, leaving him with four children, one of whom was a blind daughter. This little daughter, gentle, loving, thoughtful, and kind, became her father's special delight.

Bunyan soon married again, and his second wife was a faithful wife, a help to him in his ministry, and a mother to his children. It seems, however, that he never had any children by her.

When Charles II came to the throne, he put forth every effort to silence dissent and to conform all England to the Prayer Book. Dissenters were forbidden to preach, and John Bunyan was soon

thrown into the prison in Bedford for disobeying the command of the king.

Twelve-and-a-half long years he spent in the prison, in spite of many efforts to secure his release and in spite of many attempts on the part of his wife to persuade the courts to show mercy. Although his imprisonment and separation from his family were dreadful, Bunyan's suffering was never as bad as was the suffering of others in far more horrible prisons. His wife was cared for, if meagerly, by his congregation; the jailer was a kind man who did not, as some, vent his brutality on his prisoners; and in the later years Bunyan was even permitted to leave prison to see his wife and children, to preach in his congregation, to visit his parishioners, and even to travel to London—although the jailer was severely censured for the latter extravagance. He was not deprived of his books, paper, and pen, and it was during these years in prison that Bunyan wrote a number of books, including the classic *The Pilgrim's Progress,* published in 1678. His blind daughter came to visit him nearly every day.

Finally, after twelve-and-a-half years, and when Charles II relented a bit, Bunyan was released. He put his affairs in order and resumed his labors in the congregation. It was under his leadership that his congregation organized and became the first legal congregation of dissenters in England.

His fame as a preacher grew, and the small chapel had to be repeatedly enlarged. Branch meetings were held in the surrounding villages and the first preaching circuits were established. Bunyan became a kind of "bishop" of the churches and was even sometimes affectionately called "Bishop Bunyan."

His influence spread, and even in London, when he preached, he attracted throngs of people. The story is told that Dr. Owen was one of his frequent hearers in London. When that erudite and highly educated divine was sneeringly asked by Charles II how he could go to hear a tinker preach, Owen responded, "I would give all my learning to be able to preach as well as the tinker."

Bunyan's ministry was not long. During a time when he was very ill, he departed on a long trip through stormy and wet weather to engage in pastoral work. From this he never recovered, and he died in the home of a friend. The year was 1688. He was sixty years old. His wife outlived him by four years.

## The Pilgrim's Progress

Bunyan's views accurately reflect the theology of Puritans in these days. He was strong on doctrine and even satirized the Anglican church in Mr. Worldly Wiseman, who wanted to reduce Christianity to mere ethics. He held firmly to the doctrines of grace but preached these doctrines from the Lutheran viewpoint of justification by faith alone rather than from the Calvinistic viewpoint of sovereign grace.

Especially in his view of conversion, Bunyan reflected Puritan views, and without a solid doctrine of the covenant, he had no room for the salvation of elect children in the line of the covenant; he also somewhat deemphasized the daily conversion to which a child of God is called. In his spiritual biography, *Grace Abounding to the Chief of Sinners* (1666), he spoke of conversion as involving conviction of sin, attempts to appease God with legal righteousness, subsequent despair, a long and drawn-out period of temptation and struggle, and finally peace in the way of faith in Christ. Such a conversion, though indeed the means God uses to bring some to salvation, has become the norm for genuine conversion even in many Reformed circles, but only in those circles where there is no biblical doctrine of the covenant.

Bunyan wrote over fifty books, the better known of which are *The Holy War* and *Grace Abounding to the Chief of Sinners,* yet it is *The Pilgrim's Progress* that is most associated in the minds of many saints with John Bunyan. It has gone through countless editions, and every Christmas season seems to bring out a new one. It has been translated into many foreign languages, including all the languages and dialects of continental Europe. It was, in past years, almost always found on the shelf of godly homes, even when the only other book was the Bible.

Even Mark Twain's Huckleberry Finn gives a concise description of the book: "Interesting, but tough." Who among us who has read *The Pilgrim's Progress* can ever forget Mr. Valiant-for-Truth and Mr. Worldly-Wiseman? And who, having traveled with Pilgrim, can erase from his mind the Slough of Despond and House Beautiful? It will live yet many generations, if the Lord tarries, as the pilgrim's guide on his way to the Celestial City.

*Part Six*

# Post-Reformation Period in the Netherlands
## 1600-1920

# Part Six:

## Post-Reformation Period in the Netherlands (1600-1920)

**1560**

Belgic Confession 1562.........
Heidelberg Catechism 1563...
First Reformed Synod in the
   Netherlands 1571.............

**Franciscus Gomarus** 1563-1641

**1575**

**William Ames** 1576-1633

**Johannes Maccovius** 1588-1644
**Gijsbertus Voetius** c.1588-1676

**1600**

**Johannes Cocceius** 1603-1669

Synod of Dordrecht
   1618-1619.....................
Thirty Years' War
   1618-1648.....................

Peace of Westphalia 1648.......

**1650**   **William III of Orange** 1650-1720

**1700**

**1800**   **Hendrik DeCock** 1801-1842

Separation or Secession
   *(De Afscheiding)* 1834........

**Abraham Kuyper** 1837-1920

Aggrieved Ones
   *(De Doleantie)* 1886.........

**1900**

## Chapter 42

# William Ames
## Puritan in the Netherlands

*Introduction*
*Almost from the*
*beginning of the*
*history of the*
*Reformation in the*
*Netherlands, a*
*Puritan strain could*
*be found in the*
*Dutch Reformed*
*churches. This*
*Puritan influence*
*was to continue for*
*many years, and it*
*made an indelible*
*mark on Dutch*
*thought.*
*The reason why a*
*Puritan influence*
*could be found*

among the Dutch was the close contact, throughout the centuries, between the Dutch and the English.

The English came to the help of the Dutch in the war for Dutch independence under William the Silent. The English sent representatives to the Synod of Dordt (although it is a matter of debate whether they were of any assistance in the battle against Arminianism). During the time of Spanish persecution in the Netherlands, many Hollanders fled to England and found refuge there; and during the efforts of the Stuart kings in England to impose prelacy on all the churches, many English refugees found a haven in the Netherlands. One need only think of the Pilgrims who, after fleeing England, lived for a time in and near Leyden before sailing for America. English scholars were recognized for their learning and were invited to Dutch universities to teach, and Dutch scholars found positions in English universities. Dutch ministers preached in English churches, and English preachers found many years of enjoyable labor in Dutch churches. The contacts were of many kinds, very close, and frequent.

All this brought into the Netherlands a "Dutch Puritanism" which remains in the Dutch churches today.

William Ames was one of the Dutch Puritans.

### *Life in England*

Almost nothing is known of the early life of William Ames; not any of the details of his early life have come down to us. He was born in 1576 in Ipswich, Suffolk, a town about seventy miles northeast of London near the Sea. He was born when Queen Elizabeth sat on the throne of England as the last of the Tudors. She had already seen to it that Parliament passed the Act of Conformity, which required that all churches follow the pattern of the Church of England, both in worship and church government, a policy which made life difficult for Puritans.

These circumstances of Ames' birth are so important that his entire life was controlled by them. We shall have to say a few things, also, about the struggle which went on in England as a result of Elizabeth's rule.

The Church of England was, at least officially, quite Calvinistic, as expressed in the Thirty-nine Articles of the Church of England—the official creed of the church. In government, the church was strictly hierarchical and had the same structure of archbishops, bishops, and priests (along with a multitude of other offices) as Rome had—except for cardinals and a pope. In worship, most of the trappings, ceremonies, robes, liturgies, and symbols which were a part of Romish worship, while abolished in the first rush of reformation, gradually crept back into the church.

Within the Anglican church was a large group of clergy and people who wanted more complete reformation, not only in doctrine, but also in church polity and worship. They made every effort to change the Anglican church but were blocked in their efforts by Elizabeth, who insisted on uniformity throughout her realm. Most clergy, when forced to sign the 1571 Act of Uniformity, did so. Some did not. They became known as Puritans because they wanted to purify the church beyond what had so far been accomplished. Later, in about 1619, they were called Non-conformists, a name which stuck for many years.

For the most part, the Non-conformists stayed in the Church of England although they continued to promote their Non-conformity and refused to sign any Acts of Uniformity. Where else could they

go? It was not until the Great Ejection that Non-conformists were expelled from the Anglican church and that Non-conformist churches sprang up throughout England.

William Ames was a Puritan in the Anglican church, outspoken and vocal, and one who refused to bow before the dictates of Elizabeth. Nor could Archbishop Bancroft's most strenuous opposition to Non-conformity move him. I suppose that if Ames had been content to moderate his protests and keep his objections to himself, he would have survived within the Anglican church and would have been able to keep his post in Cambridge, but that was not in his nature. He believed deeply that prelacy, hierarchy, and all the remnants of Rome that remained in the Anglican church dishonored God and made the church a wicked institution. His deep commitment to his principles came to expression in his strong opposition to practices of the established church and made him a passionate defender of Puritan goals.

Ames received the majority of his education at Christ's College, Cambridge, where he studied under the famous Puritan supralapsarian William Perkins. Being an ardent Puritan, he could hope for no advancement within Anglican circles. Hence, when an opportunity arose to become chaplain of Cambridge University, he took it.

Ames' stay in Cambridge did not last long. The very nature of an established state church in England was conducive to careless and profane living. The students in Cambridge were no exceptions. When Ames preached a sermon against various evil practices among the students, such as card-playing and gambling, his enemies took the opportunity to work for his censure. Hating him for his Non-conformity, they used Ames' sermon as an excuse to get rid of him.

Ames quite clearly saw that he would be expelled from the university if he fought his case; and so he left the university and made his way to the Netherlands. After a brief stay in Leyden, he went to The Hague.

An interesting anecdote describing an event which took place prior to Ames' departure from the university shows how clearly the issue was really one of Non-conformity. While the storm over his sermon was still raging, Ames was called before Dr. Carey, the master of the college, and told he should wear a surplice, which was a robe worn by clerics to add to the dignity of their office. The Puritans had rejected the use of such "papal" garments, but the Anglicans were then and are now favorable to such clothing. Dr. Carey insisted that Scripture required him to wear it, and when Ames, rather astonished, asked for the text where such a command was found, Carey quoted the passage "Put on the armour of light," which, Carey insisted, referred to a white surplice. Ames' refusal to be swayed by such exegesis infuriated the master.

## Ames' Labors in the Netherlands

It was in The Hague that Ames found employment as chaplain to Sir Horace Vere, the commander of the English troops in the Netherlands. At the same time, Ames served as minister of the English church in The Hague.

But the long arm of Ames' enemies in England reached across the channel. The archbishop of Canterbury wrote a letter to Sir Ralph Winwood, the English ambassador to the Netherlands, to see to it that Ames was removed from his position. His letter ended with these words: "I wish the removing of him to be as *privately* and as *cleanly carried* as the matter will permit. We are also acquainted what *English preachers* are entertained in Zeeland, whereunto in convenient time we hope to give a redress."

Ames' persecutors could not finally keep him from finding employment in the land where he had chosen to make his home, although they tried desperately. Because of his vast learning and great ability, Ames was called to be divinity professor at Franeker in Friesland in 1622. Twelve years he served in this prestigious school, and his fame spread throughout all Europe. Students came from remote parts of the continent to study under him, and the school itself, in recognition of his contributions to the university, made him rector in 1626. During this time he had the privilege and pleasure of serving with Maccovius, of whom we will speak in a later chapter.

Sadly, though, Ames' abilities were not recognized by his countrymen, and the adage mentioned in Scripture that a prophet is not without honor, save in his own country, was true of him.

During the years of his stay in Franeker, Ames served the Dutch Reformed churches well. He did battle against the high church prelates in England and continued to write against their superstitious ceremonies and Romish practices, while defending vigorously the regulative principle of worship. Richard Baxter, famous for his still popular book *The Reformed Pastor,* left Anglicanism to join the Nonconformist movement because of the writings of William Ames.

Ames also wrote extensively against Roman Catholic error and took on the great Bellarmine, perhaps the greatest of all Roman Catholic theologians since the time of the Reformation.

But Ames' chief enemies were always the Arminians, whose theology he detested as rationalistic and humanistic, which it truly is. Not only were the Arminians subjected to his scathing attacks in print, but Ames was chosen to attend the Synod of Dordt, where he participated in their trial and condemnation. He was, in fact, paid four florins a day to attend the synod, and he served with distinction as assistant and private secretary to the president, the fiery Johannes Bogerman. Ames' work there was chiefly behind the scenes.

But William Ames always loved above all the pastoral ministry and wanted to return to it. Added to this was a severe case of asthma, which made it difficult for him to breathe in the winter months. He was, in fact, so stricken that he feared every winter in the cold and damp northern provinces would be his last.

Thinking perhaps that the southern part of the Netherlands would be better for his health, Ames took a call to the church in Rotterdam, where he served the Lord for a brief time, but the climate there did not make much difference in his asthma, and Ames made plans to move to America to settle among the Dutch churches in New York or New Jersey. He died before he could make the move, however, and finished his work on earth November 14, 1633, at the age of fifty-seven.

Ames' wife and family did move to the new world after Ames' death and took his extremely valuable library with them. This library was an extraordinarily valuable legacy in America, for he had one of the finest libraries in the country, and America, at this time in her history, was almost entirely without books.

Ames' son William returned from America to England and was vocal in the Non-conformist movement in England until he, along with so many others, was ejected from the Anglican church and suffered the awful persecution that was the lot of the ejected ministers.

Although Ames was by no means well known, the Dutch Reformed churches owe him a great debt for his unwavering and uncompromising stand against Arminianism. The Puritanism for which he fought in England was also to be his legacy in the Netherlands as it lived on in various branches of the Reformed churches.

Chapter 43

# Franciscus Gomarus

## Stubborn Champion of God's Glory

### Introduction

*It is a surprising fact of history that oftentimes, in doctrinal controversy, the heretic is a nice man, while the defender of the faith is, from many points of view, a miserable character. Arius versus Athanasius: Arius the suave, diplomatic, likeable denier of Christ's divinity; Athanasius the stubborn and implacable defender of the Nicene Creed.*

Nestorius versus Cyril: Nestorius the popular, gifted heretic who insisted Christ had two persons; Cyril the haughty and cruel defender of the unity of Christ's natures in the one divine person. Pelagius versus Augustine: Pelagius the urbane and witty defender of freedom of the will; Augustine the crabby defender of the sovereignty of grace. Hincmar versus Gotteschalk: Hincmar the learned and powerful archbishop of Rheims; Gotteschalk the stern and unfriendly follower of Augustine who rotted in prison for his recalcitrance. And so the list could go on: Erasmus the humanist versus Luther; Bolsec the heretic versus Calvin; Mary, queen of the Scots, versus Knox. Those who know their history can find others, perhaps within their own particular denominational history.

So it was also with Gomarus. Even his friends found him obnoxious at times and barely tolerable. His opponent, Jacobus Arminius, popular with students and ministers, gracious, kind, tolerant, filled with concern for friend and foe alike, presents quite a contrast. But Arminius was the heretic, and Gomarus stood for the truth.

Why does God work this way in the history of the church? Why is the pleasant fellow so often the enemy of the faith, while the old curmudgeon is the champion of the truth of God? I do not think that we can find a complete answer to this question, but part of it is that the truth is not popular, and defenders of the truth can sometimes become crabby because of the fierce and unrelenting attacks of opponents. Sometimes the deceit and double-tongued language of heretics who hide their heresy with honey-coated words can be exposed only by sharp and impolitic language. Sometimes the defense of the faith requires a stubborn man who will not budge no matter what the consequences; yet he is presented by his enemies as being unreasonable and wickedly stubborn, so that the truth for which he fights may be maligned along with him. Always God uses weakest means to fulfill his will.

There is an important truth here, a truth to which few pay attention. So many are persuaded of their position by the character of the men involved: the nice man must be right; the nasty fellow cannot possibly be correct. Yet the truth must be decided on other grounds than that of personalities; it must be decided by the Scriptures alone, regardless of any personal likes and dislikes. Without excusing what is sometimes wicked conduct on the part of orthodox men, it is important that the church remember that the truth is determined by God's Word alone. Gomarus, for all his shortcomings, was a champion of the Reformed faith. One must, for the truth's sake, overlook personal faults.

### *Early Life and Education*

The family into which Gomarus was born lived in Bruges, a city in the province of Flanders, which was then a part of the Lowlands but is now a part of Belgium. Gomarus was the oldest child in the family, born January 30, 1563. He had two younger brothers and possibly a younger sister. Sometime before 1570, although probably after Gomarus' birth, his family embraced the Reformed faith.

Gomarus began his studies in Bruges and at an early age learned Latin and Greek. In 1577, because of the severity of the Spanish persecution in the Lowlands, the family sought refuge in Germany in the Palatinate. Because of the nearness of the family to the city of Strassburg, Gomarus was able to study under Johann Sturm, a second-generation reformer, in the city where Calvin had lived in the years of his exile from Geneva.

When Frederick (the Pious), the Calvinist elector of the Palatinate, died, his brother Louis (Ludwig) came to the electorate. He was a Lutheran and hated Calvinism passionately. He drove out of the University of Heidelberg all the Calvinist professors, including Ursinus and Olevianus, the authors of the Heidelberg Catechism. Some of these professors settled in Neustadt, and to Neustadt Gomarus went to study under Ursinus and Zanchius. His studies included Hebrew, Greek, Latin, and philosophy.

From 1582 to 1584 Gomarus broadened his education by a trip to England, where he studied first in Oxford, then in Cambridge. In 1585 Louis died, and his brother, Prince Casimir, became elector. He restored to the university the professors from Heidelberg who were still living. Gomarus, seeking Reformed instruction, spent two years there.

## *Ministry and Professorship*

Gomarus had received a wide and excellent education and had become an expert in languages, including Hebrew. His education was first of all to be put to use in the pastoral ministry, to which he also aspired. He became pastor of a Dutch congregation in Germany in Frankfurt-on-the-Main. The church had been established in 1555 by Martinus Micronius and John à Lasco, two second-generation reformers. John à Lasco had played a significant role in the formation of the liturgy of the Dutch Reformed churches.

Work in Frankfurt-on-the-Main did not last very long. The church was dissolved because of Lutheran persecution. The Lutherans were always angry that Calvinism had taken hold in Germany, which they considered their own private preserve.

While in Frankfurt-on-the-Main, Gomarus married Emerentia, a daughter of Gilles and sister of Abraham Muysenhol. They did not have long together: she died in childbirth with their first child in 1591, very shortly after they were married. Two years later Gomarus married again, to a woman named Maria, a daughter of local nobility. He lived with her for many years.

Although the congregation in Frankfurt-on-the-Main was dissolved and Gomarus was left without a pastorate, within a few months he was asked to become professor of theology in the University of Leyden. His reputation for wide learning and his devotion to orthodoxy were already well known.

While it is not known exactly what was Gomarus' wage while in Leyden, the town records indicate that he was probably rather well-off. He owned a house adjacent to the university. The taxes in the city were levied on the basis of the number of chimneys on the house, and Gomarus was charged for eleven chimneys.

The early years in the university were probably some of the happiest in Gomarus' life. He enjoyed his work, had opportunity to advance his studies, and found a congenial home where his colleagues were all one with him in the faith. His students respected him, also for his vast learning, and his work was beneficial for the churches.

All this changed in 1603. In that year, over the strong protests of Gomarus, Jacobus Harmsen, known as Jacob Arminius, was appointed professor of theology in the university to work with Gomarus in that faculty of learning. This proved to be the beginning of the trouble which finally resulted in a country-wide split in the Dutch churches and was only resolved by the great Synod of Dordt.

## Controversy with Arminius

It may surprise us somewhat that Gomarus fought hard against the appointment of Arminius as professor in theology. But this surprise will evaporate when we realize that Arminius was under strong suspicion for his views before he was considered for a professorship. After he completed his studies, Arminius became minister in the church of Amsterdam. It was not long after the beginning of his ministry that he began a series of sermons on the book of Romans. In connection with his treatment of Romans 7:14–25, Arminius took the position that Paul was describing in this passage his spiritual state prior to his conversion. One can readily recognize that this implies that Paul, before being converted, was able to will the good: "The good that I would..." Such a view was a denial of the total depravity of man and paved the way for the doctrine of the freedom of the human will in the work of salvation.

These views were challenged by Plancius, one of Arminius' fellow ministers in Amsterdam. A controversy arose in the church there which intensified when Arminius began preaching on Romans 9. It was in the middle of the controversy that the appointment came which Gomarus, aware of the controversy, opposed. But Arminius had powerful friends in the highest reaches of government, and his appointment went through.

In the end, Gomarus agreed to the appointment. A conference was held between him and Arminius, prior to the final approval of Arminius, sponsored by the States-General of the Dutch government. The interpretation of Romans 7 was discussed, but Arminius so managed to hide his true beliefs that Gomarus was satisfied and approved the appointment. Gomarus later spoke of regretting that approval.

The controversy broke out again on February 7, 1604, when Arminius propounded various theses on the doctrine of predestination. The sum of these theses can be found in the following quotation from them.

> Divine predestination is the decree of God in Christ by which he has decreed with himself from eternity to justify, adopt, and gift with eternal life, to the praise of his glorious grace, the faithful whom he has decreed to gift with faith. On the other hand, reprobation is the decree of the anger or severe will of God, by which he has determined from eternity, for the purpose of showing his anger and power, to condemn to eternal death, as placed out of union with Christ, the unbelieving who, by their own fault and the just judgment of God, are not to believe.

It is my guess that the majority of our readers might be hard-pressed to find any fault with this statement of Arminius. The difficulty in finding its error is probably due in part to the fact that Arminius was capable of cloaking his error in a deceptive way to make it appear Reformed; but the difficulty in detecting what is wrong may also, sadly enough, be explained by the lack of theological sensitivity in today's church.

At any rate, the problem with the statement of Arminius just quoted lies in the fact that Arminius is teaching in this paragraph a conditional predestination: "[God] has decreed...to justify...the faithful..." That is, God has decreed to justify those who have faith, which makes faith a condition to election. And: "Reprobation is the decree...of God...to condemn...the unbelieving..." That is, also reprobation is a conditional decree, the condition of which is unbelief.

Gomarus attacked these statements, and the result was bitter and prolonged controversy. Arminius continued to present himself as a faithful defender of the Reformed faith while attempting to cast Gomarus in the bad light of an enemy of true Calvinism. It is not hard to understand that Gomarus received a bad reputation for his opposition to Arminius. After all, the point seemed insignificant, as even the leaders in government were later to say. Why fight about it? And Arminius was such a nice man! He protested his innocence time and again and assured everyone that he was soundly Reformed and deeply committed to the confessions. How could Gomarus, that man who never smiled, be such a stubborn man?

The controversy raged for four years and finally engulfed the churches. In 1608 Gomarus and Arminius conducted a public debate before the Supreme Court of The Hague in an effort on the part of the government to resolve the problems. At the conclusion of the debate, Barneveldt, a friend of Arminius and head of the government, in a short address to the two combatants, declared that he thanked God that their contentions did not affect the fundamental articles of the Christian religion. To this Gomarus replied in characteristic fashion, "I would not appear before the throne of God with Arminius' errors." The Court judged the matters in dispute to be matters of little significance.

In further efforts to resolve the disagreements, a conference was arranged at which Gomarus and Arminius were to submit papers outlining their respective positions on the doctrine of predestination. Each was given 250 guilders to cover the expense of preparing the papers. The conference was never held because Arminius died in 1609 of what was probably tuberculosis.

It is not our purpose in this chapter to trace the history of the controversy any further than Gomarus' involvement in it. As anyone with even a passing knowledge of the controversy knows, the issues were the great issues of salvation by sovereign grace alone versus salvation based on the works of man. Ten years after the death of Arminius the controversy was settled at the Synod of Dordrecht, where Gomarus' position was vindicated.

In 1611 Gomarus resigned from his position in the University of Leyden. The reason for his resignation is not known, but it may be that the controversy and the support of Arminius by the government wore beyond endurance the strength of the old warrior. At any rate, upon his resignation, he became pastor of a Reformed congregation in Middelburg, where he also lectured in theology and Hebrew in the local university.

In 1614 Gomarus went to Saumur in France, where he became professor of theology. It is a bit disconcerting to know that the school in Saumur, not long after Dordt, became a hotbed of Amyrauldianism, a heresy not unlike Arminianism.

In 1618–1619 Gomarus was at the Synod of Dordt along with other professor advisors. He took an active role in the synod's proceedings and was instrumental in the victory of the truth of Scripture that salvation is by sovereign grace and not by choice of man's free will.

An interesting sidelight to Gomarus' role at the Synod of Dordt was his work on a committee to investigate the teachings of Maccovius. Maccovius also held strongly to the doctrine of sovereign predestination but was charged with carrying the doctrine to such an extreme that he made God the author of sin. The synod handed the case to government representatives, who were unable to resolve the conflict. A committee was appointed to deal with the matter, on which committee Gomarus served. Later in the proceedings of the synod, the committee reported that the matter had been amicably resolved, and Maccovius was cautioned not to make radical and biblically unwarranted statements.

After the synod, Gomarus went to the University of Groningen, where he became professor of divinity and Hebrew.

In 1633 Gomarus took part in the revision of the translation of the Bible, which work was done in Leyden. During these meetings he argued strenuously against including the apocryphal books in the Bible but was overruled. This translation, authorized by the Synod of Dordt, was for many years to the Dutch what the Authorized Version was (and is) to the English. Gomarus stayed in Leyden until his death on January 11, 1641.

## Conclusion

There can be no question about it that Gomarus was a difficult man, hard to get along with, prone to extreme statements, sometimes violent in his opposition to Arminius and Arminianism. He never "beat around the bush." He never left any doubt in anyone's mind as to what he believed. He never worried about "stepping on people's toes" or offending them if they were not, heart and mind, committed to the truth.

Sometimes descriptions of him are biased, and bitterness against his staunch defense of the faith pours out in diatribes against his personality. Thus, one author can write, "[He] displayed a most violent, virulent, and intolerant spirit, and endeavored by various publications to excite the indignation of the States of Holland against his rival."

Some of this was true. Even Junius, later related to Gomarus through marriage, said, "That man pleases himself most wonderfully by his own remarks. He derives all his stock of knowledge from others; he brings forward nothing of his own: or, if at any time he varies from his usual practice, he is exceedingly infelicitous in those occasional changes."

There is a story somewhere, whether true or apocryphal it is hard to say, that at the Synod of Dordt, one elder was appointed to sit alongside Gomarus to tug him back into his seat when he would leap to his feet and too forcibly made a point.

Nevertheless, Gomarus was a staunch defender of the faith. Perhaps it took a man such as he to stand against the growing tide of Arminianism. God's providence prepares men who are "stubborn" about the right things. And if this seems to condone their sins, the fact is that, though it does not, God can, as the proverb has it, draw a straight line with a crooked stick. Sometimes only very strong language will do to put to flight the clever designs of heretics.

At the Synod of Dordt Gomarus defended not only orthodoxy but supralapsarian orthodoxy. And, although his views in this respect did not prevail on the synod, for the Canons are infralapsarian, his supralapsarianism was not condemned by the synod and his defense of the faith was of inestimable service as the synod struggled with the errors of Arminianism.

Gomarus cared only about one thing: the glory of God. He would allow only one book to determine his theology: the Sacred Scriptures. In an album in which he kept various letters, tokens of friendship, and something of a diary, Gomarus had written in Hebrew, "Thy [God's] Word is Light."

Gomarus was of the stripe of Calvin, Gotteschalk, Augustine, and Athanasius. He was the forerunner of others to follow, one of whom must be Herman Hoeksema, whose life is summarized in Chapter 51. We need not always approve of the way in which they did things (although we must take a long and hard look at ourselves in this respect), but we ought to thank God for them, for they were men of courage and conviction who fought for truth and right against all odds. To concentrate on their weaknesses and foibles, so as to condemn their defense of the faith, is to be unfaithful to the truth. To look beyond personalities and weigh all in the light of Scripture is to be faithful. To fight is the courage of faith. May God grant men like these to the church today, even if they sometimes have difficult personalities. The church needs more than nice men.

## Chapter 44

# *Johannes Maccovius*

## *Supralapsarian*

### *Introduction*

*The pages of the history of the church of Christ are filled with large figures who dominate their age and who cast a long shadow over subsequent history. By no means, however, does God make use only of towering men who are gifted beyond us and who have a work given them of God which is remembered throughout the ages. God uses other men, lesser figures, whose names might*
appear in a footnote or two of some learned and seldom-read volume but who are not forgotten in heaven, because their names appear in the book of life. I am not speaking here of that noble and exalted company of saints whose names no one knows but God alone, whose deeds went mostly unrecognized in the time they lived and whose graves are forgotten. They are the "last" which Scripture assures us shall be the "first" in the kingdom of heaven. But I am speaking of others, who in their own time were recognized as men of leadership and outstanding ability, whom God used sometimes in rather strange ways, but who are, for the most part, unknown today. It is worth our while to recall from oblivion some of these men.

Johannes Maccovius was one such man. Perhaps his importance lies especially in a "case" brought against him which was treated at the great Synod of Dordt and which had ramifications that touch on theological questions of our own day.

### *His Life*

Johannes Maccovius was born at Lobzenic, in Poland, in the year 1588. That means, if we would put him in the context of

some well-known events of the Reformation, that he was born about twenty-five years after the writing of the Belgic Confession and the Heidelberg Catechism, and that at his birth the error of Arminianism was already taking hold in the soil of the Netherlands.

The name "Johannes Maccovius" is his Latin name, which he took, as was the custom in those days, when he became professor in a university. The name given him by his parents was Jan Makowsky, a name clearly indicating his Polish ancestry.

The Calvin Reformation had influenced Poland to some extent, and Maccovius was by no means the only influential early reformer to come from that land. After his early education, Maccovius was sent to Germany, where he studied at the principal universities. After completing his studies, he returned to Poland, where he visited various universities in his fatherland as tutor to young Polish nobles. Somewhere he had become acquainted with that system of doctrine known as Calvinism, and he had eagerly embraced it and remained faithful to it all his life.

Maccovius' activities were not limited to the tutoring of spoiled sons of foppish nobles. He began to engage various heretics in disputations. The Socinian heresy, which denied the truth of the Trinity, and the Jesuit heresies, which sought to reintroduce Roman Catholic teachings, were the objects of his hatred. Powerful and influential Socinians and Jesuits matched their debating skills with this defender of Calvinistic orthodoxy.

It was especially through such disputations that his fame spread to other lands, and Maccovius soon received an invitation from the University of Franeker in the Netherlands to teach theology at that prestigious university. In 1614 he became a doctor of theology, and in 1615 he was appointed professor of theology. There he remained for the rest of his life, dying in Franeker on June 24, 1644.

The man who was his colleague and chief promoter was Sybrandus Lubbertus, who also became his enemy and accuser in the "Maccovius Case."

We are told that though Maccovius was an extraordinarily homely man, he was a gifted teacher and well-liked by his students. In fact, he was so popular that his fame spread throughout Europe, and his reputation attracted students to Franeker from all parts of the continent. The outstanding feature of his life was his controversy with Lubbertus; and in that controversy lie significant events which are important for us today.

## *His Controversy with Lubbertus*

Although it is not so easy to sort out precisely the issues in the controversy, it is clear that Maccovius applied what became known as the scholastic method to teaching theology. In brief, the scholastic method of teaching was a method of applying the principles of logic to theology and teaching theology as a logical system of truth. In fact, it was the logical clarity of Maccovius' teaching which made him popular with his students.

The difficulty seemed to be, however, that he sometimes carried the system of logical analysis and development too far. He was accused, for example, of giving the same authority to logical deductions from the biblical truths as he gave to Scripture itself. But here again, it is hard to tell whether he actually did this, and even whether, in doing this, he was far from orthodoxy.

At any rate, Maccovius was a bitter and implacable foe of Arminianism, and he fought it hammer and tongs. The war which he waged against Arminianism made him a despised enemy of the Remonstrants, for in him was found no compromise. Enemies of the truth are often willing to show friendship to defenders of the faith as long as there is the slightest hope of compromise. Perhaps there was no single theologian, other than Gomarus, more deeply resented by these heretics than Maccovius.

In the course of his battles against Arminianism, Maccovius was particularly determined to defend the truths of sovereign and double predestination. He made his defense over against Arminian efforts to teach that Christ willed the salvation of all men, but in the defense of the orthodox Calvinistic position, he went, in the opinion of his colleague Lubbertus, too far—too far in teaching that God decreed the reprobate unto sin; too far in teaching that the reprobate sin out of necessity.

The views of Maccovius came to the attention of Lubbertus and others in the examination of a student who, in 1616, was defending various theses involved in the supralapsarian position. The examiners traced the views of this student, whose name has been buried in oblivion, to his teacher Maccovius. Thus, that with which Maccovius was charged came really from one of his students.

It cannot be denied that Maccovius, brilliant scholar that he was, carried, by his scholastic method, the doctrines of sovereign and double predestination too far, and that he did not properly teach the relation between reprobation and sin. It is also true that Lubbertus,

whether he over-reacted to Maccovius' teaching or whether he himself did not always have things straight, made statements which seemed to support a desire on God's part to save all men, the heart of the error of the well-meant offer of the gospel.

Whatever may be the precise truth of the matter, the case was brought to the Friesland States-Deputies, which decided against Maccovius. Convinced he had said nothing wrong, Maccovius appealed to the Synod of Dordt. And so, while the synod was doing battle with Arminian heresy, it had on the table as well the case of Maccovius.

In the initial stages of the case, the matter was given to a political commission which attempted to settle the matter by trying to bring about agreement between Maccovius and his colleague Lubbertus. These efforts failed totally.

After the lack of success was reported back to synod, synod appointed another committee to study the matter, attempt to settle it, and come, if necessary, with recommendations to synod. The committee consisted of Dutch and foreign delegates: Scultetus from Heidelberg in Germany, Stein from Kassel, Breytinger from Zurich in Switzerland, and Gomarus, Thysius, and à Meyen, all from the Netherlands.

It was striking that Gomarus, himself an ardent supralapsarian, was also on the committee. The committee met with Maccovius himself, as well as with Lubbertus. What happened in the meetings was never revealed, but the committee succeeded in reconciling these two warring colleagues. The committee reported to synod that the matter was amicably resolved by a decision in which Maccovius himself had participated; that the committee had exonerated Maccovius from all error of any kind; but that Maccovius was reprimanded for his manner of teaching, for some rash statements which he had made, and for his one-sided supralapsarianism.

And so the matter was laid to rest.

## Conclusion

This action of the Synod of Dordt in the Maccovius matter has significance today.

All who know anything about the Canons of Dordt know also that these Canons are infralapsarian. It has been said by those who support infralapsarianism that supralapsarianism is anti-confessional. That would mean that members today of the Protestant Reformed

Churches, who are predominantly supralapsarian, are, in fact, anti-confessional.

But the Maccovius case proves that this is not so.

While it is surely true that the Canons are infralapsarian, the framers of the Canons deliberately and consciously refused to condemn supralapsarianism. The issues of "supra" versus "infra" were vigorously debated on the floor of the synod, and each position had its staunch defenders. The synod had the perfect opportunity in the Maccovius case, and could very well have used Maccovius' rash statements as an occasion to condemn supralapsarianism in the Dutch church, if they had so desired. By refusing to do this, and by exonerating Maccovius, the synod insisted that there was room in the Reformed churches for the supralapsarian viewpoint. This has continued to the present.

In the early years of the Protestant Reformed Churches in America, the fathers and grandfathers could argue long and furiously over the relative merits of the two viewpoints debated at Dordt, though now almost no one cares any longer about such questions. Within the Protestant Reformed churches, however, there was always room for both viewpoints, and the defenders of the one never sought ecclesiastical penalties against the other.

Gomarus, himself a strong supralapsarian, did join the committee in warning Maccovius against using unbiblical methods and making rash statements. These same rash statements are condemned in the Canons themselves, which tell us in no uncertain terms that we may not make God the author of sin.

At the same time, Gomarus, along with the rest of the committee, brought reconciliation between Maccovius and Lubbertus. This could only have been done by showing Lubbertus that Maccovius, in his opposition to a universal love of God, was Reformed.

NOTE: We add here a note for those who are interested in the issues of supralapsarianism versus infralapsarianism. The question has to do with the order of God's decrees in His counsel. Both positions agree that the sole purpose of God's counsel is the glory of God's name. The "infras" believe that God determined to glorify His name by the following order of decrees: man's creation, man's fall, predestination, salvation in Christ. The "supras" believe that God determined to glorify His name through Jesus Christ and in Him the salvation of an elect church. To accomplish that end, God determined the creation and fall of man along with the decree of reprobation. That the Canons are written from the infralapsarian viewpoint appears from such statements as "Election is the unchangeable purpose of God, whereby...he hath...chosen from the whole human race, which had fallen through their own fault...a certain number of persons..." (I, 7); "[God] leaves the non-elect in his just judgment to their own wickedness and obduracy" (I, 6). The "infras" have always feared the "supra" teaching because it could lead to making God the author of sin. The "supras" have always feared the "infra" teaching because it seemed to make the fall a mistake over which God had no control, so that salvation in Christ is Plan B when Plan A failed. The Reformed churches have always insisted that both viewpoints are acceptable if they do not go to extremes.

## Chapter 45

# Gijsbertus Voetius

## Defender of Orthodoxy

**Introduction**
*The Lord has promised the church, purchased with His own blood, that the gates of hell shall never prevail against it. To accomplish this, Christ raises men in the church who are strong and passionate defenders of the faith. These men, qualified by Christ, placed at crucial times in the church and equipped spiritually for the task, do battle with heresies that threaten the church's welfare.*

After all, one crucial means used by Satan to destroy the church is the introduction of heresy into the church's ministry and teaching.

These men are not always the most liked; indeed, they must often suffer abuse at the hands of their own fellow members in the church. They are not free from sin: in His church God is pleased to use even the weaknesses of sinful saints to fulfill His will. But they are men of courage and faithfulness, and through them Christ preserves the cause of His church in the world.

It is quite amazing that almost as soon as the delegates from the great Synod of Dordrecht said farewell to their fellow delegates and returned to their homes and churches, serious heresies arose in the churches of the Netherlands which threatened their orthodoxy. The echo of the ringing bells in Dordrecht which marked the end of the synod had not yet died away, and errors of almost every conceivable sort entered the universities and pastorates. Only through the courageous battles of some staunch men of God were these errors turned away, and then only for a time.

One of the most ardent defenders of the faith was a man by the name of Gijsbertus

Voetius, or if we would abandon his Latinized name, Gijsbert Voet—
the surname being the Dutch word for "foot." Gijs Foot. He was a
man who stood head and shoulders above his contemporaries.

## Early Life

Gijsbert Voetius was the son of a Dutch Reformed minister in the
town of Heusden, the Netherlands. His birth was March 3, 1588 or
1589; biographers are not sure; apparently some mishap clouded the
town records. The date of his birth tells us that he lived in some of
Holland's most troublous, though prosperous, times. Holland had
become a naval power, and Holland's navy sailed the seven seas.
Colonies were established by these navies in the West Indies, the East
Indies, America, and South Africa. Exotic silks, spices, and woods
flowed in an unending stream into the country. The growing trade of
Europe passed through its ports. Merchantmen and craftsmen filled
the cities. The nation's navy could stand before the mighty sea
powers of England and France without flinching. It was enough to
make any Dutchman proud.

Politics, however, were troubled. The Eighty Years War with Spain
was still raging, and the borders to the south were dangerous places
to live. The nation was divided between Orangeists (who wanted the
House of Orange on the throne of Holland) and Republicans (who
wanted nothing resembling a monarchy). The divisions were deep
and bitter.

The Reformed faith had taken root in the nation and had, within a
few decades, become the dominant religion of the Lowlands. That
Reformed faith, born and nurtured in Geneva, had found particularly
rich soil among the fiercely independent Dutch but was being
threatened by a growing attachment of many ministers and leaders to
the evil heresy of Arminianism. Arminianism had been spawned in
the fertile though shallow brain of Arminius, minister in Amsterdam
and later professor of theology in the University of Leyden.

Voetius' father was a sturdy defender of the Reformed faith, and
his son imbibed this doctrine from youth.

Gijsbert was a brilliant lad who soon outshone his fellow students
in his studies. Leyden was his home school, and there he studied
under Gomarus and Arminius, though Gomarus did more than any
other to shape his mind. He was industrious and possessed what we
would call today a photographic memory. So rapidly did he advance
in his studies that, while still in the university, he was appointed

lecturer in logic. In his classes he defended the strictest Calvinism and already in these years showed his disdain for any viewpoint which challenged the teachings of the reformer from Geneva.

Because of his many gifts, he was, upon graduation, called soon to the ministry of the Word of God in Vlijmen. The year was 1611, seven years before the great Synod of Dordt. After serving many years in the pastorate, he became professor in the University of Utrecht where he spent the rest of his life, a professor for no less than forty-two years.

### *His Effective Pastoral Ministry*

Before Voetius became professor, he served two congregations. He spent about six years in Vlijmen, where he was first called, and about seventeen years in Heusden, the town of his birth.

During the years of his ministry, Voetius preached eight times a week—and we think we are busy when we preach twice a week. While it was the custom in those days for an elder to read the Scriptures and for a precentor to lead the singing, Voetius often did both for his congregation.

He was faithful in his pastoral labors, and the congregations he served came to love him deeply.

Voetius' ministry was not limited to the work of the congregation; he was intensely interested in evangelism and missions. While in Vlijmen, a village in which were still many Roman Catholics, he was instrumental in bringing a large number of them to the Reformed faith. While minister in Heusden, he was influential in persuading the large trading companies to send missionaries with the Dutch ships to distant parts of the world so that mission work could be done in these far-off islands and lands.

If all this were not enough, Voetius gave himself over to the study of Arabic, the better to understand the Semitic languages, one of which was the Hebrew of the Old Testament Scriptures.

### *His Influential Professorship*

In 1634 Voetius accepted the call to become professor in the new Academy of Utrecht. When in 1636 the academy became a university, Voetius preached the inaugural sermon on Luke 2:46: "And it came to pass, that after three days they found him in the temple, sitting in the midst of the doctors, both hearing them, and asking them questions."

During the years of his labors in Utrecht, Voetius taught theology, logic, physics, metaphysics, and Semitic languages: Hebrew, Arabic, and Syraic, surely a heavy load. In addition to this massive load of teaching, he also became the pastor of the church in Utrecht, and the street on which he lived bears his name to this day.

Voetius was also a prolific writer in many different fields, although those who have read his writings complain that they were almost impossibly boring and difficult to read.

To accomplish all his work, Voetius rose at 4:00 A.M. to begin his studies for the day and prepare for his many lectures.

Voetius has often been accused of being "scholastic" in his theology; in fact, one author calls him "the greatest of the scholastics." This was meant, of course, as criticism. Many today complain that the theologians of the Dutch Reformed tradition, beginning with Theodore Beza and continuing through Herman Hoeksema, have altered fundamentally the theology of Calvin with their "scholasticism." Before we become too critical of these supposed "scholastic" theologians, however, we do well to listen to a more balanced view, which points out that it was not the theology itself of the early Dutch theologians that was scholastic; rather, the method in which they developed their theology was the method used by the medieval scholastic theologians. That is, these Dutch theologians were intent on developing Reformed thought by careful analysis, detailed definition, thorough development of each theological concept, careful repudiation of every heresy, and logical organization which was intended to show the relationships between all the truths of Scripture. It was not, by any means, all bad. But that is another story.

### *His Battle Against Arminianism*

Voetius hated Arminianism. He saw it for what it was: a wholesale attack on the very heart of the Reformed faith and, fundamentally, a return to Roman Catholicism and its doctrine of salvation by works.

He began his battle against Arminianism already before Dordt as the Arminians increasingly began to influence the theology of the Dutch churches. In fact, more than likely, Voetius took the call to become pastor in Heusden because this city had become a hotbed of Arminian thinking.

As Arminianism gained ground prior to Dordt, Voetius traveled to other cities (such as Gouda and Bois-le-Duc on the Belgian border) to do battle with enemies of the Reformed faith.

So trustworthy was he considered to be, that he was voted delegate to the Synod of Dordt (1618–19). At the synod he made major contributions to the defeat of the Arminians and the writing of its precious Canons. When Bogerman, the president of the synod, angrily dismissed the Arminians from the assembly and forbade them to return, Voetius supported his actions.

Although Dordt was a mighty victory for the Reformed faith, Arminian poison continued to affect the churches, and Voetius spent all his life doing what he could to root out this pernicious evil.

Voetius' interest in the Reformed faith was not merely in its intellectual coherence and internal harmony. He was a godly and pious man. One of his earliest books was entitled *Proof of the Power of Godliness*. His thesis in this book was that, while Arminianism is destructive of Christian morality, the orthodox faith gives attestation to itself in a godly and upright life. The book was not the writings of a man who did not live what he believed. He was firmly convinced, and showed it in his own life, that the Reformed faith, when embraced wholeheartedly, led to Christian piety.

### *Other Battles*

Voetius did not do battle only with Arminianism. Other heresies appeared soon after Dordt, and Voetius took up the weapons of his spiritual warfare against them.

We mention three.

Strange as it may seem to us, soon after the Synod of Dordt, the philosophy of the French philosopher René Descartes was beginning to have an impact in Holland, even in the University of Utrecht. Descartes firmly believed that the Christian faith could be supported by reason alone and really had no need of faith to bolster its tenets. This was rationalism, pure and simple. Against it Voetius waged bitter war; in fact, he secured the dismissal of Regius, his own colleague at Utrecht, a defender of Cartesianism. So biting was his attack that Descartes himself, in lonely isolation in France but adored by all Europe, considered it necessary to respond to Voetius. Sadly, Voetius, while winning the battle in his own lifetime, lost it in the long run of Dutch theology.

When the French Calvinists were persecuted in France, many of them fled to the Lowlands, where they could find political asylum. Among them were mystics, who found a congenial home in some parts of Holland. Their spokesman at the time of Voetius was Jean de Labadie, who was not only deeply imbued with mysticism but also preached and practiced separation from the instituted church, as mystics usually do. It was the valiant efforts of Voetius which held these miserable mystics at bay.

Voetius' greatest battle, though, was with Cocceius, a colleague in the ministry. In a way, this controversy was sad because Cocceius himself was an important figure in the development of Reformed thought. Cocceius was disturbed by the "scholasticism" of his colleagues and developed what later became known as Biblical Theology. In the course of his work, Cocceius made such a sharp distinction between the Old and New Testaments that he denied the validity of the New Testament Sabbath. Although Voetius attacked him for this, the controversy involved other points as well, including various political questions. Voetius promoted strongly the need for Holland to be ruled by the royal House of Orange, while Cocceius wanted a more republican form of government.

The controversy became very bitter, and the church was divided into a Voetian party and a Cocceian party. Actually, the controversy was never settled. It continued beyond the death of the two opponents and only gradually died out.

After producing three sons, two of whom became professors and one a minister, and after seeing even a grandson become a professor, Voetius died on November 1, 1676.

Voetius has often been charged with "using the end to hallow the means." He "was vehement, and not careful as respects the choice of his weapons." He has even been charged with dishonesty by some biographers, a reference to his debate with Descartes when he denied authorship of a book that was published under another man's name. That Voetius was a vehement defender of orthodoxy cannot be denied, and one author, not a friend, pays this tribute to Voetius: "With all the faults of his character, Voetius was an earnest and sincere Christian, and a most devoted servant of the Church. Few men have in any age exercised greater influence over the Church of their time and country."

It is a man who himself loves the church and the cause of God's truth who can see beyond a man's character and stand with him in the defense of the faith.

## Chapter 46
# *Johannes Cocceius*
## Biblical Theologian

*Introduction*
*In the last chapter
we talked about one
of the great
theologians in the
Netherlands during
and shortly after the
Synod of Dordrecht
(Dordt) held in
1618–1619. His
name was Gijsbert
Voetius. We
mentioned the fact
that Voetius
engaged in a very
bitter quarrel with
Johannes Cocceius,
a quarrel that*

continued beyond their lives and nearly tore apart the Dutch Reformed churches.

Now we want to talk a bit about that quarrel.

### *Early Life and Education*

Johannes Cocceius was not born in the Netherlands but in Germany. It was probably for this reason that he never felt quite at home among the Dutchmen, even though he spent a large part of his adult life with them. His date of birth was either August 9, 1603, or July 30 of the same year (the records contain both dates).

Johannes was the son of the municipal secretary in Bremen: Timann Coch. When Johannes finally Latinized his name, as so many did in those days, he did not change it much. He had one brother, and from their early youth they were together known as "Cocceii," or as we would say, "the Cochs." So all Johannes did was change this Latin plural into a singular and come up with Cocceius (pronounced: cock-SAY-us).

Bremen, though a part of Germany, was solidly in the Reformed camp. In fact, it had sent delegates to the Synod of Dordt, although the delegates from Bremen were known by all at the synod as being the weakest in their convictions and the most sympathetic to the Arminians.

The Coch family was an ancient and honorable family that had a tradition of service to church and state, many of Coch's ancestors holding high political and ecclesiastical offices.

Johannes' upbringing was very strict in moral and religious matters. The lessons he learned apparently made a great impression on him. Later in life he began an autobiography which he never finished. In it he tells us of two incidents from his childhood that illustrated this upbringing.

On one occasion, Johannes was chastised at school for some boyish falsehood; he tells us that after that incident, he despised lying so completely and gained such a reputation for truthfulness that no oath was ever required of him. At another time he used God's name irreverently at mealtime. His father hit him on the mouth with a spoon, and he never again took God's name in vain.

From the early days of Johannes' education he showed a remarkable ability to learn and a special aptitude for languages. Although he studied theology, he also so completely mastered Greek that he could read widely in Greek literature for pure enjoyment, though he was still a lad. Fascinated by ancient languages, he learned Hebrew, Chaldee, and Arabic, mostly on his own. While still a student, he wrote a Greek oration on the religion of the Turks and read the Koran in preparation for it.

In 1625, at twenty-two years of age, Cocceius went to Hamburg in Germany for Greek and Rabbinic studies under learned Jews. But he was most unhappy with university life in Germany, chiefly, as he tells us, because of the dissolute life of the students.

In 1629 Johannes left Germany and went to the University of Franeker in the Netherlands. Here he studied under Maccovius and William Ames, two men of whom we wrote earlier. He also studied under a man by the name of Sixtinus Amana, a world-renowned Orientalist. Under Amana, he concentrated his studies in the Jewish Talmud.

The learning of many of these Dutch theologians is quite astounding. They devoted their lives entirely to studies and the discipline of learning. They were highly educated and masters in their field beyond most in our day.

## His Academic Life

From Cocceius' twenty-seventh year, his life was completely devoted to teaching. His first teaching post was back in his native city of Bremen, where he was professor of biblical theology and philosophy for about six years. But the Netherlands soon beckoned him, and he returned to Franeker, where he taught Hebrew and theology. He stayed in Franeker for fourteen years, after which he moved to Leyden. In Leyden, after serving the churches as professor in the university, he died at the age of sixty-six on November 4, 1669, at the height of his powers. He was suddenly struck by a fever, and after only nineteen days of illness, he departed this life to be with God.

Cocceius spent all his life in academia and never knew the hurly-burly of the life of the pastorate with its incessant demands, crowded schedules, and bitter struggles in the forward trenches of the spiritual warfare of the church. But in the sheltered life of academia he drove himself relentlessly and produced an abundance of work which was to be of benefit to the church in subsequent years.

Cocceius was of the old German Pietistic tradition, and he reflected that tradition in his life. He was not only himself a godly and pious man, acknowledged by all to be such, but he also gave a practical and experiential bent to all his writings. His piety manifested itself also in his insistence that the interpreter of Scripture must be a man who never imposes his own ideas on God's Word but is willing, in a spirit of meekness and humility, to bow before the Scriptures.

Cocceius did extensive work in the field of biblical interpretation and developed such important principles as the organic unity of Sacred Scripture, the interpretation of Scripture according to the analogy of faith, the importance of interpreting passages of Scripture in the light of their context, and the relation between the Old and New Testaments expressed in the rhyme "The New is in the Old concealed; the Old is in the New revealed."

Cocceius' studies of Scripture ranged over the whole of the Bible, and he wrote commentaries on almost all the books. One biographer speaks of his exegetical abilities, in an unforgettable phrase, as being of "penetrating insight and robust judgment."

The greatest contribution of Cocceius lies in his work on God's covenant. Although much had been written on covenant theology

prior to his lifetime, his contributions are so respected that he is sometimes called the father of covenant theology.

In 1995 I had opportunity to hear a professor from the Netherlands, an expert in the theology of Cocceius, speak on this aspect of Cocceius' work. Without being aware apparently of the Protestant Reformed Churches' position on the covenant, the professor made clear that though Cocceius never completely escaped the idea of the covenant as a pact or agreement, he nevertheless spoke of it as primarily a bond of fellowship. For that reason alone we owe Cocceius a debt of gratitude.

### His Controversy

In spite of all his accomplishments, Cocceius is mostly remembered for his bitter quarrel with Voetius, and we now turn to that quarrel.

Strangely enough, the controversy centered in the question of Sabbath observance. Cocceius was charged with being weak on the question of the Sabbath. This is surprising if we consider that Cocceius was a godly and pious man and probably observed the Sabbath scrupulously. The difficulty, though, was in his theology, not in his practice. Cocceius taught that the Sabbath was Jewish, a part of Jewish law, abolished with the coming of Christ, and without any force in the new dispensation. He was not opposed to Sabbath observance and the worship of God on the Sabbath, but he claimed it was a matter of expediency, not principle. For this he was charged with Antinomianism, that is, with denying that the law of God was valid for saints in the new dispensation as well as the old.

A story lay behind the position which Cocceius took. Up to his time, the theologians in Europe and in the Netherlands were systematic theologians. That is, they worked hard to arrange all the doctrines of Scripture in a system of doctrine in which all the relationships between various doctrines were set forth clearly. They did work much like the *Reformed Dogmatics* of Herman Hoeksema.

In the systematizing of doctrine, however, some theologians were guilty of some exaggerations of this method. Instead of searching the Scriptures and working at careful exegesis so that the doctrines of the Reformed faith could be developed and enriched, they were content to systematize, to analyze what was already known, to pick apart and dissect by means of endless distinctions, and to raise objections against doctrines, only then to show the error of the objections.

While this description is probably an exaggeration, the danger was that doctrines became cold and sterile and lacked the warmth and passion of confession and life. When texts were referred to, it was often by way of mere "proof-texting," or using texts to "prove" points, without any solid exegesis.

Cocceius objected to this kind of work in theology and wanted something more warm, experiential, personal, and practical. He wanted to attain this by way of exegesis. He was concerned that the proof-texting often used did not do justice to the historical development of God's revelation in the four millennia of the Old Testament time of shadows, which development culminated in Christ. For example, theologians would quote a text from the time of Abraham without taking into account that God's revelation then was not as full as in later Old Testament times and in the new dispensation. Cocceius wanted exegesis to be honest with the text in the sense that it was explained as it was meant in the time the revelation was given to God's people.

To accomplish this end, Cocceius did not write a "Systematic Theology" but a "Biblical Theology." That is, he started at Genesis 1:1 and worked his way through the Bible from beginning to end in such a way that his theology followed the order of biblical books.

Some of his objections to the theology that was written at that time certainly were valid. But Cocceius did not really solve any problems. Such a method of working at theology as Cocceius employed, though still practiced today by some and though used in some seminaries, has serious weaknesses. We cannot go into all of them here but, for one thing, such a method of doing things loses the unity of the truth. Systematic theology shows how all the truth is one because God is one and the truth is of God. Biblical theology does not do that.

More seriously, such a way of doing things really divides the Old Testament from the New and makes a separation between the two. This is what Cocceius did. Especially when he was busy developing the doctrine of the covenant in the way he did, he made such separation between the two dispensations that he became a dispensationalist of sorts. As a dispensationalist, he denied the validity of the Sabbath for New Testament times.

The quarrel between Cocceius and Voetius was prolonged and bitter, and it did not end with their deaths. In fact, it only increased in intensity and became, at last, so fierce that it nearly tore the church apart. At times, if Cocceians were in the majority in a university, all the Voetians were expelled. If Voetians gained control, Cocceians were driven out. The situation worsened until the government forced the universities to appoint an equal number from the Voetian and Cocceian parties as professors in the schools.

Perhaps the most serious of all, and the real weak spot in Cocceian theology but something which flowed directly from his position, was Cocceius' teaching that the justification of the Old Testament saints was imperfect, for it was by way of promise, administered through the sacrifices, and was not the perfect justification of the new dispensational saints.

The controversy actually died out of itself after many years. It died out because the combatants wearied of the battle, and the church became so liberal that it didn't really care any more about such problems.

The questions raised by Cocceius and Voetius is on church agendas today, however, though mostly fought out in seminaries. We may be thankful that our churches, under the leadership of our spiritual fathers, have a systematic theology given to us as our heritage which does justice to exegesis in both Testaments, and which is warm and vibrant. The warmth and vibrancy of our theology is surely due to the place which the doctrine of the covenant holds among us, a doctrine which was developed so fully by Herman Hoeksema but which came, in part, from Johannes Cocceius.

## Chapter 47

# William III of Orange

## Warrior of the Faith

### Introduction

*There was a time in the history of the church of our Lord Jesus Christ when the fortunes of the church in the Netherlands were inextricably tied to the fortunes of the church in Great Britain. This was the time of William III of the House of Orange.*

*The times were extremely perilous for countries which had become Calvinistic.*

Through the efforts of the Roman Catholic Counter-Reformation, the Protestant Reformation had not only been stopped in its tracks, but the Roman Catholics had once again taken the offensive in Europe. Spain had always been firmly on the side of the Romish church. France, by slaughtering the Huguenots and forcing the faithful to escape torture and death by seeking refuge in other countries, had become an ally of the papacy in the battle against Protestantism. The Roman Catholic party was still strong in the British Isles, where God's people were well acquainted with suffering and death for Christ's sake. Rome's servants were ready to launch powerful armies to subdue Protestant kingdoms and force Europe once again to bow before the papal throne. Even in the Netherlands, that bulwark of the Reformed faith, there were those who, weary of war, sought compromise with the enemy.

The one man whom God used to thwart these papal purposes was William III of the House of Orange, stadholder in Holland. His story is an intriguing one, though no less intriguing than the man himself. His impenetrable reserve made him something of a mystery even to his closest associates.

## *Birth and Early Years*

William was the third by that name in the notable line of Dutch rulers which began with William the Silent. He was born in The Hague, the Netherlands, on November 14, 1650, to William II, prince of Orange, and Mary, daughter of Charles I of England. He was thus in the direct line of Dutch royalty and had close ties to the royal line of the Stuarts in England. Charles I was the king of England who was beheaded by Parliament with the approval of Oliver Cromwell during England's civil war. Charles II, another Stuart, was proclaimed king in Edinburgh, Scotland, in 1649, and in London in 1660. He was William's uncle.

William was born eight days after his father died and was left an orphan in his early youth. Although he was by a recently passed law prevented from assuming the rule of the United Provinces of Holland, his university education was geared towards acquainting him with the responsibilities of the throne. When sixteen years old, he was made a ward of the States-General, the ruling body in the Netherlands. Under Johan de Witte, grand pensionary of Holland, he received a knowledge of the intricate affairs of government and the niceties of diplomacy and rule.

## *William's Early Wars*

In 1671, the perfidious Charles II of England and the equally untrustworthy Louis XIV of France joined in a plot to invade the Netherlands. Their purpose was to destroy the strongest bastion of Calvinism in all Europe. This was particularly treacherous of Charles, for he had professed repeatedly to be a friend of the Hollanders. It was not strange that Louis XIV was a part of the plot, for the king of France was constantly searching in all the corners of Europe for places in which to meddle and for countries to bring under his rule. Of more importance, both Charles II and Louis XIV hated with a passion the deep and staunch Calvinism which was the religion of the Lowlands.

When the plot to invade the Netherlands was discovered, alarm spread through the country, and William was appointed captain-general of the nation's forces. However, the appointment was not to include stadholder, even though his father and grandfather had held both positions. The Dutch, always fearful of giving too much power

to their rulers and being staunch lovers of liberty, had passed a law preventing the same man from holding both positions.

The French immediately invaded the southern provinces and captured three of them in as many weeks. In defense of their country, the Dutch opened the dikes and flooded the polders to stop further French advance. William was ordered to hold the "water-line." Although the Dutch navy was able to hold England at bay and prevent an immediate invasion from across the channel, William had all he could do to slow the French advance.

Alarmed at the threat of being overrun by foreign powers, the people clamored for the States-General to make William stadholder in spite of the recently passed law. The States-General reluctantly proceeded to do so. Thus, William held the same posts which his father and grandfather had held and was now responsible for the defense of the country and its administration.

Charles and Louis, thinking they had the Netherlands at their mercy, made offers of peace which many in the Netherlands, weary of war, wanted to accept. Because the peace offers included ruinous conditions for the Lowlands, William refused them, although he had, almost by sheer will-power, to impose his determination upon the people. The Netherlands stood alone against two of Europe's greatest powers. William managed to hold out by dint of great courage. Such courage was born out of a firm conviction that the Netherlands had to remain Calvinistic and ought not return to the bondage of Romanism.

In 1673, with help from the emperor, Leopold I, William was able to rebuild his army and defeat the French in key battles which restored to him a few strategic cities. But war continued sporadically, and William was by no means successful in every battle fought.

In 1677, through a strange twist of history and through intricate diplomatic maneuvers, William married Mary, daughter of James, duke of York (later to be James II, king of England) and niece of Charles I. Because Mary was in the line of succession, this marriage not only established a pact between the Netherlands and England but made William a potential heir to England's throne.

Much has been written about the relation between William and Mary, and what has been written is by no means complimentary. It is not always easy to sort fact from fiction and determine correctly the nature of their relationship, but the following seems true.

William determined to make Mary his wife because he thought it to would result in an alliance between the Netherlands and England, which would make the lot of his people easier in their wars with France. When he married Mary, he took her away from a frivolous, opulent, giddy court and from the only life she knew and enjoyed. The thought of leaving the palace in London and living in dark and damp Holland and the relatively ascetic life of William's court filled her with dismay. She wanted neither William nor life in Holland, even in her husband's court. Her first years were miserable in the extreme.

Equally, William hated life in London. He did not fit well in the English court because his plainness stood in sharp contrast to the opulence of the palace; his plain speaking was considered vulgar in comparison with the smooth flattery and hypocritical blandishments of London society; his Calvinism was an abomination to those who, though members of the Anglican church, possessed no religion at all; and his obvious sincerity could not be tolerated amidst the frivolity of life in the king's palace.

For these and other reasons the marriage was, in its early years, a marriage of convenience in which the two rarely saw each other. But gradually Mary came to admire the steely determination of her husband and even came to adopt the faith which was the driving force of all he did. Her loyalty to him was above question, and when William came to see it and appreciate it, she became the object of his admiration and attention. They became, after a rocky start, a devoted couple.

### *William's Rule in England*

Shortly after William's marriage, his father-in-law came to the throne in England, but he was a true Roman Catholic and was determined to restore Roman Catholicism to the British Isles. This meant that his own son-in-law and daughter had to be pushed out of the way and the staunch Calvinism of the Netherlands made ineffective.

James' rule of the British Isles was so cruel, so heavy-handed, so obviously an effort to restore the papacy to England, Scotland, Wales, and Ireland, that his own people rose against him. By delegations from the nobility, William was invited to become the king.

The only way in which William could become king of England was through invasion. This was also carried out. We shall allow another to tell the story.

> On the 19th of October, William went on board, and the Dutch fleet, consisting of fifty-two men-of-war, twenty-five frigates, as many fire-ships, with four hundred victuallers, and other vessels for the transportation of 3,660 horse, and 10,692 foot, put to sea from the flats near the Brielle, with a wind at south-west by south. Admiral Herbert led the van, and Vice-Admiral Evertzen brought up the rear. The prince placed himself in the centre, carrying an English flag, emblazoned with his arms, surrounded with the legend, "For the Protestant Religion and Liberties of England." Underneath was the motto of the House of Nassau, *Je Maintiendray* (I will maintain).

Since the days when a storm destroyed the Spanish armada, the British have always maintained that God fought for Britain and for the Protestant cause in that land. Again the wind helped William. Although the wind first veered to the north and drove the Dutch fleet back to its ports, it became "a Protestant wind" once again. It not only brought the ships of William to the southern coast of England, but held the British navy at bay to the north and enabled the Dutch to land their troops unmolested in Tor Bay near Devon.

After landing successfully and without opposition (indeed, after being jubilantly welcomed by the British), William marched on London and forced James to flee to France. The throne was declared vacant by abdication, and William was pronounced king of all Britain. The date was February of 1689. In April the throne of Scotland was offered him, and opposition to William was quelled.

Determined to maintain the Stuarts on the throne, James resisted, landing in Ireland with the promise of French help. Soon he launched attacks against key cities in Ulster with the purpose of making Ireland a launching pad to recover England and Scotland.

After Londonderry and Enniskillen were successfully defended by James, William took his troops across the Irish Sea and landed at Carrickfergus, where to this day a stone marks the place where he first set foot on Irish soil. James was soundly defeated at the great Battle of the Boyne on July 1, 1690, and Ireland was subdued. This day is still celebrated by Ulster's Protestants with parades and speeches recalling God's deliverance of Ireland from Roman Catholicism.

William was now king of all Britain, and Mary, his wife, had returned to her homeland.

William could not stay long in Britain, however, for Louis XIV was still meddling in continental affairs and was determined to restore Europe to papal rule. Showing his diplomatic skill, William forged an alliance with Brandenburg, Hanover, Saxony, Bavaria, and Savoy (all Protestant provinces), with England as the linchpin of the federation, to defeat the nefarious purposes of Louis. Because Spain, thoroughly Roman Catholic, hated France with a passion, William was sometimes able to solicit the help of Spain, but this help was of dubious value.

Through many efforts towards peace and through many broken treaties, William, by sheer determination of his own will, was able to protect Protestant countries from the schemes of popery.

He died a weary and broken man on March 19, 1720.

### William's Place in History

God uses strange and sometimes sinful ways to accomplish His purpose. It cannot be denied that much of William's efforts were based on the principle that the cause of God is advanced by the sword. Even given the fact that in William's days the relation between church and state was so close that one could hardly avoid resorting to the sword in defense of the faith, the fact remains that the cause of the gospel is not advanced by human might and power.

William's accomplishments were many, although his critics constitute a multitude.

One forceful criticism lodged against William is against his character. He is portrayed by biographers as stiff, withdrawn, stern, taciturn, and reserved to the point of coldness. There is some truth to this charge. All his life William was an alien among the ruling class in England, which scorned him and ridiculed him behind his back, but it is often forgotten that William had no patience with the intrigue, double-dealing, duplicity, and double-crossing which so characterized diplomacy in those days. He was honest, forthright, and single-minded in purpose, and he said what was on his mind, whatever may have been the consequences.

Further, William was a man of iron will and deep principle who would stand by his principles though all were against him. He fought on against the powers of the papacy when his own people counseled compromise and dishonorable peace, and when his cause seemed on the brink of defeat. He believed passionately that he was God's instrument to protect Calvinism from Rome, and he unwaveringly stood for what he was sure was God's cause. Scorned by the nobility, he was loved by the common people, both in the Netherlands and the British Isles.

His courage bore fruits. Even those who hate Calvinism speak glowingly of his vast accomplishments. The freedom, union, and prosperity of Holland were due to him. He preserved the crown in England by judicious rule and gave England the stability and continuity it enjoys to the present. He was a patron of the arts, kind to the tenants on his royal estates, a brave general who commanded intense loyalty from his troops, and a friend and helper of thousands of refugees fleeing Roman persecution. He spent himself in affairs of state and ruined his health in the defense of the cause of the Reformed faith. His irritability and sometimes ungracious conduct were due to ill-health and overwork. He could also be kind, courteous, and forbearing.

His deepest drive was to create religious toleration in Europe. With that, he envisioned a cessation of religious wars, a curbing of papal power, and a European citizenry which could live in quietness and peace.

These ends he accomplished. The cause of Calvinism, though again at low ebb, was successfully defended by the fortitude of William III of Orange.

## Chapter 48

# Hendrik De Cock
## Reformed Reformer

### Introduction

*The times when true reformation comes to the church of Jesus Christ are not often. But when those times, according to God's clock, actually arrive, they come in unexpected ways. Already in the Old Testament God had reminded His people of this. He had emphatically impressed upon the mind of the moody and depressed*

Elijah that He did not work through stirring events such as took place on Carmel (God was not in the earthquake, nor the fire, nor the wind); rather God worked quietly and unnoticed by His Spirit in the hearts of the 7000 who had not bowed the knee to Baal. To Zechariah the prophet, who worried about the building of the temple after the return of the captives, God had laid down a fundamental principle: "Not by might, nor by power, but by my Spirit, saith the Lord of Hosts" (Zech. 4:6).

The great Reformation of the sixteenth century, while eventually it shook Europe to its foundations, began with the quiet nailing of Ninety-five Theses on a chapel door by an obscure monk out of the forests of Saxon Germany. The reformation of 1834 in the Reformed churches of the Netherlands began in a dark and smoke-filled consistory room of a country church of no importance, where five men gathered to sign a single sheet of paper to protest what had happened to their minister. It is in that reformation of 1834 that many Reformed churches throughout the world find their roots.

The man who is called the father of the Secession of 1834 is Hendrik De Cock, the pastor of the small church in Ulrum whose elders and deacons protested what the churches had done. Here God began His work.

It would in this way be forever evident, as it always must be evident, that the care of the church is God's work, and His alone, so that He may receive all the glory.

In perfect harmony with this truth, it is also an interesting fact that reformers are strange people. They do not seem at first glance to be cut out for the role. As a matter of fact, if one measures their abilities by human standards, they are often the world's least likely people for the work into which they are thrust.

When we look at this fact from the viewpoint of those who do the work of reformation, we discover that this great truth translates into a naive unawareness on the part of reformers that they have been thrust into the role which they occupy. They never gave thought to being reformers; they had no intention of becoming reformers; indeed, if the idea had been suggested to them, they would have considered it preposterous. Luther spoke of being carried along by a tidal wave of events over which he had no control. And the last thing De Cock was thinking about was himself as a reformer in the church. For Luther, Calvin, De Cock, or anyone else to think of himself as a reformer would immediately have disqualified him for the work. Such is the irony of God's ways.

Thus, such men do not set about the work of reforming. They have been conquered in their hearts by the Holy Spirit, who has sealed the truth indelibly upon their consciousness and who has given them the determination (often courageous) to go quietly about their business of doing what has to be done—which consists mostly of the simple act of preaching good, Bible-centered sermons.

Those selected by God to reform the church were sometimes astonished and not a little afraid at the forces that had been unleashed in the church through their work. Nor did they "count noses" to see how many would go along or postpone moving ahead in the work until they were assured of a following. They simply did what had to be done in humble reliance on divine grace. God did the rest.

## The Need for Reformation

That the church of that day needed reformation could hardly be debated. Although the church of which we are speaking was the church of the Reformation and of Dordrecht, it had become only a shell of what it formerly was. Even the great truths of Scripture were denied by many in the universities, seminaries, and pulpits. I refer to the truths of the virgin birth of Christ, the atoning sacrifice of our Lord on the cross, and His bodily resurrection from the dead. In the place of the religion of salvation by grace alone through Jesus Christ had come a religion which was interested in little more than living a good life, walking morally, and contributing to society's good through upright ethical conduct. The confessions were ignored or denied; hymns had been introduced in the place of the Psalms of the church; church government after the principles of the Church Order of Dordt was long forgotten; and the church was ruled by committees which had total and decisive power.

All this apostasy did not mean that there were no people of God anywhere to be found. They were there, scattered about, starving spiritually, groaning beneath the tyranny of apostate preachers, desperately casting about to find places to feed their souls. Many of them gathered in small "conventicles" which were little more than groups of believers who would meet in private homes to read the old Reformed writers, study the Scriptures, discuss the sad state of the church and what could be done about it, and listen to an "exhorter" (if they had one) explain from Scripture the ancient truths of the faith.

Hendrik De Cock was a perfect example of the sad situation in the Reformed churches. Born in Veendam on April 12, 1801, he was brought up in a home where the only religion that was taught was the worldly and quasi-religion of living a decent life. The churches and schools he attended did not do better. His minister in Wildervank, where the family moved shortly after his birth, and his teachers in school had no idea of what the Reformed faith was all about; or if they did know anything at all about it, they failed to teach it.

The same situation was found at the University of Groningen where Hendrik went to prepare for the ministry of the gospel. He graduated and entered the ministry as a thoroughly modern minister, equipped only to preach a modern gospel of Jesus, the good example, whose life could serve as a pattern for us. Of sin, salvation, and grace, Hendrik knew nothing.

This did not mean that during these years God was not working in His own mysterious ways to prepare Hendrik for greater things. Already as a boy he received some catechetical instruction from one of his teachers, who insisted that a man is saved only by the sovereign grace of God. While such teaching made no apparent impression on Hendrik, God used it to put ideas of a different sort into his soul, even though these ideas would not come to fruition until later.

Thus at ordination De Cock was little more than a mediocre modernist minister, destined to serve in a series of modernist congregations, though his denomination still bore the proud name of "Reformed." Both the church and De Cock were in need of reformation.

## *Introduction to Reformed Thought*

Little changed in De Cock's first two charges. Three years in Eppenhuizen and two years in Noordlaren did little to alter his views. He was, in fact, so thoroughly under the influence of the modernists in his church that he made no use of the Statenvertaling, the translation of the Bible authorized by the Synod of Dordt and filled with important marginal notes which would have helped him understand the Reformed faith. He had never read the creeds. He paid no attention to the old Reformed writers. He did not even know that such a book as Calvin's *Institutes* existed.

Perhaps the only influence on his life at this time which was of any value was the influence of a godly and pious wife whom he married shortly before his ordination to the ministry. Her name was Frouwe Venema, and while we do not know the extent of her knowledge of the Reformed faith, she was a pillar of strength to Hendrik throughout his life when troubles all but overwhelmed him.

It was in the small country church in Ulrum, however, that God changed De Cock into the man He would use to bring reformation to an apostate church.

De Cock had come to Ulrum because of the influence of an old university friend, a modernist like himself, his predecessor in Ulrum, and an influential man by the name of Hofstede de Groot.

In Ulrum were people who were starving for biblical and God-centered preaching and who would not be put off with moralistic sermons about doing good. They had not been happy with de Groot; they were not happy with De Cock. In fact, de Groot had viewed these people as odd and in need of special pastoral care. He had urged De Cock to pay special attention to them.

Though De Cock did this and attempted to show his parishioners that the key to living a good life lay in education, they were not persuaded. One common laborer, a faithful visitor at the parsonage to be catechized by his pastor, had not dared make confession of faith under de Groot because of his unease with de Groot's teachings. He kept telling De Cock that his instruction did no good because, he said, "Should I be required to contribute a mere sigh to my salvation, I would be forever lost." The man's name was Klaas Pieters Kuipenga, a simple, uneducated saint whose soul thirsted for salvation in Christ but who had none to give him drink. The sad part was that thousands like him could be found throughout the Netherlands.

De Cock was a serious pastor and longed to help these troubled sheep. How to do it became the question.

In his search for answers, De Cock found himself in the study of a fellow minister in a neighboring village. The minister turned to Calvin's *Institutes* to prove a point which had come up in the conversation. Calvin's remarks so impressed De Cock that he asked to borrow the book and, having done so, proceeded to read it through several times in amazement and growing consternation.

During this period of drinking at the fountain of Calvin's great work, De Cock also became acquainted with the Canons of Dordt, writings from earlier Reformed Dutch theologians, and the devotional writings of a more recent writer, Cornelis Baron van Zuylen van Nijveldt. The latter had written "De Eenige Redding" (The Only Salvation), a pamphlet which opened De Cock's eyes to the truth that all godly living is rooted in doctrine.

It is not surprising that De Cock's preaching began to change radically. The more he came to understand the great historic doctrines of God's sovereign and particular grace, the clearer became his sermons as they set forth salvation by grace through faith in Christ and His atoning sacrifice. It is not surprising that, as word of this kind of preaching spread like wildfire through the surrounding countryside, people starving for the Bread of Life streamed to Ulrum to hear De Cock preach.

All this does not mean that De Cock now became a conquering hero. He was opposed, sometimes strenuously, by those who

cherished the modernistic and liberal preaching so prevalent in the state church. His colleagues in the area made every effort to dissuade him from the path he had chosen to follow and ridiculed the people who hung on De Cock's preaching as more ignorant than cattle in the cow shed.

De Cock's own close friend and predecessor in Ulrum came especially to visit him to try to alter his thinking, but De Cock had found peace for his own soul and was not about to turn from that which was the heart of Reformation truth and the faith of the fathers. Hofstede de Groot wrote De Cock in chagrin:

> De Cock! De Cock! Such a bitter and unchristian writing contains your confession of faith [The reference is to another brochure by C. Baron van Zuylen van Nijeveldt entitled *De Hervormde Leer* (Reformed Doctrine)]. How deep, deep have you fallen, and how dark is to me the counsel of God that such a doctrine is now being taught the congregation that once was mine. I have prayed to God many a time that He would grant me the spirit of moderation in order that I might exercise truth and love and avoid Van Zuylen's abusive tone.

But De Cock would not budge. We sing in our versification of Psalm 8 this line: "Weakest means fulfill Thy will." So it was that the obscure and [by human standards] mediocre minister of a small country church became a stubborn defender of the truths of sovereign grace and a mighty reformer in the church of Christ.

And so Hendrik De Cock preached to growing crowds in the small church in Ulrum.

## The Work of Reformation

A number of events, each somewhat small in itself, brought De Cock's work to its climax.

The more emphatic De Cock became in his preaching, the larger grew the crowds. The larger grew the crowds, the stronger was the opposition. The growing throngs forced the consistory to propose enlarging the auditorium. Even though the people themselves brought up the money, the wardens responsible for all building projects refused permission and overruled the desires of the congregation. It was the first hint of persecution.

Astounded at the discovery that the Canons were a creed of the churches in which he was minister, De Cock published in 1833 a pamphlet which included the Canons of Dordt. In the introduction to the pamphlet De Cock spoke of "a return...to the true service of

God...which had been forsaken by a majority of the population as it had turned to the idols of man's corrupted and darkened reason." This did not endear those who wanted nothing so much as the Canons forgotten in the churches.

As the crowds grew, many people from other congregations wanted De Cock to baptize their babies. They could not, in good conscience, have their babies baptized in their own churches, partly because the old baptism form had been replaced with other heretical practices and liturgy, and partly because, if the old form was still used, they could not answer "Yes" to the question whether they believed that the doctrine taught in their church was the truth of God's Word. After careful consideration, consultation with others and with his consistory, and through anxious prayer, De Cock baptized these children. This infuriated the authorities. In fact, it was this issue which was brought to classis by De Cock's colleagues in protest against him.

A committee of classis was appointed to investigate, during which investigation De Cock came out with a pamphlet with an imposing title page and one not calculated to appease the enemies of the truth: "Defense of the True Reformed Doctrine and of the True Reformed Believers, Attacked and Exposed by Two So-called Reformed Teachers, or the Sheepfold of Christ Attacked by Two Wolves and Defended by H. De Cock, Reformed Teacher at Ulrum." Both men referred to were colleagues who had themselves written against De Cock and the things for which he stood.

In the meantime, the classis met. De Cock pleaded with classis to permit him to defend his views on the basis of Scripture, but he was refused, and in an illegal meeting he was suspended from office

> ...in order to maintain law and order in the Reformed Church, to protect the name and honor of the ministers of the Gospel, and to prevent more disorders, divisions, and revolutions in several congregations in our Fatherland;...if preachers as De Cock were not halted in their reckless enterprise, this Board fears the worst.

While ecclesiastical machinery was grinding along, De Cock submitted to his suspension and stayed off his pulpit. But as the case wound its way through the assemblies, another issue was added: that of hymn singing. De Cock had written the preface to a pamphlet in which the author, a layman, had attacked the singing of hymns in the church. The title of the pamphlet is intriguing: "The Evangelical Hymns Weighed, Tested and Found to be Too Light." It was

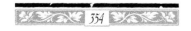

De Cock's conviction, and correctly so, that heresy had come singing into the church through hymns which had taken the place of the Psalms in the worship services.

Tensions continued to rise. They reached a kind of climax when Rev. Heinrich Scholte (later to settle and establish a colony in Pella, Iowa), known to be friendly to De Cock, was forbidden to preach for him so that a modernist could occupy the pulpit instead. The congregation did not take kindly to this, and the police were called in to prevent what was a near riot.

### Secession

Though De Cock had patiently and humbly submitted for nearly a year to the illegal suspension of the classis, he remained the object of hatred. His colleagues did everything they could to make his life miserable. Slanderous talk was everywhere published about him and his wife. The ecclesiastical assemblies forced him to pay the expenses of their case against him. He was never granted a hearing and was told to submit unconditionally to the assemblies or he would never preach again. When he asked for a transcript of the decision, he was mockingly told to copy it himself, and the president openly derided him as he proceeded to do so.

But the faithful people of God in the country were appalled that an honest and godly pastor could be treated in such a way for doing nothing but urging faithfulness to the historic Reformed faith. And God in heaven worked His sovereign work to do what had to be done to preserve and defend His church.

Upon returning from the assembly to his home, De Cock found his two-year-old daughter very ill. She died six days later, and the burden of great grief at the loss of a covenant child was added to his grief at the apostasy of his church.

Scholte came to comfort the grieving family. The consistory asked him to preach that Friday night, October 10, 1834. The Provincial Board refused him permission to preach on the Lord's day; so he preached in an open field from a wagon. Finally De Cock saw that the only hope for his sheep lay in secession.

And so it came about. It was Monday evening, October 13th, that the consistory came together. The "Act of Secession" was drawn up after some discussion, signed by the two elders and three deacons, and presented to the congregation, where it was signed by sixty-seven members and sixty-three heads of families who had not made profession of faith—a total of 247 souls.

The document is so important that parts of it ought to be quoted. Using Article 29 of the Belgic Confession of Faith as its guide, it declared that the church of which the congregation had been a part had lost the marks of the true church and that, therefore, "it has now become more than plain, that the Netherlands Reformed Church is not the True, but the False Church, according to God's Word and Article 29 of our confessions." The document binds those who sign it to be obedient to Article 28 of the same confession and "separate themselves from those who are not of the Church, and therefore will have no more fellowship with the Netherlands Reformed Church, until it returns to the true service of the Lord." The document expresses the "willingness" of those who sign it "to exercise fellowship with all true Reformed members, and to unite themselves with every gathering founded on God's infallible Word, in whatever place God has also united the same." It specifically states that the congregation is determined to be faithful to Scripture, to return to the Three Forms of Unity which are "founded on that Word," to "order our public religious services according to the ancient ecclesiastical liturgy," and to return to the Church Order of Dordrecht.

"Finally, we hereby declare," so the document concludes, "that we continue to acknowledge our unjustly suspended Pastor.

"Ulrum, the 13th of October, 1834. (signed) J. J. Beukema, Elder; K. J. Barkema, Elder; K. A. van der Laan, Deacon; D. P. Ritsema, Deacon; Geert K. Bos, Deacon."

## *Persecution*

Neither De Cock nor his congregation escaped the heavy hand of persecution. They thought they would be free to go their own way and worship in peace, for the government had an official policy of religious toleration, and every heresy under the face of the heavens was taught in the Netherlands and in the state Reformed Church. But this is not the way it goes for the cause of Christ. Every heresy is indeed tolerated—but the truth is not. There is no room for God's truth in this world nor in the apostate church.

De Cock was not long alone. He had been joined already by Rev. Scholte, and he was to be joined by four other ministers, one of whom was Albertus Van Raalte, who brought some of the Seceders to Holland, Michigan. The number of people who followed the leaders grew rapidly so that Seceder churches were organized throughout the land.

But it was a bitter and difficult struggle. De Cock himself was forbidden to preach in his own congregation, was expelled from the parsonage, and was finally forced to settle elsewhere among friends. Soldiers were sent to Ulrum and to other places where the Seceders had established separate congregations and were billeted in the homes of the Seceders. These people, usually from the poor, were forced to feed and shelter the soldiers, tend to their needs, live their lives with the soldiers always present, and try to endure their cruelty, godlessness, and depravity. The Seceders were also forbidden to hold any meetings with more than a few people present, so that it was difficult, if not impossible, to gather in worship on the Lord's day. If any regulations imposed on them were broken, they were fined vast sums of money. If they were unable to pay the fines (true of most of them), their possessions were sold in sheriff's sales so that their fines could be paid to the government. If even this did not suffice, they were imprisoned. De Cock himself spent three months in prison, separated from wife and family. These saints paid the price of faithfulness.

It was only after two or three decades and many concessions to the government that persecution eased. But many came to America where they could live in peace and enjoy the freedom to worship God according to the Scriptures. In them lies the roots of the Protestant Reformed Churches in America.

De Cock died at the age of forty-one on November 14, 1842, in the province of Groningen. He did not live long, nor did he see his followers gain rest from suffering. But he had served his purpose according to the will of God, and the time came for others to continue the work.

De Cock was a man of humble life and, from a natural point of view, unfitted for the greatness of the work. His followers were, for the most part, the poor, the uneducated, the despised, the ignoble of the land. For all that, they were the godly, the pious, the upright who genuinely thirsted for that one true heavenly Bread which is Christ Jesus our Lord.

Together God used them to bring genuine reformation to His church.

**Chapter 49**

# *Abraham Kuyper*
## *Dutch Calvinist*

### *Introduction*

*There are times when God is pleased to raise up in His church men of such outstanding ability and conviction that their work leaves an indelible mark on subsequent history. It is as if, by them, God alters significantly the course of events. Augustine was such a man; so was Martin Luther; and so was John Calvin. One hesitates somewhat to put Abraham Kuyper in such lofty company, and there are*

reasons why he does not completely fit. Nevertheless, Abraham Kuyper came close to being one of them.

Usually such men as God is pleased to use are not only men of extraordinary ability but also men of forceful personality. They are men towards whom it is impossible to be neutral. Every acquaintance either loves them deeply or hates them passionately. Augustine was such a man. Calvin and Luther, too, were hated by many and loved by many. Kuyper, perhaps more than any other person of his generation, was devoutly loved and profoundly hated.

His shadow over the church is long. It reaches to the present.

### *Childhood and Youth*

Abraham Kuyper was born in a parsonage on October 29, 1837, to Rev. and Mrs. J. F. Kuyper in the small fishing village of Maassluis, the Netherlands. The Reformed churches in the Netherlands had fallen on bad times. Over the course of the centuries they had become thoroughly apostate. Modernists occupied thousands of pulpits and held all the significant posts in the universities and seminaries. While Reformed people could be found and Reformed

ministers still preached here and there, the church itself was in the hands of and directed by those who had become enemies of the faith.

Abraham's father, a pastor in this denomination, was himself somewhere between liberal modernism and orthodox Reformed.

Two significant reformatory movements had swept the Netherlands. The first was called *De Reveil* (the Renewal), a movement which was found in every country in Europe in which Protestantism had taken root. It bore, however, some marks of humanism in the Netherlands, and it refused to engage in true church reformation, believing that the state church could be reformed from within. The second was called *De Afscheiding* (the Separation, or Secession), in which Hendrik De Cock was the leader. The movement had demonstrated powerfully that the common people thirsted for a return to Scripture and the confessions, to sound, biblical preaching, and to a holy walk. It spread like wildfire through the Netherlands but soon became the object of the persecution and oppression of the government. It was a movement that attracted thousands, mainly of the common folk, the simple and uneducated people, those on the lower rungs of society, those whom Kuyper himself was later to call *De Kleine Luyden* (the Small Folk). This Secession was three years old when Kuyper was born. That hardly any mention of it can be found in Kuyper's writings in the first twenty to twenty-five years of his life is perhaps indicative of the fact that it was scorned by the educated and ignored by the majority in the state church; after all, the sophisticated leaders in the church could not take seriously a movement which attracted such lowly and despised throngs! Neither the influences of *De Reveil* or the Secession seemed to have touched Kuyper.

Bram (as he was called) did not attend grade school but was instructed by his parents in his home. Particularly his mother was his instructor, from whom he learned French. His father, fluent in German, taught him that language. Early in life Kuyper showed an aptitude for languages and the ability to master any subject.

In 1841 the family moved to Middelburg, the capital of the province of Zeeland. This historic city is on the sea, and while growing up there, Kuyper developed a strong love for the sea and a strong desire to spend his life on board ship.

In 1849 the family moved to Leiden, where Rev. Kuyper took up new ministerial duties. Abraham had access to excellent schools. For six years he attended "gymnasium," a school which was geared to the

preparation of students for university studies. He graduated in 1855 and delivered the valedictory address, but delivered it in German and spoke on the topic "Ulfilas, the bishop of the Visigoths, and His Gothic Translation of the Bible."

Upon completion of his studies in the gymnasium, Kuyper entered the University of Leiden, a university 280 years old with an enrollment of 500–600 students. He earned sufficient money to support himself during his three years of university studies by doing private tutoring.

It seems as if all the influences on Kuyper at this time were bad, something not so strange when one considers the sad state of orthodoxy in the nation's universities. His most influential teacher was Dr. Matthias DeVries, professor of literary studies, under whom Kuyper learned the beauty and power of good writing and under whose tutorship he developed a unique and forceful style of writing that was to stand him in good stead all his life.

Kuyper graduated in 1858 *summa cum laude,* but as a modernist from a modernistic school. What little orthodoxy his parents may have communicated to him was lost in the swirl of liberal thought.

In 1858 Kuyper entered the Leiden Divinity School to study for the ministry. Again the influences were uniformly bad. Dr. L. W. Rauwenhoff, committed to an evolutionistic view of history, taught church history. Dr. Abraham Keunen, a higher critic, taught Bible studies. Dr. Joannes Henricus Scholten, an arch-heretic who denied the bodily resurrection of Christ, taught dogmatics.

In addition to these influences, two current schools of thought in the Netherlands also moved Kuyper in the direction of modernism. One was the Groningen School of thought, which really was nothing else but a promoter of a "Christian humanism" after the order of Erasmus, the humanist of Reformation times. The other school was the so-called Ethical School, which promoted an ecumenical religion of wide tolerance on the basis of an emphasis on the inner, ethical life of man.

It is no wonder that when Kuyper graduated on December 6, 1861, he came out of the school a rather thorough modernist. Even during these years, however, God governed events in such a way that Kuyper's surrender to modernism was not complete.

From divinity school, Kuyper went on to gain his doctorate, something which he accomplished in 1863.

## Conversion and Early Ministry

God made Abraham Kuyper a powerful, Reformed preacher and an amazingly effective defender of the Reformed faith. How did all this come about?

Three events in Kuyper's life were elements in his conversion.

The first took place during Kuyper's university days. The University of Groningen was offering a prize for the best essay submitted on the subject of a comparison of Calvin's and à Lasco's views of the church. With characteristic thoroughness and zeal, Kuyper devoted all his time and energy to the researching of this subject and the development of the thought. Not content with secondary sources, he scoured Europe's libraries to find the writings of à Lasco, but to no avail. Finally, in desperation, he went to the home of his old teacher, Dr. DeVries, who sent Kuyper to DeVries' father, now an old man, but one with a good library. The old minister was too old to remember what he did and did not have in his library but asked Kuyper to return in a week. Not expecting any help from this source, Kuyper was astounded to find on the table a high pile of à Lasco's works. Kuyper considered this so wonderful, especially in the light of the fact that this was apparently the only collection in Europe, that he received it as a special miracle, a miracle which forced him to consider the reality of God's providential direction of his life and the lives of men.

The second event was directly related to the first.

Kuyper plunged into his studies of à Lasco with such vigor that he hardly slept at all. The result was that although he completed his paper (written in Latin) and won the coveted prize, he suffered a total nervous collapse from overwork. He could not read or write but had to content himself with trying to build a model ship while vacationing in Germany in an effort to recoup his strength.

It was towards the end of this eight months of recuperation that Kuyper read Charlotte M. Yonge's book *The Heir of Redcliffe*. The story of a proud, successful man who is humbled, and a poor and lowly man who is exalted, had a profound effect on him. He himself said, "What I lived through in my soul in that moment I fully understood only later, yet from that hour, after that moment, I scorned what I formerly esteemed; I sought what I once dared to despise."

The third event came during Kuyper's ministry.

After completing his doctorate (his thesis was a modification of his prize-winning work on à Lasco and Calvin), he took the call to a congregation in Beesd and married Johanna Hendrika Schaay, a girl from Rotterdam.

The congregation, a small village church, was composed of simple villagers, some of whom were themselves modern and worldly, but some of whom were orthodox and sincere. In an effort to get to know his parishioners, Kuyper visited each in turn. He was surprised and chagrined when one peasant girl of thirty, Pietronella Baltus, refused to shake his hand. Finally Kuyper prevailed upon her to do so, but she made it clear she would do this only because he was a fellow human being, not a brother in Christ.

It is amazing that Kuyper had the grace and humility not only to inquire why Pietronella said this, but also to return again and again to her home when she told him that he was preaching false doctrine and that his soul was in danger of eternal hell. It was at the feet of these humble parishioners that Kuyper was led back to Calvin and the Reformed fathers, and from them to the Scriptures: the one great fountain of the Reformed faith.

### *The Preacher*

Kuyper was a powerful and effective preacher. As he moved steadily towards the Reformed faith, his preaching reflected his commitment to the truth of Scripture and the heritage of the Reformed fathers. His sermons attracted others: some because they could delight in his oratorical skills and his masterful use of the Dutch language; others because Kuyper preached a gospel for which their souls thirsted. It was difficult to find such preaching in any other place in the Netherlands.

That Kuyper's influence upon his times and subsequent history was so great was undoubtedly due to the fact that he was first of all a preacher. God uses preachers: Augustines and Calvins and Luthers and Knoxes. The power of reformation in the church is the power of preaching, above all else.

Kuyper soon moved (in 1867) from Beesd to Utrecht, a church of 35,000 members and eleven ministers. The year was 1867. It was a ministry of about three years, filled with many events. Here Kuyper met Groen Van Prinsterer and cast his lot with the Anti-revolutionary Party. Here he became an editor of *De Heraut* (the Herald), a post he was to hold for the rest of his life. And here his church

reformation work really began, although at the time there was little evidence of it.

The work of church reformation began when Kuyper's consistory refused to answer a questionnaire sent by a committee of the classis that substituted the questionnaire in place of church visitation. The consistory refused to answer: first, on the grounds that the work was not properly being done when done by questionnaire; and secondly, that the work was hypocritical when an apostate body was inquiring into the spiritual health of a congregation. This refusal could have been construed as an act of rebellion, punishable by the classis, but the broader ecclesiastical assemblies chose not to force the issue and backed down without requiring compliance.

In 1870 Kuyper went to Amsterdam, a church of 140,000 members, 136 officebearers, twenty-eight ministers, ten sanctuaries, and four chapels. It was the most prestigious church in the country, the most influential, and the most venerable. It was a strategic place for Kuyper to continue his work.

Without any doubt, Kuyper was the most popular minister of his day, and he drew throngs of people whenever and wherever he preached. Not only were his sermons powerful defenses of the Reformed faith, but they were also masterpieces of literary style and oratorical delivery. Always his preaching was directed towards the common folk. Kuyper had the ability to address his preaching and teaching to every one—a trait of great preachers. He could teach the children in catechism in a way that would pull them to the edges of their seats, and he took the time and made the effort to visit regularly the orphanages where the orphans could also be taught the Word of God.

Not only were Kuyper's sermons powerful and masterful, his liturgical work in the pulpit was meticulously done and carefully delivered. His prayers were eloquent and led the soul of the humble saint to God. His reading of Scripture was an experience in itself. One fellow professor, Dr. Rutgers, said once that hearing Kuyper read, just read Psalm 148, was clearer exposition of that Psalm than most sermons preached on it and that it brought tears to his eyes.

It was during Kuyper's work as minister in Amsterdam that he strove mightily for the renewal and reformation of that church. It was a time of struggle and bitter infighting, but the result was that the church in Amsterdam became a strong Reformed church with the majority of the elders and ministers supporting Kuyper. This did not mean that the modernists and liberals were expelled from the church: this was impossible in a state church. It did mean, however, that the orthodox were in the majority and could control the affairs of the church so that Reformed preaching and instruction became the order rather than the exception.

Polarization was, however, the result. When Kuyper preached a sermon on "The Assurance of Election," a modernist minister followed immediately with a sermon on "Let Anyone Who Comes With Another Gospel Than That Christ Died For All Men Be Accursed." Nevertheless, for the first time in years and years, the Reformed faith and the truth of the confessions were being proclaimed and defended from the pulpits in Amsterdam.

Because of Kuyper's great ability as a preacher, it is more than sad that he laid down his office so soon to give himself to politics.

Personally, I have never been able to understand this move of Kuyper. One who is called to be a minister is called for life, and this highest of all callings has such a grip on the soul of the faithful ambassador of Christ that to leave it is impossible. Paul himself struck the only possible note: "Woe is me if I preach not the gospel." Kuyper resigned in 1874. He had been elected to Parliament and he could not take his seat in that body without leaving the ministry.

A case can be made for the fact that Kuyper's departure from the ministry was in some respects the beginning of his loss of power. That may strike some who have read his biographies as strange and untenable; it is, however, arguable, and we shall take a closer look at some aspects of this question.

### The Journalist and Writer

It is largely through Kuyper's writings that his influence has continued over the years. Article after article, and volume after volume, poured from his pen. It is almost impossible to imagine that Kuyper, as busy as he was, could write as much as he did.

The only reason he did succeed in writing so much was his highly structured and disciplined life. Not only those who loved him, but also his enemies, wondered if Kuyper ever slept. He wrote in long hand everything he published, preached, and spoke. His mornings were reserved for his writing. He absolutely refused to be interrupted during these hours and gave strict instructions to his wife and servants that only a grave emergency could interfere with his morning's work. In the afternoon he lectured. From 5:30–6:30 was

dinner hour and time to spend with his family. In the evenings he corrected proofs from the printer. And his work often continued far into the night. Kuyper spent himself in the cause of the church and the kingdom of Christ.

Kuyper's literary career really began in 1866 with the publication of à Lasco's works, which he had used in the writing of his award-winning essay during university days. He prepared a lengthy introduction to the set and did the church an invaluable service by making available these important treasures from the past. His life could have been profitably spent as a historian; he later edited and published selected writings of Junius and Voetius.

Kuyper had become an associate editor of the weekly *De Heraut* (the Herald) in 1869; in 1871 he assumed the full editorship of this paper. Its character could easily be determined by the motto carried on its masthead: "For a free church and a free school in a free land." In 1872 he also became editor of *De Standaard* (the Standard), a Christian daily newspaper. He continued to function as editor of both these papers until he was eighty-two years old, a span of almost fifty years. Both papers took considerable time, not only for editorial responsibilities, but also for filling the pages with his own writings. Many of the series of articles he wrote in them were later published in book form. The papers were widely read by friend and foe, and they exerted considerable influence on the nation, especially in the area of politics.

It has been said that Kuyper could have been an expert in anything to which he set his hands. There is truth to this. His writings are not only vast, but are on many different subjects. He wrote widely in the field of theology; his lectures on dogmatics were published under the title *Dictaten Dogmatiek* (Dictated Dogmatics). He wrote hundreds of meditations, these being perhaps some of his most enjoyable writings. He prepared many articles on practical Christianity, material that remains of value to the present. He was a student of history and philosophy, of politics and aesthetics, and his writings embrace all these subjects. He prepared expositions of the confessions, the most famous being his exposition of the Heidelberg Catechism, *E Voto Dordraceno* (According to the Will of Dordt). After touring the lands surrounding the Mediterranean Sea, he wrote two extensive volumes on the geography, history, and cultural life of the many peoples who lived in these lands. Some of his writings indicate that he was not a cold intellectual as some charged;

emerging from his facile pen are many writings which can only be classified as "Reformed Mysticism." *Nabij God to Zijn* (Nearness to God) is perhaps his most widely known book in this field.

His writings (as well as his speeches and sermons) abounded in illustrations and figures of speech. Some of his illustrations are memorable, although there are times when one wonders whether the illustrations were intended to prove a point rather than illustrate a point.

Kuyper was a man of most unusual gifts. His learning was vast; his knowledge of history, philosophy, the natural sciences, and politics was wide and profound. He was capable of speaking fluently many of the languages spoken in Europe. He was thoroughly versed in Greek and Hebrew. He lectured and wrote in Latin.

There can be no question about the fact that Kuyper's vast writings have continued to influence the thinking of countless people.

## Church Reformer

After his conversion, Kuyper became an unrelenting foe of the modernism which had captured the universities and divinity schools in the Netherlands, and which had sapped the church of its spiritual life.

The separation which had taken place in 1834 under De Cock and others had been a true reformation in the Netherlands. But by virtue of its very character, it had attracted only the lower classes of people; it had never had any strong theological leadership; many of its members had migrated to America under the heavy burdens of poverty and persecution; and it was itself torn by strife, internal division, and ecclesiastical separation. Christians in other classes of society who were faithful to the Scriptures and the Reformed creeds had remained in the state church.

Kuyper's battle against the evils of doctrine and life in the church brought him into conflict with the theologians, professors, and leaders. They hated him and fought against him bitterly. But opposition never deterred Kuyper from doing what he believed right. He did battle with liberalism and modernism through his preaching and writing, and as his influence grew, his work led to an increasing polarization of the orthodox and liberals.

The first open conflict was over the aforementioned questionnaire sent to the consistory at Utrecht while Kuyper was minister in Utrecht. Although the classical board did not censure Kuyper and

the consistory, it noted Kuyper as one unwilling to go along with the status quo.

It was only after Kuyper had resigned from the ministry and had become in 1882 an elder in the consistory of the church of Amsterdam, that other issues were added until the troubles finally came to a head.

The issues were these:

The Formula of Subscription, which formerly had bound all ministers, elders, deacons, and professors to faithfulness to the creeds, was changed to require of those signing it only a promise "to promote the interests of the kingdom of God in general and especially those of the State Church." Presumably, "the interests of the State Church" would be decided by those who held positions of power. The consistory of Amsterdam, under the leadership of Kuyper, insisted on confessional integrity of its ministers and officebearers.

Furthermore, within the consistory arose the question whether unbelieving young people ought to be admitted into full membership in the church and ought to be received at the Lord's Supper. The consistory refused to allow such desecration of the Lord's table even though the practice was common in the state church.

The result was inevitable. The assemblies acted against them. Five ministers, forty-two elders, and thirty-three deacons were suspended by the classical board. The board also changed the locks in the cathedral consistory room and put steel panels on the inside, taking possession of all the property and the archives. These actions were upheld by the synod, which deposed all of the officebearers. Two hundred congregations left with about 100,000 people. This movement was called *De Doleantie* (the Grieving Ones, or the Aggrieved Ones). Kuyper and his followers chose this name for two reasons: 1) it expressed their sorrow over the apostasy in their denomination; 2) it identified them as still a part of the denomination, while not in agreement with it.

Although this too was a genuine reformation of the church of Christ, Kuyper came to recognize the fact that the Separation (Secession) of 1834 was also a true reformation. Although not immediately involved in seeking contact with the people of the Separation, eventually he became a supporter of it.

The efforts to bring about union were successful, and in 1892 the two denominations merged. Four hundred congregations of the

Secession of 1834 and three hundred congregations of the Kuyperian churches came together to form De Gereformeerde Kerk (the Reformed Church).

In some respects, the marriage was a forced one. The doctrinal differences were many and significant, although the basic difference had to do with God's covenant.

The co-existence of these two denominations in one church structure resulted in a great deal of tension. The people distinguished between the two by speaking of the churches of the Secession as the A-churches, and the churches of the Kuyperian group as the B-churches. It often happened in various cities and villages that neither the people nor the ministers of the one group would want to appear in the company or church buildings of the other.

Although immigrants from the churches of the Secession had begun their trek to North America in the 1840s, churches of the Kuyper group soon followed. In their adopted country, they joined the same church and became the Christian Reformed Church.

### The Politician

Perhaps Kuyper's role in the political affairs of the Netherlands, more than anything else, has had its effect on subsequent generations. His goal was to restore the Netherlands to what it had once been in the golden days of its history when the Reformed church was truly Reformed and the government was a strong supporter of orthodoxy. As a by-product of this goal, Kuyper saw that the advantage would be an alleviation of the difficult lot of the common people.

We have noticed before that Kuyper was a man of the common people, who spoke to them in a way they could understand. He loved them with a deep love. Throughout his entire life he sought the spiritual, material, and political welfare of the common folk.

In 1869 Kuyper joined the Anti-revolutionary Party, the party of Groen Van Prinsterer. In keeping with his character, Kuyper threw himself into the work of the party with vigor and enthusiasm, and eventually stood for election in the Second Chamber of Parliament. After being defeated twice at the polls, he was elected from Gouda in 1874. It was at this point that he resigned his position as minister of the church of Amsterdam and assumed the role of emeritus minister so as to give himself completely to the work of Parliament. The law forbade anyone from being both a member of Parliament and an active minister of a church.

In 1875 he was reelected, but this term was interrupted by his second major nervous breakdown from overwork. For fifteen months he was incapacitated, months which he spent mainly in Italy and Switzerland.

Upon his return and through his efforts, the Anti-revolutionary Party was thoroughly organized, with a constitution, a "Statement of Principles," national and local organization, and a well-formulated platform. Such organization paid dividends, and the party continued to increase its membership in Parliament.

Nevertheless, as Kuyper and his policies were more and more hated by the opposition, the two main parties in Parliament united against him, and it soon became clear that the only way for the Anti-revolutionary Party to break the hold of the liberals on the country was to form a coalition with the Roman Catholics. This coalition was effected and was victorious in the election of 1888; but its victory was temporary, and it lost the election of 1891. It was not until 1901 that the coalition once again came to power. This time Kuyper was asked to head the new government as prime minister. After the dissolution of the government and the defeat of the coalition in the election of 1905, Kuyper's brief term as prime minister came to an end. Twice more he served briefly, once in the Second Chamber and once in the First Chamber of Parliament. But his age and infirmities were catching up with him and his terms were ineffective.

Although the goals of the Anti-revolutionary Party were never fully achieved, some accomplishments of note resulted from the years in which the party of Kuyper was a force with which the opposition had to reckon. Perhaps most importantly, a school bill was passed which gave the Christian schools legal parity with the government schools. Prior to Kuyper's labors on behalf of Christian education, the situation in the Netherlands was very much as it is in the United States today: government schools were supported by all taxpayers; Christians schools had to be supported by the people who did not want their children taught in government schools; thus, a double burden of taxation and tuition fell upon them. Kuyper succeeded in getting legislation passed which gave government subsidy also to Christian schools.

Kuyper pressed hard and long for the Christianizing of the colonies under Netherlands' rule, and he sought legislation which

would alleviate the hard lot of the working man and abolish child labor. Kuyper was astounded to learn that little children were required to work seventy to eighty hours a week, and had to be wakened in the morning by being doused with cold water.

That Kuyper came to power at all involved a compromise of his own position. Early in his work with the Anti-revolutionary Party, Kuyper refused cooperation with the Conservative Party (its name is deceptive; though called "Conservative," it was closely allied with the Liberal Party and was bitterly opposed to anything the orthodox stood for) because they "subjected even the honor of the holy God to calculations of political advantage." Yet Kuyper could form a coalition with Roman Catholics in order to gain political advantage.

As he became older, Kuyper not only did not actively participate in party affairs as he once had done, but he became more and more critical of his party, criticisms he publicly voiced in *De Heraut* and *De Standaard*. He sometimes left the impression, rightly or wrongly, that he was becoming a bitter old man who could not tolerate the leadership of others, especially when they disagreed with him. Many complained of his autocratic leadership.

## *The Educator*

Kuyper was deeply interested in and concerned for Christian education. Not only was he concerned that the children of believers receive instruction in the ways of God's covenant, but he labored long and hard to make Christian education available for the common folk whose financial burdens were often very great.

Kuyper's interests in education went beyond the instruction offered in what we would call grade schools and high schools. Dissatisfied with the apostasy in the universities (schools under government control), Kuyper set his sights on the establishment of a Christian university free from government control. After much labor on his part, the Free University was established on October 20, 1880. It was a school for the orthodox, free from any governmental or ecclesiastical control, operated as a parental institution, and supported by the gifts and prayers of the people of God.

The university was organized under five disciplines: theology, medicine, jurisprudence, natural science, and philosophy. Its first professors were Dr. Kuyper, Dr. F. L. Rutgers, and Dr. Hoedemaker (all three in theology); Mr. D. P. D. Fabius (in law); and Dr. F. W. J. Dilloo (in letters). Five students were enrolled at the beginning, but

it continued to grow and served to supply Reformed ministers to the new denomination which Kuyper had been instrumental in forming.

In this university Kuyper lectured in dogmatics until he was forced to retire for health reasons.

His interests in university education led him to America. He was invited to deliver the Stone Lectures at Princeton University in 1898 and to receive an honorary degree. These lectures, by no means Kuyper's better work, were later published under the title *Calvinism*.

## The Theologian

That Kuyper was a theologian of note goes without saying. His many years of teaching Reformed theology in the Free University, the publication of his *Dictaten Dogmatiek,* and his many theological writings give abundant testimony to his theological acumen.

He was a *Reformed* theologian, unsparing in his attacks on the liberals whose hatred and fury he incurred, and he was unwearying in his defense of the Reformed faith.

In theology as well as in preaching, Kuyper was a theologian of the people. He taught and wrote in a way that could be understood by the least educated of the church, and he could make the most profound truths unmistakably clear; he rallied the scattered sheep of the church of Christ around the banner of the Reformed faith.

Yet Kuyper's work as theologian was somewhat limited. These limitations were, in large measure, due to his wide interests, his overwhelming work load, and his involvement in all the affairs of the Netherlands, political, ecclesiastical, and social. Although Kuyper was an articulate and powerful defender of the Reformed faith, he made few significant contributions to the organic body of the faith as it had been delivered to the church of his time by the fathers from the past.

I suppose this statement will be sharply challenged, for there are many who see Kuyper as one of the greatest of all original theologians. Nevertheless, where Kuyper did introduce new ideas, they were often outside the mainstream of the Reformed faith of the past and innovative in the sense that they could be challenged as unbiblical, unconfessional, and, therefore, wrong. This was true of his view of presumptive regeneration (the idea that one must presume the regeneration of all the children born of believing parents). This doctrine became a major bone of contention in later years, and it was rejected by the church after him. This was also true of his views on common grace, although here his influence was very wide, and his ideas of common grace are still widely held both in the Netherlands and in this country.

Although attempts have been made to prove that Kuyper, also in the doctrine of common grace, stood in the line of Reformed thought beginning with Calvin, it must be admitted that Kuyper introduced into Reformed thinking a novelty which can hardly stand up under the test of Scripture and the Reformed confessions. Kuyper's world-view was closely connected to his views on common grace.

Kuyper was a man of the antithesis. He believed strongly that the antithesis requires absolute separation of the church from the world in all areas of endeavor, to the point that he himself labored mightily for a Christian labor union, a Christian political party, a Christian system of education free from any government control. Yet he formed a political coalition with the Roman Catholics and taught a doctrine of common grace which paved the way for cooperation between believers and unbelievers in many areas of life.

But all this is not to minimize his strenuous efforts, blessed by God, to return churches in his country to the faith of their fathers.

### *The Christian Man*

Kuyper was also a man among men and a Christian man among Christian men.

He was a family man who reveled in the life of his own covenant family. To him and his wife were born five sons and two daughters. Family devotions were important to Kuyper. During the evening meal, Kuyper would gather also the servants into the family circle, read the Scriptures with them, explain these Scriptures to them, and lead the household in prayers to God. Mealtime was a time of discussion, fellowship, laughter, and fun.

The old year passed away and the new year entered with Kuyper and his family reading the Scriptures and praying together. This was a family custom preserved until nearly the end of Kuyper's life.

The amount of work Kuyper did was incredible, but he was, after all, human. The heavy load of work twice brought him to complete nervous exhaustion. When he finally learned his own limitations, he took three vacations a year, usually spent in Europe and often involving mountain climbing. He had learned to love mountain climbing when he was in Switzerland after his second collapse.

Kuyper was also a man of most unusual gifts. His learning was vast; his knowledge of history, philosophy, the natural sciences, and politics was wide and profound. He was capable of speaking fluently many of the languages spoken in Europe. He was thoroughly versed in Greek and Hebrew. He lectured and wrote in Latin.

Sorrow also touched his life when in 1892 his nine-year-old son died, and in 1899 when his beloved wife died at the age of fifty-eight. Kuyper never married again and bore the sorrow of these losses to the grave.

Though short of stature, Kuyper had a commanding presence, and his eyes were piercing. He preached and spoke literally hundreds and hundreds of times. But he could hold his audience spellbound with his marvelous voice and forceful oratorical style. He was uncompromising in his convictions and conveyed what he believed with passion and sincerity. He had the ability to move people deeply.

Kuyper's own spiritual life was one of devotion and reflection on the Word of God. Though no mystic in the wrong sense of that word, Kuyper spoke often and eloquently of the union of the soul with Christ. That was the joy of his life and the hope that sustained him as he looked beyond this life to glory.

Kuyper was not without flaws, however. It is probably characteristic of a forceful personality, as it was of Kuyper, that he not only held strongly to his convictions, but was intolerant of anyone who disagreed with him. He tended to be dictatorial in ecclesiastical and political affairs, and could not easily abide contradiction from those who were with him in the same cause. As he grew older, these weaknesses became sharper, and the last years of his life were not the happiest. It seems as if the temptations of old age for one who has labored long and hard in the cause of Christ are uniquely temptations to succumb to bitterness. Kuyper did not always successfully resist these temptations.

He died November 8, 1920. The funeral was attended by thousands, yet the services were simple. Not even one flower or sprig adorned the casket. The climax was the singing by the throng of Kuyper's favorite Psalm: Psalm 89:7, 8 of the Dutch Psalm book. On his tombstone were engraved the words [translated]:

Dr. A. Kuyper

Born October 29, 1837

And fallen asleep in his Saviour

November 8, 1920

*Part Seven*

*Twentieth Century Reformers
in the United States
1920-1965*

*Part Seven:*

# Twentieth Century Reformers in the United States (1920-1965)

Dutch Immigration to USA
for religious freedom
1840s-1900....................

Christian Reformed Church
in USA 1857...................

Aggrieved Ones
*(De Doleantie)*1886.............

World War I 1914-1918........

League of Nations 1919........

Auburn Affirmation 1924......
Protestant Reformed
Churches in America 1925..
Scopes "Monkey" Trial 1925..
Westminster Theological
Seminary 1929.................

Orthodox Presbyterian
Church 1936...................

World War II 1939-1945.......

United Nations Charter 1945..
World Council of Churches
Organized 1948.................

*1840*

*1850*

*1860*

*1880*   **J. Gresham Machen** 1881-1937

**Herman Hoeksema** 1886-1965

**George M. Ophoff** 1891-1962

*1900*

*1920*

*1925*

*1930*

*1940*

*1965*

# Chapter 50

# J. Gresham Machen

## Presbyterian Reformer

*Introduction*
*The Reformation of the sixteenth century, under the leadership of John Calvin, separated, in the providence of God, into two streams: the one the stream of Presbyterianism, which dominated in the British Isles; the other the stream of Reformed thought, which was found primarily on the continent of Europe and which had its center in the Netherlands.*

The two were not fundamentally different. Both were strongly Calvinistic in doctrine, liturgy, and church government. The differences were due to the different circumstances under which the Reformation took place and the different cultures in which God had planted these witnesses to His truth. They were not at odds; they complemented each other.

Presbyterianism reached its high water mark in the British Isles with the great Westminster Assembly (1643–1652) and the formulation of the Westminster Standards; the Reformed branch of the Calvin Reformation reached its zenith at the Synod of Dordt (1618–1619).

Both came early to North America, prior even to the Revolutionary War. And both flourished on the new soil. Presbyterianism, especially, grew in both the South and North and became the mighty Presbyterian Church in the U.S.A.

The Civil War split Presbyterianism into a southern church, the church of Thornwell and Dabney, and a northern church, the church of Princeton where Samuel Miller, Benjamin B. Warfield, and the Hodges taught and gave to the church hundreds of solid Calvinistic preachers.

Just as in the Reformed churches in America there was doctrinal decline and apostasy, so was it true in the Presbyterian churches that apostasy crept in and eventually took over the churches. In both, God raised men to bring reformation to the church. In the northern branch of the Presbyterian church, this apostasy all but destroyed Presbyterianism. But God gave the church a champion of Calvinistic orthodoxy, J. Gresham Machen, a man courageous in his defense of the truth, persecuted sometimes unmercifully for his uncompromising stand, but faithful to the end. Through his struggles and trials, orthodoxy triumphed in the formation of what is today known as the Orthodox Presbyterian Church.

It is Machen's story that needs to be told in this chapter.

### *Early Life and Education*

John Gresham Machen's birth and early life seemed unlikely to fit him, according to our standards, for the important calling which God had in store for him. He was born to Arthur Machen and Mary Gresham on July 28, 1881, the second of three sons. His father was a successful lawyer from Baltimore, Maryland, and his mother an aristocratic lady from the "genteel" Southern city of Macon, Georgia. Both father and mother were from high society and moved in intellectual and political circles, and their friends included many men famous in American politics.

Nevertheless, the Machen home was a godly home: both parents were "Old School" Presbyterians, deeply committed to the Westminster Standards, involved in church affairs, and concerned about the religious education of their sons. At his mother's knees, Machen learned the Scriptures and the Shorter Catechism.

Because it will be necessary to say something more about Old School Presbyterianism, it is well that the term be explained a bit before we proceed.

A split had taken place within the Presbyterian Church in 1837 between what became known as "Old School Presbyterians" and "New School Presbyterians." The former were determined to maintain Presbyterian distinctives as outlined in the Westminster Confession, while the latter were more broadly evangelical, more interested in church union—often at the price of doctrinal integrity— and not sharply Calvinistic in their theology, as was evident from their support of revivalism even as it was preached by such an enemy of Calvinism as Charles Finney. The differences were so deep that a split was the only cure.

Nevertheless, in 1869, after years of negotiations, the "New School" churches rejoined the "Old School" denomination without substantially changing the position which had brought about a split a little more than thirty years earlier. The union came about in spite of the fact that many "New School" churches were doctrinally unsound.

Machen was raised in "Old School Presbyterianism."

Though his father was fifty-five years old at John's birth, he still exerted considerable influence on his son, for he lived to be an old man. But the greatest influence was from his mother, who taught him in his youth, lived until just five years before John died, and was his correspondent and confidante until her death. Their correspondence was lengthy and continuous, and to no one did Machen reveal his thoughts more fully than to his mother. The fact that Machen never married made his mother's influence all the more profound.

Machen went to a private school for the first six years of his education, and received a classical education in Latin, Greek, mathematics, and the natural sciences in university.

In 1896 Gresham professed his faith, became a full member of the Presbyterian Church, and began to wonder whether he was called to the ministry of the gospel. For some reason, this was a perplexing question to Machen, and he came to no decision on it for many years.

In 1902, after a trip to Europe, Machen enrolled in Princeton Theological Seminary. These were the glory days of Princeton when Dick Wilson, Geerhardus Vos, and Caspar Wistar Hodge, among others, were teaching there. Nevertheless, Machen found studies in Princeton unbearably boring. He often skipped classes, spent the afternoons in fun, enjoyed the boisterous pleasures of fun-loving college students, traveled to New York City and elsewhere, and found particular pleasure in the college football games then already common in the East.

A few words about Princeton might be in order here. The school was a strong "Old School" Presbyterian seminary, affiliated with Princeton University, perhaps the most conservative of all the northern church's seminaries. It was typically Presbyterian, however, in that it emphasized the rational nature of Christianity and was influenced by the philosophy of Scottish common sense realism, which held to the basic reliability of ordinary human perception. It was interested in furnishing various rational proofs of Christianity by means of the inductive method. Still, it remained solidly Calvinistic in its commitment to the truth, and its professors insisted on strict subscription to the Westminster Confession. While a rational approach to the doctrines of Scripture was characteristic of Presbyterianism, it had the effect on Machen of creating in him a life-long commitment to the intellectual aspects of Christianity and to the need for a thorough intellectual training for the ministry in the Presbyterian Church.

After a summer studying Greek at the University of Chicago, Machen went to Germany to improve his German. He concentrated on New Testament studies in Marburg and Göttingen. Machen was profoundly moved by Wilhelm Herrmann, a liberal higher critic, who nevertheless displayed a deeply religious character. Machen was disturbed by an apparent conflict in Herrmann between a liberal theology and a deep Christian piety. How could one deny the fundamentals of Scripture and remain genuinely pious? Herrmann's ability to hold these two in tension remained a puzzle for Machen all his life.

In 1906 Machen accepted a position in Princeton Seminary teaching New Testament.

## *Early Years In Princeton*

Before Machen agreed to teach in the New Testament Department of Princeton, he had to be assured that he would be permitted to do this without committing himself to ordination. He had not yet resolved in his mind whether or not to become an ordained minister of the gospel. The resolution to these problems would come later.

Princeton was, in those days, under some pressure to alter its curriculum. Many students were dissatisfied with the strong intellectual emphasis in the seminary and wanted more practical studies, less demanding on their time and energies, and more suited to their own views of the practical aspects of the ministry. Some students, for example, no longer wanted to be forced into the discipline of mastering the original languages of Scripture, Hebrew and Greek. Already in those days students often did not appreciate the rigor of intellectual disciplines and sought the easy road to the ministry. Times do not change appreciably.

But Machen found teaching strenuous work, not only because of the demands of teaching, but also because of deep-seated disinterest on the part of some students. Perhaps this was partly the reason why Machen developed some idiosyncrasies in his classroom lecturing. He sometimes lectured while banging his head against a wall. At other times he lectured balancing a book on his head. He often opened his morning mail while correcting Greek mistakes in the recitation of students. And he seemed fond of writing Greek conjugations backwards on the blackboard.

Nevertheless, he was a serious scholar who devoted himself to his work. And the fruits of his work soon appeared in a scholarly work entitled *The Origin of Paul's Religion.* Perhaps the value of this work can best be summarized by H. L. Mencken's opinion of Machen. Mencken was an agnostic, hateful of Christianity, and bitterly satirical in his writings. But for some reason he was impressed with Machen's work and remained an admirer of Machen all his life. After reading Machen's book, Mencken compared Machen and Machen's colleague William Jennings Bryan (an influential elder in the church, attorney for the prosecution in the famous Scopes Trial, and twice Democratic nominee for the President of the United States) as analogous to a comparison between the Matterhorn and a wart.

Machen's years in Princeton were some of his most productive. In addition to the book mentioned above, Machen also wrote two other books which were widely hailed, *The Virgin Birth* and *What is Faith,* although both appeared somewhat later in his career.

In addition to his writing, Machen also taught full time, concentrating on Greek, exegesis, and studies of various New Testament books. Many articles from his pen appeared in the prestigious *Princeton Theological Review,* and he wrote extensively for the Sunday school program of his church. His mastery of New Testament Greek was complete, and he crowned his studies in this field with the preparation of a *Greek Grammar of the New Testament,* which is still widely used today.

As his popularity increased, so also did invitations to speak and to preach (he "preached" as a "lay preacher" prior to his ordination), and the invitations to teach in various Bible schools, colleges, and seminaries came with regularity into his post box. One of the most difficult invitations to turn down was an invitation to Columbia, a Southern Presbyterian seminary in South Carolina.

This might be an appropriate place to mention two other events in Machen's life. The first was the resolution of his problems with becoming an ordained minister. Whatever may have been the reasons for his reluctance to choose this path, finally, in 1914, he sought ordination. This was granted him, as well as a full professorship at Princeton. It was the end of a long struggle and brought great peace to his soul.

The second was his determination to serve his country during the years of World War I. He wanted to serve in some sort of religious capacity, but finally could find a place only in the Y.M.C.A. Although he was near the front lines and sometimes under fire, it was a measure of his humility as a servant of Christ that he served without complaint in canteens mixing and serving chocolate, providing as best he could for the little comforts the soldiers could find near the front and ministering to their spiritual needs when that was possible. It was, in God's unfathomable ways, a strange preparation for the great work ahead of him.

### Early Troubles

But serious troubles were appearing on the horizon, troubles which would soon engulf the church and would affect Machen personally.

A latitudinarian party appeared in the church which favored toleration of departures from the truth, was inclusive in its attitude towards other denominations, and wanted very loose subscription to the creeds in order to make room for its sympathy for other religious viewpoints. But Machen led a party in the church (which included most of the Princeton Seminary faculty) which was opposed to all these things. Machen spoke for doctrinal integrity and forthright defense of the great truths of the Calvin Reformation. He argued strict subscriptionism, that is, insistence on adherence to the Westminster Standards in all matters of faith.

This position made Machen a marked man. Because he was outspoken in his convictions and was not fearful of expressing his concern for the church, he soon became the object of what can only be called a propaganda campaign to discredit him.

It is worth our while to trace the history of those troubles which led to Machen's separation from the church, for there is a pattern here often followed in church struggles, a pattern from which we can well learn.

The first step in the process by which liberals often gain control of the church is to reduce differences to emotional issues. This happened in Machen's church. The liberals accused Machen of questioning their sincerity and their commitment to the church, but all the while, they made no effort to answer his arguments. They insisted they were only pleading for a bit of tolerance for their position, although such a plea did not prevent them from being impossibly intolerant once they gained the majority. Walter Lippmann, the famous newspaper columnist, was right when he pointed out that being friendly with and tolerant of liberals was akin to "smiling and committing suicide." In the meantime, anyone who spoke against the liberals was accused by them of bigotry, intolerance, and a hateful attitude towards brothers.

But other events hastened the process of decay. It was ominous for the church when in 1903 a revision of the Westminster Standards took place which modified the doctrines of Calvinism to include a love of God for all, an atonement of Christ for all, and a desire on God's part to save all. Such an alteration of the creeds paved the way for the return of the Cumberland Presbytery, which had left the Presbyterian Church in the United States of America in 1810 because of the strong Calvinism in the latter denomination.

In 1914 J. Ross Stevenson was elected to the presidency of Princeton Seminary. He was one of the first ecumenists and later attended the initial meetings of the formation of the World Council of Churches in 1948. Dr. Stevenson supported a more practical emphasis in the curriculum. Surprisingly, Machen concurred, but Warfield was bitterly opposed to the change. Warfield never attended another faculty meeting because of his disgust with this turn of events.

In 1920 Machen attended his first General Assembly meeting, but was appalled to discover that the church was ready to adopt a Plan of Union with twenty other denominations. The plan seriously compromised the truth for which Machen's church stood. More disconcerting was the fact that two professors from Princeton favored the plan: Dr. Stevenson and Dr. Charles Erdman. The plan ultimately failed on the level of presbytery, and this failure may be attributed to the fact that Machen fought it fiercely in speeches and articles.

But the tide of liberalizing theology rolled on, nonetheless.

## Continued Apostasy in the Church

Perhaps the catalyst which brought matters to a head was the preaching of Harry Emerson Fosdick in the First Presbyterian Church of New York City. It was strange and already disconcerting that Fosdick should be preaching there at all. He was not a Presbyterian, but a Baptist; yet he was stated supply in First Church in New York.

Fosdick's sermon, which burst like a bomb over the church, was entitled "Shall the Fundamentalists Win?" It was an open attack on the conservatives in the church, a bold statement of modernist belief, and a trumpet blast summoning the liberals to do battle with the conservatives. The trumpet blast branded the conservatives as intolerant men, and it pleaded for tolerance in the church on such issues as the virgin birth of Christ and our Lord's second coming.

Individuals, especially in the Philadelphia Presbytery, and finally the presbytery itself; protested the sermon and asked for discipline. With this protest the General Assembly agreed. It condemned Fosdick's position and sermon, and it advised the presbytery in which First Church resided to see to it that the preaching conformed to the Westminster Standards.

But the presbytery not only refused to follow the instructions from the General Assembly; they openly defied it. The liberal forces were becoming increasingly vocal and better organized.

In early January of 1924, a document was published by the liberals, which became known as the "Auburn Affirmation," a notorious and shameful document in the history of Presbyterianism. Its immediate occasion was the condemnation of Fosdick by the General Assembly; its significance lay in the fact that it openly espoused a position completely contrary to everything Presbyterianism had stood for. It stated that five cardinal doctrines of the Christian faith—the virgin birth, the inspiration of Scripture, the substitutionary atonement of the Lord Jesus Christ, the bodily resurrection of Christ from the dead, and the miracles recorded in Scripture—were not essential to the system of doctrine found in Scripture, but were mere theories. It was eventually signed by 1,274 ministers, about 13% of the total clergy.

Although many protests were made against the Auburn Affirmation, and although the cries were loud and furious, the General Assembly of 1924, though tossing a few sops in the direction of the conservatives, refused to condemn Fosdick. A kind of

a footnote to the whole matter is the role which John Foster Dulles played in the affair. Many will remember him as one of the most powerful Secretaries of State that the United States has seen, who served under President Eisenhower during the worst days of the Cold War. Dulles was, perhaps more than any other, responsible for steering all protests into various standing committees where they could die untreated.

The protests continued, however, and Machen stood in the forefront of the battle. In this crucial position he, and those who stood with him, were the objects of fierce attacks. It was almost as if the liberals were determined at all costs to dispense with Machen himself. They made use of politics, misrepresentations, and personal attacks, the meanwhile presenting themselves as martyrs who only wanted peace and quietness in the church. The conservatives were branded as bigoted and enemies of the good of the denomination. The liberals pleaded for tolerance until they were in positions of power; then, as liberals will always do, they rammed their views down the throats of the church members ruthlessly and intolerantly.

The General Assembly of 1925 took the easy way out of the difficulties, but a way favored by liberals throughout history. It gives time to consolidate one's position. The assembly appointed a committee to study the state of the church to learn, if possible, the causes of division. In the mind of any fair-minded person, the reason for unrest was as clear as the sun on a cloudless day: the modernism of a large percentage of the clergy. But the committee reported back that the conservatives were to blame for the unrest, for—the committee piously concluded—the Presbyterian Church had always been pluralistic, no liberalism could be found in the church, and the charges of the conservatives bordered on libel and slander.

At the General Assembly meeting of 1926 another matter came up which boded ill for Machen. He had been appointed to the chair of apologetics and ethics at Princeton, and his appointment had to be approved by the assembly. The assembly postponed a decision on the matter on the grounds that Machen's qualifications were in doubt, not intellectually, but because of Machen's personality and harshness. That was ominous in the extreme. The assembly had quite obviously agreed to be led by the liberals and modernists and concentrate its attack on the most outspoken defender of the faith in the church.

Rather than approve Machen's appointment, the assembly appointed another committee, this time to look into matters at

Princeton itself and to ascertain the reasons for and the cure of Princeton's problems. The problems, of course, were, as everyone knew, due to the presence of modernistic sympathizers on the faculty. But the committee did not see it that way and recommended, instead, a complete reorganization of the seminary, which would effectively give the seminary to the control of the Modernists. Machen was fingered as the leading figure in disturbing the peace of the seminary. The report was approved, and the seminary reorganized in 1927 and 1929.

That did it. Machen had been effectively made an outcast in his own church and seminary, and the ruthless forces of opposition to his strong stand had won the day.

### *Westminster Seminary*

Machen resigned from his position when this reorganization was complete. He could do little else. His willingness to sacrifice his prestigious position in Princeton for the sake of the truth may have given the modernists reason to gloat, but it was an act of faithfulness to Almighty God and to the cause of God's church, which he served with distinction.

This courageous act of Machen was all the more admirable because his friends, fellow conservatives, and ardent supporters in Princeton chose to remain in the school. This was true of his personal friend of many years, Dr. Armstrong, as well as Dr. Caspar Wistar Hodge and Geerhardus Vos. Machen stood almost alone.

Nevertheless, there were those in the church who supported him, and a group made up predominantly of laymen met in order to start an alternative seminary. The money was subscribed, and Westminster Theological Seminary began to prepare for classes in the fall of 1929. The men who agreed to work and teach in the seminary were a notable group: Paul Wooley as secretary and registrar, as well as professor of church history; Dick Wilson, O. T. Allis, and Alan MacRae in Old Testament studies; and Machen and Ned Stonehouse in New Testament studies. A bit later, Cornelius Van Til was added to the staff in apologetics, and R. B. Kuiper came to teach dogmatics and practical theology. The latter two were from the Christian Reformed Church.

It was too bad that the seminary became an independent institution, for the preparation of men for the ministry of the gospel is the work of the church itself and ought to be under the direction

and supervision of the church of Christ. Westminster has remained an independent seminary to the present.

Even during Machen's lifetime the seminary was beset by difficulties. To understand these difficulties, it is well to back up a bit to take another look at Machen's position in another area.

Machen had often been branded as a fundamentalist, when in fact he really was nothing of the kind. He rejected fundamentalism for several reasons. While he certainly approved of the firm position of fundamentalism on the crucial questions of the virgin birth, the inspiration of Scripture, the bodily resurrection, etc., he dissented in some important areas. In the first place, Machen was deeply committed to the Westminster Standards and wanted a strongly creedal church, something to which fundamentalism tended to give little more than lip service. Secondly, Machen did not agree with fundamentalism's eschatology, which tended to be dispensational and pre-millennarian. And finally, Machen was opposed to the stringent position of fundamentalists that all smoking and drinking of alcoholic beverages was wrong. He had made his own position on the latter point publicly clear when he had opposed Prohibition.

For this last scriptural position, Machen had suffered a great deal of criticism, and he continued to do so. After the founding of Westminster, for example, reports were circulated that the students in the seminary smoked and drank, as if the seminary had become a den of iniquity.

The fundamentalist position was crucial to some who followed Machen. In 1935 Dr. O. T. Allis left with thirteen members of the Board, and in 1937 Oliver J. Buswell Jr., Carl McIntyre, and Alan McRae left Westminster to form the Bible Presbyterian Church.

## *Machen's Deposition*

All this time, Machen remained a member in good standing in the Presbyterian Church in the U.S.A. But his dissatisfaction with the church continued. It concentrated especially on the mission labors of the church, for many missionaries had been imbued with the same modernistic heresies as ministers stateside. Especially was this true in China where Pearl Buck, an influential missionary, was teaching that all religions had good elements in them, including the pagan religions, and that Christ was nothing more than a great teacher and leader.

Machen filed a protest against these teachings with the New Brunswick Presbytery, and it eventually reached the General Assembly. In both courts Machen's protest failed. In response to this failure of his objections, Machen, along with others, organized a new mission board, The Independent Board of Presbyterian Foreign Missions. This was a fatal step.

Support for the board grew rapidly and its influence in the churches constituted a real threat to the power of the regular board; the leaders in Machen's denomination were forced to do something about it. Machen was accused of acting unconstitutionally by his participation in the activities of his board; and that became the standard accusation made against all others whom the church wanted to discipline.

It is not so easy to evaluate all this. It would seem that the charge made against Machen, even under Presbyterian church polity, was correct. It is hard to imagine how a group of individuals can form its own mission board within a denomination, and proceed to do the same work as the official board. In any case, it is clear enough that the work of missions, because it is the official preaching of the gospel, is the work of the church and may not be performed by an independent board outside of church control. Machen's horror at the corruption of the current board could not outweigh the serious mistake he made in forming this independent board.

There remains an irony here, however. These same men who were so intent on the letter of the constitution in condemning Machen rode roughshod over every principle of justice and righteousness when they used Machen's participation in the work of this board as the occasion to discipline him. How often has it not happened in the church that righteous men are condemned while the wicked are approved. Machen's case was no different from countless others.

The General Assembly in 1934 condemned Machen's participation in the board, and the New Brunswick Presbytery held its trial of Machen in February and March of 1935. It might be worthwhile to quote a part of Machen's defense:

> Having been ordered by the General Assembly of the Presbyterian Church in the U.S.A., to sever my connection with The Independent Board of Presbyterian Foreign Missions, I desire to say, very respectfully:

I. I cannot obey the order.

    A. Obedience to the order in the way demanded by the General Assembly would involve support of a propaganda that is contrary to the gospel of Christ.

    B. Obedience to the order in the way demanded by the General Assembly would involve substitution of a human authority for the authority of the Word of God.

    C. Obedience to the order in the way demanded by the General Assembly would mean acquiescence in the principle that support of the benevolences of the Church is not a matter of free-will but the payment of a tax enforced by penalties.

    D. All three of the above mentioned courses of conduct are forbidden by the Bible, and therefore I cannot engage in any of them. I cannot, no matter what any human authority bids me do, support a propaganda that is contrary to the gospel of Christ; I cannot substitute a human authority for the authority of the Word of God, and I cannot regard support of the benevolences of the Church as a tax enforced by penalties, but must continue to regard them as a matter of free-will and a thing with regard to which a man is responsible to God alone.

II. Though disobeying an order of the General Assembly, I have a full right to remain in the Presbyterian Church in the U.S.A. because I am in accord with the constitution of that Church and can appeal from the General Assembly to the Constitution.

Eighty pages followed in which Machen defended his position in careful detail. The assembly had made up its mind, and swiftly and efficiently Machen's case was judged; he was found guilty on all counts, and he was summarily defrocked. Those who dared to stand with him were quickly punished by their respective presbyteries.

## New Denomination

With that action, the assembly paved the way for the establishment of a new denomination, first called The Presbyterian Church in America, but later, the Orthodox Presbyterian Church.

On June 11, 1936, when the new denomination was formed, it was made up of about 5,000 people who left with Machen; this out of a denomination which numbered nearly 2,000,000. And with him thirty-four ministers and seventeen elders left as well.

In the years prior to this action, the Presbyterian Church in the U.S.A. had come to the evil condition in which it found itself because good men kept silent. During the height of the struggle, these same good men did not have the courage to come out openly in their support of those who were leading the fight. When push came to shove, and the time came to stand up and be counted, it was again the good men who, while encouraging Machen in private to stand for his convictions, refused to go along. A mere handful finally were willing to act on their principles. And this, too, is the way things go in times of crisis in the church of Christ.

Although it grew rapidly to about seventy-five ministers, the Orthodox Presbyterian Church had its problems in its early history which paralleled those in Westminster Seminary. But the denomination continues to the present.

J. Gresham Machen's story is almost over. He did not live long after the formation of the new denomination. Enormous demands were placed upon him in the seminary and by the newly established churches. And determined to do all he could for the cause of the church, Machen exhausted himself in the work.

On a preaching trip to North Dakota, which he made in spite of a severe cold, he became ill with pleurisy and died of pneumonia in a hospital in Bismarck.

To a friend at his bedside he spoke of a view of heaven which had been granted him and cried, "Sam, it was glorious, it was glorious." A bit later, he said, "Sam, isn't the Reformed faith grand?" The next day, mostly unconscious, he nevertheless was clear enough to dictate a telegram to another colleague at the seminary, John Murray. It read simply, "I'm so thankful for the active obedience of Christ. No hope without it." It was the last he spoke. He died on January 1, 1937.

## Conclusion

J. Gresham Machen remained a bachelor all his life and enjoyed only one close attachment with a member of the opposite sex. She was from New England, and the two became very close. Marriage, however, was out of the question because she was a Unitarian and could not bring herself to embrace the faith which Machen held dear. Yet, they remained friends all Machen's life.

It was undoubtedly his bachelor status which made the tie between him and his mother all the closer. When he could confide in

no one else, he confided in her, and her death, five years before his own, was a severe blow.

The history of Machen's involvement in the struggles with modernism in the Presbyterian Church brings up an interesting question: Why was the battle with modernism? How can it be that a church came to a point where such doctrines as the divinity of Christ and His bodily resurrection from the dead were denied before anyone challenged their presence and teachings? A church does not become modernistic over night. Apostasy is a gradual thing. Modernism is not the beginning of decline; it is the end.

And herein lies the sad part of the struggle. Although Machen and those with him, in their allegiance to the Westminster Standards, had stood firmly for a strong Calvinism, their spiritual forebears had not been willing to fight when Arminianism had made its inroads into the church many years earlier. That Arminianism had, in fact, been given official sanction to some extent when the Old School Presbyterians had welcomed into their fellowship the New School churches, which were doctrinally inclusive in their views of evangelism and shot through with Arminianism.

This grave weakness in the church had become manifest in the open espousal of revivalistic movements, which were ecumenical in all the bad senses of the word, and in the difficulties the church faced in dealing with a man such as Charles Finney, who openly repudiated his church's Calvinism and preached a crass form of Arminianism of the worst kind.

Arminianism is incipient modernism. That is the lesson of all history. The failure of the church to deal with Arminianism leads inevitably to rampant modernism, which can no longer be rooted out when some begin to see that a battle has to be fought. By that time it truly is too late.

The failure of the Presbyterian Church to deal with Arminianism in the 1800s opened the door to on-going Arminianism which even today is tolerated in Presbyterian churches as another acceptable version of the gospel, even though it may be inferior.

Does this mean that if a church should wait until Arminianism has become modernism to engage the enemy, it is too late? Does this mean that failure to engage the enemy at the beginning means that the battle is lost before it begins?

Often that is the case. Nevertheless, in the Netherlands in the days of Hendrik De Cock, the State Church, in which De Cock was a

minister, had itself become thoroughly modern. The same truths later denied in the Presbyterian Church in the U.S.A. were being denied in the Hervormde Kerk. But there was one significant difference between De Cock's reformation of the church and the reformation performed under Machen: De Cock took himself and the churches which followed him back to Dordt and Dordt's Canons. That is, De Cock saw clearly that the battle against modernism could be fought successfully only if the church would go back, prior to modernism, to battle Arminianism and reaffirm, on the basis of the creeds of the church, the truth of the absolute sovereignty of God in salvation. Machen wrote *The Virgin Birth*. De Cock said, "We need the Canons." This is a great difference.

It was also to be regretted that Machen refused to commit himself on the question of evolutionism. His Princeton colleague Charles Hodge had considered it perfectly possible that evolutionism was the way in which the worlds came into being, as long as one put these evolutionary processes under the providential control of God and as long as one was willing to accept the creation of the soul in man as a divine and miraculous intervention in evolutionary processes. Machen refused to become involved in these discussions, claiming that they were outside his field of expertise. But such issues are not outside the field of a theologian's concerns, for they involve the basic doctrines of the infallible inspiration and trustworthiness of Sacred Scripture. These compromises that were made in the late 1800s opened the door to crasser forms of evolutionism which have plagued the church ever since.

Nevertheless, anyone who reads the history can only be thankful for the courage of a man who was willing to sacrifice all for the cause of the truth and who was instrumental in preserving that truth as embodied in the Westminster Confession of Faith.

## Chapter 51

# Herman Hoeksema
## Theologian and Reformer

### Introduction

*I shall have to write this sketch of someone whom I knew. I did not and could not know him as his family knew him. I did not and could not know him as his colleagues knew him. But he was my pastor for nearly twenty years, and he was my professor in the Protestant Reformed Seminary for at least six years. His students knew him in the classroom, in the coffee room at break time, during the*

informalities of Student Club, and in the banter and give-and-take of seminary life.

Yes, it was six years, not the normal three of a full seminary course. While I was still in college but making plans to go to seminary, Herman Hoeksema suffered a stroke. The Lord gave him a remarkable, though not complete, recovery. We were concerned that by the time we were ready to enter seminary Hoeksema would no longer be capable of teaching, and we wanted to study dogmatics under him. I and several others asked permission from the Theological School Committee to take dogmatics with him even if it meant only auditing the courses. This permission was granted, and we studied dogmatics with him during three years of college studies. The Lord spared him for additional years, and we were given the privilege of studying dogmatics (as well as other subjects) with him for an additional three years. So we went through the six loci of dogmatics with him twice. Not a day of these studies was wasted.

It is not, I am sure, possible to balance praise with blame and to be just and right in both. God uses sinful means to accomplish His will. We hold our treasure, Paul tells the Corinthians, in clay pots. But these things are not my primary concern. What is of interest to me and ought to be of interest to all of us is the fact that God used Hoeksema in remarkable ways in the church. That God uses sinners is a given. That God used Herman Hoeksema is reason for gratitude on the part of all who love the Reformed faith.

Gertrude Hoeksema, a daughter-in-law of Herman Hoeksema, has written the one biography of him, and the readers of this sketch are urged to read that book. Its title is *Therefore Have I Spoken*. On it I must rely for much information not available in other sources.

## Hoeksema's Early Life

Herman Hoeksema was born on March 12, 1886, to Johanna Bakema and Tiele Hoeksema in Hoogezand, in the province of Groningen, the Netherlands. The date of his birth, 1886, will attract the attention of any who have knowledge of and appreciation for the history of the church in the Netherlands. It was the year that Dr. Abraham Kuyper led the faithful in the apostate state church out to form a new denomination and thus reform the church in that land.

Dr. Kuyper's work, however, was not the first reformation brought about in the state church; Hendrik De Cock, as we discussed in an earlier chapter, had also led faithful people of God out of the state church, but fifty years earlier in 1834. Hoeksema was born from parents who belonged to the churches that De Cock had formed, known as *De Afscheiding*, or the Secession.

The people of these churches were the common folk, the poor day-laborers, the people without influence, but they possessed something more important: a godliness and piety which had deep roots in Scripture and in a prayer-filled life.

Hoeksema had a very godly mother. Her godliness and spirituality were all the stronger because of the husband to whom she was united. He was a drunkard who forsook his family to enlist in foreign service, and who spent what little he earned in sin. He returned home only occasionally, and when Herman was nine years old, he forcibly took him from his home. Mrs. Hoeksema had to get a court order to prevent this from recurring.

His mother was required to take in sewing and to work long hours to support her family. Even with hard work, money was always in short supply. It was not easy to feed three growing boys and one girl and to provide a Christian education for them besides. The result was that the family often went hungry, and Herman took to running around with the town ruffians, who sometimes engaged in stealing food to ease their hunger pangs.

It was possible for Herman to continue his education only because he was given support from the town. This education was in a trade school, which qualified him to serve as apprentice for a blacksmith. He obtained work away from home where, at fifteen years old, he worked from 4:00 A.M. to 10:00 P.M. for $30.00 a year plus room and board. The work was hard and the food he received meager and insufficient to sustain his growing body. For a year he worked here, but at the end of the year he found a better job in his hometown making wrought-iron fences.

The poverty and hard work of his youth gave to Herman a sympathy for the poor and a distaste for the selfish employer who refused to pay his help a living wage but demanded long hours and hard work. His preaching during his years in the ministry often reflected these childhood experiences.

Although he received his religious training in a church of *De Afscheiding*, Hoeksema had a friend who belonged to the churches of the Kuyper movement. Through this friend, he came to hear Dr. Kuyper preach and speak, and was influenced by Kuyper's strong and uncompromising emphasis on salvation by sovereign and particular grace. It was an influence that was to be the standard of his life.

At eighteen years of age, Hoeksema left the Netherlands and the poverty he knew there to find a home in America. He stayed in Chicago with his sister who had preceded him. After holding a variety of jobs and saving what he could, he was able to get his mother and brothers to the United States, while he himself departed for Grand Rapids and Calvin College to study for the ministry of the Word.

### *Early Ministry*

Hoeksema had received gifts from God that equipped him for more than just working with his hands. He was a man of towering intellect, penetrating insight, and originality of thought. His studies came easily to him, and he was able to absorb vast amounts of material. His interest was in Dutch Reformed theology, and because he knew the Dutch language thoroughly, he was able to read with ease that ocean of Reformed Dutch thought, so rich and fertile, but so inaccessible to most believers today.

In addition to the gifts of intellect, he was an artist of some ability. Later in life, when he took up painting for relaxation, he became skillful in oils. His artistic skills extended also into literary achievements. He wrote a dramatic production in poetry while in school; he composed a sonnet at the time of his twenty-fifth anniversary; and all his writing (and there was much of it) was characterized by a clarity and literary grace to which few attain. The clarity of his writing (and his preaching and speaking) was of such a kind that, although there were many who disagreed with his theology, no one ever complained that they could not understand what he meant. He could express profound ideas in simple language.

Hoeksema was a man of iron will and steely determination. This was characteristic of his own life, which was highly disciplined; but it was especially evident in his commitment to the truth. Having once set himself upon the course of service to the church of Christ and the truth of God, he could not be swerved him from it. No one, friend or foe, would dispute the fact that Hoeksema stood firmly for what he believed. This was so true that the word that came most often from the mouths of his detractors was "stubborn."

The evidences of his commitment to the church appeared already during his days as a seminary student. When he was scheduled as a student to bring a word of edification to the congregation of Maple Avenue Christian Reformed Church in Holland, Michigan, he knew that the congregation was opposed in large measure to Christian education. Aware of the implications of what he was doing, he prayed in his congregational prayer that God's covenant people might not in the education of their children deliver them over to the gates of hell—his forceful characterization of the public school system. So infuriated did the congregation become that his hosts did not reappear in their own home until he had departed, and the consistory made an effort to keep him from their pulpit—an effort that failed only because the student body of Calvin Seminary decided that no student would go to Maple Avenue if Hoeksema could not go.

It was, however, the beginning of a long life of controversy.

### Controversy in His First Charge

From the day Hoeksema entered the ministry in Fourteenth Street Christian Reformed Church in Holland, Michigan, to the day he died, his life was a life of controversy.

It has been alleged that his controversy-filled life was due to his own constant efforts to "pick a fight." He was, so it has been said, willing "to go to the mat" for anything and everything. This is a grievous slander and one which will not stand the scrutiny of unbiased men.

One must understand a bit the background in the church in America of which Hoeksema became a part.

The members of the Christian Reformed Church (CRC) in the first half-century of its existence were almost exclusively from *De Afscheiding*. While indeed this movement in the Netherlands was a true reformation of the church and while several of its leaders were strongly Reformed, weaknesses in doctrine also ran through the movement, and not all the leaders were equally Reformed. These strengths and weaknesses were also present in the Christian Reformed Church: it was not as Reformed as it should have been. Specifically, strains of Arminianism were present in some parts of it. Doctrines such as the well-meant offer of the gospel, a universal love of God, and salvation dependent on the free will of man were openly taught. In some places there was strong opposition to Christian education, and in other places the urge to "Americanize" the church led the church into unholy unions with un-Reformed organizations.

Around the turn of the century, immigrants from the *Doleantie* movement of Dr. Abraham Kuyper in the Netherlands also joined the Christian Reformed Church. They were a different kind of folk. Many of them held to Kuyper's rejection of the well-meant offer of the gospel, but others had been taken in by Kuyper's teaching of common grace, a common grace which was quite different in emphasis from that of the earlier immigrants. Both groups were present in the church, and the struggle for control of the church was long and sometimes bitter.

Hoeksema, an heir to the piety of the people of *De Afscheiding* and to the doctrines of sovereign and particular grace in the Kuyper followers, had early come to the conclusion that the battle for the future of the church was to be fought—as it had been throughout the ages—in defense of sovereign and particular grace over against Arminianism and Pelagianism. But he saw, early in his ministry, that the truths of sovereign grace applied not only to the sovereignty of God in the work of salvation, but equally strongly to the antithetical walk of God's covenant people in the world. The common grace of the well-meant offer was a threat to the former; Kuyper's common grace was a threat to the latter.

Into the ministry in this denomination Hoeksema entered, and through the maze of conflicting ideas he had to find his way, which,

he was determined, would be the way of the historic Reformed faith. This brought him into controversy.

Conflict started early. In his very first charge he faced opposition over two matters: his strong support of Christian schools and the emphasis in his preaching on sovereign grace rooted in double predestination. His steady hand on the tiller of the congregation, however, steered the people of God through many dangerous shoals. Those who were not persuaded left for elsewhere, while many learned to be thankful for a man who would direct them in a way consistently Reformed.

The years were those of World War I. Patriotism became all but an idol and blind patriotism the order of the day. In bursts of patriotic fervor, churches put the United States flag on the pulpit. Hoeksema refused to do this, not because he was not aware of his calling to be in subjection to the magistracy, but because the church's business was conducted in the sanctuary of the church, and that church is catholic, not bound to one country. Threatened by zealots in the community, he was forced for a while to carry a pistol in self-defense.

One great doctrinal controversy in the Christian Reformed Church at large involved Hoeksema during this time. It was a dispute over dispensational pre-millennialism. Hoeksema took a leading role in pointing out to the church the fact that such a position was contrary to the Reformed confessions because it denied that Christ is the King of the church. His efforts were instrumental in protecting the church from a dangerous heresy.

### Continuing Controversy

Hoeksema's second charge was in Eastern Avenue Christian Reformed Church in Grand Rapids, Michigan. This was the church where my father and paternal grandparents were members.

Here, too, conflict soon came.

The first controversy was in no respect of Hoeksema's making. It involved the teachings of Dr. Ralph Janssen in the Calvin Seminary. This professor of Old Testament denied the infallible inspiration of Scripture and brought into his instruction higher critical methods. His four colleagues in the seminary objected to his teachings but could not secure a condemnation of his views by the churches in their broader assemblies. Hoeksema was finally brought into the battle, even though Dr. Janssen was a member of his congregation.

Hoeksema's careful and thorough work as part of a study committee, presented to the synod of 1922, was the basis for Janssen's condemnation.

The irony of it was that Dr. Janssen used Kuyperian common grace to justify his higher critical methods, knowing full well that Hoeksema, already then, repudiated the doctrine. Although the issue of common grace was not faced by the synod of 1922, it later became the occasion for Hoeksema's expulsion from the Christian Reformed Church.

This brief biography is not the place either to discuss the issues or to trace in detail the history. We can only briefly describe what happened.

Faced with several protests against Hoeksema's denial of common grace and various overtures asking for a statement on common grace, the synod of the Christian Reformed Church meeting in Kalamazoo, Michigan, adopted a doctrinal statement that combined the well-meant offer of the gospel and Kuyperian common grace into one decision. Although informed by Hoeksema that he would never subscribe to such an unbiblical and anti-confessional statement, the synod refused to discipline him and, in fact, pronounced him fundamentally Reformed—although with a tendency towards one-sidedness.

Hoeksema's critics were not satisfied, and they finally prevailed upon the classis of which Hoeksema was a part to require absolute subscription to the doctrine of common grace or to face suspension from the office of the ministry.

Upon Hoeksema's refusal, the classis suspended him and set his consistory and the congregation outside the denomination.

Two other ministers, from a different classis, Rev. Henry Danhof and Rev. George M. Ophoff, were deposed shortly thereafter for the same reasons, and their congregations were expelled with them.

These congregations, and others in the Christian Reformed Church that believed as they did, formed a new denomination, the Protestant Reformed Churches in America, in 1925.

These were busy years. Herman Hoeksema was the pastor of a congregation numbering more than 500 families; he taught dogmatics and all New Testament subjects in the seminary which was formed immediately after 1925 to train the denomination's own ministers; he wrote extensively for the *Standard Bearer*, a bi-monthly Reformed periodical, and served as its editor; he traveled around the country speaking in the many places to which he had been invited;

he was full-time radio pastor from 1940 to 1963; and he wrote a number of books, most of which are in print today.

The enormous amount of work which Hoeksema performed took its toll, and in June of 1947 he suffered a massive stroke in Sioux Falls, South Dakota, on his way to Manhattan, Montana, where my father was pastor and I lived with my family.

The Lord gave Hoeksema recovery from the stroke—never complete, but sufficient that he could take up his work once more in his church and for the denomination.

### *The Last Battle*

It was evident that the Lord gave Hoeksema recovery because one more battle in defense of sovereign grace had to be fought. It happened in the early 1950s. The battle was over the question whether salvation is conditional—a clear and forceful attack against the doctrine of sovereign grace.

Dr. Klaas Schilder in the Netherlands had suffered at the hands of the Reformed churches in his own country. He had been unjustly deposed from office in 1944 in the same way as Hoeksema. Twice, in 1939 and in 1947, Schilder had visited the States. Hoeksema had struck up a friendship with him and had been influential in seeing to it that the pulpits of Protestant Reformed churches were open to him. Although Schilder and Hoeksema had much in common, they differed radically on the doctrine of the covenant. Hoeksema insisted that a unilateral and unconditional covenant was taught in Scripture and the confessions; Schilder taught a bilateral and conditional covenant. Hoeksema insisted that only the elect children of believers were included in that covenant. Schilder insisted that all the children of believers had some place in it.

Many of the ministers in the Protestant Reformed Churches began to teach and preach Schilder's views, until the church was rocked with controversy. In 1953 the debate was settled only through a difficult split, which took nearly two-thirds of the ministers and members out of the Protestant Reformed Churches. Another denomination was formed by those who departed, which eventually returned to the Christian Reformed Church.

In that controversy Hoeksema played a major role—in his preaching, in his writing, and in his defense of the faith on the floor of the assemblies. He understood that the conditional theology of Schilder and his followers constituted a serious threat to the

doctrines of sovereign grace. He also knew that the very right of existence for the Protestant Reformed Churches demanded that they hold unswervingly to the truth of unconditional salvation. It was what Hoeksema had fought for in his battle against common grace; it was still what had to be defended if the churches of which he was a part would survive, faithful to their heritage.

God gave the Protestant Reformed Churches the victory. It is true that the numbers of the denomination were severely diminished. It is also true that the controversy was bitter and difficult. But God preserved the cause of the Protestant Reformed Churches, that there might be a denomination which uncompromisingly continued to teach the same truths which the whole church of Christ throughout the ages has loved.

It was, indeed, the last battle for an old and weary warrior.

Although Hoeksema lived for another twelve years and took part in rebuilding a shattered denomination, God ended his work before He ended his life. He died in September of 1965 and went to his eternal resting place.

## Conclusion

It is hard to imagine the amount of work which Herman Hoeksema produced. But that is true of many whom God uses in His church. They spend themselves in the cause of the gospel and do work that indeed derives its power from heaven.

Above all, Hoeksema was a preacher. It is difficult for us to understand how anyone who heard his preaching could leave his congregation. He was clear, concise, biblical, and confessional. A little child could understand him; an adult versed in theology could be stimulated by his thought. He was eloquent, moving, forceful, and persuasive. The real power of his preaching was in careful exegesis, which unfolded the riches of the Scriptures and brought them home in countless practical ways.

One who heard him preach could never doubt that his first love was preaching. I well remember that near the end of his life he would begin a sermon in such a painfully slow manner that one wondered whether he would be able to get through it, but as he became caught up in it, his eyes would begin to sparkle, his face would light up, and he would begin to preach as one who received new life.

It was also especially toward the end of his life that Hoeksema began to preach more and more about heaven. When he spoke of

heaven, he would refer to it as "that blessed hope." This was significant because, as he was ready to explain, he did not mean that hope was a mere "shrug of the shoulders," as he called it; hope was absolute assurance which rested on the faithfulness of the promise of God. His "blessed hope" was real and certain.

Hoeksema's exegesis of Bible passages was always his strength. It is the strength of his *Reformed Dogmatics* and of his many other books, and it was the strength of his instruction in the seminary. He would debate with us with great patience and long-suffering and would bear with our immaturity with grace and kindness, but he insisted that we bolster every argument with Scripture. If we did not want to take the time or put forth the effort to do that, he would not permit us to waste his time.

Hoeksema was a man of great physical strength who wore himself out in his work. He was a man of great mental strength as well. He never ceased to amaze us in seminary with his ability to show the falsity of a theological argument with a few sure and probing remarks that exposed the hollow character of much theological thought.

He was also a man of enormous spiritual strength. Some called it "stubbornness"; the Bible calls it "steadfastness." He loved the Scriptures, was committed to the defense of the Reformed faith, and would not be moved, no matter what the price. And he paid a very dear price indeed.

Hoeksema was a sinful man—as we all are. He knew how great is the miracle of grace that God uses sinners in His church. He had his weaknesses. He was not above making fun of shoddy thinkers who passed themselves off as profound theologians and made bold but unproved assertions. He sometimes walked his own path without due consideration of those who were one with him and determined to support the cause for which he stood.

But he was absolutely convinced that the truth which he preached was the truth of Scripture and the Reformed faith. He said in my hearing more than once that he would stand firm for that truth, even if all others turned away. His conviction was unshakable, and his commitment to faithfulness was total.

Yet, when he was in the circle of friends and fellow saints, he was jovial, with a robust laughter, a ready wit, a warm spirit of camaraderie. Some never came to know this side of his character, but even within the congregation he showed it in moments of relaxation.

Two illustrations of Hoeksema's character stand out in my memory. The first had to do with our seminary training.

Hoeksema was content all his life to teach in a single room in the basement of First Protestant Reformed Church, a room which was dark, dingy, cold, damp, and wholly unattractive, when with some compromise he could have been an outstanding theologian in the ecclesiastical world and a blazing star in the ecclesiastical firmament. He never complained that he was squandering his gifts when he spent his life with two or three students patiently teaching them theology in what was little more than a walled hole in the ground. The only explanation for this can be a total commitment to the truth of Scripture and the Reformed faith.

The second incident is of a different kind. It took place when in 1953 we had to seek other quarters for the seminary and were using Adams Street Protestant Reformed Christian School. It was Hoeksema's seventieth birthday. It was coffee time. We were in the teachers' lounge. Hoeksema was soliloquizing. His remarks went like this:

"Now that I am seventy years old I sometimes wish that I could live another seventy years. If the Lord would give me another seventy years, I think I could finally come to understand the truth a bit. Now I know almost nothing."

I do not know whether he saw our jaws drop in amazement. I doubt it. But then he added, almost to himself, "No, I am glad that I won't live very long anymore, because I shall soon go to heaven. Then I shall understand perfectly."

It was an important evidence of the fact that Hoeksema well understood that, because the truth of Scripture is the truth of God Himself, it is unfathomable, and we mere men can know only very little of it. Hoeksema would often conclude a sermon with a remark to the effect that he had succeeded only in scratching the surface of a text; and he often said in his prayer at the end of the sermon that all he had done was mutter and stutter a bit about the truth. It was all rooted in that great governing principle of his life that God is God, great and glorious and greatly to be praised.

Nor was he a man who gloried in an isolated ecclesiastical life. It was forced upon him because of his defense of the faith, but it was not his wish.

He would have enjoyed seeing sister-church relationships established between the Protestant Reformed Churches and the

churches formed under Dr. Schilder's leadership if a common basis
could have been found in the truth. That enjoyment was rooted, in
part, in a personal affection for Dr. Schilder himself. Hoeksema was
saddened by the rift between himself and Schilder and between the
churches they represented. He was genuinely sorrowful when
Schilder died. Hoeksema preached in other churches when the
opportunity was given him. Dr. Henry Atherton's Grove Chapel in
London is one example. The Orthodox Presbyterian Church of
Portland, Maine, near the place where Hoeksema vacationed, was
another. He sought out and eagerly participated in a conference with
ministers from the German Reformed Churches of Eureka Classis.
He willingly participated in a conference with Christian Reformed
ministers called to try to heal the breach. He urged the synod at one
point to send observers to the Reformed Ecumenical Council. But he
permitted no compromise when it came to questions of the truth.

Hoeksema hated church politics in any form. His firm belief that
Christ preserves His church kept him from the evil of playing
political games in the church, soliciting support through ways other
than debate, attempting to influence decisions by maneuvering, and
"counting noses" to be assured of sufficient support before making a
move. All the things so important in today's church world were
abhorrent to him.

Above all, Hoeksema was used by God to bring reformation to the
church. With the adoption of common grace, the Christian
Reformed Church chose a path of apostasy which would (and has)
led the denomination astray. It is understandable that common grace
would receive a great deal of attention in the early years of the
Protestant Reformed Churches. Unlike men who lead sects who
never get beyond criticism of heresy, who are always and only against
things, who have an obsession to write critically of others without
producing anything positive, Hoeksema wanted more than anything
else to see the Christian Reformed Church reject the false doctrine it
had adopted. When it would not, when it cast Hoeksema out after
stripping him of his office, and when it persisted in going its own
way, Hoeksema turned to the positive work of church reformation.
Such reformation was surely in the area of church government and
liturgy. The Christian Reformed Church had departed from the
Reformed line in introducing hymns into worship, and the church
polity had been corrupted when the broader assemblies engaged in

discipline of Hoeksema. Hoeksema's reforming efforts were especially in doctrine.

I cannot spell it out here. But as Hoeksema stood for the truths of sovereign and particular grace, he developed those truths in some important areas. Undoubtedly because of his experience in the case of Dr. Janssen, who denied the miracles in Scripture and did so on the grounds of common grace, Hoeksema developed those truths of sovereign and particular grace in the area of miracles. In his *Reformed Dogmatics* one will find one of the best, most biblical, and most beautiful developments of miracles that one can find anywhere.

Hoeksema applied the truth of particular grace to the concept of revelation and subjected the doctrine of "general revelation"—especially as many wanted to relate it to common grace—to rigorous scrutiny in the light of Scripture.

Most importantly, Hoeksema saw the implications of the doctrine of sovereign and particular grace, rooted in eternal election, for the doctrine of the covenant. Here is his greatest work. He gave the church an inheritance of the truth which is powerful, throbbing with life, filled with practical implications for an antithetical walk on the part of God's covenant people, and which gives all glory to God. It is a biblical doctrine of the covenant which begins with God and ends with God and has as its theme Glory to God. If Hoeksema had done nothing else but this, it would have been enough.

Herman Hoeksema has not been recognized by the church world, yet for him, having God's approval was the important thing. Mostly he knew opposition, hatred, and slander, or cold and disdainful ignoring of him and his theology. Records are kept in heaven, the only records which count. The sins are there too, of course. They are covered in the blood of Christ. But the suffering and the persecution are noted as well. God, who had His own place in the church militant for Herman Hoeksema, has His own place in the church triumphant for a man who fought a good fight, finished the course, and kept the faith. He received the crown of righteousness which God gave to him and will give to all who love Christ's appearing.

## Chapter 52

# George Martin Ophoff

### Humble Servant of the Truth

***Introduction***
*Apart from my parents, the two men who had the most influence on my life were my two professors in the Protestant Reformed Seminary. The one was Rev. Herman Hoeksema; the other was Professor George M. Ophoff. From Rev. Hoeksema I learned Reformed dogmatics and how to exegete the New Testament;*

from Professor Ophoff I learned the history of the church of Christ and how to exegete the Old Testament. They determined the nature of my ministry in the church of Christ.

For most of the time I was studying for the ministry, the seminary was meeting in the basement of First Protestant Reformed Church in Grand Rapids, Michigan. The one room set aside for seminary had nothing to commend it as a classroom conducive to study. The student body was small. The library was all but non-existent. The seminary boasted no support staff: no secretary, no administrator, no registrar, no department heads, no records or filing cabinets. Just two professors and a handful of students.

I am bold to say that we received some of the best theological education available in this country if not abroad. Yet this seemingly bold statement is true only if one weighs the value of theological education in the scales of the one thing theological education is all about: learning to preach the gospel of Jesus Christ according to the Scriptures and the Reformed confessions. I never wanted to study elsewhere and did not, in fact, give it even a thought. I have never had one moment's regret that the place where

I studied was the dingy "seminary room" in the basement of First Church.

The only possible explanation of all this is the fact that the two professors who taught us everything we knew about theology and preaching were two gifted preachers who were wholly committed to the Reformed faith and the cause of our Lord Jesus Christ.

In all the world no two men could be found working together who were so different from each other. It was itself a miracle of divine grace that both not only worked together from the beginning of the history of the Protestant Reformed Churches in 1924 to the late 1950s—a period of over 35 years—but did so in unity, harmony, singleness of purpose, and equal devotion to the cause of Christ.

I have written of Rev. Herman Hoeksema. The delightful task of writing of Rev. George Ophoff now awaits me. It is the story of a man whom I respected greatly and whom I learned to love deeply. That his name may not be forgotten by those who love the Reformed faith, I write these lines with thankfulness to God for Professor Ophoff.

## Early Life and Training

George Martin Ophoff was born in the city of Grand Rapids, Michigan, on January 25, 1891. He was the oldest of eight children born to Frederick H. Ophoff and Yeta Hemkes Ophoff. Frederick Ophoff worked in a furniture factory in downtown Grand Rapids, to and from which place he walked to save the five-cent streetcar fare. The hours were long: from 6:00 in the morning to 5:00 in the afternoon, six days a week. The meager wages could barely support the family and provide Christian school tuition for the children.

The household lived a normal life for a second-generation immigrant family. The Dutch communities in Grand Rapids were close-knit, and life centered in the church. The churches were composed of immigrants from the Netherlands and their children and grandchildren; and they were scattered throughout the city. Almost all of them had roots in the Secession, the reforming movement in the Netherlands which had been launched by Hendrik De Cock. The first generation of immigrants had come to Michigan under the leadership of Albertus C. Van Raalte.

In keeping with the traditions of those who belonged to this particular group of Dutch immigrants, the family was a godly and pious family willing to sacrifice for the cause of Christian instruction.

Ophoff received his instruction in the home, in Oakdale Christian School, and in Franklin Street and Oakdale Park Christian Reformed Churches. It was truly a covenantal instruction which Ophoff himself, in all his life, considered a great blessing. In his later years in seminary, Ophoff was wont to speak of what he called *Gereformeerde gevoelhoren,* that is, "Reformed antennae." By this expression he referred to one who had a deep sense of what was included in the Reformed faith and an ability to detect unerringly that which was opposed to it. Ophoff firmly believed that such a sense for what is truly Reformed could be gained only through covenantal instruction given to the children of God's covenant in church, home, and school.

While George, as a boy, was not himself a brawler but something of a loner, he nevertheless did not run from a good fight, and he was quick to come to the defense of one who was being unjustly or cruelly taunted on the playground, even if this involved a battle with his peers. His mother despaired of the many ruined clothes in which he came home—in days when one pair of trousers and one shirt was worn all week long, to be washed on Saturday and put on again on Monday. Ophoff had on his right hand a crooked index finger with which he often gestured on the pulpit and in class, the legacy of one such brawl in which his finger was broken.

At the time Ophoff graduated from grade school, there was as yet no Christian high school. Calvin College, organized exclusively for the training of teachers and ministers, incorporated various high school subjects into its curriculum. To this school Ophoff went with his mind set upon being a minister of the gospel. He graduated from the high school part of it in 1909 at the age of eighteen.

### *Preparation for the Ministry*

From that point on, Ophoff's education was repeatedly interrupted. Apparently the reason, in part, was a lack of finances in the Ophoff household, which forced him to drop out of school and seek employment with a local ice company.

Another event was to alter his life significantly. Between his college studies and seminary work, while laboring at the ice company, his maternal grandfather fell and broke his hip.

Ophoff's grandfather, Gerrit Hemkes, had been born and raised in the Netherlands, had entered the ministry of the churches of the Secession led by De Cock, and had come to the United States. At

first he took a call extended to him from the Christian Reformed congregation in Vriesland, Michigan. Because of his many abilities, he had been called to be assistant professor in the Calvin Seminary in Grand Rapids, where he had served with distinction.

When as a relatively old man Hemkes fell and broke his hip, George was sent by his parents to the home of his grandfather, to live with him and care for him. Ophoff never returned again to his own home.

God has his purpose in all our sufferings, sorrows, and disappointments. So it was in this instance. Because of the care of his grandson, Professor Hemkes was able to remain at his home until he died. But George also benefited. It was Hemkes who encouraged him to return to school, who helped him with his studies, and who provided a quiet place for George to pursue his studies. Furthermore, Hemkes, a very gifted man, was able to give George a great deal of instruction in and a deep and abiding love for the Reformed faith.

In 1918, at twenty-seven years of age, George entered Calvin Seminary. Two events of these years must be recorded.

The first was tragedy in the Ophoff family. George's father was fatally injured in a fire which broke out in his place of work. Although he escaped from the building when it began to burn, he rushed back in to rescue a very precious watch which he had left on the shelf in his department. An explosion tore to pieces that part of the building, and Frederick Ophoff was badly burned. He died the same day, at the age of fifty-two, leaving a widow and eight children.

The second incident was somewhat revealing with regard to Ophoff's understanding of theology. As one of his course requirements, he was assigned a paper on common grace, an issue under discussion in the churches. He had a great deal of difficulty with the paper, chiefly because of the fact that he could not fit the current teachings on common grace into the organic body of Reformed thought. It seemed to conflict with everything he knew of the Reformed heritage of the truth.

Finally, in sheer desperation, he decided to approach the subject from the viewpoint of its being a doctrine contrary to Scripture. Unaware of questions concerning its biblical character which had already appeared in some places in the church, and using a denial of common grace only as a "working hypothesis," he discovered that this approach solved all his problems. To use his own words,

"Suddenly the light went on," and all the pieces began to fall into place. The paper became easy to write.

Whatever may have been the reaction of his professor to this paper, Ophoff himself became subjectively convinced that common grace was contrary to Scripture and the Reformed confessions, long before the controversy became public in the churches. That conviction was to remain unalterable throughout his life.

During his seminary years, George met and married Jane Boom, with whom he had four sons. God gave him a wife who was truly a help *meet* for him. She was a beautiful woman of amazing character. Born in a Reformed home and brought up in the Reformed faith, she completely devoted herself to her husband. She was to be his support and encouragement in the unbelievably difficult years that lay ahead. Because Ophoff's grandfather, Professor Hemkes, was still living, the newly married couple moved in with him. George and Jane were married in August of 1920, and in December of that year Professor Hemkes died.

In May of 1921 George graduated from the seminary, and in January of 1922, he assumed the responsibilities of his first pastorate in a Christian Reformed Church in Riverbend, Michigan. The congregation is now the Hope Protestant Reformed Church in Walker and has its sanctuary within a long block of where the old church once stood.

### Ophoff's Pastoral Work

George Ophoff was ordained into the ministry of the Word and sacraments on January 26, 1922 in the Hope Christian Reformed Church during the evening worship service. The congregation had been in existence since 1916, though it had never had a pastor. It belonged to Classis Grand Rapids West, and had been receiving pulpit supply from ministers within the classis and from students and professors in the seminary. It was a rural congregation numbering between thirty and thirty-five families, most of whom farmed.

In many ways and from many viewpoints, Ophoff's strengths were not best utilized in the pastoral aspects of the ministry. It is always a marvel that God gives sovereignly to each man his gifts and abilities, that the particular place of each man within the church is determined by God, and that the two so perfectly match. It soon became evident that Ophoff's gifts and abilities lay in teaching.

He was a forceful teacher in Catechism classes, although he did not usually succeed in remembering all the names of his catechumens, and they could easily "pull the wool over his eyes" by reading the answers to the questions they were supposed to memorize without his being aware of it.

Ophoff was, nevertheless, extremely interested in the spiritual welfare of the children, a welfare rooted, he was convinced, in their thorough understanding of the Reformed faith. After Ophoff was deposed from the ministry in the Christian Reformed Church (though he continued to be a minister in the Hope Protestant Reformed Church), it came to his attention that a nearby local Christian Reformed minister was attempting to persuade some of Ophoff's catechumens to attend Catechism in the Christian Reformed Church. Ophoff's solution to this problem was to take his entire Catechism class to the home of the "proselytizing" minister and proceed, in the presence of his class, to instruct the local minister in the error of common grace and in the necessity of the children to learn the Reformed faith over against this pernicious error.

The same strength of Ophoff appeared in his preaching. His preaching, especially on the Old Testament, was powerful, Reformed, unique, and gripping. He could bring the whole congregation, including the children, into the lives and history of the saints described in Scripture. He could unfold, in an unforgettable way, the riches of Christ crucified as the salvation of God's people in every age.

But Ophoff was rarely on time for anything—a weakness that plagued him all his life. In concern for the congregation, the elders would often start the service, and the minister would appear some time during the preliminary acts of worship.

Ophoff's life was, especially after 1924, unbelievably difficult as he attempted to combine the full-time care of a congregation with the heavy responsibilities of seminary instruction, when the full curriculum fell on just two men. The result was that his sermons were not always as carefully prepared as they would have been if he had sufficient time to spend on them; he often failed to finish a sermon in the allotted time, and it was not unusual that he would complete a sermon in the afternoon worship service which he had begun in the morning.

Ophoff sometimes would reprimand from the pulpit individual members of the congregation who had sinned, and his condemnation

of sin, though stern and unbending, was not always touched by a shepherd's love for the sheep. Because bulletins were unheard of and the minister was required to read the announcements, Ophoff often became entangled in the difficult task of finding the correct piece of paper containing the current announcements among a welter of slips of paper found in every pocket of his coat.

Jacob was his favorite Bible character—what Ophoff himself would call his "favorite personage." He admitted that this was true because he saw himself in Jacob, who illustrated so vividly that sovereign election and grace makes a saint from a very miserable character. Because his sermons were filled with illustrations and homely, down-to-earth expressions taken from everyday life, even today those who heard him preach remember many of his sermons and the points he was making in them.

After the controversy over common grace, which was the occasion for the beginning of the Protestant Reformed Churches, Rev. Ophoff was pastor for sixteen years in Byron Center, Michigan. Partly because of controversy in the congregation, the church was dissolved, and Ophoff was able to devote all his time to his work in the seminary. His work in a congregation after that was limited to faithful and dedicated service in the office of elder in First Protestant Reformed Church.

### Ophoff's Deposition

George Ophoff was involved early in the events which led up to the formation of the Protestant Reformed Churches. Although the PRC were not formally established until January of 1925, Rev. Ophoff joined the staff of the *Standard Bearer* in October 1924 and wrote his first article in the November issue. It was entitled "A Declaration" and was intended to explain his action:

> And thus it happens that I, the undersigned, am of the group editing this periodical. The fact that I agree to serve upon the editorial staff of the "Standard Bearer" amounts to an admission on my part that I too reject the views and conception of things which the term common grace stands for. For me it is quite impossible to adhere to the principles embedded in the term common grace and remain on friendly terms with Scripture.

To write for the *Standard Bearer* and to write this kind of language was an act of courage born out of faith. The times were troubled and dangerous. A few months before, in June, the synod of the Christian Reformed Church had adopted a statement concerning common grace which made the doctrine official dogma in the church. While the synod had not required the discipline of those who disagreed with its decision, many had started movements to rid the church of all those who dared express disagreement with what synod said. Ophoff must have known that such writing would eventually lead to trouble for him.

And it did. Rev. Herman Hoeksema was disciplined in December 1924 by Classis Grand Rapids East. Classis Grand Rapids West followed in January. A reading of the minutes of both classes will show that the same men who had sought the ouster of Hoeksema would not rest until also Ophoff was put out of the church. The material presented to Classis West was much the same as that which had appeared in Classis East. From the first day of the meeting it was obvious that the classis had not come together as a deliberative body to discuss the issues; it had one purpose in mind, namely to rid the church once and for all of anyone who disagreed with the synodical pronouncements. It had one question to ask Ophoff: Will you sign the three points of common grace or not?

The demand came to Ophoff via the insistence of the classis that Ophoff's consistory confront its pastor with these demands. The missive read,

> Dear Brethren,
> The Classis Grand Rapids West hereby requires you to require of your minister:
> 1) That he declare himself unequivocally whether he is in full agreement, yes or no, with the three points [of common grace] of the Synod of Kalamazoo.
>
> 2) An unconditional promise that in the matter of the three points, he will submit (with the right of appeal) to the Confessional Standards of the Church as interpreted by the Synod of 1924, in other words, neither publicly nor privately propose, teach or defend either by preaching or writing any sentiment contrary to the Confessional Standards of the Church as interpreted by the Synod of 1924 and in case of an appeal that he in the interim will acquiesce in the judgment already passed by the Synod of 1924.
>
> The Classis further requests you to furnish the Classis by 10:00 A.M., Wednesday morning, Jan. 21, 1925, with a definite written answer of your pastor to the twofold requirement of the Consistory.

The classis brushed aside the detailed answer of Hope's consistory and proceeded to depose from office Rev. Ophoff himself and his

elders. One deacon also was deposed, while another agreed to common grace.

From an earthly point of view, the results were disastrous. Ophoff was stripped of his office, as were his elders; the congregation was reduced to a small group of about seven or eight families; the whole movement numbered only three ministers and three congregations; Ophoff's relatives all remained in the Christian Reformed Church, and what had been a close-knit family was torn apart by the split.

Nevertheless, God used this seemingly hopeless situation to bring reformation to His church. Common grace is an unwarranted departure from Scripture and the Reformed confessions and an introduction into the church of deadly heresy. The deposition of faithful ministers was a terrible sin. Ophoff was determined to remain true to Scripture and to his God. Nothing else mattered. At the time of his deposition the *Grand Rapids Press* published an edition with the headline "OPHOFF PREFERS DEATH." The reference was to a statement which Ophoff had made on the floor of the classis during the course of proceedings. He had informed the classis that he would rather be shot than to sign the three points. The paragraph from the *Press* reported Ophoff's words:

> Mr. President, if you were to place me before a gun to be shot or set before me the three points to adhere to, I would choose the former. I cannot sign the three points. If I did I would be tearing the Bible into shreds. I would be stamping the Word under foot. I would be slapping God in the face.

It was not a vain and empty boast. The truth was more important to him than life itself. The courage to stand alone, as saints before him had so often done, was a courage born in an unshakable faith that Christ's cause always has the victory.

### *Ophoff as Professor*

From the beginning of the Protestant Reformed Churches, a seminary was established and operated under the firm conviction that the survival of the fledgling denomination depended upon the training of its own ministers. And so, in addition to his pastoral work, Ophoff began teaching church history and Old Testament subjects in the seminary. Although the seminary could not begin to compare with other seminaries in facilities, organization, size of student body, and prestige, the simple fact is that it turned out ministers who in ability to preach and shepherd the church of Christ were head and shoulders above every other seminary in the land.

While the academic aspect of the training was good, the success of the seminary was, without doubt, due to the deep spirituality of its teachers.

I consider it one of the God-given, great privileges in my life that I could study under Professors Ophoff and Hoeksema. This part of a seminary education was better than anything obtainable elsewhere. I look back on those years with gratitude.

I am compelled to look at this aspect of Ophoff's work from my own perspective because it was in the seminary that I best knew him.

In the first year I attended seminary, the school was rather large, with students from the Protestant Reformed Churches, interested young men and college students who audited various courses, students from the Netherlands, and students from the Eureka Classis of the German Reformed Churches. After the controversy of 1953, the number of students was significantly reduced.

My first impression, formed already in those years, and one which continues to the present, is Ophoff's immense dedication to the cause, a dedication which became especially evident in his willingness to sacrifice almost all earthly goods and position for the sake of the truth. Such enormous dedication left an indelible mark.

My second impression was that our education was of the highest possible caliber. This was true even from an academic viewpoint. Ophoff, for example, taught us our Hebrew grammar and reading. He taught it well, and he taught it thoroughly. We could not have learned it better anywhere else. We had to study, and we had to study hard. The sleepless nights were many, and the work was demanding. We had good courses.

The education was especially good because it was, throughout, from the perspective of Scripture and the confessions. Ophoff had insights which were unique and powerful. In Old Testament studies he opened to us the history of Israel in a way which could not be learned from any book. He did not rely upon what others had said; he did not use the same old notes over and over, year after year. He was fresh, vigorous, new, insightful, and interesting. In church history he showed us something I had never learned in all my college days: the fundamental spiritual difference between the Reformation and the Renaissance that created a sharp antithesis between them. And this is but one example.

My third impression was that Ophoff was disorganized in much of his life. It must be remembered that the workload he carried was enormous and the obligations many and varied. Ophoff's absorption in a given subject at a given time made him so preoccupied that he was often oblivious to what was going on about him. Nevertheless, he was not a man who claimed organization as his strength. His study, to anyone entering it, was a disorganized place (although he seemed to know fairly well where everything was). His notes were disorganized in a way that no one else could possibly have used them. His instruction was disorganized, and the students used to joke that we stayed longer at Mt. Sinai than the children of Israel. We never covered all the material. The clock, governing the beginning and the end of class periods, did not exist for him. I am sure we would have had the same class all morning if we had not reminded him of the time. But we received from him insights which were principial; we learned viewpoints and methods of working that were distinctively Reformed; we were subjected to a man whose concentration on a given subject was at any moment total; and we could not help but be moved repeatedly by a spiritual dedication that stood above all else. If later in life we had to continue our studies in subjects we only began with him in seminary, we found that we had been given the proper starting point and that the way was carefully charted so that we would never get lost. And that, after all, is what counts.

The same characteristics appeared in Ophoff's writings. He wrote syllabi for classroom use and wrote volumes for the *Standard Bearer*. But what was true of his teaching was equally true of his writing. During my seminary years when I worked in the print shop which printed the *Standard Bearer*, Ophoff's material was always late. His typewriter always needed a new ribbon. His manuscript was so heavily edited by pencil or pen that it was difficult to read. Arrows directing one to all other parts of the manuscript, pieces chopped off or cut out of pages, pages renumbered, bits of paper glued on to other pages—all of these made setting his articles on the linotype a real challenge.

His writings were studded with startling insights into the text of Scripture and magnificent truths developed at length in stirring rhetoric. But the organization was uniformly poor and the writing impossibly long-winded and detailed.

His writings remain a treasured part of our heritage, but someone needs to take his best pieces and edit them by a rigorous shortening

process. The Reformed churches could benefit tremendously from such work.

## Ophoff the Polemicist

Deep commitment to the truth of Scripture leads to warfare, for there are not many who love the faith with fire and passion. Ophoff fought for the Reformed faith.

He did that already in the years surrounding the origin of the Protestant Reformed Churches. He wrote oftentimes in a polemical style, for he saw in so many writings by men who claimed to be Reformed froth and blather, talk without substance, and higher critical attacks upon Scripture. Against all these he raged with vehemence.

Ophoff led the fight in 1953 when conditional theology threatened to engulf the churches. He was the first to detect a different "spirit" in the churches than that which had characterized the PRC at its inception. When Dr. Klaas Schilder came to this country from the Netherlands, Ophoff saw what most did not see, that Schilder's covenant views were at odds with those views developed in our churches. Schilder promoted a bilateral and conditional covenant, and such teachings, Ophoff saw, were directly in conflict with the truths of particular and sovereign grace.

In fact, when Hoeksema urged Ophoff to be cautious and to withdraw charges against a minister (Hubert De Wolf) in First Church, Ophoff persisted in pressing the charges, and these charges eventually became the occasion for De Wolf's suspension from office. When defenders within the Protestant Reformed Churches openly wrote with approval of a conditional covenant, Ophoff's defense of the Reformed faith was vigorous and unyielding.

At the same time, Ophoff never attacked someone's person. He wrote against false views, and he often did so in such controlled fury that his enemies were incensed. But it was heresy against which he wrote, not people. He was often a prophet whom few would hear.

Yet his work was extraordinarily important, for it was used by God, not only to defeat a calculated attempt to drive the PRC in a direction different from that in which it had gone, but also to develop truths which became the heart of the Reformed faith as taught in the Protestant Reformed Churches.

### *Ophoff's Last Days*

The valiant defense of the faith which led to the split in the Protestant Reformed Churches in 1953 was Ophoff's last battle. It seemed as if God had preserved him for it, and that when the shouting and the tumult died and peace returned, Ophoff's work was over.

Already prior to the split in 1953, Ophoff entered the hospital for stomach surgery. Although the surgery was successful, the doctors warned him that he would have to lighten his work load. He never did. A lifetime of work had developed a habit which could not be broken.

In the summer of 1958, while Rev. and Mrs. Ophoff were returning from a vacation in Canada, Ophoff suffered a massive stroke in Toledo, Ohio. He was moved by ambulance to Grand Rapids, but it proved the end of his work. Although he recovered from some of the effects of the stroke, he gradually lost his sight. While it was possible for him to think about theology and understand the theology that others read to him, it was no longer possible for him to read or write it.

In February of 1962 Rev. and Mrs. Ophoff were moved to a nursing home. One week before he died, Rev. Ophoff was moved to Pine Rest Christian Hospital. His death came on June 12, 1962, and a little more than two years later, his wife followed him to glory. It was a little more than three years before his colleague, Rev. Hoeksema, went to his eternal reward.

### *Conclusion*

George Ophoff stood about five feet, nine inches tall and was rather well-proportioned. Although he surely put on weight in his later years, he was never overly heavy. He had a natural dignity in his bearing, in the look on his face, and in his head of pure white hair. He was a handsome man, although he was completely oblivious to this. His eyes behind iron-rimmed glasses were sharp and penetrating. His head was massive, and his chin had the set of a bulldog, so that his whole appearance was one of tenacity and courage.

On the one hand, Ophoff could be surprisingly indifferent to his appearance, and he often came to school looking rumpled and disheveled—most often because he had been in his study all night. His wife had a difficult time of it keeping him presentable. At certain times, though, he could be surprisingly concerned about his clothing.

If we would comment that the tie he wore did not go well with his suit, he would never wear the combination again. And his wife took great pains to attempt to keep him in clean, neatly ironed shirts suits.

An outstanding feature of his life was his meekness. We often thought of Moses when we thought of Ophoff. Of Moses it is said in Sacred Scripture that he was the meekest man on the earth. Ophoff came in, we thought, a close second. His meekness was expressed not only in his total dedication to the glory of God, but in his willingness, all his life, to labor with his considerable gifts in the shadow of Herman Hoeksema—and to do so without a word of complaint or a tinge of jealousy. Ophoff never received the recognition which was due him, and his considerable gifts often went unnoticed, but the deeds of a man are noted in heaven, and records there are kept with infallible precision so that God may reward His servants in due time.

The relation between Ophoff and Hoeksema was unique. They worked together for over thirty-five years in the seminary and in the work of the churches. They were about as different as it is possible for two people to be, yet they worked in harmony and unison, with a common cause and purpose. Both had nothing but respect for the other. Each always called the other by his last name.

But that meekness, as was the case with Moses, could sometimes be dispelled by a burst of fierce temper and violent rage, although it was an attack on the truth which most often provoked it. But if he did wrong to someone, Ophoff would be the first to apologize, beg forgiveness, and express his heartfelt sorrow for his bad conduct.

His forgetfulness is legendary and remains to this day the subject of loving conversations that turn to his work in the churches. But that forgetfulness was often the fruit of total absorption in what was occupying his thoughts at the moment. His concentration was total. I personally witnessed evidences of this more than once. In the course of an ecclesiastical assembly a motion would be vigorously discussed, into which discussion Ophoff would enter. But while he was pondering the implications of the motion, it would be passed and the assembly would go on to other business. Suddenly he would jump to his feet and ask for the floor to discuss the recently passed motion. He never noticed the progress of the body, and if the matter was important, did not notice what else was happening in the body as he sank back into his own thoughts.

Ophoff had a tenacity that showed in remarkable ways. He could be relentless in pursuing the logical consequences of a proposition; he could hold to a point like a bulldog when others abandoned it; he could maintain a position against everyone else. But it was this very tenacity which enabled him to be the fit servant of Christ that he was in the defense of the faith. Nonetheless, when he became convinced that he was wrong in his thinking, he was quick to admit it, for he was, above all, loyal to the Word.

While Ophoff seemed so often to be completely oblivious to all that was going on around him, he had a penetrating insight into human nature and events in history. He taught me things about the powers of sin, human character as depraved and saved, and relationships in life which I shall never forget.

In the second chapter of the book of Judges we read that when Joshua died and all his generation, "there arose another generation after them, which knew not the Lord, nor yet the works which he had done for Israel" (v. 10). That is Scripture's way of introducing the sad history of the judges. The generation that led the Protestant Reformed Churches to the marvelous truths of Scripture that are our heritage has died and been gathered unto their fathers. Shall another generation arise which knows not the Lord? May God forbid it.

# Suggested Reading

The works listed here are not intended to be a bibliography. Although I have consulted these works from time to time, the preparation of the book led me to consult many more sources than one can list here. Many of these sources, for obvious reasons, were in the Dutch language, to which most readers have no access. Books listed are provided for those who wish to read more extensively on any given subject. They are intended for the general reader whose interest may have been whetted by various chapters. The few quotations found in the book are also from these writings. Although I have not included additional reading suggestions for all those whose lives are described, a general work on church history will give the reader additional biographies and works to consult.

## General Works:

Daniel-Rops, Henri. *The Church of Apostles and Martyrs*, translated from the French by Audrey Butler. 2 vols. New York: Image Books, 1962.

Hoeksema, Herman. History of Dogma, unpublished notes, ed. Herman Hanko. Grandville, Mich., Theological School of the Protestant Reformed Churches, 1982.

Kurtz, Johannes. *Church History*, translated by John Macpherson. 3 vols. in *The Foreign Biblical Library*, edited by W. Robertson Nicoli. New York: Funk & Wagnalls, 1888–1890.

M'Lintock, John and James Strong, ed. *Cyclopedia of Biblical, Theological, and Ecclesiastical Literature*. Grand Rapids, Mich.: Baker Book House, 1968.

Presbyterian Board of Publication (PCUSA, Old School). *The Lives of the British Reformers*. 12 vols. Philadelphia: Presbyterian Board of Publication, n.d. (selections from a collection of tracts originally published by the London Tract Society in 12 vols. as *Lives and Writings of the British Reformers*).

## General Works (continued):

Schaff, Philip. *The Creeds of Christendom with a History and Critical Notes by Philip Schaff.* 3 vols. New York: Harper & Brothers, 1919 (consulted for information about the creeds and quotations from them).

Schaff, Philip. *History of the Christian Church.* 8 vols. Grand Rapids, Mich.: Wm. B. Eerdmans Publishing Co., 1950.

Schaff, Philip, ed. *A Select Library of the Nicene and Post-Nicene Fathers of the Christian Church.* 14 vols. Grand Rapids, Mich.: Wm. B. Eerdmans Publishing Co., 1979-1989.

Steinmetz, David C. *Reformers in the Wings.* Grand Rapids, Mich.: Baker Book House, 1981.

Woodbridge, John D., ed. *Great Leaders of the Christian Church.* Chicago: Moody Press, c. 1988.

Wylie, J. A. *The History of Protestantism.* 3 vols. London: Cassell, Petter, & Galpin, n.d.

## Church Fathers (A.D. 10–50):

Eusebius, Pamphili. *The History of the Church from Christ to Constantine*, translated with an introduction by G.A. Williamson. Harmondsworth, England: Penguin Classics, 1965.

## Books about Selected Saints:

### Anselm

Anselm. *The Prayers and Meditations of St. Anselm*, translated [from the Latin] by Benedicta Ward. Harmondsworth, England: Penguin Classics, 1984.

### Augustine

Augustine, *The Confessions*, translated by E. B. Pusey. New York: E. P. Dutton & Co., Inc., 1950.

Bonner, Edgar. *The Life and Teachings of Augustine.* Canterbury Press Norwich, 1996.

### Calvin, John

McGrath, Alister E. *A Life of John Calvin: A Study in the Shaping of Western Culture*. Cambridge, Mass.: Basil Blackwell, Inc., 1990.

Parker, T.H.L. *John Calvin: A Biography*. Philadelphia: Westminster Press, 1975.

Penning, L. Genius of Geneva: *A Popular Account of the Life and Times of John Calvin*. Grand Rapids, Mich.: Wm B. Eerdmans Publishing Co., 1954.

### Columba

Cahill, Thomas. *How the Irish Saved Civilization: The Untold Story of Ireland's Heroic Role from the Fall of Rome to the Rise of Medieval Europe*. vol. 1 of *The Hinges of History* by Thomas Cahill. New York: Doubleday, 1995.

McNeill, John T. *The Celtic Churches: A History A.D. 200 to 1200*. Chicago: University of Chicago Press, 1974.

Stokes, George T. *Ireland and the Celtic Church: A History of Ireland From St. Patrick to the English Conquest in 1172*. London: Society for Promoting Christian Knowledge, 1907.

### Cranmer, Thomas

Webb, Charles. *The Life of Archbishop Cranmer*. 2 vols. London: J. G. & F. Rivington, 1833.

### de Brès, Guido

Van Halsema, Thea B. *Glorious Heretic: The Story of Guido de Brès*. Grand Rapids, Mich.: Baker Book House, 1982.

### Farel, William

Bevan, Frances. *The Life of William Farel: A Spiritual Force in the Great Reformation Who Nobly Endured the Reproach of Christ*. London: Pickering & Inglis, n.d.

Blackburn, Wm. M. *William Farel and the Story of the Swiss Reform*. Philadelphia: Presbyterian Board of Publication (PCUSA, Old School), c. 1865.

## Gotteschalk

Gotteschalk, [first name unknown]. Portions of Gotteschalk's Confessions, translated by Ronald Hanko, pp. 34ff in "Gotteschalk's Doctrine of Double Predestination," by Ronald Hanko. *Protestant Reformed Theological Journal,* Vol. 12 #1 (Nov. 1978), pp. 31-64 (also contains bibliography and summary of the life and teachings of Gotteschalk). Note: Last name has an alternate spelling of "Gottschalk."

## Hoeksema, Herman

Hoeksema, Gertrude. *Therefore Have I Spoken: A Biography of Herman Hoeksema.* Grand Rapids, Mich.: Reformed Free Publishing Association, c. 1969.

## Hus, John

Budgen, Victor. *On Fire For God: The Story of John Hus.* Welwyn, England: Evangelical Press, 1983.

## Knox, John

Reid, W. Stanford. *Trumpeter of God: A Biography of John Knox.* Grand Rapids, Mich.: Baker Book House, 1982.

## Kuyper, Abraham

Vanden Berg, Frank. *Abraham Kuyper: A Biography.* Grand Rapids, Mich.: Wm. B. Eerdmans Publishing Co., 1960.

## Latimer, Hugh

Demaus, Robert. *Hugh Latimer: A Biography.* London: Religious Tract Society, 1869.
Wood, Douglas C. *Such A Candle: The Story of Hugh Latimer.* Welwyn, England: Evangelical Press, 1980.

## Luther, Martin

Bainton, Roland H. *Here I Stand: A Life of Martin Luther.* New York: Abingdon Press, 1950.
Brecht, Martin. *Martin Luther: His Road to Reformation,* translated by James L. Schaaf. 3 vols. Minneapolis: Fortress Press, 1985 (vol. 1), 1994 (vol. 2), and 1993 (vol. 3).

## Machen, J. Gresham

Hart, D.G., *Defending the Faith: J. Gresham Machen and the Crisis of Conservative Protestantism in Modern America*. Grand Rapids, Mich., Baker Books, 1995.

Stonehouse, Ned B., *J. Gresham Machen: A Biographical Memoir*. Grand Rapids, Mich.: Wm. B. Eerdmans, 1954.

Rian, Edwin H., *The Presbyterian Conflict*. Horsham, Pa.: Committee for the Historian of the Orthodox Presbyterian Church, 1992.

## Patrick

Cahill, Thomas. *How the Irish Saved Civilization: The Untold Story of Ireland's Heroic Role from the Fall of Rome to the Rise of Medieval Europe*. vol. 1 of *The Hinges of History* by Thomas Cahill. New York: Doubleday, 1995.

McNiell, John T. *The Celtic Churches: A History A.D. 200 to 1200*. Chicago: University of Chicago Press, 1974.

Stokes, George T. *Ireland and the Celtic Church: A History of Ireland From St. Patrick to the English Conquest in 1172*. London: Society for Promoting Christian Knowledge, 1907.

## Scottish Presbyterians

Howie, John *The Scots Worthies according to Howie's Second Edition, 1781...*, ed. Andrew A. Bonar. Glasgow: John M'Gready, n.d.

## Tyndale, William

Demaus, Robert. *William Tindale: A Biography, Being a Contribution to the Early History of the English Bible*. London: Religious Tract Society, 1871. Note: Earlier spelling of last name was Tindale.

Edwards, Brian H. *God's Outlaw: The Story of William Tyndale and the English Bible*. Welwyn, England: Evangelical Press, 1988.

## Ursinus, Zacharias

Van Halsema, Thea B. *Three Men Came To Heidelberg*. Grand Rapids, Mich.: Baker Book House, 1982 (also includes material on Caspar Olevianus and Frederick the Pious).

## Vermigli, Peter Martyr

Simler, Josiah. *Peter Martyr*, ed. J. C. McLelland and G. E.
Duffield. n.p.: Sutton Courtenay Press, 1989.

## Waldensians

Wylie, J. A. *History of the Waldensians.* Mountain View, Calif.:
Pacific Press Publishing Assn., 1977.

## William III of Orange (1650-1720)

Bowen, Marjorie. See titles of 3 vols. below in series entitled
William & Mary Trilogy, Dealing with the Life of William of
Orange, Afterwards William III of England. Edited from early
U.S. editions of 1911 (vols. 1 & 2) and seventh edition of
1922. Neerlandia, Alberta, Canada: Inheritance Publications.
vol. 1 – I Will Maintain, c. 1993.
vol. 2 – Defender of the Faith, c. 1994
vol. 3 – For God and the King, c. 1995

## Wycliffe, John

Fountain, David G. *John Wycliffe: The Dawn of the Reformation.*
Southampton, England: Mayflower Christian Books, c. 1984.
Wood, Douglas C. *The Evangelical Doctor: John Wycliffe and the
Lollards.* Welwyn, England: Evangelical Press, 1984.

# Index of Selected People, Places, and Religious Terms

*NOTE: Portions of the book indexed include the main text of the book and timelines but not chapter titles and subheadings. Persons indexed are the saints about whom the chapters are written (last names in all capital letters) and important Reformers, rulers, and key people who supported or opposed these saints. Place names are not, for the most part, indexed, except to indicate boundaries or facts that influence the lives of the saints. Indexing of religious terminology includes the names of denominations, movements and doctrines, especially those related to the Reformed faith and to views differing from it.*

Anabaptists:
  criticized by Reformers, 163, 177
  converted to Calvinism, 224
  Lowlands (settlement in), 223, 224
  radicalism of brings persecution on
    other Protestants, 220, 224
Anglican Church. *See* Church of
  England
ANSELM (archbishop):
  birth, 74
  birth & death dates on timeline, 62
  boyhood spirituality, 74
  character, 75, 76
  charity, works of, 75
  counselor for distressed, 75
  doctrine of atoning sacrifice of
    Christ, 77
  education, 74
  exile, 76
  Huguenot involvement, 183
  investiture controversy, 76
  monastery organization in England,
    74, 75
  monk, 74
  offices held, 74, 75
  ontological proof of God, 76, 77
  papal loyalty, 76
  parentage, 74
  prayer lacking assurance, 77, 78
  writings, 74, 77
ANTHONY (ascetic):
  appearance, 23, 24
  Athanasius and, 24
  birth, 23
  birth & death dates on timeline, 2
  care for sister, 23
  death, 25
  distrust of learning, 25
  emergence from desert, 24
  founder of asceticism, 23
  life in desert solitude, 23
  miracles ascribed to, 25
  self-denial, 23, 24
  temptations, 24
antinomianism, 338
antithesis, 43, 372
Arianism, 24, 30, 31
Arius, 29, 30
Armagh, Ireland, 48

Arminianism, 44, 282, 289, 313,
  324, 329, 331, 332, 391, 392, 397
Arminius, Jacobus:
  academy in Geneva (study under
    Beza), 182
  Amsterdam ministry questioned,
    317
  appointment to University of
    Leyden contested by Gomarus,
    317, 318
  death, 319
  name, 319
  popularity, 314
  Synod of Dordt (condemnation of
    views at), 319, 320
Articles of Faith, Sixty-Seven (by
  Zwingli), 138
ascetic practices harmful to one's
  health, 36, 81, 92, 123
ascetics and asceticism, 22-26
ATHANASIUS:
  Alexander and, 28
  Anthony and, 24, 33
  appearance, 32
  ascetic life, 33
  banishments, 31, 32, 208
  birth, 27
  birth & death dates on timeline, 2
  canon of Scripture, 33
  childhood, 28
  *contra mundum*, 27
  Council of Nicea, 29, 30
  death, 32
  doctrine of divinity of Christ,
    27-30, 32, 33
  merciful acts, 33
  offices held, 28, 30
  parentage, 27
  Synods of Tyre & Constantinople,
    31
atheism (Roman Empire's definition
  of), 14
Auburn Affirmation, 376, 384, 385
Augsburg. *See* Diet of Augsburg. *See*
  Peace of Augsburg
AUGUSTINE (bishop of Hippo):
  Ambrose's sermons bring
    conviction to, 41
  (continued next page)

(continued next page)

(continued next page)

441

mysticism, 20, 74, 90-95, 123, 129, 170, 223, 224, 333, 366, 373

Roman Catholic Church (continued):
  comfortless doctrine of, 194, 195
  Council of Trent dates, 120, 132
  elevation of sacraments above
    preaching, 98, 108
  remorse never shown regarding
    centuries of persecution, 71,
    100, 117
  refutation of double predestination
    and truth of Scripture at Synod
    of Mainz (A.D. 848), 70, 71
  ruling church of Middle Ages, 73
  Scripture in vernacular not allowed
    by, 108
  Semi-Pelagian doctrine of, 68, 69
  Synod of Chiersy's adoption of
    conditional reprobation &
    universal atonement, 70
  wealth of papacy at expense of
    others, 103, 104, 106
  See also ascetics and asceticism
  See also friars and monks.
  See also Inquisition.
  See also monasticism.
  See also pope(s) and papacy
Roman Empire:
  boundaries of, 47
  persecution of Christians by, 6, 7,
    29
  See also Caesars (Roman)
Rome (fall of city), 2, 63
Roundheads, 284
Rufus, William, 76
RUTHERFORD, Samuel:
  banishment to Aberdeen for stand
    against Arminianism & prelacy,
    289
  birth, 286
  birth&death dates on timeline, 280
  character, 293
  conversion, 287, 288
  death, 293
  dismissal from teaching post, 287
  education, 287
  letters & poetry, 289, 293
  ministry (study for), 288
  parentage, 286, 287

(continued next column)

RUTHERFORD (continued):
  pastorate (first), 288, 289
  preaching, 289, 290, 294
  St. Andrews' work, 290, 292
  Westminster Assembly (work for
    establishment of Presbyterian
    form of government in church),
    290, 291, 294
  wives, 289, 290
  writings (including *Lex Rex*), 280,
    292, 293, 294

## S

Sadolet, Cardinal, 145, 148
St. Bartholomew's massacre of
  Huguenots, 120, 183
Schilder, Dr. Klaas, 400, 404, 417
scholastic method, 324, 325
scholasticism, 331, 333
Scholte, Heinrich, 355, 356
Scopes "monkey" trial, 376, 381
Scottish common sense realism, 379
Scottish Confession of Faith, 248,
  258, 259
Scottish General Assembly. *See*
  General Assemblies of Scottish
  church
Scottish National League and
  Covenant. *See* National League and
  Covenant
Scripture interpretation (literal vs.
  allegorical), 36
Seceders, 356, 357
Secession. *See* Afscheiding
Secession, Act of, 355
Semi-Pelagianism, 19, 22, 43, 44, 68,
  69, 136
Separation. *See* Afscheiding
Servetus (heretic in Geneva), 150,
  184
Shorter Catechism, 378
Sigismund, Holy Roman Emperor
  (reign 1411-1437), 115, 116,
  128
Smith, Richard, 171
Socinian heresy, 323
state church of Netherlands
  (Hervormde Kerk), 228, 353, 359,
  364, 366, 367, 391, 392, 394

Stevenson, J. Ross, 383
Stylites (ascetics), 25, 26
subscriptionism, 382, 399. *See also* Formula of Subscription
supralapsarianism, 311, 325-27
Symeon (ascetic), 25
Synod, Christian Reformed Church, 399, 412
Synod, First French Reformed in Paris (1559), 211
Synod, First Reformed in Netherlands at Emden (1571), 120, 224, 308
Synod, French Reformed in La Rochelle, 183
Synod of Chanforans (Waldensian), 158
Synod of Chiersy (in A.D. 849), 70
Synod of Constantinople, 31
Synod of Dordrecht (Dordt, 1578, Second Reformed Synod in Netherlands), 224, 235, 237
Synod of Dordrecht (Dordt, 1618-1619):
  Ames, William (assistant to Synod president), 313
  baptism form, 235
  Bible translation in Dutch ordered by Synod, 320, 351
  dates of on timeline, 308
  Form for the Administration of the Lord's Supper, 235
  Gomarus (against Arminianism), 317, 319-21
  Maccovius (defending supralapsarian position), 322, 323, 325
  Representatives to Synod from England, 309, and Bremen, Germany, 335, 336
  Voetius (against Arminianism and helping to write Canons), 332
Synod of Mainz (A.D. 829), 69, 70, 82
Synod of Mainz (A.D. 848), 70
Synod of Reformed Churches in Antwerp (adoption of Confession of Faith), 219
Synod of Rockingham (1095), 76
Synod of Tyre, 31

systematic theology, 338, 339

# T

TERTULLIAN:
  birth, 17
  birth & death dates on timeline, 2
  "blood of martyrs is seed of church" saying, 17
  boyhood, 16, 17
  conversion, 17, 18
  death, 20
  doctrines developed by:
    anthropology, 19
    divinity of Christ, 19, 20
    soteriology, 19
    traducianism, 19
    Trinity, 19, 20
  Montanist sect (membership in), 20, 21
  office of, 18
  parentage, 17
  Scripture (defense of), 18
  wife, 18
  writings, 18
Tetrapolitan Confession, 166
Tetzel (monk selling indulgences), 125
Thirty Years' War, 308
Thirty-nine Articles, 205, 271, 310
Three Forms of Unity, 356
traducianism, 19
transubstantiation, 172, 264
Trent. *See* Council of Trent
Trinity, docrine of, 19, 20, 43, 150, 184, 323
TYNDALE, William:
  Bible translation in English, 248, 251-54
  birth, 249
  birth & death dates on timeline, 248
  bishop of London (run-in with), 250
  conversion to Lutheranism, 250
  education, 249
  imprisonment; 253
  martyrdom, 253, 254
  parentage, 249
  (continued next page)

# About the Author

Professor Herman Hanko holds an A.B. degree from Calvin College and a Th.M. degree from Calvin Seminary, Grand Rapids, Mich. He received an M.Div. from the Theological School of the Protestant Reformed Churches in Grand Rapids, now located in Grandville, Mich. In 1955 he was ordained as a minister of the gospel in the Protestant Reformed Churches. He served ten years in the pastoral ministry, first at Hope PR Church, Grand Rapids, then at Doon PR Church, Doon, Iowa. While at Doon, he accepted a call to teach at the Protestant Reformed Seminary, where for thirty-three years he was professor of New Testament and church history.

In addition to his work at the seminary, Professor Hanko preached and lectured on behalf of the churches, both in the United States and abroad, and he continues to do this in retirement. Over the years he has written countless articles for the *Standard Bearer* magazine. In addition, he has authored the following works:

*Books:*
*Far Above Rubies: Today's Virtuous Woman* (editor)
*God's Everlasting Covenant of Grace*
*The Mysteries of the Kingdom: An Exposition of the Parables*
*Ready To Give An Answer: A Catechism of Reformed*
 *Distinctives* (co-author)
*We and Our Children: The Reformed Doctrine of Infant Baptism*

*Pamphlets:*
"The Battle for the Bible"
"Biblical Ecumenicity"
"The Building of a Home"
"The Christian and the Film Arts"
"The Christian and the Social Gospel"
"Creation: Fact or Fiction"
"Ought the Church to Pray for Revival?"
"Phoebe: An Example for the Christian Woman"
"What It Means to Be Reformed"